# Relationship Marketing

*To my most beloved friend*
*most*
*most*

*Sushmita & Esther*

*[signature]*

# Relationship Marketing
## Concepts, Theories and Cases

### Supriya Biswas

Formerly, Visiting Faculty, Marketing
Indian Institute of Social Welfare and Business Management
(IISWBM)
Kolkata

**PHI Learning** Private Limited

New Delhi-110001
2011

₹ 375.00

**RELATIONSHIP MARKETING: Concepts, Theories and Cases**
Supriya Biswas

**ISBN-978-81-203-3983-5**

Published by Asoke K. Ghosh, PHI Learning Private Limited, M-97, Connaught Circus, New Delhi-110001 and Printed by Baba Barkha Nath Printers, Bahadurgarh, Haryana-124507.

*In memory of*
*my father Late Kanti Chandra Biswas*

# Contents

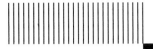

# Preface

Marketing in the new millennium has evolved with a host of new ideas and changes. The synthesis of these ideas, changes and transformations culminated in finer segmentation of customers, deeper insight into their likes and dislikes, greater emphasis on value added products and services, innovative strategies for retention and application of technology to facilitate these processes. What eventually transpired out of this metamorphosis is the concept of Relationship Marketing. Although conceived in the mid-eighty's, its flavour started pervading into the academics and business space since the nineties. The purpose of this book is to provide the readers an overview of diverse perspectives that constitute the foundation of Relationship Marketing.

The book is organized into seventeen chapters.

Chapter 1 is an introduction to relationship marketing covering historical framework of relationship marketing, various definitions of relationship marketing, differences between conventional marketing and relationship marketing, different levels of relationship marketing, six market models, relationship planning and building, concepts of permission, retention and database marketing, customer relationship management, and advantages of relationship marketing.

Chapter 2 discusses the role of customer experience and emotion in relationship marketing, emotion in business relationship, emotion and customer experience, customer experience management, 3Ds of customer experience, rational emotional behaviour manifestation, FCB grid, emotion in buying decisions, body chemistry matter in relationship, and emotional loyalty.

Chapter 3 describes the concepts of relationship brands touching upon various dimensions of parasocial relationship, effects of brand relationship norms, brands as relationship partners, norms of behaviour and their role in social interaction, and brand relationship style monitor.

Chapter 4 focues upon various aspects of customer value chain, with discussions on the framework of user value, value proposition, customer value chain, value profit chain, relationship marketing and lifetime value, RFM model, measurement of customer lifetime value, enhancing customer value, co-branding, cross-promotion, Keiretsu concepts, and global value chain.

Customer equity is one such concept which has found strong association with the philosophy of relationship marketing. Chapter 5 has explored various components of customer equity, models of customer equity, implementation of customer equity, elaboration of brand equity, customer equity and relationship equity—the three factors that drive customer equity, measurements and benefits.

Chapter 6 deals with the strategies and techniques of cross-selling and up-selling, its conceptual background, its definitions, procedures and rules for cross-selling and up-selling, emotion factors in cross-selling and up-selling, building profit improvement and critical success factors.

Chapter 7 highlights the temperament of business relations covering discussions on relationship signals, effect of client categories on brand equity, trend of business temperament, relationship constructs, relationship temperament matrix, and analysis of relationship temperament matrix.

Quality is the strength that ascertains the confidence of the customer on the products and services. Chapter 8 discusses on systems and standards managing customer satisfaction through quality, difference between quality control and quality assurance, business tools and business quality standards, quality standards in IT Industry, difference between ISO and CMM, and concepts of Six Sigma with case study.

Chapter 9 provides an exclusive coverage on various aspects of customer loyalty with discussion on its historical framework, definitions, models of loyalty, measuring loyalty, loyalty analysis, social bonding in loyalty, attachment and loyalty, relationship ladder, entry and exit barrier concluding with the issues and concerns in loyalty.

Chapter 10 discusses concepts on measuring relationship effectiveness with emphasis on measurement parameters, relationship quality survey, customer satisfaction index, ServQual model, American Customer Satisfaction Index (ASCI) and Balanced Scorecard (BSC) perspective of measuring effectiveness.

Chapter 11 elaborately describes the importance, role and responsibilities with respect to the position of the relationship manager in an organization. This chapter also discusses the functional categories of the relationship manager.

Technology plays a critical role in facilitating the application of relationship marketing in business. Chapter 12 examines the considerations for technology deployment, descriptions of various technology areas for promoting relationship marketing, for example, contact centre, data warehousing, data mart, data mining, CRM, Knowledge Management System, Self-service kiosks and portals.

Chapter 13 broaches the areas of new age relationship marketing, that is, virtual relationship marketing, relationship marketing in the virtual space, real and virtual relationship, virtual organization and virtual relationship, virtual relationship cycle and virtual value chain.

Customer Management of Relationship or CMR is a new age philosophy indicating the future directions of relationship marketing. Chapter 14 describes the conceptual framework of CMR, CMR versus CRM, CMR approach, trends of perfect market and the elements of successful CMR marketing

Chapter 15 discusses how nurturing relationship with various stakeholders of the business can enhance the enterprise image. On the basis of a graphic framework of business relationship, the chapter has examined the importance of relationship with the stakeholders, namely investors, clients, employees, government, media, society and international community.

Chapter 16 is a consolidation of various real-life examples, thoughts that depict in the lay man's language the quintessential expression about how relationship marketing is perceived in different walks of life and business.

Chapter 17, the concluding chapter, provides the names of some of the premier international institutes dedicated to the promotion of relationship marketing.

I would like to express my gratitude to Dr. Jagdish N. Sheth and Dr Atul Parvatiyar because their books and my subsequent interactions with them inspired me to get involved with the philosophy of relationship marketing. I would also like to thank my friend and mentor, Mr Rathin Ray of CMC Ltd. and my colleagues at CMC for my learning experience.

In case readers have any suggestion, they can mail me on this id: supriya_biswas@hotmail.com.

**Supriya Biswas**

# CHAPTER 1

# Framework of Relationship Marketing

## INTRODUCTION

There is an astounding transformation in the mood of business in the new millennium with its heart driven by the 'consumer power'. Today's consumers are impatient and want everything everywhere, anytime. There are numerous instances to uphold this belief, for example, while watching TV, if the viewers find the channel a little boring, they flick the button of the remote and switch channels (channel surfing) without much ado. However great the image of the star, the viewers must like them, else he would be wiped out of the screen. Similarly, a few minutes more for a website to land on the workstation, users have the option of clicking to an alternative site. Consumers are well aware that the market has enough capable people to cater to their needs who are right there to knock on the doors in times of need. And here begins the genesis of relationship. Relationship is a relatively new terminology in business. The term 'client' or 'customer' (including even the consumers in not too distant future!) is gradually getting replaced by the more progressive term 'relationship' because it implies a long-term affair very

1

much like a family bonding. Today, the focus of the organization is much on relationship building, and positions have been created in many organizations to promote the relationship building process. Relationship definitely plays a positive and constructive role towards long-term business successes. This chapter covers discussions on the historical artifacts of relationship marketing, significance of relationship in the context of business transactions, definitions and examples of relationship marketing, levels of relationship marketing and its advantages.

## RELATIONSHIP IN BUSINESS

The word 'customer' is derived from the root word *custom*, which is defined as "to render a thing customary or usual" and "to practice habitually". A customer is a person who becomes accustomed to buying from those who sell. This custom is established through purchase and interaction on frequent occasions over a period of time. Without a strong track record of contact and repeat purchase, this person is not your customer; he is a buyer. A true customer is grown over time (Griffin 2002).

What relationship has got to do with customers? What are its impacts on the business? The following facts and figures, which have been observed through various research and studies to account for the lost customers, would give the answer (LeBoeuf 1989):

- One per cent die.
- Three per cent move away.
- Four per cent just naturally float.
- Five per cent change on a friend's advice.
- Nine per cent can buy cheaper elsewhere.
- Ten per cent are chronic complainers.
- Sixty-eight per cent go elsewhere because the people they deal with are indifferent to their needs.
- Only 4 per cent of dissatisfied customers tell us, 96 per cent tell to other people.

Despite the fact that many companies tout their focus on service in advertising, the research showed that overall customer satisfaction is declining. A global benchmarking study showed a reduction in customer service satisfaction from 82 per cent to 68 per cent in the year 2006. Additional studies show that 68 per cent of customers leave a business relationship because of a perceived attitude of indifference on the part of the company (Klein et al. 2007).

There is also another set of information, which reveals even more interesting facts:

- Each unhappy customer tells on an average 10 or more people.
- Resolving a problem quickly will turn 95 per cent of unhappy customers into return customers.

One of the most common and significant reasons for customer switching and disloyalty is the indifference and inattention of the business and, from the customer's point of view, the lack of any real reason to stay. The focus of the relationship in business lies in the fact that 68 per cent customers go elsewhere because the people they deal with are indifferent to their needs. This is interpreted in some other sense—it is complacency and not competition that kills business.

If we look in more detail at what is meant by 'indifference', both through the research statistics and our own experience, it becomes clear that there are many critical aspects behind any customer defection, including:

- Too little contact.
- Too little attention.
- Poor quality attention—especially when problems are encountered
- Generally poor service levels and standards (Roberts-Phelps 2003).

But further studies show that there is something beyond the satisfaction of customers:

Forum Corporation reports that up to 40 per cent of the customer in its study who claimed to be satisfied, switched suppliers without hesitation (Stum & Thiry 1991). *Harvard Business Review* reports that between 65 per cent and 85 per cent of customers who chose a new supplier say they were satisfied or very satisfied with the former one (Reichheld 1993).

Research conducted by the Juran Institute reveals that in excess of 90 per cent of top managers from more than two hundred of America's largest companies agree with the statement, "maximizing customer satisfaction will maximize profitability and market share." Yet, fewer than 2 per cent of the two-hundred-plus respondents were able to measure a bottom-line improvement from a documented increase in the level of customer satisfaction (Fay 1996). Albeit these figures, Relationship Marketing is a fast growing concept in marketing that is patronized by the corporate world for growth and expansion.

## RELATIONSHIP MARKETING—HISTORICAL FRAMEWORK

In 1983, Leonard L. Berry, a distinguished Professor of Marketing at Texas A&M University, coined the word 'Relationship Marketing' when he presented a paper entitled 'Relationship Marketing' at the American

Marketing Association's Services Marketing Conference. The paper was published in the conference proceedings and for the first time, the word Relationship Marketing appeared in the Marketing literature. Later, Jackson (1985) used the concept in Business-to-Business context.

Another opinion is that Relationship Marketing is a gradual extension of the "Nordic School" approach to services marketing and management (Gummesson 1997). There are ample examples to prove long-term relationship emphasized by the Nordic School researchers (Grönroos 2000), but without using the term 'Relationship Marketing' as early as 1977, before Berry and Jackson used the term 'Relationship Marketing'.

Added to this, the scholarly contributions of thought-leaders, namely, B. Schneider, Theodore Levitt, Jagdish Sheth and Atul Parvatiyar, Evert Gummesson, Michael Porter, Adrian Payne and others, to enrich the concept of Relationship Marketing in terms of its academic importance as well as industry applications, lent a differentiated status of Relationship Marketing as another vertical in the discipline of Marketing.

In 1980, B. Schneider wrote: What is surprising is that researchers and businessmen have far more concentrated on how to attract customers to products and services than on retaining customers. In 1983, Theodore Levitt, the exponent of Relationship Marketing, wrote: In a great and increasing proportion of transactions, the relationship actually intensifies subsequent to the sale. This becomes the central factor of the buyer's choice of the seller next time. Relationship Marketing is an approach that emphasizes the continuing relationships between the organization and its customers. It emphasizes the importance of customer service and quality, and of developing a series of transactions with the consumers.

Levitt described his article 'Marketing Myopia' as a manifesto. It challenged the conventional thinking of the time by putting forward a persuasive case for the importance of the marketing approach and the short-sightedness of failing to incorporate it into business strategy.

In an era in which post-war shortages contributed to a concentration on production, most companies had developed a product orientation which, Levitt believed, was too narrow a philosophy to allow continued business success. A drive to increase the efficiency and volume of production took place at the expense of monitoring whether the company was actually producing what the customer wanted. Marketing Myopia stressed that customer wants and desires should be a central consideration of any business.

"The organization must learn to think of itself not as producing goods or services but as buying customers, as doing the things that will make people want to do business with it" (Marketing Myopia).

In order to achieve this, "... the entire corporation must be viewed as a customer-creating and customer satisfying organism. Management must think of itself not as providing products but as providing customer-creating value satisfactions. It must push this idea (and everything it means and requires) into every nook and cranny of the organization."

Of late, the marketers have restructured their strategy to track and monitor activities that address specifics of customer requirements in multiple market segments. This is prevalent, particularly with the world economy moving towards the service economy from product economy. As a result, the new approach to marketing has emerged, which is commonly referred to as *Relationship Marketing*. The concept of Relationship Marketing spread like wildfire during the 1990s. In its wake followed first One to One, then Customer Relationship Management.

Relationship Marketing though conceptually recent, its practice existed earlier in an unformatted and unstructured fashion, which was devoid of any disciplinary value. Till the early 1970s, organizations handling high value outsourced business of clients were largely labelled as *contractors*, often *managing agents* and ones handling low value business known as *vendors* or *suppliers*. These terminologies are still being used, but with the change of mindset, many prefer to address them as *business partners* today.

## GOING BEYOND MARKETING

If Relationship Marketing is taken as an offshoot of Marketing Practice, it would not be unjustified. Because it is not confined to only using the force of relationship in marketing process; rather it implies:

(a) 'Relationship' as a specialized service which needs to be identified with all factors of business, for example, client, society, government, partner, employee and investors.

(b) To identify the areas of development of relationship and making a complete plan and strategy for implementation. The outlook of corporate houses should be oriented to address and augment the relationship development process within the organization.

(c) Maintain and improve the level of relationship accomplished through periodic review.

For example, a growing relationship with any of the factors of business can ease the business acquisition process further and minimize a lot of tasks that need to be undertaken as a starter. The client, who is currently one of the many senior managers of the organization, may likely become the chief executive or one of the major decision-makers in the near future. Therefore, it makes a lot of difference in having the relationship with different interacting stakeholders of business when an organization operates with a long-term business goal.

Sheth and Parvatiyar (2002) ascribed five micro-environmental factors for the growth of relationship orientation in marketing, such as,

- Rapid technological advancements
- Adoption of total quality programme by companies
- Growth of service economy
- Organizational development processes leading to empower-ment of individuals and teams
- An increase in competitive intensity leading to concern for customer retention.

## A NEW DISCIPLINE OF MARKETING

Relationship marketing has become a fundamental concept within modern marketing thought. Some authors even suggest it is the fundamental concept (Stavros 2005).

For academicians, Relationship Marketing is a paradigm shift in marketing philosophy urging the importance of long-term relationship and retaining existing customers over getting new customers; since a bird in hand is worth two in the bush (Saravanan & Ramkumar 2007). Relationship Marketing is a relatively new discipline still in search of its roots. Various sciences have contributed to the systematization of marketing into a viable research and teaching discipline, for example, economics, psychology, sociology, political science and mathematics. Relationship Marketing draws upon these sources as well (Houggard & Bjerre 2002).

However, in view of its growing academic importance and its acceptance across the industries, Relationship Marketing has successfully emerged as one of the key branches of marketing discipline.

Figure 1.1 depicts the position of Relationship Marketing as a unique entity under the aegis of Marketing along with its other branches, such as Marketing Management, Sales Management, Sales Promotion, Advertising and Communications Management, Public Relations, Marketing Research and Consumer Behaviour.

It may also be noted here that Relationship Marketing is functionally related to HR, Finance and Production disciplines because of its cross-functional contribution in the value creation process. Thus, Relationship Marketing stands connected with cross-functional disciplines in the way it acts with cross-functional departments. This has been corroborated in the concept of six markets model of Relationship Marketing.

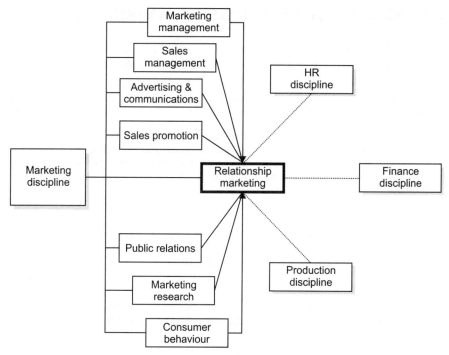

**Figure 1.1  Relationship marketing—a discipline of marketing.**

In the past three decades, there have been at least three successes and three failures in the journey from domain to discipline. The three successes are: consumer behaviour, marketing strategy, and services marketing. The three that have failed to become a distinct discipline even though domain knowledge exists are international marketing, social marketing, and business marketing. By analyzing and understanding why they failed or succeeded in becoming disciplines of marketing, we may get some insights and even engage in intervention to make sure that relationship marketing becomes a distinct discipline in marketing (Sheth & Parvatiyar 2002).

Relationship Marketing is "as much about management as it is about marketing." Indeed, the propeller of the Relationship Marketing school of thought is the recognition by academicians and practitioners alike of the need for some measure of "customer," and "partner," relationship management in the marketing system. Therefore, proposing a new name for the newest school of thought in marketing, "Relationship Marketing Management" would be meaningful. While Relationship Marketing Management will not rise to the status of a discipline, it will replace traditional Marketing Management as the mainstream school of marketing thought (Adel 2005).

# DEFINITIONS OF RELATIONSHIP MARKETING

Definitions of Relationship Marketing have been formulated by eminent thought leaders of this discipline through exhaustive research works, and some of these are discussed here. The following definition, given by Sheth & Parvatiyar (2002), brings clarity on the understanding of Relationship Marketing:

> Relationship Marketing is the ongoing process of engaging in collaborative and cooperative activities, programmes with immediate and end user customers to create and enhance mutual economic value at reduced cost. The emphasis is on the words "ongoing" and "collaborative".

Evert Gummesson (2002):

> Relationship Marketing is marketing based on interactions within networks of relationships. A network is a set of relationships that can grow into enormously complex pattern.

Leonard. L. Berry (1983):

> Relationship Marketing is attracting, maintaining and—in multi-service organizations—enhancing customer relationships.

B. Jackson (1985):

> Relationship Marketing is marketing to win, build and maintain strong lasting relationships with industrial customer.

Morgan and Hunt (1994):

> Relationship Marketing refers to all marketing activities directed to establishing, developing and maintaining successful relational exchanges.

Porter (1993):

> Relationship Marketing is the process whereby both parties—the buyer and the provider—establish an effective, efficient, enjoyable, enthusiastic and ethical relationship: one that is personally, professionally and profitably rewarding to both parties.

Research shows that there is a direct relation between the customer retention and corporate profitability. The cost of acquiring a new customer is 9 to 12 times that of holding on to an existing customer (Brown et al. 1993).

# CONVENTIONAL MARKETING AND RELATIONSHIP MARKETING

Conventional marketing practice envisages product oriented marketing planning and strategy implying a uni-directional involvement, where the market, marketers and end-users, their spokespersons are contented with whatever is embodied in the product. This is possibly because of the following reasons:

- There was absence of stiff competition.
- Price pressure on the producers was less.
- Knowledge/information dissemination process/technology was not in place.

Conventional marketing practice functioned on the principles of 4Ps of marketing, namely product, price, place and promotion, whereas relationship marketing functions on 7Ps of marketing, namely, people, process and physical evidence, in addition to those 4Ps of marketing (Booms & Bitner 1981). In the service industry, *people* determine the success of the product. Training, attitude building, right compensation and company ownership of the people lead to the growth of the best persons. A set of excellent people can create market reputation of an organization. The importance of the *Process* enriches the competence of the firm to differentiate the offer and customize the product and services to leverage maximum client satisfaction. International bodies, Quality Assurance Institutes, International Standards Organizations, etc. award Quality Certifications after a thorough evaluation of the processes undertaken by the organization. *Physical evidence* implies the ambience in which the customer is being served. This implies not only the quality of the food but also the plate on which the food is served, the décor of the room, the surrounding—all these add to the value of physical evidence. When a customer is invited for a product demonstration or training, the ambience of the place, the facilities arranged for the demo must suit the customer's taste or expectations. Or, take the case of reference. The reference should be good enough to provide adequate supporting evidence to the partner's good work to the prospect.

Modern marketing is bi-directional—it has focus on every aspect of the end-users and their spokespersons. Hence, it is relationship that plays a pivotal role when the feedback from the other end starts flowing in. Figure 1.2 illustrates the difference between these two and how important is relationship in the context of cross-functionality based marketing (Mitra & Chatterjee 2000).

According to Kotler et al. (2009), marketing is a societal process by which individuals and groups obtain what they need and want through creating, offering, and freely exchanging products and services of value with others. A very crucial question arises here as to what should be this value? Generally, the monetary value is considered but it is not entirely and only monetary value that is involved. The monetary value is only the material and physical aspect. The underlying significant fact is being the value of the particular need that has to be satisfied. It is the value that a potential customer perceives in his mind. The money he would be ready to part with depends entirely upon the degree of intensity for that

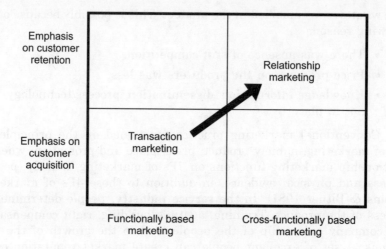

**Figure 1.2  Transition to relationship marketing.**

*Source:*   Professor Adrian Payne (1997), adopted with permission.

need to be fulfilled, the quality of the solution that he has received from the seller and the satisfaction that he gets from it. Looking at the basics of the marketing function, till date exchange has been the main objective of all marketing programmes. This exchange could be more precisely classified as exchange of value in the form of money (especially with reference to physical products) (Grönroos 1990).

Consequently, the main focus of the marketers is to make customers buy, regardless of the fact whether they exist or new customers. Organizations following the traditional marketing philosophy generally feel that a small proportion of the marketing budget can be directed towards retaining existing customers. This type of marketing with the focus on one-time sale and exchange orientation is called *transaction marketing* in the marketing literature. Transaction is a one-time phenomenon and it is basically done for getting financial profits. Each transaction is anew and independent one, irrespective of whether the customer is a repeat customer or a new one. There is no difference in any two customers from the company's point. The transaction approach to marketing is inherently *seller-oriented*; and personal selling is a major activity in transaction marketing (Borden 1964) with focus on optimizing the economic gain in an exchange process between seller and buyer (Gronroos 1994). In addition such calculated exchange ignores humanism that positions people at the center of the social interaction (Smith and Higgins 2000). Table 1.1 shows the difference between Conventional and Relationship Marketing.

**Table 1.1** Difference between Conventional Marketing and Relationship Marketing

| Conventional Marketing | Relationship Marketing |
|---|---|
| One to many transactions without any predictability factor | Focus on one to one transaction; study and analysis of transactions to forecast future trend |
| Defined life cycle that concludes with sale | Continued life cycle after sales; continuous exploration of future requirements, as well as ways and means to address them |
| Driven by 4Ps of marketing mix, namely, product, price, promotion and place | 4Ps are supplemented with another 3Ps, known as people, process and physical evidence to facilitate one to one transaction |
| Moderate customer contact | High customer contact |
| Product-centric marketing | Customer-centric marketing |
| Repeat sales are incidental | Apart from repeat sale, it triggers cross-sell and up-sell |
| Limited use of technology | Exhaustive use of technology as it is considered to be the major enabler of the concept |
| Production-centric quality control | Quality assurance involving cross-functional team |
| Weak initiative to promote customer loyalty | Greater emphasis on customer loyalty |
| Customer handling by business development executive or manager | Relationship manager is dedicated for client servicing |
| Driven by brand equity | Along with brand equity, it is driven by value equity and retention or relationship equity |
| Confined in marketing function | Aligned with organization and other functions of management in terms of business goals and objectives |

Traditionally, organizations encourage their marketing departments to get new customers. It is indeed important to acquire new customers, but it is equally important to retain the existing ones, provided they are profitable enough. Practical examples show that the Customer Life Time Value is greater than the cost of acquisition of new customers. It is quite possible that if the latter is taken care of, the former comes automatically. The present customers, if satisfied, would refer the product to the people they know and also spread a positive word of mouth.

Finally, Relationship Marketing and Transactional Marketing are not mutually exclusive and there is no need for a conflict between them.

However, one approach may be more suitable in some situations than in others. Transactional Marketing is most appropriate when marketing relatively low value consumer products, when the product is a commodity, when switching costs are low, when customers prefer single transactions to relationships, and when customer involvement in production is low. When the reverse of all the above is true, as in typical industrial and service markets, then Relationship Marketing can be more appropriate. Most firms should be blending the two approaches to match their portfolio of products and services. Virtually all products have a service component to them and this service component has been getting larger in recent decades (Wikipedia).

## LEVELS OF RELATIONSHIP MARKETING

Relationship Marketing is a multi-level activity. As Grönroos (1995) cautioned, 'Neither there is a single paradigm of Relationship Marketing nor should one expect it to work that way'. Berry et al. (1991) identified the following three levels of Relationship Marketing:

**Level 1: Price-preference based Relationship Marketing,** where economic incentives are offered to customers to forge a relationship. Examples of this approach are the frequent-flyers schemes, price-off coupons to repeat purchasers, credit facility, etc.

**Level 2: Feelings-based Relationship Marketing,**  where emotional gains are offered to customers to forge a relationship. Here the customers receive such emotional rewards as easy recognition, greetings on personal and professional important dates, etc.

**Level 3: Structure-oriented Relationship,** where the values, policies and systems of the sellers are re-configured to forge a relationship with the customers. Here the whole organization is dedicated to Relationship Marketing. Specific individuals are no longer critical in achieving its goals in the organization since the structure takes over and is re-engineered to Relationship Marketing. This is an organization where relationship orientation is practised at all levels and in all departments (Ruckert & Walker 1991).

In other words, Relationship Marketing has a continuum (Grönroos 1995). It can be tailored to suit the individual needs and intent of the participating service organizations.

## SIX MARKETS MODEL FOR RELATIONSHIP PLANNING

Based on the level of relationship an organization plans to operate, strategic planning for relationship marketing is undertaken accordingly.

This calls for analysis of various networked entities predominant in the specific segment or level chosen for operations.

Adrian Payne (1991, 1997) identifies six markets which he claims are central to Relationship Marketing. They are: internal markets, supplier markets, recruitment markets, referral markets, influence markets, and customer markets.

The traditional marketing plan has focused upon customers or consumers without recognizing the importance of supplier development, recruitment markets, referral sources or 'influencers'. However, each of these 'external' markets can have considerable impact upon performance in the customer/consumer market place (Payne et al. 1995).

**Internal marketing** refers to using marketing techniques within the organization itself. It is claimed that many of the traditional marketing concepts can be used to determine what the needs of "internal customers" are. According to this theory, every employee, team, or department in the company is simultaneously a supplier and a customer of services and products. An employee obtains a service at a point in the value chain and then provides a service to another employee further along the value chain. If internal marketing is effective, every employee will both provide and receive exceptional service from and to other employees. It also helps employees understand the significance of their roles and how their roles relate to others. If implemented well, it can also encourage every employee to see the process in terms of the customer's perception of value added, and the organization's strategic mission.

Recruitment market is best explored through recruitment practices of an organization. A number of research studies have highlighted the importance that **recruitment** practices can have upon the company's performance. This is particularly important if one seeks to develop a certain culture and style within the company. The aim should be to become an organization that attracts the type and calibre of person that matches the profile that the company seeks to sustain in the eyes of the customer.

To do an excellent job of managing *external relationships*, service firms must be prepared to do an excellent job of managing *internal relationships*. This effort begins with recruiting, selecting, and retaining employees who are likely to serve customers well. While service firms strive to match the knowledge, ability, and skills of potential employees to the requirements of the job, most organizations do not have the time or the resources to implement elaborate recruitment and selection systems. This is especially true among services where relatively high turnover levels mandate that recruitment and selection processes be fast and inexpensive. To meet this challenge, managers often focus on a set of easily identifiable individual characteristics, such as experience, job tenure, age, or education that can be assessed during the time of an interview or scan of a job application. Research results indicate that satisfied and committed service employees tend to be older, better educated, and possess a great deal of service experience. These employees also appear to be better able to handle the stress associated with service positions. These characteristics are atypical of the service industry, where employees tend to be younger, possess relatively little experience in any one industry. Implications for managing the recruitment, selection, and retention of service employees are offered, as are directions for future research (Hartline et al. 2003).

**Referral marketing** is developing and implementing a marketing plan to stimulate referrals. Although it may take months before one can see the effect of referral marketing, this is often the most effective part of an overall marketing plan and the best use of resources.

**Marketing to suppliers** is aimed at ensuring a long-term conflict-free relationship in which all parties understand each other's needs and exceed each other's expectations. Such a strategy can reduce costs and improve quality.

**Influence markets** involve a wide range of sub-markets including: government regulators, standards bodies, lobbyists, stockholders, bankers, venture capitalists, financial analysts, stockbrokers, consumer associations, environmental associations, and labour associations. These activities are typically carried out by the public relations department, but relationship marketers feel that marketing to all six markets is the responsibility of everyone in the organization.

Because of the need to ensure that all the dimensions of both external and internal markets are addressed in an integrated and cohesive way and to achieve a sharper focus on the goal of building long-term customer relationship, the development of Relationship Marketing plan is advocated. The purpose of the plan is to ensure the highest degree of integration and focus across six critical markets that form the platform for successful customer relationship. Relationship Marketing plan will begin with a clearly expressed definition of the customer-retention goals of the organization.

## STRATEGIES FOR PRACTISING RELATIONSHIP MARKETING

In the context of service, Relationship Marketing has been defined as attracting, maintaining and in multi-service organizations, enhancing the customer relationships. Here attracting customers is considered to be an intermediary step in the relationship.

Berry (1983) has recommended the following five strategies for practising Relationship Marketing:

- Developing a core service around which to build a customer relationship
- Customizing the relationship to the individual customer
- Augmenting the core service with extra benefits
- Pricing services to encourage customer loyalty
- Marketing to employees so that they would perform as well for customers.

Successful implementation of Relationship Marketing practices requires a strategic approach, which encompasses developing customer-centric processes, selecting and implementing technology solutions, employee empowerment, customer information and knowledge generation capabilities to differentiate them and the ability to learn from the best practices.

Gummesson (2002) has transformed the underlying philosophy of Relationship Marketing into practice with his proposition 30Rs, that is, thirty tangible relationships. The relationships are grouped in the following way. The first two types are market relationships. These are relationships between suppliers, customers, competitors and others who operate in the market. They constitute the basis for marketing, they are externally oriented and apply to the market proper. Some of them concern relationships to both consumers and other organization, others are focused on either consumers or they are interorganizational relationships. The market relationships are:

- *Classic market relationships* (R1–R3): These are the supplier-customer dyad, the triad of supplier-customer-competitor and the physical distribution network, which are treated extensively in general marketing theory.
- *Special market relationships* (R4–R17): They represent certain aspects of the classic relationships, such as the interaction in the service encounter or the customer as the member of a loyalty programme, parasocial relationship leading to relation-ship with brands and objects, etc.

The next two types are non-market relationships, which indirectly influence the efficiency of market relationships:

- *Mega relationships* (R18–R23): These exist above the market relationships. They provide a platform for market relationships and concern the economy and society in general. Among these are mega marketing (lobbying, public opinion and political power), mega alliances (such as the NAFTA, SAFTA) and social relationships (such as friendship and ethnic bonds).
- *Nano relationships* (R24–R30): These are found below the market relationships, that is, relationships inside an organization (intraorganization relationships). All internal

activities influence the externally bound relationships. Examples of nano relationships are the relationships between internal customers, and between internal markets, that arise as a consequence of the increasing use of independent profit centres, divisions and business areas inside organizations. The boundary between the externally and internally directed relationships is sometimes fuzzy; it is a matter of emphasis. For example, the physical distribution network (R3) is part of a logistics flow, concerning internal as well as external customers.

---

*Case Study:*   **Relationship Marketing Strategy–EMI's New Tune Wins New Fans**

---

**Background:** EMI Music is one of the top global recorded music companies, representing artists spanning all musical tastes and genres including Lily Allen, The Beach Boys, The Beatles, Coldplay, Norah Jones, Kylie Minogue, Pink Floyd and The Rolling Stones. Traditionally relying on mass market brick-and-mortar retailers to drive market share and revenues, the emergence of digital media formats and the popularity of online retailers like iTunes dramatically impacted EMI Music's margins. As the sales of CDs began to plummet, the music industry as a whole was left scrambling to reinvent itself.

**Objective:** Facing declining revenues and lagging consumer demand, EMI Music Europe moved to embrace the digital music age. However, it quickly recognized that if its business model was undergoing a transformation, so too would its marketing and sales strategies. No longer able to rely on mass marketing to drive in-store sales, EMI Music had to figure out who, exactly, was downloading its artists' music, and how to maximize communications with those consumers on the right channel to strengthen relationships and drive more revenue.

**Solution:** EMI Music opted for enterprise marketing software from Neolane. Neolane helped EMI to organize customer data derived from different databases, from numerous data capture systems, and from various channels, including registration cards, email, direct mail and artist websites. Neolane's platform allows EMI Music to capture and store customer data in a centralized database, and to continually merge, purge and de-duplicate the information. Subsequently, EMI Music's marketing staff is able to precisely target customers according to media habits and preferences, musical tastes, online behaviour, shopping habits and sociodemographics. Today, nearly 100 targeted campaigns are launched each month on the basis of these criteria.

Now, EMI Music can work seamlessly across multiple channels including direct, email and mobile, enabling EMI Music to send SMS (Short Message Service or text) messages to alert fans about upcoming events, new ringtones and screensavers.

*"We needed to bring all of this data together to gain better insight into our fans' purchasing behaviour and preferences. As a result, we are able to drive better customer interactions across multiple channels, including email and SMS in particular,"* said Guillaume Pech-Gourg, Head of Content and Customer Relationship Management at EMI Music, France.

**Results:** Just 18 months after implementing Neolane's automated marketing solution, EMI Music's digital revenues have nearly offset the decline in physical sales, which demonstrated the effectiveness of its new marketing approach. Now the company is on track to meet the projected goals of ensuring 25 per cent of sales revenue come from legitimate music downloads by 2010.

Today, EMI Music depends on Neolane to help execute its relationship marketing strategies, promote its artists, maintain fan clubs, run surveys and draws, and to encourage customer loyalty. Neolane's enterprise marketing platform works seamlessly across various direct, email and mobile marketing channels, allowing EMI Music to send SMS messages to music fans that have opted in through email or direct mail, alerting them to upcoming concerts, new ringtones and screensavers. And later this year, the company will begin rolling out MMS (Multimedia Messaging Service) campaigns that offer access to artist's photos and video clips on 3G wireless devices, and allow music downloads directly to new generation multimedia cell phones.

*Source:* www.mmaglobal.com.

## RELATIONSHIP BUILDING

In the business-to-business world, relationships are very important (and take even longer to form) for several reasons. As the cost and complexity of a purchase go up, decision-makers place more emphasis on forming a strong relationship with a partner who will do more than quoting prices and taking orders. Relationship building can be possible through quality delivery of service; leading service providers see quality as a strategic tool.

The process of taking prospective customers from the point of initial interest to where they become loyal is where the service quality comes into play. By delivering excellent quality, service providers can receive benefits including increased growth through improved customer retention and increased customer acquisition.

On the other hand, repeat customers depend heavily on building a relationship of trust (Allen, C.). Each individual gathers information on the Web and changes his or her attitude along the way. There are a number of variables that can affect how fast a relationship can be developed.

A person's acceptance or rejection of new products affects how fast he or she will form a relationship with a company and buy its products. In addition, the way the marketers communicate with others can affect how quickly they are accepted.

For example, a person can be interpreted in several different ways if he or she uses words with multiple meanings, and this can slow down the relationship-building process. Companies can have the same communication problem, especially when common, everyday words take on complex, technical meanings.

Take the word 'personalization.' What could be easier to understand than personalization? It is all about creating an experience, specifically for one individual. However, in the personalization industry, the word means different things to different companies.

Understanding how customers gather information and make decisions is especially important for online marketers, because Web visitors can click to another website faster than TV viewers can find their remotes. Fortunately, marketers can use their own shopping experiences to learn how information is gathered and examine how relationships are formed.

Think about when you bought your last car. You may have started by gathering information about the model either on the Web or from magazines. What followed next was a visit by a local dealer, a test drive, negotiating the price, and finally making a purchase decision. Through this process, you were not only gathering information, you were also building a relationship with the manufacturer and the local dealer.

Throughout the process, you were making decisions about trust, reliability, consistency, and other aspects of a relationship. In the end, the dealer with the lowest price does not always get the sale, especially if he or she has not forged a relationship with the customer.

## Online Relationship

It is interesting that Web retailers and manufacturers think that buying relationships can be created faster online than in the offline world.

But are companies able to build trust any faster online than offline? It is a little early to tell for sure, but it appears that the speed of building these profitable customer relationships is tied to how well a company understands the needs of its online visitors.

Many online merchants have been surprised at the high ratio of page views compared to the number of orders. It is well known that shoppers are using the Web to gather information before making important purchases; therefore, it should not be surprising that people are viewing a large number of pages to gather that information.

One can take advantage of this by providing more informative and educational content than the competitors. This not only encourages visitors to spend more time at their site, but it helps them understand that there is enough care taken to create a positive shopping experience when they buy. And that is what building a strong customer relationship is all about.

## Relationship Blog

Relationship Marketing is based on the idea that people prefer to do business with those who they know and like. After all, it is easier to buy from a friend than from someone you have never heard of before. It is a matter of building trust. It is said that people need to hear an offer at least seven times before they buy. That concept certainly works against the single step marketing method (Shah 2007).

That is where a business blog can be really helpful. A reader can be reached seven times with ease, and many more times besides, through the blogging interaction. As you write your daily blog entries, your readers get to know you and your business on a more personal level. Your blog begins that all-important relationship with your prospects and current customers. You have started a blogging conversation.

As they read about your daily business activities, your problem solving ideas, your business advice, and your various products, they begin to think of themselves as a part of the company. In fact, they are!

Your existing customers will remain loyal to your business, through the regular personal contact of your blog. Your customers will not only stay loyal, but they will often bring tons of valuable referral business to your company. Happy customers are your best marketing friends. They will become customer brand evangelists for your business and its products and services.

## Voting in Reality (Talent Search) Shows

'Send your vote through SMS'—now a very common practice to select the best performer in any entertainment 'reality show' hosted by reputed channels like Zee, Sony or Star. Raj TV Network of Chennai is one of the pioneering channels to promote this concept in their talent search programme—'Rajageetham' for Tamil songs. It started in the late 90s and polling votes for selecting the best singer at the end of that episode through physical distribution of small voting slips and their collection from the audience present in the programme. This programme is not only popular among the Tamil speaking people in India, but there are instances of non-Tamil speaking people enjoying and participating in the programme.

## Relationship Building Process in Pharmaceutical Industry

Although the practice and the process vary from industry to industry, the guidelines remain the same (Lal 2000). In the pharmaceutical industry, the practice is different where the customer is not the actual consumer of the product. Here the customer is the doctor. More personalized interactions can lead to higher customer satisfaction, that is, the knowledge of the Medical Representative (MR) about the doctor at an intimate level, for example, his hobbies, likes and dislikes, family details. The fundamental premise is that the doctor is as human as anybody else is and hence we should recognize his individuality. It is of utmost importance that it is decided beforehand what kind of information would be collected and, much more importantly, how it will be used. Interactions can be at two levels:

1. *Personally at the MR level:* The most productive would be using human intervention. The MR can easily collect most of the information from his day-to-day interactions with his customer. Alternatively, a formal structured questionnaire can also be administered.

2. *Direct at the corporate level:* The structured questionnaires requesting further details can also be mailed to doctors with each response entitled to a token gift, etc. This approach typically would yield a lower rate of return but the quality of information would be superior to the first approach as it is coming directly from the doctor.

The information collected is then incorporated to the basic database earlier formed. Just to give an idea of the type of information collected by companies, consider the following:

- *Personal information:* Place and date of birth, marriage anniversary, details of children, qualification and experience.
- *Hobbies and interests:* activities during spare time, TV channels watched, general interest, magazines read, and favourite vacation destinations.
- *Professional interests:* Type and name of medical journals read, professional membership of association(s), attendance of national conferences.
- *Ownership details:* Household durable owned, vehicle ownership.

Companies have been able to collect enormous amount of such data through either of the means enumerated earlier. What is important to note that they have been able to demonstrate their sincerity in actually using this data.

According to Sergio Zyman, former Chief Marketing Officer of Coca Cola, if you build enough of a reservoir of goodwill for your brand, when you have problems your customers are going to be a lot more forgiving. Besides, if you have a relationship with your customers, they are more likely to stick to you when your products come under attack by another brand. How does this forgiving look come from the client with whom there is purely a business relation? It is the same chemistry that works in the family and its success lies in the art of living underneath their skin.

There are certain other marketing strategies adopted to build effective relationship with the client. Some of the terminologies are recent in nature, namely:

- Permission marketing
- Database marketing
- Retention marketing

# PERMISSION MARKETING

Permission Marketing centred on obtaining customer consent to receive information from a company. It states that when communicating with customers, one should be anticipated, be personal, and be relevant. The customer's definition of these three ideas would naturally change over time, so you have to listen to the customer and engage in a dialogue.

This has the effect of upgrading the quality of your customer base because, in theory, only the people who really want something from you grant permission. This is definitely in the customer profiling camp, where the focus is on improving the value of customers and not spending money on customers who are not interested.

Coined and popularized by Seth Godin, *permission marketing* is about building an ongoing relationship of increasing depth with customers. In the words of Seth Godin, it is "turning strangers into friends, and friends into customers."

Permission marketing has been hailed as a way for marketers to succeed in a world increasingly cluttered with marketing messages.

# SOLICITED AND UNSOLICITED EMAILS

To somehow get a tick in the box that says you can email the prospect or customer something, anything, at some time turns to be an irritant to client or prospect.

This approach of 'tick and mail' sees permission as something negative; a constraint to business or an entry fee to the email marketing game. This misses the whole point; permission, properly gained and used, benefits the marketer.

Anyone taking this negative approach will inevitably end up sending emails to people who do not really expect or want them. The results are—negative word of mouth, spam complaints, blacklisting and more.

A second approach sees permission as a valuable but flexible concept. This is the type of permission marketing often practiced by companies with strong brands or reputations, and deep pockets. In the initial engagement with the customer or prospect, they seek and get genuine and clear permission to send specific marketing messages.

Then they fall victim to the temptation to extend and redefine the permission granted; "You signed up to a newsletter about X. Well, if you like X, you'll probably be interested in Y, too. So we signed you up to our newsletter about Y."

The marketer often justifies this arbitrary extension of permission by claiming that it is acceptable in the context of the relationship they have built with the customer or prospect, or that it is somehow in the customer's best interests.

If you made the right inferences about their interests, attitudes and perceived relationship with you, then you are OK. But that is a huge "if". It is all too easy to misjudge all three. More usually, this justification is just a public relations exercise. But you are still putting those brands and those relationships—two of the most valuable assets you have—on the line, every time you take the decision to unilaterally extend the permission granted. If you have misjudged your customers or prospects, then it is perdition marketing again.

In a third approach, marketers do not see permission as about meeting some kind of administrative, contractual or even ethical standards. They see permission as a way of initiating and building a profitable long-term relationship with an attentive and responsive customer or prospect, for as long as you respect the integrity of the permission granted.

This approach labels you, as a company the customer or prospect can trust, one who respects their wishes, one who delivers on promises. It is a risk-free business proposition with staying power.

So, ask yourself three questions to decide which kind of permission marketing you practice?

1.   *Are you requesting permission because you want to, or because you have to?*

2.   *Do you see permission as an asset to be nurtured or one to be exploited?*

3.   *Are you practising permission marketing or perdition marketing?*

## DATABASE MARKETING

Database Marketing is a form of direct marketing using databases of customers or potential customers to generate personalized communications in order to promote a product or service for marketing purposes.

The method of communication can be any addressable medium, as in direct marketing.

The distinction between direct and database marketing stems primarily from the attention paid to the analysis of data. Database marketing emphasizes gathering all available customer, lead, and prospect information into a central database and using statistical techniques to develop models of customer behaviour, which are then used to select customers for communications. As a consequence, database marketers also tend to be heavy users of *data warehouses*, because having a greater amount of data about customers increases the likelihood that a more accurate model can be built.

The "database" is usually name, address, and transaction history details from internal sales or delivery systems, or a bought-in compiled 'list' from another organization, which has captured that information from its customers. Typical sources of compiled lists are charity donation forms, application forms for any free product or contest, product warranty cards, subscription forms, and credit application forms.

The communications generated by database marketing may be described as junk mail or spam, if it is unwanted by the addressee. Direct and database marketing organizations, on the other hand, argue that a targeted letter or e-mail to a customer, who wants to be contacted about offerings that may interest the customer, benefits both the customer and the marketer.

Although organizations of any size can employ database marketing, it is particularly well-suited to companies with a large number of customers. This is because a large population provides a greater opportunity to find segments of customers or prospects that can be communicated in a customized manner. In smaller (and more homogeneous) databases, it will be difficult to justify on economic terms the investment required to differentiate messages. As a result, database marketing has flourished in sectors, such as financial services, telecommunications, and retail, all of which have the ability to generate significant amounts of transaction data for millions of customers.

Database marketing applications can be divided logically between those marketing programmes that reach existing customers and those that are aimed at prospective customers.

## Consumer Data

In general, database marketers seek to have as much data available about customers and prospects as possible. For marketing to existing customers, more sophisticated marketers often build elaborate databases of customer information. These may include a variety of data, including name and address, history of shopping and purchases, demographics, and the history of past communications to and from customers. For larger companies with millions of customers, such data warehouses can often be multiple terabytes in size.

## Business Data

For many business-to-business (B2B) company marketers, the number of customers and prospects will be smaller than that of comparable business-to-consumer (B2C) companies. Also, their relationships with customers will often rely on intermediaries, such as salespeople, agents, dealers, and the number of transactions per customer may be small. As a result, business-to-business marketers may not have as much data at their disposal. Another complication is that they may have many contacts for a single organization, and determining which contact to communicate with through direct marketing may be difficult. On the other hand, the database of business-to-business marketers often include data on the business activity of the respective client that can be used to segment markets, e.g. special software packages for transport companies, for lawyers, etc. Customers in business-to-business environments often tend to be loyal since they need after-sales service for their products and appreciate information on product upgrades and service offerings. Sources of customer data often come from the sales force employed by the company and from the service engineers. Increasingly, online interactions with customers are providing business-to-business marketers with a lower cost source of customer information.

*Source:* www.wikipedia.com.

# RETENTION MARKETING

Retention Marketing and Zero defection emphasize the relationship to existing customers. The latter term is paraphrasing the 'zero defects' quality strategy. This strategy says that a company should continuously improve its quality and deliver defect-free goods and services. Zero defection means a defect-free relationship, reducing a loss of customer to zero. This strategy, however, does not imply that the customer should be kept at all costs. If a customer is unprofitable, defection should be encouraged. What the zero defection strategy really says that a good customer should not leave because of disinterest from the supplier, late delivery, sloppy service or wrong pricing (Gummesson 2002).

# PERDITION MARKETING

As opposed to Retention and Permission marketing, the dictionary defines perdition as total destruction, or the loss of happiness at a future date. Particularly, in a down economy, the pressure of posting glittering figures in the balance sheet, often forces the companies in resorting to stringent short cut measures that might have adverse effects on the long term sustenence of business.

Sometime back, PricewaterhouseCoopers (PwC) issued its Trendsetter Barometer Survey, which encompasses interviews with the CEOs of 407 product and service companies identified in the media as the fastest growing over the last five years. More than 75 per cent rated their companies as better at innovation than their competitors, which they considered their biggest competitive advantage. Yet buried in the report was another statistic—less than half considered their companies better at marketing than their competitors, or higher in brand recognition. Which once again begs the question—if you build it, will they come?

The tech landscape is littered with companies who built superior products, placed all of their faith in "innovation" and "product development," and then found themselves out-flanked by lesser products with superior marketing efforts.

One of the best-known examples is WordPerfect, which in the early 1990s was the premier word processing program. When Microsoft bundled Word with its Excel spreadsheet program and PowerPoint presentation software and called the entire suite Office, IT decision-makers chose convenience and interoperability over performance. It was a pure marketing ploy that paid off. Today, Microsoft Office is on 90 per cent of corporate and government desktops, and WordPerfect is primarily a niche player in the legal industry.

For many in the tech sector, it is all about the technology. Make it better, faster, cheaper than the competition. These are quantifiable results, and engineers like hard data. So do CEOs who are focused on the balance sheet. There is also an element of competitive spirit in focusing on products.

The trouble is, products cannot exist in a vacuum. In order to keep making new and better ones, you first have to sell the ones you have. That is Economics. But how can people buy what they do not know about? Word of mouth is a good thing, but it is slow and imprecise. Without a concerted marketing effort, the best product in the world remains a best-kept secret.

An interesting phenomenon occurs in a down economy. At this point, where risk is amplified, IT decision-makers look for the familiar. Referring Scott Nelson, Vice President and Research Director at Gartner Group, it seems that "The market is drifting toward safe choices. If clients are struck with some dilemma about a vendor, they drift to the big-name players, even if the solution is not adequate to their needs."

So what happens? At the very point smaller organizations need to be most aggressive in order to inspire confidence in potential customers, they often cut their marketing budgets and disappear from the landscape. This is done because marketing is viewed as an expense, and expenses must be trimmed in order to meet the numbers for the quarter. Never mind the impact on sales of such a move—it is not easily quantifiable. But the impact of a budget reduction is easy to see—it is decisive, and immediate.

Think of it another way. If you are in a room with 50 people and they all start shouting different things at once, it is difficult to make out any one thing being shouted. But empty the room down to two people, and it is a lot easier to hear what either one is saying. The same goes for marketing. In boom times, where everyone is making noise, it is tough to get heard above the crowd. But in times of relative quiet, a clear, concise message stands out against the silence.

## RELATIONSHIP MARKETING DURING ECONOMIC DOWNTURN

Economic downturn is one such alarming phase in business cycle that poses severe threats to business operations, and in some extreme cases collapse of the enterprise is not unknown. During boom, when economy is upbeat with soaring stock market index, no one knows what may follow a couple of months later—no wonder it is recession that sends shockwave along its spine. Trim, prune, and downsize become hard-hitting catchphrases during slowdown. Management acts rough and tough to beat the business adversities—pink slips, job cuts, salary cuts, cost control, price cut, highly optimized use of resources, plummeting of interest rate, etc. are some of the measures taken to protect business because recession has its all pervasive manifestations on the economic growth and stability of any business enterprise. Large entrepreneurs readjust their business strategies in the wake of faltering low consumer confidence and economic instability within the financial markets; companies have to develop new business opportunities to replace those hardest hit.

During recession, when money is tight, it is critical that businesses find effective ways to communicate with their market if they are to continue to prosper and grow. It is easy in these hard economic times to attribute slow sales to the economy, but the problem can be exacerbated if business fails to meet new people and networking. Even more important is relationship marketing.

By pulling in the purse string and limiting expenses, one can do away with the relationships. History has shown that businesses often reduce or completely stop the money spent on marketing and advertising during economic slowdowns. The economy may have something to do with fewer people spending money, but there is nothing one can do about the plight of the economy. The preferred option in such circumstances is to practice relationship marketing with people in ones own sphere of influence to boost up sales.

Building relationships requires finding new prospects and making your name first in their minds so that when they have a need for promotional products, they turn to you first. Particularly, when we build strong networks and nurture meaningful relationships with the people we serve, we garner unlimited referrals and are less affected by economic down cycles.

Joe Girard earned recognition in *The Guinness Book of World Records* as the "World's Greatest Retail Salesman" for 12 consecutive years. Joe was not born with a silver spoon in his mouth. Joe was abused by his father as a child, lost jobs as an adult and then went bankrupt. He finally landed a job at a Chevrolet dealership. Joe did very well, personally selling more cars than most dealers. In fact, people stood in line to buy cars from Joe.

What was his secret? Joe practised relationship marketing. Here is how he did it. He sent 13 handwritten cards to each of his clients and prospects every year—one card each month and one on Christmas. These cards communicated appreciation, tips and giveaways—never special sales, discounts or promotions. During his 15 years, Joe sent 13,000 handwritten cards! Every recipient began anticipating a card from Joe every month, and he was the first person on their mind when they were ready to buy a car.

What can we learn from Joe's story and how can we expand upon it? Strategic objectives can be put in place, so that businesses can better withstand the impact of economic downswings (Saunders 2008).

McGraw-Hill Research's Laboratory of Advertising Performance studied recessions in the United States. Following the 1981–1982 recessions, it analyzed the performance of some 600 industrial companies during that economic downturn. It found that "business-to-business firms that maintained or increased their marketing expenditures during the 1981–1982 recessions averaged significantly higher sales growth both during the recession and for the following three years than those which eliminated or decreased marketing."

Business consultants and marketing experts realize the need for business to find innovative marketing channels leveraging the philosophy of relationship marketing during a recession. It is suggested that marketing executives and entrepreneurs take a new approach to marketing in the downturn as it is the time to think outside the usual realms of traditional marketing.

Because it leverages online social media and networks, relationship marketing is an incredibly cost-effective means of communicating with the market. Thanks to the rapid spread of new Internet technology, the emerging area of relationship marketing is a boon for small and medium sized businesses looking for cost-effective marketing strategies.

The basic tools of relationship marketing—email, blogs, online social networks like Facebook, or online video via YouTube—have extremely low costs in comparison to traditional marketing.

Thus, technology acts as a facilitator for the businesses techniques to get connected directly with the audience, en masse, on a low budget. It is time to look at the price points, for example, because customer spending and behaviour changes during economic lean times, businesses could benefit from offering a lower cost stripped back version of their popular products. Alternatively, other products could be marketed as 'micro luxuries', offering an affordable escape from the doom and gloom.

Hence, strong consideration should be given to the idea that relationship marketing can play a critical role in times of recessions. While the role of marketing was once more informational than brand identity building, and considering that never more than today has the clutter factor been so great, relationships between customers and brands are critical. Relationship marketing has surged to the top of effective marketing campaigns as a means to keep an appropriate level of share of mind for purchase loyalty and thereby serves to foster and maintain consumer-brand relationships.

## LEARNING RELATIONSHIP

One-to-one marketing can be thought of quite simply as "treating different customers differently"—that is, telling them apart and remembering them individually, interacting with them, and then customizing the product or service to each customer's own, individual needs. This implies three distinct computer capabilities—the database, interactivity, and mass customization.

When these three capabilities are used together, the firm can keep track of its customer individually and remember him or her. The customer can interact with the firm and say what he wants, or how he wants to be served. And then the firm, masscustomizes its product or service, in order to meet these needs. At this point, yet another interaction takes place, and the customer tells the firm how to better adjust the service or better fit the product. Over time, as the customer *teaches* the firm how he wants to be served, and the firm incorporates this knowledge into its actual behaviour towards that customer, a "Learning Relationship" is created. It is this relationship that ensures the customer's continued loyalty and protects the firm's unit margins.

A Learning Relationship is a relationship with a customer that gets "smarter" with every interaction. If every time you interact with a customer you can tailor your service or product a little bit better, based on what the customer told you the last time, then after a while you will have set up a barrier to competition that will be nearly insurmountable. After all, even if your competitor offers the same exact quality of product and the same level of customization as you do, if your customer wants an equivalent product he must first *re-teach* the competitor what he has already gone to the trouble of teaching you (Peppers and Rogers 1999).

Not only will a Learning Relationship make a customer inherently more loyal, but it will tend to protect a firm's margins as well. The single biggest threat to unit margins at most businesses today is the "commoditization" that comes from competitive marketing. Other firms imitate your product or service, offering the same features and benefits to the market, and rendering your product less unique. In such a market, prices fall as competitors scramble to build and protect their own share.

But by using individual customer input to tailor a product or service—or just to tailor some aspect of the product-service "bundle"—an enterprise can escape the trap of commoditization and protect its margins. A custom product, driven by individualized interaction, is inherently unique. Moreover, if every time you interact with a customer your product can be better tailored to that customer's needs, then with every interaction the product you render will become more convenient, and therefore more valuable, to *that* customer.

## TIPS ON RELATIONSHIP BUILDING

### Example from SAE—Building Relationship

Servicios Automotrices Echegaray (SAE) is a proprietary firm owned by Alfredo Gomez Luna, a mechanical engineer of 30 years' standing. Specializing in the repair of automotive vehicles, SAE is located over the Avenida Gustavo Baz Na 181, in Echegaray, Naucalpan, a state of Mexico, in densely populated neighbourhood with settlers from the middle-income group (Chowdhary 2002).

At Servicios Automotrices Echegaray, proprietor Alfredo Gomez impresses upon his employees, through personal example, that customers must be treated as friends. The following are his guiding principles:

- You do not make abnormal and unfair profits out of friends. SAE bases its repair pricing on labour costs plus a 40 per cent margin. As most of its customers are themselves automotive experts, there is no point in trying to hoodwink them.

- Do not make a margin on a friend's cause. The discounts offered by suppliers should be passed on to friends.

- Do whatever is possible to help a friend. It may mean working overnight or even on weekends. Remember, a friend in need is a friend indeed.

- Try to share your friend's concerns. Learn more and more about his vehicle—what is causing him trouble and keep him cautioned on what could cause a problem in future. Take a ride with him in his vehicle to understand his concerns fully.

- Drive with him when he comes to collect the car, and ensure that he is fully satisfied with the repair. Do not compromise on this.

- Friends need to be in touch. Maintain a database and call your friends when it is time for routine maintenance.

- Friends should spend time together. So make a party of your job. Allow your friends to participate in what you are doing and how you are doing it. Share with them whatever you do and plan to do. Encourage them to help you fix their cars and maintain them.

- Friends will give you the chance, for they know no one is perfect. Even if you make mistakes, they may be willing to overlook them. Just let them know that you are doing your best. Track your performance and keep improving so as to help your friends better. If needed, get back to school (to learn new advances and update on technology).

# ENCOURAGING RELATIONSHIP FEEDBACK

Feedback reflects the current value of the product and services received by the end users. It spells in clear terms the level of satisfaction or dissatisfaction with the product and services offered by an organization. In business-to-business scenario, it also depends on the person who is responsible for collecting the feedback.

Why is the person collecting feedback so important? If the customer does not open up before the person, then the meaning of product, value, services, etc. lose their ground. Depending on the modus operandi, we may be faced with one or some of these categories of feedback:

**Category A:** Clients feel free to open themselves before the partner and help the partner in having feedback. The business partner nicely clarifies everything. Even any lapse from client side is tackled very gently.

**Category B:** Clients may still hesitate to open up before the partner because they are not sure of things.

**Category C:** Some of them do not like to open up lest the partner may react harshly if there is a lapse in the information.

**Category D:** The client feels disinterested in opening up because there is always a 'shut up' look from the partner.

Good business partners always facilitate and work for creating an environment that encourages Category 'A' feedback. Customer feedback for evaluation of relationship has been discussed in Chapter 10 (Measuring Relationship Effectiveness).

# TREND OF CUSTOMER ASPIRATIONS

Feedback is one such means to assess customer satisfaction. At the same time, to understand customer satisfaction, it is important to gauze the trend of clients/customers needs. In this context, it is apparent that the customer's need is a dynamic entity. The customer may be happy today and expected to be happy tomorrow. In spite of the satisfaction with the product or service, customer may switch elsewhere when they ask for more and someone else offers 'the extra satisfaction' quicker and faster through innovation. Some of the simplest and easily identifiable trends of customer's aspiration are listed below:

(a) Smaller

(b) Cheaper

(c) Faster

(d) Easier to learn

(e) Simple to use

(f) Easy to maintain

(g) Latest (technology).

In fact, the last point, that is, latest technology has become more pertinent in view of knowledge explosion through the Internet. Now, everyone is aware of technology and there is no wonder about it. Consumers, customers would prefer to have something new for enjoying the advantages of latest technology.

Most of those seven points are valid irrespective of any industry type. The commercial success of the product lies in its acceptance by the average consumers/users. Convenience of use is important here and the more the product reaches the average persons, there are higher volume sales, resulting in greater revenue.

The awareness and inclination for capturing the customer's urge to have more is possible, only when there is relationship and intimacy with the customer. Conventional or transaction marketing does not take into account the nuances of the customer's behavioural pattern with changing time whereas Relationship Marketing has opened up the scope of achieving the same. According to conventional marketing philosophy, the customer was thought of as a segment of the population rather than an individual. As a result, on most occasions, the offers failed to meet the needs of individual customers (Mukherjee 2007). The marketing orientation was regarded as a method to enable firms to achieve better understanding of customers. Kohli and Jaworski (1990) suggested that the firm that possesses marketing orientation would go about generating an organization-wide market intelligence pertaining to customers' needs; the intelligence would be assessable to the people within the firm and the organization would respond to the intelligence that has been collated in a holistic manner. In this regard, Hunt and Morgan (1995) suggest that firms need to consider not just the customer but also the competitors. Day (1994) further elaborates by adding issues like market sensing, customer linking, channel bonding and technology monitoring. The moot point here is of keeping track of change and responding to the changes appropriately thereby meeting customers' aspirations.

## CUSTOMER RELATIONSHIP MANAGEMENT (CRM)

The study of Relationship Marketing is never complete without CRM. Conversely speaking, CRM has its roots in Relationship Marketing. Relationship Marketing is a philosophy and orientation towards customer retention and CRM is regarded as the practical implementation of Relationship Marketing (Christopher et al. 1991). Precisely, it is a result of marriage between Relationship Marketing and Information Technology. Nevertheless, there are conceptual foundations of CRM emerged out of research and analytical studies. One of the most accepted definitions of CRM is:

A comprehensive strategy and process of acquiring, retaining and partnering with selective customers to create superior value for the company and customer (Sheth & Parvatiyar 2001).

The purpose of CRM is to improve marketing productivity. Marketing productivity is achieved by increasing marketing efficiency and by enhancing marketing effectiveness (Sheth & Sisodia 1995). As a result of co-operative and collaborative processes from both client and partner ends, there is a creation of superior mutual value chain.

According to Bob Thompson, founder of CRMGuru.com, CRM is a business strategy to acquire and manage the most valuable customer relationships. CRM requires a customer-centric business philosophy and culture to support effective marketing, sales and service processes. CRM applications can enable effective customer relationship management, provided that an enterprise has the right leadership, strategy and culture.

There are three key elements to a successful CRM initiative: people, process, and technology. The people throughout a company— from the CEO to each and every customer service representative—need to buy in to and support CRM. A company's business processes must be reengineered to bolster its CRM initiative; often from the view of, how can this process better serve the customer? Firms must select the right technology to drive these improved processes, provide the best data to the employees, and be easy enough to operate that users would not balk. If one of these three foundations is not sound, the entire CRM structure will crumble. In a nutshell, CRM is just an enabler of Relationship Marketing and hence it would be wrong to assume that more technology leads to a more effective CRM programme (Batterly 2003). CRM has been discussed in detail in Chapter 12 (Technology in Relationship Marketing).

## e-CRM

In simplest terms, e-CRM provides companies with a means to conduct interactive, personalized and relevant communications with customers across both electronic and traditional channels. It utilizes a complete view of the customer to make decisions about messaging, offers and channel delivery. It synchronizes communications across otherwise disjoint customer facing systems.

e-CRM adheres to permission-based practices, respecting individuals preferences regarding how and whether they wish to communicate with the partner and it focuses on understanding how the economies of customer relationships affect the business (Chaturvedi & Bhatia 2000).

Table 1.2 shows how Relationship Marketing and Customer Relationship Management differ from each other in terms of concept and practice.

**Table 1.2**   Difference between Relationship Marketing and Customer Relationship Management

| Relationship Marketing | Customer Relationship Management (CRM) |
|---|---|
| A philosophy that helps to draw a marketing strategy embodying the spirit of relationship | More about technology, putting strategy into practice as regards how relationship marketing can be implemented in the organization using the IT product and solutions |
| Business interactions with clients across the organization to understand clients' present and future needs and ways and means to address them | Collaborative and operational CRM facilitates interactions with end clients using technology tools, such as call centre, IVRS, portal, etc. |
| Relationship Marketing acts as a source of more authentic business data about prospects and clients | Pervasive use of IT tools for customer profiling and business data analysis |
| Outcomes of successful Relationship Marketing are cross-sell, up-sell and repeat sale | CRM outputs using Business Intelligence, Data Warehouse, etc. tools support top management in taking strategic business decisions |

**Table 1.2** Difference between Relationship Marketing and Customer Relationship Management (*contd.*)

| Relationship Marketing | Customer Relationship Management (CRM) |
|---|---|
| More of person to person interactions, handling critical situations to win customer confidence | Highly process-oriented activity originating from strategy |
| Activities coordinated by relationship manager | Responsibilities lie predominantly with technology team led by IT Head in functional co-ordination with Relationship Manager |
| Functions with the objective of long-term profitable relationship with the client | Support the internal team with analytical figures to achieve business goals and objectives |

## ADVANTAGES OF RELATIONSHIP MARKETING

The secret is creating brands that listen and learn from the consumers. It is about looking relationship rather than transactions. It means providing information that has a unique value to customers based on information from them. This is the centrepiece of Relationship Marketing and the following are the benefits:

**Increase loyalty**. Customers who have a relationship with your brand are less likely to migrate to your competitors.

**Decrease acquisition costs**. It is much more profitable to keep your best customers and to upgrade them rather than acquiring new customers who have no link to your brand.

**More business from existing customers**. When you know what they want from you, it is much easier to cross and up-sell. Information is the "oxygen of the modern age". It is changing the way consumers look at your brands. You need to use it to change the way you look at your consumers.

Studies have shown that while manufacturing costs have declined from 55 per cent to 30 per cent, management costs from 25 per cent to 15 per cent, the marketing costs have increased from 20 per cent to 55 per cent. The practice of relationship has the potential to improve marketing productivity through improved marketing effectiveness.

**Cross-selling and up-selling.** Cross-selling and up-selling are some of the major derivatives of Relationship Marketing. Cross-selling and up-selling techniques are deployed to provide customers easy access to products they may want or need. This has been discussed in detail in Chapter 6.

*Cross-selling* consists of displaying or linking to products related to the one(s) the user is already viewing or in possession. For example, in the garment store, after you choose a ready-made shirt, the counter salesperson shows you a variety of ties or else if you buy a trouser, you are offered to buy a shirt.

*Up-selling* consists of displaying or linking to a more expensive alternative to the one the customer has chosen. Up-selling can help users understand what is available at the next higher price level, and how much the additional function or quality would cost. For instance, if the customer chooses an expensive trouser, he may be offered a suit.

To sum up the advantages, business firms would adopt Relationship Marketing only if it has the potential to benefit them. Some business consultants feel that Relationship Marketing is one of the rescue options during economic downturn. When the customers enter into a relationship with a firm, they are willingly foregoing other options and limiting their choice. Some of the personal motivations to do so result from (a) greater efficiency in decision making, (b) reduction in information processing, (c) achieving more cognitive in decisions, and (d) deduction of perceived risk with future decisions (Shajahan 2004).

## CONCLUSION

Relationship Marketing is an emerging concept that facilitates the business community to view their customer's requirements in a more personalized way so that the chances of defection are minimized to the best possible extent. It is different from the conventional marketing where the client and the producer position each other to achieve short-term business goals. There are three distinct levels of Relationship Marketing and each level has its own characteristics and importance in terms of addressing relationship aspects in the specific business segment, and accordingly the relationship marketing strategy is framed. Planning for relationship marketing is based on six market models, namely customer, internal, referral, recruitment, marketing to suppliers and influence. There are many ways in which relation-building process is facilitated. Taking customer to a level of a friend has its positive aspects. Feedback is one such activity that provides the relationship marketers the profile of relationship and ways and means to rework on it for a better look and shape. Feedback from the client helps the partner to evaluate relationship status for strategic actions. At the outset of building relationship, it is important for the partner to solicit permission of the customer for every 'client-sensitive' move in taking the relationship forward. Such client handling strategy, in other words, is referred as Permission Marketing. Customer Relationship Management is the outcome of blending Relationship Marketing with technology and it provides an effective foundation in the practice of the discipline. During economic downturn, Relationship Marketing stands to the rescue of the marketers. Finally, relationship marketing has certain advantages, for example, it helps to increase loyalty, decrease acquisition cost, to acquire more business from existing clients through cross-sell and up-sell.

> **Keywords:** *Conventional Marketing, Relationship Marketing, Relationship Planning, Relationship Building, Permission Marketing, Retention Marketing, Database Marketing, Perdition Marketing, Customer Relationship Management*

## Exercises

1. How do you interpret 'indifference' to a customer? Give three examples which show signs of indifference to the customers. What are the measures that can be taken to prevent such act of indifference?

2. How do you differentiate between Conventional Marketing and Relationship Marketing practice? What are the specific pitfalls in Conventional Marketing that are addressed in Relationship Marketing?

3. Why is the role of Relationship Marketing uniquely identified in the discipline of marketing? How does it relate and contribute to the other disciplines of marketing?

4. What are the mutual benefits that a client, who is in power sector, and the partner, who is in the IT sector, are expected to leverage in the relationship building process?

5. From your experience, describe two examples where one-to-one marketing is strongly practised.

6. What is the difference between Relationship Marketing and Customer Relationship Management?

7. What are the advantages of Relationship Marketing with particular reference to service industry?

8. "The trend of customer aspirations is acquiring costly items, which entail difficult and complex process of learning to use". Justify your answer with suitable examples.

9. Why does the learning relation turn a customer inherently more loyal?

Fill up the blanks:

10. _____Marketing is the ongoing process of engaging in _____ and _____ activities, programmes with immediate and end user customers to create and enhance _____ at _____ _____.

11. Six markets which are central to Relationship Marketing are:
    _____ markets, _____ markets, _____ markets, _____ markets, _____ markets, and _____ markets.

12. The key advantages of Relationship Marketing are:

    (a) _____, (b) _____, and

    (c) _____.

## *References*

Adel, I. El-Ansary, 2005. Relationship Marketing Management: A School in the History of Marketing Thought, *Journal of Relationship Marketing*, Vol. 4, No. 1&2, pp. 43–56.

Batterly, R., 2003. *Leading Through Relationship Marketing*, Tata McGraw Hill, New Delhi.

Berry, A., Parasuraman, A. and Zeithaml, V., 1991. *Marketing Services*, Free Press, New York.

Berry, L.L., 1983. 'Relationship Marketing', in *Emerging Perspectives on Service Marketing*, L.L. Berry, G.L. Shostack and G.D. Upah (Eds.). Chicago, Illinois: American Marketing Association.

*Ibid.*, p. 25.

Booms, B. and Bitner, M., 1981. "Marketing Strategies and Organization Structures for Service Firms", in *Marketing of Services*, J. Donnelly and W. George (Eds.), Chicago: AMA Proceedings Series.

Borden, N.H., 1964. The concept of Marketing Mix, Journal of Advertising Research, Vol. 4, No. 2, pp. 2–7.

Brown, T.J., Churchill, G.A. and Peter, P., 1993. Improving the Measurement of Service Quality, *Journal of Retailing*, Vol. 69, pp. 127–139.

Chaturvedi, R. and Bhatia, Anil, 2000. eCRM: Deriving Value of Customer Relationship, in *Customer Relationship Management, Emerging Concepts, Tools and Applications*, Jagdish N. Sheth, Atul Parvatiyar and G. Sainesh (Eds.), Tata McGraw Hill, New Delhi, pp. 118–119.

Chowdhary, Nimit, 2002. Serving Customers Like Friends, *Indian Management*, Vol. 41, No. 9, Dec. 2002, pp. 76–79.

Christopher, M., Payne, A. and Ballantyne, D., 1991. *Relationship Marketing*, Butterworth-Heinemann, Oxford.

Cliff Allen is the co-author of the book *One-to-One Web Marketing*, 2nd ed., published by John Wiley & Sons. and is president of Coravue, Inc. Coravue provides marketers with a line of Web personalization, content management, and customer relationship management software and hosting services.

Day, G., 1994. 'The Capabilities of Market Driven Organizations', *Journal of Marketing*, Vol. 58, No. 4, pp. 37–52.

Diane Berenbaum, Senior Vice President of Communico, a customer service consultancy company in Smart Answers to Keren E. Klein in *Business Week*, June 1, 2007.

Fay, C., 1996. Can't Get No Satisfaction? Perhaps you should stop trying (White Paper). Wilton, Conn: Juran Institute.

Gartner Group, 1999. Enterprise Management Alert: Five e-Business Myths that can destroy a Business, US.

Griffin, Jill, 2002. Customer loyalty "Growing a loyal customer—the seven key stages", Jossey–Bass, a Wiley Imprint, San Fransisco, p. 31.

Grönroos, C., 1990. *Service Management and Marketing: Managing the Moments of Truth in Service Competition.* Massachusetts, Lexington.

Grönroos, C., 1994. From Marketing Mix to Relationship Marketing: Towards a Paradigm Shift in Marketing, *Management Decision*, Vo. 32, No. 2, pp. 4–20.

Grönroos, C., 1995. Relationship Marketing, The Strategy Continuum, *Journal of Academy of Marketing Science*, Vol. 23, No. 4, pp. 252–254.

Grönroos, C., 2000. 'Relationship Marketing: the Nordic School Perspective', in *Handbook of Relationship Marketing*, J.N. Sheth and A. Parvatiyar (Eds.), Sage: Thousand Oaks, CA, pp. 95–118.

Gummesson, Evert, 1997. 'Relationship Marketing as a Paradigm Shift: Some Conclusions from the 30R Approach', *Management Decisions*, Vol. 35, No. 4, pp. 267–272.

Gummesson, Evert, 2002. Total Relationship Marketing, Marketing Management, Relationship and Strategy and CRM Approaches for the Network Economy, Butterworth-Heinemann, Oxford, UK, p. 36.

*Ibid.*, pp. 27–30.

Hartline, Michael D. and Witt, Tom De., 2003. Individual Differences Among Service Employees: The Conundrum of Employee Recruitment, Selection and Retention, *Journal of Relationship Marketing*, Vol. 3, No. 2/3, pp. 25–42.

Houggard, S. and Bjerre, Mogens, 2002. *Strategic Relationship Marketing*, Springer-Verlag, Denmark, p. 45.

Hunt, S.D. and Morgan, R.M., 1995. The Comparative Advantage— Theory of Competition, *Journal of Marketing*, Vol. 59, No. 2, pp. 1–15.

Jackson, Barbara B., 1985. Build Customer Relationships that Last, *Harvard Business Review*, Vol. 63, Nov.-Dec., pp. 120–128.

*Ibid.,* p. 165.

Jill, Griffin, 2002. "Customer Defined: Growing a Loyal Customer", Customer Loyalty—How to earn, how to keep it, Jossey-Bass, A Wiley Imprint, San Francisco, CA.

Kohli, A.K. and Jaworski, B.J., 1990. Market Orientation the Construct, Research Propositions and Managerial Implications, *Journal of Marketing*, Vol. 54, pp. 1–18.

Kotler, Philip, Keller, Kevin Lane, Koshy, Abraham, and Jha, Mithileswar, 2009. *Marketing Management—A South Asian Perspective,* 13th ed., Prentice-Hall, New Delhi, p. 6.

Lal, Sameer, 2000. Building Relationships with Doctors for Effective Marketing: The Case of the Pharmaceutical Industry" in *Customer Relationship Management, Emerging Concepts, Tools and Applications,* Jagdish N. Sheth, Atul Parvatiyar and G. Sainesh (Eds.), Tata McGraw Hill, New Delhi, p. 210.

LeBoeuf, Michael., 1989. How to win customers and keep them for life, Berkley Trade, March 1.

Levitt, Theodore, 1960. Marketing Myopia, *Harvard Business Review*, Vol. 38, No. 4, Jul./Aug., pp. 45–56.

Levitt, Theodore, 1983. After the Sale is Over, *Harvard Business Review*, Vol. 61,No. 5, Sept.-Oct., p. 87–93.

Mark, Brownlow, 1999. E-mail Marketing Reports, mark@email-marketing-reports.com Portal versus Retailers, A&M, Vol. XI, No. VIII, 16–31 July, pp. 70–72.

Mitra, Subrata and Chatterjee, A.K., 2000. Managing Relationship in Supply Chains of the 21st Century, in *Customer Relationship Management, Emerging Concepts, Tools and Applications,* Jagdish N. Sheth, Atul Parvatiyar and G. Sainesh (Eds.), Tata McGraw Hill, New Delhi, p. 338.

Morgan, R.M. and Hunt, Shelby D., 1994. The Commitment-Trust Theory of Relationship Marketing, *Journal of Marketing*, No. 58, July, p. 22.

Mukherjee, Kaushik, 2007. *CRM—A Strategic Approach to Marketing*, Prentice-Hall of India, New Delhi.

Nikolich, Mike, President and CEO, Tech Image My 2 Cents' Worth, The Real Road to Perdition.

Payne, A., 1991. Relationship Marketing: The six markets framework (working paper). Cranfield, England: Cranfield University, School of Management.

Payne, A., 1997. Relationship Marketing, A Broadened View of Marketing, in *Advances in Relationship Marketing*, ed. Payne, A. Kogan Page, London, pp. 29–40.

Payne, A., Christopher, Martin, Clark, M. and Peek, Helen, 1995. *Relationship Marketing for Competitive Advantage: Winning and Keeping Customer*, Butterworth-Heinemann, Oxford, pp. 10–11.

Peppers, Don and Rogers Martha, 1999. Which came first: The Web or the Business Model, Marketing1to1, Peppers and Rogers Group, The Business Forum online http://www.businessforum.com/m1to1.

Porter, Clive, 1993. Quoted in the The Marketing Strategy Letter, May, p. 14.

Reichheld, F.F., 1993. Loyalty Based Management, *Harvard Business Review*, Mar.-Apr., p. 71.

Roberts-Phelps, Graham, 2003. '*Customer Relationship Management— How to Turn a Good Business into a Great One*, Viva Books Private Ltd., Delhi, pp. 17–19.

Ruckert, Robert W. and Walker, Orville C., 1991. Shared Marketing Programmes and the Performance of Different Business Strategies, Marketing Science Institute, June.

Saunders, Keren, 2008. How Relationship Marketing can Help Your Business during Bad Economic Times, website: www.ducttapemarketing.com/article, www.macgraphics.net

Shajahan, S., 2004. *Relationship Marketing: Cases and Concepts*, Tata McGraw-Hill, New Delhi, pp. 17–18.

Saravanan, S. and Ramkumar, D., 2007. The Dark Side of Relationship Marketing, International Marketing Conference on Marketing and Society, IIMK, April.

Schneider, B., 1980. The Service Organization Climate is Critical, *Organizational Dynamics*.

Shah, Malay, 2007. Relationship Marketing: Business Blogs are the Keys, Dec., website: zahir.in.

Seth, Godin, 1999. Permission Marketing: Turing Strangers into Friends and Friends into customers, Simon and Schuster, New York, p. 4–75, 189–192.

Sheth, N. Jagdish and Parvatiyar, Atul, 2001. *Customer Relationship Management: Emerging Concepts, Tools and Applications*, in Jagdish N. Sheth, Atul Parvatiyar, and G. Sainesh, (Eds.), Tata McGraw Hill, New Delhi.

Sheth, N. Jagdish and Parvatiyar, Atul, 2002. Towards a definition of Relationship Marketing, in *Handbook of Relationship Marketing*, Jagdish N. Sheth, and Atul Parvatiyar, (Eds.), Response Books, A division of Sage Publications, New Delhi, p. 9.

Sheth, N. Jagdish and Parvatiyar, Atul, 2002. Orientation of marketing practice in the post-industrial era, in *Handbook of Relationship Marketing*, Response Books, p. 133.

Sheth, N. Jagdish and Parvatiyar, Atul, 2002. Evolving Relationship Marketing into a Discipline, *Journal of Relationship Marketing*, Vol. I, No. 1, Haworth Press, pp. 4–5.

Sheth, N. Jagdish and Sisodia, R.S., 1995. Improving Marketing Productivity, in *Encyclopedia of Marketing for the Year 2000*, J. Heilbrunn (Ed.), Chicago: American Marketing Association/NTC.

Sheth, W & Higgins, M., 2000. Reconsidering the Relationship Analogy, *Journal of Marketing*, Vol. 16, No. 1, pp. 81–94.

Smith, W. and Higgins, M., 2000. Reconsidering the Relationship Analogy, *Journal* of *Marketing*, Vol. 16, No. 1, pp. 81–94.

Stavros, Constantino, 2005. Research Abstract, Relationship Marketing in Australian Professional Sport: An Organizational Perspective, Griffith University.

Stum, T. and Thiry, A., 1991. Building Customer Loyalty, *Training and Development Journal*, Apr., p. 34.

Zyman, Sergio. The End of Marketing As We Know It, *Harper Busines*, IBD, Delhi 1999.

Websites

www.wikipedia.com
www.businessforum.com/m1to1 (o1)
www.businessweek.com
www.CRMguru.com
www.mmaglobal.com
www.ducttapemarketing.com/article
www.macgraphics.net

# CHAPTER 2

# Customer Experience and Emotion

## INTRODUCTION

While talking about relationship, irrespective of business or non-business activities, the context of emotion surfaces with its own natural manifestations. No relationship can be visualized or comprehended without a touch of emotion. Because customers are people first. The root cause of most of the strain in relationship originates from emotional disturbance of behaviour. In business transactions, emotion has a major role to play, particularly in the era of 'experience economy'. Customer experience is manifested in positive or negative emotion that either helps in retention or termination of business relationship. Starting with the psychological concepts and definition of emotion, this chapter examines different dimensions of emotion with respect to business relationship, how emotion can influence the buying decision of customers.

## EMOTION IN BUSINESS RELATIONSHIP

Relationships involve one or more exchanges over time. However, a key feature of relationship marketing is its explicit recognition that exchanges between organizations and customers extend beyond strict economic boundaries (Morgan & Hunt 1994). For example, it recognizes that emotions—as well as cognition—play a role in the relationship between the buyer and the seller. In mass markets, relationship marketing can facilitate customer intimacy by involving emotions in a variety of contexts. Broadcast media can create a sense of identification or affiliation with the organization. Organization procedures can influence customers' perceptions of the fairness of the exchange relationship (Lind & Tyler 1988). Substantively personalized service can influence customers' perceptions of the helpfulness and friendliness of the organization (Supranant & Solomon 1987). In favourable situations, these circumstances can evoke emotions such as happiness, pride, and achievement. In unfavourable situations, these same circumstances can evoke emotions such as anger and frustration. Customers and employees in organizations who engage in favourable relationships feel as sense of "commitment" or "connection" towards one another (Morgan & Hunt 1994).

## Emotions Defined

Emotion is one of the strategic tools that work towards the development of Relationship Marketing. According to the general agreement by the scientists, emotions involve three major components: (a) Physiological changes within our bodies—shifts in heart rate, blood pressure, and so on; (b) subjective cognitive states—the personal experiences we label as emotions; and (c) expressive behaviour—outward signs of these internal reactions (Tangney et al. 1996; Zajonc & McIntosh 1992). In the relationship perspective, the pertinent point is how feelings shape thought and thought shapes feeling, that is, affective states of emotion. Affect is relatively mild feelings and moods—rather than intense emotions.

The boundary between emotions and affective reactions is somewhat fuzzy. For many years, it was assumed that affective reactions are bipolar in nature; that is, positive affect and negative affect represent opposite ends of a single dimension, and our moods fall somewhere along this dimension at any point of time.

However, in recent years, this assumption has been challenged by the suggestion perhaps positive affect and negative affect are actually independent dimensions—so that we can be high on one, low in the other, high on both, or low on both. This issue has not yet been resolved, although recent findings seem to offer fairly strong evidence for the idea that positive and negative affects are indeed two ends of a single dimension (Barret & Russel 1999; Russel & Carroll 1996).

Now, there is a growing attention to Emotional Quotient (EQ) as a measure of emotional content of an individual. Daniel Goleman in 1995 defined 'Emotional Intelligence' as 'that which shapes how an individual uses intellectual ability through self-control, zeal, persistence and self motivation'. According to him, all those skills present the learners greater opportunities to use the intellectual potential they have been given genetically. EQ does not lend itself to any numeric measurement, like the way Intelligence Quotient is measured. In the corporate world, the most valued employees are those with EQ traits according to various studies conducted in the USA. It helps one to understand and manage emotions as well as in building relationship.

Emotions have their own appeal and if they are applied properly, they can produce favourable results. When passions surge, the emotional side holds the rational side captive. Emotions are hardwired directly to the body through a fast-track neural network—rational thinking is indirectly connected with the body's functioning. In fact, emotions actually simulate the mind 3000 times faster than regular thoughts. In many situations, emotion moves a person to act well before the rational mind has had a chance to catch up (Goleman 1995).

## EMOTION AND CUSTOMER EXPERIENCE

Experience is one such element in an individual that acts spontaneously to strike the chord of emotion. Irrespective of the category of product or service, it is the experiential component that builds long-term loyalty of the customer. Premium positioning and higher margins are only realized if one can deliver a really powerful and pleasant customer experience and reinforce it in as many ways as possible—so that in a consumer's mind the 'value' equation changes from 'price' to the 'pleasure' of using the product/service. In this state, relationship with the consumer transcends from purely transactional to emotional. Experiences are built around feelings, emotions, colours, spaces, sounds, human contact, branding, etc. A great experience is created—it does not happen by accident (Kumar, et al. 2007). A trend towards experience-oriented relationship has been the emerging concept in the market economy. According to Tom Peter, four stages of economy have reigned in four decades. Those are as follows:

**Raw material economy in the 1940s:** Where the market was unorganized without any concept of product or services. For example, consumers used to procure raw materials for preparing food items. The cost of making it was the lowest.

**Goods economy in the 1950s:** When the market was little organized and consumers did not have to depend fully on the raw materials. Some of those were available in packaged form. The cost was little higher.

**Service economy in the 1970s:** Professionally prepared end product used to cost higher than the goods economy.

**Experience economy in the 1990s:** The product offers an experience that lives in the memory. It is expensive and higher than the similar product offered in service economy, but the price is worth it. Table 2.1 presents the difference between service and experience economy:

**Table 2.1** Comparison between Service Economy and Experience Economy

| Service economy | Experience economy |
|---|---|
| Product or service | Experience |
| Good stuff | It is a kick, a hoot |
| It works | It leaves an indelible memory |
| I am glad I bought it | Give me more |
| Satisfied customer | Member of club |
| Repeat customer | Word of mouth—viral marketing agent |
| You get what you pay for every turn | You are surprised and delighted at |
| Agrees with your wallet | Agrees with your psyche |
| Deals with one of your needs | Helps define who you are |

# CUSTOMER EXPERIENCE MANAGEMENT

Customer Experience Management (CEM) is the process of strategically managing a customer's entire experience with a product or a company. CEM is a truly customer-focused management concept (not a "marketing" concept). It is a process-oriented satisfaction idea (not an outcome-oriented one). In addition, CEM goes far beyond CRM by moving from recording transaction to building rich relations with customers (Schimitt 2003).

CEM has a broad view of how a company and its products can be relevant to a customer's life. It connects with the customer at every touch point and calls for the integration of different outcomes of the customer's experience.

CEM also takes an integrative approach to the organization, looming internally as well as externally. A manifestation of this integration is its attention to the employee experience because employees influence customers' perceptions of the company. Therefore, to create a delightful customer experience employees must be motivated, competent at their jobs, and innovative in their thinking. To do all these, employees need to have the right experience with the company they work for.

The CEM framework has five basic steps:

- Analyzing the experiential world of customer

- Building the experiential platform
- Designing the brand experience
- Structuring customer interface
- Engaging continuous innovation

For B2B markets, it is required to analyze the business context including requirements and solutions that build the experience of customer

Experiential platform includes a dynamic, multisensory, multidimensional depiction of the desired experience (referred to as "Experiential positioning"). It also specifies the value that the customer can expect from the product (Experiential Value Promise or EVP)

Brand experience includes, first, experiential features and product aesthetics that can serve as a jumping off point for the customer's brand experience. Next, it includes an appealing "look and feel" in logos and signage, packaging. Finally, appropriate experiential messages and imagery in ads and collaterals as well as on-line complete the brand experience.

Experiential platform must also be implemented in the customer interface. Whereas the brand experience is largely static (once designed, it remains much the same for sometime), the customer experience is dynamic and interactive, e.g. face-to-face in store, check-in desk, and e-commerce in Internet.

In any service, encounter perception is a reality, i.e. how the customer interprets the encounter. There is a process that narrates how people react to sequence and duration of events and how they rationalize an experience after it has occurred.

**Sequence effects**: When people recall an experience, they do not remember every single moment of it unless it is short and traumatic. Instead, they recall a few significant moments vividly and gloss over others. They remember snapshots, not movies. It is most intriguing that the ending matters enormously. A terrible ending usually dominates a person's recollection of an experience.

**Duration effects**: Perception of time passage is subjective and the duration matters to the experience only if the activity takes much longer or much shorter than expected. The pleasurable content of the experience and how it is arranged—rather than how long it takes—seem to dominate people's assessment.

**Rationalization effects**: People want explanation they focus on things they observe—something that is concrete enough to be changed—if only in their fantasies. People often conclude that deviations from rituals and norms caused the unexpected outcome. People tend to ascribe credit or blame to individuals, not systems. They want to put a human face on the problem. However, people are far less apt to search for guilty if they think they have had some control over the process that occurred accidentally (Kumar et al. 2007).

Five operating principles are presented here, based on those behavioural findings:

**Principle 1:** The beginning and the end of an encounter are not equally weighted in the eyes of the customer. The end is far more important because that is what remains in the customer's recollections.

**Principle 2:** Get the bad experience out of the way early in a sequence involving good and bad outcomes. People prefer to have undesirable events come first and to have desirable events come at the end of a sequence.

**Principle 3:** Segment the pleasure—combine the pain. Experience seems longer when they are broken into segments. In addition, people have varied reaction to losses and gains. So it is important to break pleasant experiences into multiple stages and combine unpleasant ones into a single stage.

**Principle 4:** Build commitment through choice. People are happier and more comfortable when they believe they have some control over a process, particularly an uncomfortable one. Some airlines apply this principle by letting passengers choose when they want to have their meals served during long flights.

**Principle 5:** Give people and stick to them. People are ritualistic. They find comfort, order and meaning in repetitive, familiar activities. This is particularly important in longer term professional service encounters. Rituals like kickoff presentations, dinners, and introduction meetings of the team, etc. provide an implicit standard for evaluating service encounters. Deviation from them is often perceived as a failure (Chase & Sriram 2001). This can be related to rationalization effect.

## Sound and Smell of Customer Experience

Growing importance of customer experience has led to the concept of Experiential Marketing which can be defined as a live interaction between a brand and a consumer that is sensitive to the brand values, impactful, memorable and capable of generating lasting positive relationship. Experiential marketing is essentially concerned with the six senses: smell, vision, taste, hearing, touch and balance (Schimitt 1999). IHG (Intercontinental Hotels Group) of the USA announced recently that they are deepening the design of their customer experience by creating signature smells for their hotels as part of their guest experience. This makes a lot of sense. The sense of smell accounts for 70 per cent of what our emotional recall is based on, according to some researchers (Smith, 2008).

So, do you design the smell and other senses such as the sound of your customer experience? Most organizations do not. BMW does. They design in that 'new car smell' on purpose because research says their customers like it. They tune the exhaust to 'sound like a BMW'. They understand that the 'ultimate driving experience' is one that engages all the senses.

Kjell Nordstrom, the economist, recently explained how Chris Bangle, the former BMW design guru, took him on a tour of BMW's 'door room'—a giant hangar full of car doors mounted on rigs, with engineers all over the place slamming the doors shut and recording the sounds of the doors. It is how they get that satisfying and reassuring BMW 'thunk' sound as the door of the car closes.

Designing the 'sound' of your experience is a concept most organizations do not even address because even the word 'design' has visual origins, so it excludes sound. But, here is an example of what it can achieve: At Glasgow Airport, they play natural, ambient sounds (bird's singing, plus soothing chill-out music underneath it) over the loudspeakers to relax travellers. Sales in the airport shops went up 10%.

So, smell and sound are part of customer experience. If you do not design them in, you leave them to chance. But we know that the biggest impact on how we feel about an experience is the behaviour of the people that deal with us and yet that is often overlooked because it is intangible.

## EMOTIONAL CLUSTERS OF CUSTOMER EXPERIENCE

Experiential marketing will rise in importance (specially for marketers of intangible products) because marketing in the 21st century is more challenging then ever due to fragmented media, clever and articulated consumers, and the rise of the "free-thinking" consumer. Experiential marketing is about more than a one-off experience. The crux of experiential marketing is that a marketer should not only be concerned with customer satisfaction. He or she should be (more) concerned with making the consumer emotionally attached to the product/service (Nair 2010). Thus, customer experience is the competitive battleground, and that emotion accounts for over 50 per cent of every customer experience. There are four clusters of emotions that either drive or destroy value and these four emotional clusters (Figure 2.1) include **destroying, attention, recommendation** and **advocacy**. These have been independently and statistically proven to impact customers' short-term spend, and drive or destroy loyalty. It is possible to prove that improving customer experience generates revenues.

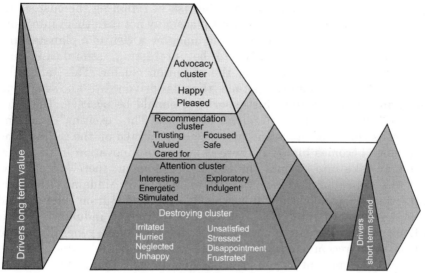

Hierarchy of Emotional Value

**Figure 2.1**

*Source:* Colin Shaw (2007), adopted with permission.

## Destroying Cluster

Once identified, destroying cluster can be the first area an organization needs to focus on when it decides to improve its customer experience. The destroying cluster represents the negative emotions that organizations may unwittingly provoke. For example, customers may feel frustrated if they do not have prompt access to a Customer Service agent or else they experience gross discomfort while interacting with the customer help desk. "Destroying" emotions include feeling *neglected, disappointed, stressed, irritated* or *unhappy.* All these features lead to strained relationship with customers resulting in frequent conflict and culminating in separation or attrition.

It is impossible to eradicate destroying emotions entirely, but wise organizations take steps to mitigate them. It is important to recognize that this cluster not only destroys value, but taxes resources and imposes other costs on an organization. Suppose, for example, delivery of a complex IT system is poorly coordinated and a few items are missing. In addition to feelings of frustration, such lapses waste the valuable time of the personnel involved with installation.

## Attention Cluster

The attention cluster contains emotions used by organizations to attract customers. Research has shown that these emotions encourage customers to explore offers and experience, and boost customers' short-term spend.

However, this cluster reveals the risk of retaining the customers. What attracts a customer in the first place may not turn them into long-term customers. As a simple example, imagine a visit to a planetarium. The very first visit is likely to be interesting, stimulating and energetic—all characteristics of the attention cluster. This takes the customer to the cognitive stage that is driven by 'knowing and perceiving' and certainly this experience should be positive. Take, for example, what happens after the 5th visit? The "exciting" emotions fade—it is the same stars and moon being projected on the ceiling. The experience becomes bland. If there is adequate innovation in the show that may take into account the latest development, there are chances that the repeat experience can be pleasant. In Madame Tussauds Attractions in London, new items, models are added from time to time to make it more interesting. With entertainment industry, it is a difficult task to recreate innovation because such items generally create impact upon recommendation with its 'one-time-usage' value. That is what people comment: If you visit London, do not forget about Madame Tussauds. For service and manu-facturing industries, such experience carries adequate importance as it aids in its transformation into recommendation stage through innovations.

## Recommendation Cluster

The recommendation cluster is where loyalty is built. This cluster includes basic human emotions like *valued, cared for* and *trusted*. It reflects a reactive, rather than proactive, state. For example, if a colleague asks you to recommend a good car dealer, you would offer your opinion, or if somebody asks about local travel in Delhi, the most obvious answer will be 'Delhi Metro'. But if they had not asked, you probably would not have brought it up.

## Advocacy Cluster

The advocacy cluster is at the top of the pyramid, and contains only two emotions, reflecting their statistical importance. *Happiness* is a primary goal for everyone. People want to be happy, thus we seek out experiences which please us. Obviously, organizations should strive to make their customers happy. Happy customers become advocates, proactively telling people about your organization without prompting, and are among the most loyal. Word of mouth, after all, is the best form of marketing.

Today's increasingly educated consumers expect companies to do more than relationship marketing. It is in this environment that the need for customer advocacy attains great importance. Customer advocacy is doing what is best for the customer and truly representing the customer's interest through a mutual dialogue and partnership. Besides, as customers become ever more demanding, less tolerant, and more skeptical, advocacy has become the favoured strategy as companies seek to deal with the changing power equation. Companies are successfully applying customer advocacy across different industries, with companies such as Starbucks and Harley Davidson being able to create high levels of customer engagement.

To realize its full potential, companies need to ensure that customer advocacy is an essential component of their corporate culture, such that it encourages employees to be committed to the customer and go beyond in-the-box customer service.

Today's customers are looking beyond device-based value propositions and are demanding solution-based value propositions, more proactive thought leadership, increased knowledge transfer, tailored offerings, and consistent quality. Customer advocacy based marketing will enable companies to help customers improve their productivity, reduce operational costs, and get their applications and services to market as quickly as possible (Kumar 2008).

## Emotional Signature

We have seen how marketers are deepening the design of their customer experience by creating signature smells for their hotels as part of their guest experience. Every organization has an Emotional Signature that measures its emotional engagement with customers.

For example: An upscale retail client 'X' wanted to compare its Emotional Signature to that of a competitor 'Y'. X was puzzled by contradictory data. Although their customer satisfaction scores showed they were ahead of Y, X was rapidly losing market share to them. Most organizations measure only the physical aspects of the Customer Experience—price, product availability, range, and so on. They ignore the other 50 per cent of an experience: the customer's emotions.

Like a graphic equalizer, a company's Emotional Signature can be altered to produce a better sound, i.e., experience. Because they are not consciously and deliberately thought-out in advance, most experiences are out of tune. Many organizations unwittingly evoke unintentional emotions. For example, customers become frustrated when their actions trigger the wrong behaviours, and organizations should take action to reverse this. To persuade the customers to feel you "care for" them—a powerful differentiator—you may need to change your recruitment process and hire people who are naturally caring. It is important to understand what your Emotional Signature is today, to enable you to take action to improve it.

## 3Ds OF CUSTOMER EXPERIENCE

Call it the dominance trap: The larger a company's market share, the greater the risk it will take its customers for granted. As the money flows in, management begins confusing customer profitability with customer loyalty, never realizing that the most lucrative buyers may also be the angriest and most alienated. Worse, traditional market research may lead the firm to view customers as statistics. Managers can become so focused on the data that they stop hearing the real voices of their customers (Allen & Hamilton 2005).

Financial software powerhouse Intuit briefly fell into this trap, despite a history of excellent customer service. In 2001, its Turbo Tax programme commanded 70 per cent of the retail market for tax-preparation software and 83 per cent of the online market. But then it began doing things that annoyed customers, such as hiking up the price of tech-support calls and limiting software licences to one computer. Store-based retail growth flattened, and as Web-based tax preparation sites sprang up, online buyers started jumping ship. In 2003, Turbo Tax's share of the online market plummeted.

A recent Bain & Company survey reveals just how commonly companies misread the market. They surveyed 362 firms and found that 80 per cent believed they delivered a "superior experience" to their customers. But when asked the customers about their own perceptions, they found that they rated only 8 per cent of the companies as truly delivering a superior experience. Clearly, it is easy for leading companies to assume they are keeping customers happy; it is quite another thing to achieve that kind of customer devotion.

So, what sets the elite 8 per cent apart? Unlike most companies, which reflexively turn to product or service design to improve customer satisfaction, the leaders pursue three imperatives simultaneously:

1. They **design the right offers and experiences** for the right customers.

2. They **deliver these propositions** by focusing the entire company on them with an emphasis on cross-functional collaboration.

3. They **develop their capabilities** to please customers again and again—by such means as revamping the planning process, training people in how to create new customer propositions, and establishing direct accountability for the customer experience.

Each of these "Three Ds" draws on and reinforces the others. Together, they transform the company into one that is continually led and informed by its customers' voices.

## EMOTION IN SURPRISE—THE 'WOW' EXPERIENCE

There are research projects that highlight the possibility of attracting and retaining customers by means of surprise, which, in other words, plays the emotional chord of clients and consumers. Interestingly, it has been suggested that positive surprise is a necessary condition for customer delight and that customer delight translates into higher customer retention levels (Rust et al. 1996; Oliver et al. 1997).

On the one hand, most studies suggest that customer satisfaction is a necessary condition for customer retention (Goderis 1998; Scheuing 1995) with customer satisfaction translating into higher customer retention (Anderson & Sullivan 1993; Fornell 1992; Oliver 1980). On the other hand, it has been reasoned that merely satisfying customers is not enough, businesses need to delight their customers, which cannot be achieved without positively surprising them (Oliver 1997; Rust et al. 1996). What is known about surprise originates from the literature on psychology. Surprise, which is a syndrome of reactions, is considered by most researchers to be a short-lived emotion (Charlesworth 1969; Derbaix & Pham 1989; Ekman & Friesen 1985; Izard 1997; Meyer 1988).

The polarity of surprise is interesting. Is surprise negative or positive? Although the emotion of surprise itself is neutral, it is often followed by another emotion that 'colours' it either positively (e.g. surprise leads to joy) or negatively (e.g. surprise leads to anger) (Ekman & Friesen 1975). Businesses have paid widespread attention to positively surprising their customers. Incidentally, the possible correlation between positive surprise and customer delight has received only little attention in the literature. The exploratory study by Oliver et al. (1997), an exception, supports the correlation. Other studies by Oliver and his colleagues also indirectly support the notion that positive surprise leads to higher satisfaction levels and repurchasing intentions. Furthermore, the literature in psychology suggests that customer delight is a second-order emotion resulting from a combination of two first order emotions, namely surprise and joy (Plutchik, 1980). According to these findings, positive surprise might thus play an important role in customers' satisfaction and ultimately retention (Vanhamme, Lindgreen & Brodie 1999).

# FIVE BARRIERS TO MEASURING CUSTOMER EXPERIENCE

Customer experience is much beyond giving customers a good time. It is a leading KPI (Key Performance Indicator) for the customer-centred organization. While many organizations have a strong desire to improve their customers' experience, barriers to effective measurement hamper them—their feedback loop is blocked (Kirkby, 2008).

The 'green field' organization enters into the world full of vision. With innovation and passion, its owners monitor what they know is important to their growth (e.g. awareness, repeat business and satisfaction) and instinctively recruit people with an understanding and feel for what they are about. And if a customer is unhappy, there is concern and they get personal attention.

But 'hands-on' entrepreneurship is not sustainable in a growing organization: scaling requires values, strategy and 'processes'. Controlling metrics are expediently put in place to steer the ship to its financial shore, but often at the expense of the traditional guiding star of vision. It is expected that employees will imbibe the vision 'on the job', but of course they do not because they are measured on unlinked budgets and targets. So while customers expect a smooth trip to Paradise Island, what they often get is a bumpy ride to 'Hell'—and quite naturally some of them complain.

> "At Virgin we look for opportunities where we can offer something better, fresher and more valuable, and we seize them." Creating a breakthrough customer experience and combining brand with the physical customer experience is what the vision should embody!
> —Richard Branson

It is in this atmosphere that the new **Head of Customer Experience** is hired to imbue a little customer focus. Their first port of call should be strategic customer metrics—but in at least 70 per cent of the cases, these will be inadequate according to Deloitte's 2007 study, 'In the Dark'.

Their second visit should then be customer complaints. If qualitative research is applied, these will provide insight into four important levels:

- The brand—"you're too expensive"
- The proposition—"you don't understand my needs"
- The experience—"you don't call me back"
- The basic resources—"your staff are rude".

Actual customer experience measures are therefore what the customer-centred organization should be tuning into: if, that is, it wants to deliver the vision of what it promises. Its first thought would then no longer be "how do we measure Interactive Voice Response System (IVRS) effectiveness?", but rather "what are our customers expecting when making a call and how so they feel when confronted by a taped voice going through messages and menus?"

## Barriers to Measuring Experience

If customer satisfaction and advocacy are to become Key Performance Indicators (KPIs), then they need a free flowing customer experience feedback loop. But there are five main barriers:

### 1. We Rely on Magic Numbers

*"Too many companies use magic numbers—measures claimed to be*

*inextricably linked to financial results, but whose actual correlation for each company is never researched or modelled".*—Professor Robert Shaw

Magic numbers are KPIs which are deemed to be important because "everyone has them"—for instance, net promoter score, customer retention and leads. They are easy to understand, collect and compare, but few really understand how to really manage them, or what drives them in a particular industry and company? "Our churn level is 40 per cent", the boards are told, but few know how many customers died. The top and the bottom of the sales funnel are common magic numbers. Leads go in at the top and sales come out of the bottom. What is frequently not known is what actually happens in between. If this 'sales process' is changed to a 'buying or engagement' process, with analysis of experience and outcomes at each stage, then the management of those 'magic numbers' becomes more apparent. *Model the processes from the customer perspective, and understand through research and feedback what happens at each stage—then put in metrics.*

## 2. Hearing without Listening

*"Selling is about listening and engaging with customers, making them feel comfortable. The best selling is a service in its own right, a source of information sharing and problem solving".*

We need to break down our propositions and services—the customer's view of process—and find out just what drives engagement, and how customers feel about each part. It is important to understand customers' emotions about the brand, about the basic proposition, about service levels. Do we listen to their tales and stories? Stories quickly convey complex thoughts and difficult emotions. How do customers feel beyond satisfied and not satisfied on a 1–10 scale? Stories give us a way of locating the desires, perceptions and attitudes of our customers.

Companies like Zara and Red Bull listen to customer stories and then use them in their brand building—always monitoring the outcome. Norwich Union (NU) uses emotional feedback measures they have found to be important, such as "do you feel appreciated as an individual" and "do you genuinely feel that NU cared about meeting your needs" and use the result back in 'customer innovation' sessions with staff.

## 3. Measuring Word of Mouth is Hard

'Word of mouth' is the new marketing communications, as people turn to trusted friends and intermediaries to share experiences and recommendations.

- The London School of Economics has found that word of mouth advocacy is a statistically significant predictor of annual sales growth.
- Typically, 15 per cent of the customer base will be influencers in the product category.

- Forrester research has revealed that 77 per cent of online shoppers seek out ratings and reviews when making a purchase.

Measuring word of mouth is in its infancy, but here is a template. The two key things to measure are **content** (think tags and web harvesting by way of technical help) and **who** (think research for influencer segmentation), then:

(a) Find and monitor the market influencers:
- Social—highly influential at all levels
- Category—influential in your product category
- Brand—the brand advocates.

(b) Measure the content as in a buzz unit, taking into account a weighted basket of:
- Brand value reflection
- Degree of positive vs. negative (5–10 point scale)
- Clarity
- Impact of vehicle, e.g. email, blog
- Timeliness

## 4. Too Much Functional Data—Too Little Insight

A company recently spent a large amount in researching a new product pilot, and at the end of it had little understanding of customers' needs, attitudes and behaviours. Internal rumour started that it had not been a success because additional sales, over normal, could not be identified. When all the research and data were combined, the product had been a huge success. It had retained a number of customers and engaged many more; indeed product take up had been fuelled by the word of mouth of satisfied customers.

The moral of this story for all organizations is to unify all research and analysis with a voice of the customer (VOC) programme. Within this there must be a clear VOC plan and process, key benchmark variables used in every study to tie the data together, an identified budget, a multi-skilled team, and internal evangelism on the benefits of customer advocacy.

## 5. Weak Visibility Beyond the Obvious and the Superficial

Recently a mobile phone company noticed that their salespeople were not engaging customers when they walked into their retail outlets. The initial reaction was that the 'salespeople' were lazy and needed to be set targets. But a totally different truth emerged from research. The systems and processes made it very difficult for salesperson to help the customer as much as they would like and they were ashamed of giving poor service. Far from being apathetic, the employees were keen to deliver a good experience, but their support let them down.

Root cause analysis, via research and piloting initiatives, goes a long way to overcoming the barrier of superficiality: just keep asking why.

There are positions created for taking special care of customer experience. One such example is given in Figure 2.2.

### *London, UK*

### Head of Customer Experience

### Retail and Telecommunications

Our client is one of the UK's leading Retail and Telecommunications companies, with an extensive and diverse product range. Already established as the market leader in the UK and with massive growth potential in Europe, the organization is focusing on delivering a more rewarding customer experience through focused and market leading Customer Management.

Working directly with the MD of Customer Management is an excellent opportunity for an ambitious individual to take ownership for the strategic review and relationship management of all the channels relating to the Customer Experience of one of the UK's fastest growing FTSE 150 organizations.

**Areas of influence:**

• **Communication:** The successful candidate will need to be an effective communicator with excellent influencing skills. This successful candidate will report directly to a Group MD and be responsible for the relationship management of a number of UK board directors who are key stakeholders in the area.

• **Operations:** You will need excellent analytical skills as you will be responsible for reviewing the operations of all the customer management functions with a view to identifying and implementing new process improvements.

• **Strategic thinking:** You will need to be able to review and influence the strategies of the Customer Management Areas: CRM, Contact Centre, Direct Marketing and Revenue Assurance—with a view to managing the cross-migration of any strategies from both a UK and European perspective.

• **Leadership:** As this is a new area brought about by business growth, the successful candidate will be responsible for developing and recruiting 4 seniors, and maintaining an overview of their teams.

**The person:**

The successful candidate will have a strong academic background, sit at a senior management level and could come from either a management consultancy or Blue Chip industry background. This role should develop into a directorship within 18 months so the successful candidate will need to be career-focused and ambitious.

Apply Now **Reflect** www.reflecthis.com

**Figure 2.2** Advertisement for the position of head of customer experience.

## RATIONAL–EMOTIONAL BEHAVIOUR MANIFESTATION

FCB Grid, known as Foote, Cone and Belding (FCB) Grid (Vaughn 1980), uses two dimensions to classify products—the level of involvement, ranging from high to low, and a continuum from thinking to feeling. This classification suggests that purchase decisions are different when thinking is mostly involved and others are dominantly involved, with feeling. In addition, different situations also exist, resulting in decision-making processes, which require either more or less involvement. The product category matrix is fabricated using these two dimensions. Vaughn indicates that the horizontal side of the matrix is based on the hypothesis that over time there is consumers' movement from thinking towards feeling. Also, Vaughn believes that high and low involvement (the vertical side of the matrix) is also a continuum, proposing that high involvement can decay to relatively low involvement over time.

Vaughn developed a planning model by pulling together the major theories of consumer behaviour and advertising to make the FCB Grid. Vaughn (1980) reviewed four traditional theories of advertising effectiveness from which effects on marketing have been noticeable. These four theories are Economic, Responsive, Psychological, and Social theories. Each theory is applicable to the four quadrants in the FCB Grid, and definitions and applications of each four traditional theories of the grid will be covered in the explanations later.

Furthermore, Berger (1986) also referred to four different theories into human behaviour in his paper to approach to the FCB Grid. According to Berger (1986), insight into human behaviour can be interpreted differently, depending on the theory.

- **Socialists** favour the theory of economic man, the search for value, the need for information with advertising seen purely as information—applicable to **Economic** theory.
- **Freudian** and other psychological theories give us the notion of behaviour governed by unconscious impulses—applicable to **Psychological** theory.
- There is also **Pavlovian** theories of purchases influenced by conditioning and repetition—applicable to the **Responsive** theory.
- Finally, there is the theory, deriving from **Veblen**, of people as consumers who buy to join, emulate or belong to a group—applicable to **Social** theory.

Four quadrants are developed in the matrix based on these two dimensions (involvement and thinking/feeling) in the FCB Grid (Figure 2.3). The quadrants summarize four substantially major goals for advertising strategy: "to be informative, affective, habit forming or to promote self-satisfaction" (Vaughn 1980). The insight from Vaughn led to the conceptualization of using a continuum of high involvement to low involvement, as well as a continuum of thinking and feeling, in order to form a space where we can position the products relative to each other.

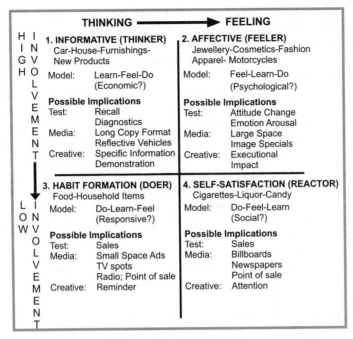

**Figure 2.3  FCB grid.**

*Source:*  Vaughn (1980).

With this FCB Grid, advertisers can develop advertising strategy according to consumers' relations towards a product according to information (learn), attitude (feel) and behaviour (do) issues. However, every theory needs scientific research, which can validate its conclusions. The primary grid validation study was conducted in the United States among 1,800 consumers across some 250 product categories. The results are that products and services were reasonably positioned as expected, and some 'think' and 'feel' items correlated with involvement, which corroborated that it was possible to have varying amounts of think and feel—high or low—depending on involvement (Vaughn 1986).

Also, international study about the Grid has been conducted by asking over 20,000 consumers in 23 countries. This study indicates that consumer mental processes are quite similar throughout different countries in spite of communication distinctions in advertising. In spite of the successful validation of the FCB Grid by thorough research, Vaughn (1986) accentuated the importance of speculation about the involvement and think-feel dimensions.

An obvious failing of the FCB grid is its contention that products like automobiles are purchased solely on 'Thinking'. A cursory look at auto ads on TV will reveal that insistent use of 'feeling' techniques through spontaneous communication cues like jingles along with product attributes. This proposition has found its relevance in ADM (Advertising Differentiation Matrix) (Chaudhury 1996) that uses rational and emotional values to categorize products into four classes. The general implications for advertising strategies are viable for all product categories.

Products such as automobiles, airlines and televisions are high in rational value and high in emotional value. The obvious failing of the FCB grid (Vaughn 1980, 1986) is its contention that products like automobiles are purchased solely on "thinking" because auto ads on TV make insistent use of "feeling" techniques for such product categories.

Services like banking, and household appliances are low in emotional value and high in rational value. But there is always an attempt to generate emotional value through the advertising of a product. FCB grid does not accommodate products that may be low in both thinking and feeling.

But certain products, such as tissues, fabric softeners, and detergents are low in emotional value and low in rational value. Ads for such products provide consumers with easy decision rules for choosing among the brands in a low involvement product category. The endorsement by celebrities is one of the common mechanism for facilitating such decision making process.

There are some products, such as chocolate, alcoholic beverages, and sodas that are high in emotional value but low in rational value. Low involvement in such cases can be increased by the use of other emotional treatments, such as 'vicarious learning', which enhance the perceived value of the product.

Pechmann and Stewart (1989) describe the process of vicarious learning through advertising. Ads that portray rewards or punishment for an actor due to use or nonuse of a particular brand arouse identification and emotion. Overall, the ADM sees emotion and reason as separate dimensions (which comprise the totality of what is called involvement) so that products can be high on both or low on both.

# RELATIONSHIP DEVELOPMENT LINE—EMOTIONAL BUYING PROCESS

With reference to the findings in ADM, it is apparent that emotion is one of the strong drivers of relationship because, with such feeling, the buyer can quickly relate himself/herself to the product or service. But this can happen once the first purchase offers an experience of comfort to the buyer. Figure 2.4 illustrates how the transition from rational buying motive to emotional buying motive is facilitated. The buying motive and the buyer behaviour have been discussed in Appendix. The trend towards emotional motive is a healthy one that is nurtured

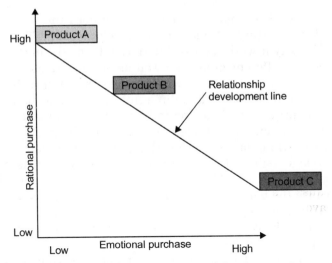

**Figure 2.4** **Transition diagram from rational buying motive to emotional buying.**

through relationship strengthening process. Besides, the process involved in such transition lies behind the success of cross-selling and up-selling endeavour of the organization.

Figure 2.4 indicates that the client's first time purchase decision of a product (Product A) fully depends on product performance and other related factors that endorse the product's credibility. This is an example of Rational Purchase where emotion has very little role to play in the buying process. Thereafter, the interactions with the partner build up the relationship constructs (Table 7.1, Chapter 7) and gradually the faith and confidence in the client lead to emotional relationship with the partner. It is because the feeling that works at the top of the client's mind: 'I know those guys for a long time—they cannot do a bad job for us.' It is a case of pleasant experience with the person and the product that sets the tone of emotion element in the relationship on the affective side.

The success of Product A coupled with emotional relationship causes Relationship Development Line's sloping towards Emotional Purchase, leading to smooth execution of cross sell or up sell of Product B and Product C.

## BODY CHEMISTRY IN RELATIONSHIP

There is something called 'body chemistry' when we talk about relationship. For example, if two persons (even in the absence of any good reason) fall out against each other, it is said that it is all because their body chemistry is not matching. Is any individual born with such body chemistry? The answer is, no. So, how does the body chemistry develop when we think of client-partner relationship? The answer is attitude. The way it works across different individuals, in the same way it works across different groups as well as organizations.

There is a saying, 'People would rather buy from a friendly and enthusiastic trainee than an indifferent expert'. The person who is friendly and enthusiastic is bound to have universal acceptance. This is not like the situation that the client asks for something, and for the heck of it, only something or some other thing is somehow delivered. But in them there is a visible effort and understanding into the depth of what the client has asked for. The pain in the face of the partner is always there, because the partner is always serious of the client's requirements and endeavours to improve in order to leverage utmost satisfaction of the client. The client feels—yes there is someone who at least tries to live underneath his or her skin.

The approach, attitude of such partners are convincing enough to make exception of circumstances. They are the winner at the end of the day.

Given the fact that attitude triggers the 'matching' or 'mismatching' body chemistry leading to an emotional bond between the client and the partner, is there any measure of such emotion in relationship? For example, what is the intensity of emotion? There may not be any straightforward answer to this question, but think of the momentary emotion the audience experienced in the mega movie 'Titanic' by James Cameron when Kate Winslet blew the whistle in the sea and the rescue boat turned around. There is a time, place and duration of emotion and those are left to the judgment of Relationship Marketers to leverage those with the clients.

## EMOTIONAL LOYALTY

The emotional loyalty approach blends the principles of operational excellence with the human touch at customer relations and creates a more positive customer experience. This approach improves customer satisfaction and retention activities and uniquely builds emotional loyalty with customers. Güngör (2007) developed the emotional loyalty concepts during his Ph.D. research at the University of Amsterdam.

The principles of the emotional loyalty approach have already been empirically tested and implemented in leading European firms from different industries, including several large banks in the Netherlands and in the United Kingdom.

Underlying research explored in the emotional, cognitive, general, and transactional dimensions of customer satisfaction and loyalty process in the customer contact environment. It is suggested that current business and CRM practice are heavily involved with cognitive and general satisfaction, and aimed at utilizing emotional and transactional satisfaction as a distinctive competitive advantage for more customer loyalty.

As customer contacts can be a source of negative emotions and it is desirable to increase positive emotions in the contact centre environment, Güngör focused on the emotional aspects of customer satisfaction, in particular on the *Emotional Satisfaction of Customer Contacts* (ESCC) (Figure 2.5). The ESCC research demonstrated that the more positive the customer contacts, the stronger the customer satisfaction and loyalty.

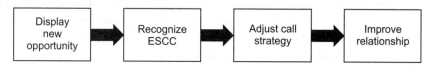

**Figure 2.5  Impact of customer contact.**
*Source:*  Huseyin Güngör (2007), adopted with permission
(www.emotionalloyalty.com).

## Emotional Satisfaction of Customer Contacts (ESCC) Model

- Emotional factors are more important than cognitive factors in customer satisfaction and loyalty.
- The more positive the customer contacts, the stronger the customer satisfaction and loyalty.
- Negative contacts have stronger impact than positive ones on customer satisfaction and loyalty.
- It is possible to shift customers from negative contact experience zones to more positive contact experience zones.
- It is possible to identify dissatisfactory issues and recover service failures proactively while creating stronger loyalty.
- The ESCC model supports continuous improvement actions as well as learning loops in the organization.

## CONCLUSION

In the era of Experience Economy, emotion is one of the strategic tools that work towards the development of Relationship Marketing. Experience can lead to emotion. Customer experience is the current trend considered for the strategies of relationship marketing. It depends on various parameters, such as duration of the experience, sequence, and rationalization. Surprise, particularly positive surprise, is one such factor that can result in joy or delight tickling emotion in the customer's perception, which ultimately culminates into a positive experience. Customer experience can be categorized into four emotional clusters, namely, destroying cluster, attention cluster, recommendation cluster, and advocacy cluster. Emotional behaviour in purchase is described in FCB Grid and advertising differentiation matrix. There are measures for customer experience and KPIs are used for such measures. There are also barriers in measuring such experience and the marketers need to devise appropriate strategy to overcome those barriers. In a buying process, emotion is not recognized at the start, but, with growing client satisfaction this becomes more pronounced and helps partners to acquire more business from the clients. Favourable customer experience through positive emotions is also responsible for emotional loyalty, which helps marketers to leverage new opportunities in business in future.

> **Keywords**: *Emotional Intelligence, Attention Cluster, Advocacy Cluster, Destruction Cluster, Recommendation Cluster, Emotional Signature, 3Ds of Customer Experience, FCB Grid.*

## Exercises

1. 'Emotion has a role to play in Relationship Marketing'. Why do you think it is important in the context of experience economy?

2. What do you understand by the term 'customer experience'? Describe its significance in the service sectors.

3. What are the major barriers in measuring customer experience? What are the ways to overcome those barriers?

4. What are the objectives of ESCC Model? Can you relate two examples where the customer's emotional loyalty has taken a pronounced stance over the rational perception?

5. Cognitive factors have greater impact in customer satisfaction and loyalty than emotional factors (True/False).

6. What is '3D' of customer experience? How would you plan to implement it in music CD?

7. Discuss the roles and responsibilities of the Head of Customer Experience you plan to propose for a company engaged in banking business.

Fill in the blank:
8. The success of Product A coupled with _____ relationship causes_____Line's sloping towards _____ _____Purchase leading to smooth execution of _____ or _____ of Product B and Product C.

# *References*

Allen, James, Reichheld, Frederick F. and Hamilton, Barney, 2005. The 3Ds of Customer Experience, Harvard Business School Working Knowledge for Business Leaders, http://hbswk.hbs.edu/archive/5075.html.

Anderson, E.W. and M. Sullivan, 1993. The Antecedents and Consequences of Customer Satisfaction for Firms, *Marketing Science*, Vol. 12, No. 2, pp. 125–143.

Barret, L.F. and Russel, J.A., 1999. The Structure of Current Affect: Controversies and Emerging Consensus. *Current Directions in Psychological Science*, Vol. 9, pp. 10–14.

Berger, D., 1986. Theory into Practice: The FCB Grid. *European Research*, Vol. 14(1), pp. 35–46.

Carrol, J.M. and Russel, J.A., 1996. Do Facial Expressions Signal Specific Emotions? Judging Emotion from the Face in Context, *Journal of Personality and Social Psychology*, Vol. 70, pp. 205–218.

Chase, Richard B. and Dasu, Sriram, 2001. Want to Perfect Your Company's Service? Use Behavioural Science, *Harvard Business Review*, June, p. 83.

Charlesworth, W.R., 1969. The role of surprise in cognitive development, in *Studies in Cognitive Development: Essays in Honour of Jean Piaget*, D. Elkind and J.H. Flavel (Eds.), Oxford University Press, Oxford.

Chaudhury, Arjun, 2007. *Theories of Learning, Emotion and Reason in Consumer Behaviour*, Butterworth-Heinemann, UK, pp. 79–80.

Derbaix, C. and Pham, M.T., 1989. "Pour un development des measures de l'affectif en marketing (For the development of measures of question in marketing", *Recherches et Applications en Marketing*, Vol. 4(4), Grenoble Cedex, France, pp. 71–87.

Ekman, P. and Friesen, W., 1975. *Unmasking the Face*. Prentice-Hall, Englewood Cliffs, New Jersey.

Ekman, P. and Friesen, W., 1985. Is the Startle Reaction an Emotion?, *Journal of Personality and Social Psychology*, Vol. 49(5), pp. 1416–1426.

Fornell, C., 1992. A National Satisfaction Barometer: the Swedish Experience, *Journal of Marketing*, Vol. 56(1), pp. 1–21.

Goderis, J.P., 1998. Barrier Marketing: from Customer Satisfaction to Customer Loyalty, *CEMS Business Review*, Vol. 2(4), pp. 285–294.

Goleman, Daniel, 1995. *Emotional Intelligence*, Bantam Books, New York.

Güngör, H., 2007. *Emotional Satisfaction of Customer Contacts*, Amsterdam University Press, Amsterdam.

Izard, C.E., 1977. *Human Emotions*. Plenum Press, New York.

Kirkby, Jennifer, 2008. The five barriers to customer experience, website www.MyCustomer.com

Kumar, Alok, Sinha, Chabi and Sharma, Rakesh, 2007. *Customer Relationship Management: Concepts and Application*, Biztantra, New Delhi, pp. 153–155.

Kumar, G.B., 2008. Being Customer Focused: The Customer Advocacy Imperative, *Business World*, April, p. 32.

Lind, E.A. and Tyler, T.R., 1988. The Social Psychology of Procedure Justice, Plenum, New York.

Meyer, W.U., 1988. After the Sale is Over, *Harvard Business Review*, Vol. 5, pp. 87–93.

Morgan, R.M. and Hunt, S.D., 1994. The Commitment Trust Theory of Relationship Marketing, *Journal of Marketing*, Vol. 58(3), pp. 20–38.

Nair, Lakshmi, 2010. Experiental Marketing: A conceptual framework for connecting with the customers, *Indian Journal of Marketing*, Vol. 40, No. 6, New Delhi, p. 32.

Oliver, R.L., 1980. A Cognitive Model of the Antecedents and Consequences of Customer Satisfaction Decisions, *Journal of Marketing Research*, Vol. 17(4), pp. 460–469.

Oliver, R.L., 1997. *Satisfaction: A Behavioral Perspective on the Consumer*, McGraw-Hill, Singapore.

Oliver, R.L. and Westbrook, R.A., 1993. Profiles of Consumer Emotions and Satisfaction in Ownership and Usage, *Journal of Consumer Satisfaction, Dissatisfaction, and Complaining Behaviour*, Vol. 6, pp. 12–27.

Oliver, R.L., Rust, R.T. and Varki, S., 1997. Customer Delight: Foundations, Findings, and Managerial Insight, *Journal of Retailing*, Vol. 73(3), pp. 311–336.

Pechmann, Cornelia and Stewart, David A., 1989. The Multidimensionality of Persuasive Communications: Theoretical and Empirical Foundations, in *Cognitive and Affective Responses to Advertising*, Patricia Cafferata and Alice M. Tybout (Eds.), Lexington Books, Lexington, MA, pp. 31–45.

Peters, Tom, 2003. *Re-imagine! Business Excellence in a Disruptive Age*, DK Publishing, London.

Plutchik, R., 1980. *Emotion: A Psychoevolutionary Synthesis*, Harper and Row, New York.

Richards, Bill, 2000. Under the Radar, *The Wall Street Journal,* Dow Jones & Co., New York.

Rust, T., Zahorik, A. and Keiningham, T.L., 1996. *Service Marketing,* Harper-Collins, New York.

Scheuing, E.E., 1995. *Creating Customers for Life,* Oregon: Productivity Press, Portland.

Schimitt, Bernd, 1999. Experiential Marketing: How to Get customers to Sense, Feel, Think, Act, Relate, Free Press, New York.

Schimitt, Bernd, 2003. *Taking the Customer Seriously—Finally, Customer Experience Management: A Revolutionary Approach to Connecting with your Customers,* John Wiley and Sons, New Jersey, pp. 17–18, 25.

Shaw, Colin, 2007. *The DNA of Customer Experience: How Emotions Drive Value,* Palgrave Macmillan. www.beyondphilosophy.com.

Smith, Shaun, 2008. What does your customer experience smell like?, www.customerthink.com.

Surprenant, C.F. and Solomon, M.R., 1987. Predictability and Personalization in the Service Encounter, *Journal of Marketing,* Vol. 51(2), pp. 86–96.

Tangney, J.P, Miller, R.S., Flicker, L. and Barlow, D.H., 1996. Are Shame, Guilt and Embarrassment Distinct Emotions? *Journal of Personality and Social Psychology,* Vol. 70, pp. 1256–1269.

Vanhamme, Joelle, Lindgreen, Adam and Brodie, R.J., 1999. Taking Relationship Marketing for a joyride: The Emotion of Surprise as Competitive Marketing Tool in *Marketing in the Third Millenniium,* J. Cadeaux and M. Unders (Eds.), Sydney, New South Wales, Australia, Univ. of New South Wales.

Vaughn, Richard, 1980. How Advertising Works: A Planning Model. *Journal of Advertising Research,* Vol. 20(5), pp. 27–33.

Vaughn, Richard, 1986. How Advertising Works: A Planning Model Revisited, *Journal of Advertising Research,* Vol. 26, No. 1, pp. 57–66.

Zajonc, R.B. and McIntosh, D.N., 1992. Emotions Research: Some Promising Questions and Some Questionable Promises. *Psychological Science,* Vol. 3, pp. 70–74.

Websites

www.customerthink.com
www.beyondphilosophy.com
www.ExperienceClinic.com
www.emotionalloyalty.com

# CHAPTER 3

||||||||||||||||||||||||||

# Relationship Brands

## INTRODUCTION

Positive experience contributes in the relationship building process. This is related to persons, products and services and hence the saga of personification of brand. The purpose of relationship branding is to help the marketers on connecting the brand with its consumers through an imaginery sense of relationship. In this chapter, the role of parasocial relationship, which is other than interpersonal relationship, in relationship building has been discussed. This is in the form of a brand, which is interpreted in terms of the brand dialects as equity, personality or anything that forms a mental bond with the consumers or customers. The categories of such relationship have been explained and apart from these, the effects of brand relationship norms on consumer attitudes and behaviour have also been discussed.

## CONCEPT OF RELATIONSHIP BRAND

It is important to pay attention to the brand-consumer relationship, which is necessary for real long-term success. The emotional part of any brand strategy is derived from what the brand stands for, and the personality of the brand that is used to build attraction, trust and loyalty. Summarily, relationships thrive on emotions; they survive or perish, depending on the emotional fit between people. Brands have therefore to reflect personalities that people like, and this means having an emotional basis or edge to them. Indeed, the best brands have personalities carefully crafted to suit them and their target audiences. People have a universal longing to be liked, given attention, and to be loved. This makes the emotional dimension of the brand-consumer relationship very important, and it is the personality and attitude of the brand that attracts and keeps people loyal to it (Temporal 2010).

Relationship branding is a strategic approach aimed at making consumers enjoy a sense of relationship, or personal connection, with a brand, usually implemented through mass customization and market segmentation. A relationship brand is also an offering tailored to a small segment of consumers. While this is true, we believe there is also much more to relationship branding. And in many ways the rhetoric of mass customization and targeting small segments (or even segments-of-one) is oversimplified. A more considered approach is necessary to realize the true potential of relationship branding (Tybout & Calkins 2005). There are six phases in the life of a brand— from commodity to brand immortality (Kapoor 2004):

1. **Commodity phase:** Every product or service starts its journey as a commodity with quality at par; the only diffentiator is the price of the product or service.

2. **Label phase:** Transition from commodity to becoming a label where the product is packed and it puts on a name. It is still not a brand, it is only packed.

3. **Recognized label:** The packed commodity with a name is familiar to people and is recognized by them. They do not find the label new or alien or unknown. However, the product or service has still not become a brand.

4. **Brand phase:** It stands for something in the perceptual map of the human mind—for example, Dettol stands for protection from germs and has gained its core value over a period of time.

5. **Brand personality phase:** The brand acts like a human being and is endowed with a character, it breathes, feels and grows like any other person.

6. **Brand immortality phase:** The final and last phase of a brand where it lives beyond generations. Brands like Coke, Pepsi, and Xerox are the examples.

In the last phase, the brand's immortality is due to the intimate relationship with the consumer community. Relationship Marketing drives the brand from the Brand Phase to the Brand Immortality Phase. Relationship helps a brand endure the highs and lows of the market. And it is only brands which endure through generations that can hope for immortality.

The problem with the simple notion of relationship brands as mass customization is that almost all brand concepts or ideas are—at least to some extent—based on mass appeal. Overall they rely on the inherent appeal of shared experience. An example of this is branded diets, such as the South Beach Diet of the early 2000s. Part of the appeal of such diets is that everyone seems to be on them. Being on the latest weight-loss regimen is like joining a club, becoming a part of a social group. It is the "next thing". Inherent in the very idea of the brand is its mass appeal. Once it loses this appeal, it is just another diet. The mass appeal of most brands is not as obvious as with the diet example. But think of a brand like Diet Coke. Part of the brand's appeal is surely that it is known, understood, and accepted by a large number of people—people who share something in common because of their experience with Diet Coke.

If relationship branding is not a mere customization to segments, a relationship brand has a shared mass appeal that can be experienced in more individualistic or idiosyncratic way by the consumer. In the South Beach Diet example, the brand is an appealing idea or concept for a segment of consumers who are either on the diet or interested in it. But consider two segments of these consumers. One, mostly female, is always on a diet and is looking to use the diet for all her meals; another, mostly male, looking to diet at breakfast and lunch during the workweek (these males figure to "relax" at night and on weekends). If the marketers find a way to allow each of these subsegments to experience the brand in their own way, the brand becomes a relationship brand. This could be as simple as giving the first subsegment a set of meal planning tips covering all meals and the other a set focusing on just the workday. Both subsegments share the same idea of the brand, and this is part of its appeal. They both buy into the diet, but they are able to relate to the brand in their own way.

To illustrate the concept another way, think of the brand as a person. We both know Mary. Now Mary is Mary, but we each have a different relationship with Mary because we have our own experiences with her. Indeed, this is what having a relationship is all about. We should think of relationship branding in the same way. Viewed as such, the key to relationship branding is to allow segments of consumers to experience the brand in a more individualistic, personal way. And this leads directly to using different contact points with each subsegment to create different experiences, and hence the relevance of Customer Relationship Management. A useful way to think about this idea comes from an integrated marketing perspective (Calder & Malthouse 2003). As diagrammed in Figure 3.1, the key notion is that the company must translate the brand idea into a series of contacts with the consumer that in turn creates the experience that underlies the brand. From this perspective, relationship branding involves creating contacts from subsegments of consumers that produce a more idiosyncratic

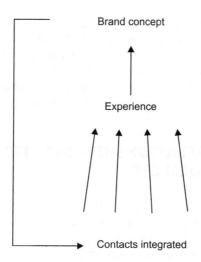

**Figure 3.1 The integrated marketing paradigm.**

*Source:* Bobby J. Calder and Edward C. Malthouse (2003), adopted with permission.

experience than would be the case if the same contacts were used for all consumers.

Rapp and Collins (1995) point to new types of brands, relationship brands:

"...with the ability to identify prospects and customers by name and address, learn more about them, interact with them in an ongoing relationship, a new form of branding is evolving: 'relationship branding'. You no longer simply brand or promote what you sell. You brand and promote the relationship as well."

In a similar vein, Duncan and Moriarty (1998) offer a Relationship Marketing model claiming the 'communication is the primary integrative element in managing brand relationships', with brand equity as the goal and core category. A relationship brand has a name, logo, usually offers membership, is advertised and includes continuing involvement.

Monopoly means that a single supplier rules the market. When there is competition, companies differentiate their offerings. One strategy is to achieve a value monopoly (DeBono 1992). There are many cities, paintings, movie directors, cartoons and awards, but only one Venice, one Mona Lisa, one Ingmar Bergman, one Donald Duck and one Nobel Prize. Patents give a temporary, innovation-based value monopoly. A corporation can dominate its industry, like IBM ruled over the computer industry up until the 1990s. Then Microsoft took over the star role and its president Bill Gates became the symbol for the new and exciting IT future. The cost of breaking a value monopoly can be so excessive that no competitor will succeed. A handful of such brands are known throughout the world: Coca-Cola, Sony, Mercedes, Kodak, Disney, Nestle, Toyota, McDonald's, IBM and Pepsi. Some brands have become so well known that they degenerate as brand names and are identified as synonymous with the generic product. 'To Xerox' now means to take copies even if the brand of machine is Canon, and Caran d'Ache, the Swiss pencil manufacturer, is used as the word for pencil in Russian.

## PARASOCIAL RELATIONSHIP—RELATIONSHIPS TO BRANDS AND OBJECTS

In her bestseller 'No Logo', Naomi Klein directs severe criticism against global brands. She points out that industry now understands that '... successful corporations must primarily produce brands, as opposed to products' (Klein 2000). Brands are old, and the core of politics and the church has often been symbols—the crown, the coronation, Buckingham Palace, the White House, the cross, the communion, the Vatican—rather than content, such as a promise or a message. When we are used to think of relationship as personal, which are primarily between people (Gummesson 2002), there are also parasocial relationships (Cowles 1994), which involve objects, symbols and other less tangible phenomenon. Our relationship to corporations, their services and products are often impersonal, yet important through the image they convey to us. These relationships are manifested in the connotations of company names, brands, trademarks and well-known business leaders or other people who symbolize a business. Just like a person, a product or a company has a soul, a personality and a body language. A limousine and French champagne have a different appeal than a taxi and beer. Russian cavier, oysters and red roses symbolize festivity, romance and wealth, respectively.

According to Linn (1987), the meta product is 'the whole of the invisible world of perceptions which we link to a branded product'. He proceeds: 'Every object has its metaphysical properties. It is sufficiently strong in symbols like the Christian cross, the David star or the hammer and the sickle for people to sacrifice their lives'. Linn gives the classic example of the Volkswagen 'Beetle': 'It was so personal that it was almost provocative...people established a relationship to the car. You had to react, it was hard to be indifferent... . If we want to see the whole in which the marketed product thrives, we must look more to men and their relationship to the products than we do today.' The perceived reality is not constituted by the product and service as independent objects, but by the relationships and interactions between the beholder and the product/service.

DeBono (1992) says that offering integrated values is the third stage of a firm's development. It has been preceded by a product-oriented stage when goods were scarce and manufacturing was the overriding issue. In stage two, competition was in focus. Companies are now approaching the third stage, but this stage is still in its infancy.

## Iconic Brand

In entertainment and culture, mass production is often a goal; the relationship between the entertainer and the consumer is rarely a personal friendship. Celebrities such as rock groups or sports champions become symbols of lifestyles, beauty, strength and smartness. Sometimes an actor's charisma, star quality, visibility and private life are equally important or much more important to the fans than her professional performance. People know them from their appearances as well as from news media and gossip columns. The fans can come close to their idols in their imagination. **It is personal relationship for one party, and a mass relationship for the other;** the fans 'know' their stars as individuals, but the stars usually know their fans as anonymous audiences. The role and the stage personality are perceived as real, and get mixed up with the private person. The fame of the star can be used to add credibility and popularity to products and services, and to boost images (Rein et al. 1987).

The strength of the parasocial relationship became blatantly obvious when Diana, Princes of Wales, died in a Paris car accident in 1997. Her beauty, love affairs, and care for the less privileged, combined with her own vulnerability, captured the minds of people around the world. They genuinely mourned her as a close friend.

According to Holt (2004), to systematically build iconic brands, companies must reinvent their marketing function. They must assemble cultural knowledge, rather than knowledge about individual consumers. They must strategize according to cultural branding principles, rather than apply the abstracted and present-tense mind-share model. For cultural branding, this knowledge differs dramatically from the standard kinds of brand and consumer knowledge that managers now rely on to guide their branding efforts. Cultural knowledge views the brand as a historical actor in society. Cultural knowledge seeks to understand the identity value of mass culture texts, rather than treating mass culture simply as trends and entertainment.

Let us look at John Lennon of the Fab4 "The Beatles" (Figure 3.2). One thing that made John Lennon an iconic brand is that he represents the populist world that stands up against the mainstream national ideology of his time. In simple words, he is simply a rebellious type of person and the world is usually amazed with such kind of human being.

The point, however, is that an icon such as John Lennon usually represents the voice of that silent majority. During the 60s and 70s, he spoke vibrantly against his own government, the Queen gave him the title, Member of the British Empire (MBE), but he rejected and returned it to Her Majesty for some reasons. During the cold war, he represented

**Figure 3.2   John Lennon—an example of iconic brand.**

all who were too sick with the killings, and imagined how the world could be living in peace, where there is no country, no hunger, no religion too.... the kind of anxiety and desire that all of us would dream of but just could not dare to speak it out loud. Well, perhaps we could speak it out, but did not think that it would be heard (Hermawan Kartajaya).

---

### Case Study: Big B as a Relationship Brand

Take the case of Indian Megastar Amitabh Bachchan, who is no less than an iconic brand in the entertainment industry. Star TV's historic 'Kaun Banega Crorepati' (KBC) in the year 2000 (Who would win INR 10 million?) game show presented episodes that morphed megastar Amitabh Bachchan into 'Big B'. In KBC, he came close to common people or the masses. By virtue of being an actor, he leveraged the opportunity of reading and learning about his prospects (the characters that played different roles) from the ground reality. In one of the episodes, a participant inadvertently dropped his handkerchief on the sets while going back. Big B's gentlemanly act was reflected when he stooped down to pick it up from the floor and handed it back to him. Millions of viewers across the country witnessed this act—nothing to do with the business, but an act that touched the heart and lent a gentler dimension to 'mass' relationship. He sensed and experienced in totality the 'Life Line' of his audience. The entire exercise on the sets of KBC infused in him a new facet on the cultural knowledge about the audience. He could sense the vibes of common audience in a one-to-one context (Figure 3.3).

What was visible in the game show was the way the participants looked at him, spoke to him—he was still their favourite and they believed in him. This established the fact that he is still the historic actor of his audience.

For any brand to attain iconic status, it has to create an identity myth. Every society invariably goes through phases of prosperity and

Figure 3.3  Amitabh Bachchan in KBC game show.

crisis. A brand that resonates and shows direction to masses through the brand stories and brand activities gets etched to the culture. These brands, by creating an identity for themselves, provide identity to the whole society (Roll 2006).

Big B is truly an identity myth who has sustained visible presence on the silver screen for more than three decades. His superhit films in post- 2000 period reaffirmed his inner potential, mastery on the craft of acting. What people envisaged as 'Big B' is now beyond the definition of a mega star but as good as a legend that would live beyond any time and tradition because Big B is now the historic or iconic brand. Apart from innumerable film awards, national awards, Honorary D.Lit from Universities, France's highest civilian award the Légion d'honneur (2007), for his contribution to Indian and international cultural life, voting of BBC Online to elect him as Star of the Millennium above Hollywood greats, replica of Big B sculpted and displayed at Madame Tussaud's wax museum in London, UNICEF's Brand Ambassador, have placed him as a sparkling icon among the historical and entertainment Hall of Fame of the world. Big B developed a broader and deeper relationship with common people in the modern day perspective of reaching the masses and KBC in a true sense facilitated 'mass customization' of his 'Brand Value'. In 2008, Amitabh Bachchan started his personal website where he invited comments from the bloggers. This seems to be an ideal strategy to promote and strengthen one-to-one relationship with his audience. Big B's ultimate transformation to an iconic brand has been possible through leveraging the success of establishing himself as 'relationship brand'.

## EFFECTS OF BRAND RELATIONSHIP NORMS ON CONSUMER ATTITUDES AND BEHAVIOUR

The key premise underlying the effects of brand relationship norms on consumer attitudes and behaviour is that, different relationships carry with them specific norms of behaviour. Three experiments tested the general hypothesis that consumers' brand evaluations are guided by the norms of consumer-brand relationships. Two types of consumer-brand relationships were examined—'exchange' relationships in which people provide benefits to others in order to get something back, and 'communal' relationships in which benefits are given to demonstrate concern for other's needs. It was hypothesized that the degree of consistency between the actions taken by a brand and the norms of the particular relationship influence consumers' evaluation of those actions (Aggarwal 2004).

A distinction is made in social psychology literature between relationships that are based primarily on economic factors and those based more on social factors (Goffman 1961). The differences between economic relationships and social relationships have been studied in some detail by Clark and Mills (Clark and Mills 1979, 1993; Clark 1986; Clark et al. 1986; Mills and Clark 1982, 1986). These authors distinguish between what they term *exchange* relationships and *communal* relationships mainly in terms of the norms governing giving of benefits to the partner.

According to other authors, more elaborate break-downs (e.g. Fiske 1992) in such norms have been suggested, but for the sake of simplicity the two relationship-type versions of Clark and Mills have been adopted. The receipt of a benefit incurs a debt or obligation to return a comparable benefit. People are concerned with how much they have received in exchange for how much they have given, and how much is still owed to the partner. Relationships between strangers and people who interact for business purposes are often characteristic of this type of relationship.

To elaborate the concepts of exchange and communal relationships, three experiments were conducted. The results of Experiment 1 showed that charging a fee for providing a special service violated communal relationship norms but not exchange relationship norms, causing communal relationship participants to evaluate the brand poorly relative to the exchange participants.

The results of Experiment 2 showed that an offer of an inexpensive gift rather than cash compensation for filling out a questionnaire is perceived as a violation of relationship norms by exchange participants but not by communal participants, leading the former to have a lower evaluation of the brand.

Relationships in which the key concern is mutual support by the partners are termed *communal relationships*. In such relationships, people give benefits to others to demonstrate a concern for that person and to express attention to their needs. They also expect others to demonstrate a similar concern for their own needs. Most family relationships, romantic relationships and friendships fall in this category. It is important to note here that communal relationships are not completely bereft of a sense of reciprocity and shared giving. Each individual interaction, however, is not scrutinized for evenness or balance of the transaction. Instead, the relationship may be evaluated over a longer time period.

Finally, the results of Experiment 3 showed that relative to communal participants, exchange participants experienced greater violation of relationship norms, and evaluated the brand lower in response to a request for help from the brand if the request was made after some time gap rather than immediately after they had sought help from the brand. Mediation analysis supported the hypothesis that a violation of relationship norms influenced participants' evaluation of the brand as well as their assessment of the relationship strength. Findings are consistent with the premise that analogous to interpersonal relations, brand-consumer relationships carry with them socially sanctioned norms of behaviour and adherence to or violation of these norms influences the appraisal of specific marketing actions.

Branding and brand-based differentiation are powerful means for creating and sustaining competitive advantage. Prior research has examined differences in how consumers perceive and evaluate brands, for example brand equity (Aaker 1991, Aaker and Biel 1993, Keller 1997, McQueen, et al. 1993), brand personality (Batra et al. 1993, Plummer 1985, Aaker 1991) and brand extensions (Nakamoto et al. 1993, Aaker & Keller 1990). More recently, researchers have noted that consumers differ not only in how they perceive brands but also in how they relate to brands (Fournier 1998, Muniz Jr. O'Guinn 2001, Blackston 1993). This line of research has suggested that people sometimes form relationships with brands in much the same way in which they form relationships with each other in a social context. For example, Fournier (1998) has argued that consumer-brand relationships cover a wide spectrum encompassing 'flings', 'courtships', 'best friendships', 'arranged marriages' and 'enmities' among others. In addition to the existing academic work, there is some support from marketing practitioners that people may sometimes form relationships with brands quite like their relationships with other people.

A recent paper published by the consulting firm Booz-Allen & Hamilton argues that some loyal consumers, called *brand zealots* experience a relationship that goes well beyond the fulfillment of a functional need (Rozanski et al. 1999). These consumers are militant in their commitment to the brand and have a strong sense of emotional loyalty to the brand. These brand zealots 'animate' the brand, giving it quasi-human qualities and relate to it in a way similar to how they relate to human beings.

In addition, there is abundant anecdotal evidence suggesting that consumers commonly interact with brands in ways that seem more appropriate for relationships between people. Most of us know some people who are 'crazy' about their cars, or their music systems or even their watches. The love affair that some consumers have with their VW

Beetle can be seen first hand on the innumerable websites where people have shared their intimate experiences with the brand (e.g. http://custom1.vw.com/ownExp/). Consumers have been known to give names to their 'bugs', and have been observed talking to them and stroking them with affection. The New Coke experience demonstrates how the millions of dollars spent on product and research failed to capture the powerful emotional undercurrents that consumers experienced with the brand. Mac users, reputed to be very passionate about their brand, have Web pages known to feature an altered picture of Bill Gates that includes devil-style horns, entitled 'Save us from the Gates of Hell' (Muniz Jr. and O'Guinn 2001). One advertising executive even got the 'Apple' logo of Macintosh tattooed on his chest—next to his heart!

All these examples suggest that people sometimes form a very close bond with brands. And in some extreme cases, a passion, that is often associated only with a close circle of friends and family. In an effort to understand the implications of forming such strong emotional bonds with brands, studies of the effect of different types of relationships on consumer attitudes, behaviours and brand evaluations have been done resulting in the central premise that relationships carry with them norms of behaviour that guide the actions of the people in the relationships and that affect their evaluation of the relationship partner. In particular, using a relational framework, it has been possible to explain differences in consumer responses to marketing actions taken by a brand. This has helped understanding of the consumer-brand relationships in order to make predictions that would not be possible using existing theories about the effects of brand personality, brand loyalty, imagery, or familiarity. One of the few sustainable differentiating tools available to marketers is the brand's equity that needs to be built. The relationship metaphor can be seen as an effort at extending the 'static' concept of equity into an interactive, dynamic process.

The concept of a brand relationship is neither novel not outrageous. It is readily understandable as an analogue—between brand and consumer—of that complex of cognitive, affective and behavioural processes which constitute a relationship between two people. Although the idea of a brand relationship may be acceptable, a few attempts have been made to develop an operational definition or a system for identifying, measuring, and building brand relationships.

We can infer the nature of the relationship between two people by observing the attitudes and behaviours they display towards each other. Unless they are involved in an elaborate deceit, an experienced analyst can make some fairly accurate inferences. Analogously, understanding the relationship between brand and consumer requires observation and analysis of:

- the consumer's attitudes and behaviour towards the brand, and
- the brand's attitudes and behaviours towards the consumer.

Just as an example, we can look at a hypothetical relationship between a doctor and a patient. If we let the doctor stand in for the brand, the chacteristics, namely skill, caring, funny, etc. constitute the patient's attitude towards the doctor—the patient's perception of the doctor's 'brand personality' and we would expect the patient to like the doctor.

However, when we uncover the crucial bit of information what the patient thinks the doctor thinks of him (a boring hypochondriac), our understanding of the nature of relationship changes completely. It does not matter what the doctor really thinks, because, for the patient, the relationship is based on what he thinks about the doctor's attitude. Like a relationship with another person, everything we need to know about the brand relationship is going on inside the customer's head. Thus, the real question we need to ask is, "What do the consumers think that the brand thinks of them?" That is the difference between a one-dimensional brand image and a brand relationship (Aaker & Biel 1993).

## BRANDS AS RELATIONSHIP PARTNERS

The types of brand relationships suggest a continuum, depending upon how close, personal and deep the relationship is perceived to be. For example, Fournier (1998) describes one of her participants' relationships with Coke Classic and Ivory as 'best friendship', but with trial size shampoos as 'flings' and with Gatorade as 'committed partnerships'. Her research shows that people describe the relationship with brands in the same terms as relationships with other people. However, the idea that people form relationships with brands is not without controversy. Prior research has noted that people and objects differ in many ways and different approaches may be needed to examine how consumers interact with each of them (Fiske & Taylor 1991; Lingle et al. 1984; Wyer et al. 1986).

For example, Kardes (1986) notes that the effect of initial judgment on subsequent judgments of products is different from the extent of this effect on social judgments and impression formation of people. Lingle et al. (1984) suggest that judgments of social stimuli (i.e. people) are likely to depend on inferred, abstract information (e.g. traits) whereas judgments of non-social stimuli (e.g. products) are likely to depend on concrete attributes. Menon and Johar (1997) find that the positivity effect in judgments of social experiences is not likely to manifest in judgments of product experiences. One reason noted for expecting non-social judgments to differ from social judgments is that people often judge others using the self as a frame of reference (Fong & Markus, 1982) whereas no such comparison is possible in judging non-social objects (Fiske & Taylor, 1991).

While acknowledging that relationships with non-social objects are different from social relationships, there may be reasons why people sometimes interact with brands in ways that parallel human interactions. First, consumers often do not distinguish between brands and manufacturers of brands. To them the company is the brand, and the brand is the company. This perception is more likely for service brands (e.g. hotels, airlines and banks), for brands that have a combination of products and services as their core offering (e.g. many online stores) and for brands in which consumers have a direct interaction with people who work for the company. When people interact with human beings as representatives of the brand, it is easy to use relationships used in human interactions for such brands. Second, even when companies focus primarily on selling physical products, some consumers may think of the brand as a living being. Animism, the belief that objects possess souls, has long been recognized in the domain of products (Gilmore 1919). McGill (1998) has looked at differences between natural and artifactual (man-made) categories and suggested that '... people treat some brands and products as if their characteristics are produced by an underlying, defining essence, analogous to DNA or a soul, and not by human design or construction'.

Moon (2000) has demonstrated that many of the social 'rules' and conventions that govern interpersonal interaction also apply to the human-computer relationship. This finding is consistent with what other writers have suggested that computers have characteristics of natural categories whereas most other artifactual categories such as tables or chairs do not (Gelman and Coley 1991; Keil 1986). Thus, even for some physical products people may think of the products as having a soul or, at least, more human-like properties. Third, the brand communicates with its consumers in a large number of ways. The dynamic and repeated interactions in the form of direct mail, ad messages, discount-coupons, and freebies have strengthened the sense of an ongoing relationship between the brand and the consumer. Over time, with the use of interactive media like the Internet and emails, this sense of two-way relationship and communication has become even stronger and more pervasive.

Finally, marketing practitioners and researchers often use projective techniques to get the consumers to describe the brands in terms of age, gender, socio-economic characteristics and other personality traits (D. Aaker 1991; Keller 1998). It is found that brands are often perceived to have a gender (Levy 1959), and three of the five dimensions used to describe brand personality are the same as those used to describe human personality traits (J. Aaker 1997). Marketers also encourage this perception by using brand mascots in advertising messages in an effort to 'bring the brand alive' (e.g. Michelin Man, Energizer Bunny, Mr. Clean, Hush Puppies, and Pillsbury Dough Boy). And once products and brands are associated with human qualities, it is easy to see how people may interact with brands in ways that parallel their 'social' relationships'.

It is important to clarify that brand relationships are different in many ways from the relationships that people form with other people. The key assertion here is not that people necessarily form relationships with brands that share the same richness and depth as those between human partners, but that consumers often behave *as if* they have relationships with brands that parallel human relationships in a social setting. And when they behave as if they have a relationship with brands, the consumer-brand interactions are mediated by the norms that govern these social relationships. Prior experience with the brand or specific marketing communication may bring the norms of different relationships to the forefront of people's minds so that they interpret the communication and the actions of the brand through the lens of the relationship norms.

## NORMS OF BEHAVIOUR AND THEIR ROLE IN SOCIAL INTERACTION

Social relationships carry with them norms of behaviour that the relationship partners are expected to follow. Norms emerge from interactions with others; they may or may not be stated explicitly, and sanctions for deviating from them come from social networks, not the legal system. These norms include general societal expectations for our behaviour, expectations of others for our behaviour, and our expectations of our own behaviour. One view of norms suggests that norms develop to balance the selfish desires of the individual with the need for social control and collective survival (Walster et al. 1978).

Thus, one of the primary functions of social norms is to allow people to live together in peace. Cialdini and Trost (1993) have argued that these norms are acquired by people in a social setting over long time periods of the socialization process. As these norms become internalized, they serve as a valuable guide for everyday behaviour and allow people to function in situations that may otherwise be new. Thus, when faced with different social situations, people use the norms that are salient at the time to guide them on the 'right' thing to do. In addition, people also tend to use these norms to judge others' behaviour. A particular action may therefore be a part of the norms of one relationship and be regarded as good and appropriate by one person, while the same action may be seen as a serious violation of the norms of another relationship and perceived to be improper by another person.

For example, keeping a close tab on how much money one spends on a relationship partner may be considered appropriate in a commercial transaction, but may appear inappropriate in interactions with family members. It is this adherence to or violation of the relationship norms that often determines our appraisals when we interact with our relationship partners. Three experiments, described earlier, this work, test the effect of adherence to or violation of the norms of relationship in the context of consumer-brand interactions. Consumers' reactions can be distinguished in instances when the relationship with the brand is thought of largely in economic terms (i.e. balanced exchange) from instances when the relationship takes on the characteristics of close personal relationships. This explains why we might sometimes observe consumer behaviour that appears irrational from a business perspective but makes perfect sense from a personal relationship perspective.

# FCB GROUP UNVEILS BRAND RELATIONSHIP STYLE MONITOR INDIA STUDY

Cogito Consulting, the brand consulting division of the FCB Group, shared key findings from the Brand Relationship Style Monitor Study. The Brand Relationship Style Monitor (BRSM) tries to understand the nature and intensity of the relationships between a brand and its customers, guiding relational branding and providing insight into how to improve these relationships, brand loyalty and profitability.

The Brand Relationship Style Monitor has been developed by FCB Worldwide through an extensive study across 342 brands and 45 categories in 7 countries, states an official release. It took over two years and a multi-million dollar investment for the model to be developed.

A rich database of around 163,000 brand customer relationships has been examined to provide insight into several global majors. The studies were conducted in Brazil, mainland China, Germany, Hong Kong, the United Kingdom and the U.S. Some of the categories that threw remarkable worldwide insights through the BRSM were packaged goods, food & beverages, computers, communications, financial services, automobiles, healthcare, toys, fashion and apparels and airlines.

The Relationship Monitor model consists of two basic components: A set of 13 relational dimensions connecting customers to brands and a set of 7 relational styles describing the nature of customer-brand relationships.

The BRSM in India was done across 1125 customers (users of brands) and revealed close to 2400 brand mapping scores. Done across two cities, the study took over 12 months to develop and fine-tune, given the complexities of the Indian market. The initial product categories of the study included automobiles, consumer durables, telecom and financial products.

FCB Ulka Advertising Mumbai ED & CEO, M.G. Parameswaran reckons, "The BRSM will be a very powerful tool for marketers to have in their quiver for great brand strategies."

Cogito Consulting COO Kinjal Medh, who presented the findings, opined, "Indian consumers are very different from the rest of the world, though a bit like consumers in Brazil. Indian consumers tend to gravitate to the two ends of the BRSM, namely consumers in a 'perfect fit' relationship with their brands as also consumers in 'price-based' equations with their brands. Both styles being highly indicative of the seriousness with which consumers here seek brands, being fairly high involved decisions at the same time being highly price-value conscious." Dorab Sopariwala, an eminent Marketing Consultant, said, "It is very a useful tool and can be used in conjunction with other brand equity measures."

Brands in categories such as telecom and consumer durables have strong skews towards the 'follow-the-leader' relationship style. The study also revealed that a few brands among financial products suffer on very important relationship styles such as 'caring' and 'reliant'. The BRSM also highlights certain 'diagnostic' measures that can be used for brands to move up the relationship ladder, for better brand equity.

*Source:* http://www.indiantelevision.com/mam/headlines/y2k5/dec/decmam67.htm

| *Case Study:* Fevicol |
|---|

Pidilite Industries is the market leader in adhesives and sealants, construction chemicals, hobby colours and polymer emulsions in India. Its brand name Fevicol has become synonymous with adhesives to millions in India and is ranked amongst the most trusted brands in India.

Consumers love Fevicol because it has created a bond with the Indian consumers over the years, which seems virtually unbreakable.

'Fevicol ka jod hai, totega nehin'. (This is joined by Fevicol and will not break apart.)

This has been made possible through a powerful relationship marketing exercise in which Fevicol has sensitively come closer to the customer and has been able to bind itself in the daily lines of Indian consumers.

A major initiative that Fevicol has embarked upon is the FCC (Fevicol Champions Club)—a relationship marketing strategy—which has over hundereds of FCC as well as over tens of thousands of carpenters and contractors club members who are helped, guided, rewarded informed as well as motivated to enhance their own businesses thereby bringing a unique closeness and affinity towards the brand Fevicol. A very well-organized network along with fruitful programme schedule helps the FCC members to be able to build their businesses and generate prosperities to their families. The FCC relationship marketing initiative is a great example of creating a bond between influencers and the brand and thereby creating a connection between the consumers and brand Fevicol through regular interactions and world-class communication. There cannot be a better example of bonding than this (Kapoor 2004).

## CONCLUSION

The key to relationship branding is to subsegment the market, which enables the marketers to create contacts that allow specific subsegments of consumers to make a more personal connection to the brand—to enable them to experience the brand in a more powerful individualistic or idiosyncratic way. This is the true power of relationship branding. Relationship branding is not a mere customization to segments, a relationship brand has a shared mass appeal that can be experienced in more individualistic or idiosyncratic way by the consumer. However, the issue of brands and image is not new, it is currently stirring up more interest than ever. By approaching the issue through the relationship eyeglasses, new marketing insights can be generated. Relationship brand leaves no doubt about the parasocial relationships supporting the concepts of integrated marketing paradigm. Brand Relationship Style Monitor (BRSM) tries to understand the nature and intensity of the relationships between a brand and its customers, guiding relational branding and providing insight into how to improve these relationships, brand loyalty and profitability.

> **Keywords**: *Integrated Marketing Paradigm, Parasocial Relationships, Brand Relationship Style Monitor (BRSM)*

## Exercises

1. How does brand immortality connect itself with the philosophy of Relationship Marketing? Explain with examples.

2. Discuss how the concept Relationship Branding has been applied in the entertainment sector in India.

3. How communal and exchange relationships are related to Relationship Branding? Present your views with reference to the banking sector.

4. How does brand act as a relationship partner?

5. What are your views in maintaining the essence of communal relationship in the exchange relationship? Does it help in promoting the business relationship?

Fill in the blanks:

6. Relationship branding is usually defined in terms of _____ _____ and _____ _____ a relationship brand is an offering tailored to a _____ _____ of _____.

7. _____ tries to understand the nature and intensity of the relationships between a brand and its customers, guiding relational branding and providing insight into how to improve these relationships, brand loyalty and profitability.

8. _____is the primary integrative element in managing brand relationships.

## References

Aaker, David A., 1991. *Managing Brand Equity*, The Free Press (a division of Simom and Schuster Inc.), New York.

Aaker, David A. and Biel, Alexander, 1993. *Brand Equity and Advertising: Advertising's Role in Building Strong Brands*, Lawrence Erlbaum Associates Inc., Publishers, New Jersey.

*Ibid.*, p. 115.

Aaker, David A. and Kevin Lane, Keller, 1990. Consumer Evaluations of Brand Extensions, *Journal of Marketing*, Vol. 54, January, pp. 27–41.

Aaker, Jennifer L., 1997. Dimensions of Brand Personality, *Journal of Marketing Research*, Vol. XXIV, August, pp. 347–356.

Aggarwal, Pankaj, 2004. The Effects of Brand Relationship Norms on Consumer Attitudes and Behaviour, *Journal of Consumer Research*, Vol. 31, June, pp. 87–101.

Batra, Rajeev, Donald, R. Lehmann and Singh, Dipinder, 1993. The Brand Personality Component of Brand Goodwill: Some Antecedents and Consequences, in *Brand Equity and Advertising's Role in Building Strong Brands*, David A. Aaker and Alexander L. Biel (Eds.) Lawrence Erlbaum Associates, New Jersey.

Blackston, Max., 1993. Beyond Brand Personality: Building Brand Relationships, in *Brand Equity and Advertising's Role in Building Strong Brands,* David A. Aaker and Alexander L. Biel (Eds.) Lawrence Erlbaum Associates, New Jersey.

Calder, Bobby J. and Malthouse, Edward C. 2003. What is Integrated Marketing, in *Kellogg on Integrated Marketing*, Dawn Iacobucci and Bobby Calder (Eds.), New York, Wiley, pp. 6–15.

Cialdini, Robert B. and Trost, Melanie R., 1993. Social Influence: Social Norms, Conformity and Compliance, *Handbook of Social Psychology*, Ch. 21, pp. 151–183.

Clark, Margaret S., 1986. Evidence for the Effectiveness of Manipulations of Communal and Exchange Relationships, *Personality and Social Psychology Bulletin*, Vol. 12, No. 4, Dec., pp. 414–425.

Clark, Margaret S. and Mills, Judson, 1979. Interpersonal Attraction in Exchange and Communal Relationships, *Journal of Personality and Social Psychology*, Vol. 37, No. 1, pp. 12–24.

Clark, Margaret S. and Mills, Judson, 1993. The Difference between Communal and Exchange Relationships: What It Is and Is Not, *Personality and Social Psychology Bulletin*, Vol. 19, No. 6, Dec., pp. 684–691.

Clark, Margaret S., Judson, Mills, and Powell, M.C., 1986. Keeping Track of Needs and Inputs of Friends and Strangers, *Personality and Social Psychology Bulletin*, Vol. 15, pp. 533–542.

Clark, S. Margaret, and Mills, Judson 1986. Communications that should Lead to Perceived Exploitation in Communal and Exchange Relationships, *Journal of Social and Clinical Psychology*, Vol. 4, pp. 225–234.

Cowles, Deborah L., 1994. Relationship Marketing for Transaction Marketing Firms: Viable Strategy via Command Performance, in *Relationship Marketing: Theory, Methods and Applications*, Jagadish N. Sheth and Atul Parvatiyar (Eds.), Research Conference Proceedings, Atlanta, GA: Center of Relationship Marketing, Emory University.

DeBono, Edward, 1992. Sur/Petition: Going Beyond Monopolies, London: Fontana.

Duncan, Tom and Moriarty, Sandra E., 1998. A Communication-based Marketing Model for Managing Relationships, *Journal of Marketing*, Vol. 62, April, pp. 1–13.

Fiske, Alan Page, 1992. The Four Elementary Forms of Sociality: Framework for a Unified Theory of Social Relations, *Psychological Review*, Vol. 99, No. 4, pp. 689–723.

Fiske, Susan T. and Taylor, Shelley E., 1991. *Social Cognition*, 2nd ed. McGraw Hill, New York.

Fong, Geoffrey T. and Hazel, Markus, 1982. Self-schemas and Judgments about Others, *Social Cognition*, Vol. 1, No. 3, pp. 191–204.

Fournier, Susan, 1998. Consumers and Their Brands: Developing Relationship Theory in Consumer Research, *Journal of Consumer Research*, Vol. 24, March, pp. 343–373.

Gelman, S.A. and Coley, J.D., 1991. Language and Categorization: The Acquisition of Natural Kind Terms, in *Perspectives on Language and Thought: Interrelations in Development*, S.A. Gelman and J.P. Byrnes (Eds.), pp. 146–196.

Gilmore, G.W., 1919. *Animism.* Marshall Jones Company, Boston.

Goffman, Erving., 1961. *Asylums: Essays on the Social Situations of Mental Patients and other Inmates,* Doubleday Anchor, New York.

Gummesson, Evert, 2002. *Total Relationship Marketing, Parasocial Relationships—Relationships to Brands and Objects,* Butterworth-Heinemann, Oxford, UK, pp. 111–115.

Holt, Douglas, 2004. *How Brands Become Icons: The Principles of Cultural Branding,* Harvard Business School Press, Boston, September 2004.

Kapoor, Jagdeep, 2004. Brand Practices: Twenty Seven Action Packed Strategies for Building Winning Brands, Macmillan India, New Delhi, pp. 142–143.

*Ibid.,* pp. 144–145.

Kardes, Frank R., 1986. Effects of Initial Product Judgments on Subsequent Memory-based Judgments, *Journal of Consumer Research,* Vol. 13, June, pp. 1–11.

Keil, F.C., 1986. The Acquisition of Natural Kind and Artifact Terms, in *Language Learning and Concept Acquisition,* D.W. Demopoulos and A. Marras (Eds.), Norwood, New Jersey, Ablex. pp. 133–153.

Keller, Kevin Lane, 1997. *Strategic Brand Management: Building, Measuring, and Managing Brand Equity,* Prentice Hall Inc., New Jersey.

Klein, Naomi., 2000. *No Logo.* Harper Collins Publishers, London.

Levy, Sidney J., 1959. Symbols for Sale, *Harvard Business Review,* Vol. 37, No. 4, pp. 117–124.

Lingle, John H., Mark, W. Altom and Douglas, L. Medin, 1984. Of Cabbages and Kings: Assessing the Extendibility of Natural Object Concept Models to Social Things, in *Handbook of Social Cognition,* Robert S. Wyer and Thomas K. Srull (Eds.), Hillside, New Jersey: Lawrence Erlbaum, Vol. 1, pp. 71–117.

Linn, Carl Eric., 1987. The Metaproduct and the Market, Kogan Page, London.

McGill, Ann L., 1998. Relative Use of Necessity and Sufficiency Information in Causal Judgments About Natural Categories, *Journal of Personality and Social Psychology,* Vol. 75, No. 1, pp. 70–81.

McQueen, Josh, Carol, Foley and Deighton, John, 1993. Decomposing a Brand's Consumer Franchise into Buyer Types, in *Brand Equity and Advertising's Role in Building Strong Brands,* David A. Aaker and Alexander L. Biel (Eds.), Lawrence Erlbaum Associates.

Menon, Geeta and Venkataramani, Johar, 1997. Antecedents of Positivity Effects in Social versus Nonsocial Judgments, *Journal of Consumer Psychology,* Vol. 6, No. 4, pp. 313–337.

Mills, Judson and Clark, S. Margaret, 1982. Communal and Exchange Relationships, *Review of Personality and Social Psychology*, Vol. 3, pp. 121–144.

Moon, Youngme, 2000. Intimate Exchange: Using Computers to Elicit Self-disclosure from Consumers, *Journal of Consumer Research*, Vol 26, March, pp. 323–339.

Muniz Jr., Albert M., O'Guinn, C., and Thomas, C., 2001. Brand Community, *Journal of Consumer Research*, Vol. 27, March, pp. 412–432.

Nakamoto, Kent, Deborah J. McInnis and Hyung-Shik Jung, 1993. Advertising Claims and Evidence as Bases for Brand Equity and Consumer Evaluations of Brand Extensions, in *Brand Equity and Advertising's Role in Building Strong Brands*, David A. Aaker and Alexander L. Biel (Eds), Lawrence Erlbaum Associates.

Plummer, Joseph T., 1985. How Personality Makes a Difference, *Journal of Advertising Research*, Vol. 24, December 1984/January 1985, pp. 27–31.

Rapp, Stan and Collins, Tom., 1995. *The New Maximarketing*. McGraw-Hill, New York, pp. 197–298.

Rein, Irving J., Kotler, Philip and Stoller, Martin R., 1987. *High Visibility,* Heinemann, London.

Roll, Martin, 2006. *Asian Brand Strategy*, Palgrave Macmillan, Hampshire, U.K.

Rozanski, Horacio D., Baum, Allen G. and Bradley, T. Wolfsen, 1999. Brand Zealots: Realizing the Full Value of Emotional Brand Loyalty, in *Strategy and Business* (Booz Allen Hamilton, USA), No. 17, Fourth Quarter.

Temporal, Paul, 2010. *Advanced Brand Management: Managing Brands in a Changing World*, 2nd ed., John Wiley & Sons (Asia), Singapore.

Tybout, Alice M. and Calkins, Tim, 2005. *Relationship Branding and CRM, Kellogg on Branding*, Wiley India, New Delhi.

Walster, E., Walster, G.W. and Berscheid, E., 1978. *Equity: Theory and Research*, Allyn and Bacon, Boston.

Wyer, Robert S., Srull, Thomas K.l. and Gordon Sallie, 1986. The Effects of Predicting a Person's Behaviour on Subsequent Trait Judgments", *Journal of Experimental Social Psychology*, Vol. 20, January, pp. 29–46.

Websites

www.indiantelevision.com/mam/headlines/y2k5/dec/decmam67.htm

Hermawan Kartajaya, http://hermawan.typepad.com/blog/2005/12/john_lennon_an_.html

# CHAPTER 4

||||||||||||||||||||||||||

# Value Creation in Relationship Marketing

## INTRODUCTION

One of the underlying themes of Relationship Marketing is to ensure value addition to the client-partner business at reduced cost. User value is explored in the product and services and this is deciphered in the value chain analysis. Using the value approach, the firm can also have an insight into the competitive edge of its products and services. As pointed out by Harvard Business School's Theodore Levitt, "competition exists not between what companies produce in their factories but between what they add to their factory output in the form of packaging, services, advertising, customer advice, financing, delivery arrangements, warehousing, and other things that people value". The value the customer attributes to these benefits is in proportion to the perceived ability of the offer to solve whatever customer problem prompted the purchase. This chapter covers the various dimensions of customer value with specific references to lifetime value as well as RFM (Recency, Frequency, Monetory value) model.

## FRAMEWORK OF USER VALUE

Value has a long and distinguished history in economics, starting with the work of John Hicks (1939, 1973) and leading on to the present work on valuation in economics, finance, and consumer behaviour (Brendl et al. 2003). Hicks conceived of capital as both input and output. To Hicks, the measurement of capital as output was value and it was "roughly equivalent to a capitalization of future net output for a given rate of return" (Hamouda 1993). Merchandise value amounts to the customer's perception of the tangible and nontangible (i.e. quality) elements of a store's products weighed against the sacrifices (i.e. price, time, etc.) that the customer has to make to obtain these products. Differentiation value is the customer's perception of the favourable uniqueness of the store's quality relative to the quality of alternative stores.

Let us come back to Relationship Marketing. From the definition of Relationship Marketing (Sheth & Parvatiyar 2002), it follows that:

- It is a collaborative business activity between a supplier and a customer.
- It is executed on a one-to-one basis.
- It helps growth of the total market.
- It generates better end user value at reduced cost.

The concept of relationship implies at least two essential conditions. First, a relationship is mutually rewarding connection between the provider and the customer, which is to say that both parties expect to obtain benefits in terms of 'real value' from the contact. Second, the parties have some sort of commitment to the relationship over time, and they are therefore willing to make adaptations in the routines with which the exchange situations deal (Ford 1980).

Thus, Relationship Marketing can also be seen as a 'continuous process dedicated to mutual need development triggering interdependence between the client and the partner on a long-term basis, augmented by the client through delivery of right solution/product in right time backed by relationship constructs, namely trust, commitment and concerns, etc.' The last point mentioned hits the fundamental note of Relationship Marketing—creation of better end user value at reduced cost.

Creating customer value is increasingly seen as a key source of competitive advantage. Value creation can be viewed as one of the key cross-functional processes, namely, strategy development process, multi-channel integration process, information management process, etc. that together constitute the strategic framework for Customer Relationship Management. Yet, despite growing attention to this aspect of strategic process, there is still conflict of agreement in the management as regards what exactly is meant by 'customer value'. Further, there is ambiguity in the understanding and interpretation of value in the organizations because most companies find it difficult to specify in sufficient detail the value they seek to deliver to clearly defined customer segments and how they propose to deliver the value.

Customer value creation is a teamwork involving innovation in terms of cost, quality, marketing, distribution and similar other factors of an enterprise by cross-functional teams. As a matter of fact, "value creation selling" does not end once the sale is made. The value-creating salesman, in fact, needs to be a strategist. It is time to comprehend that no longer should one measure one's own success first. Instead, an organization needs to measure success by how well the customers are doing with its support. Normally, large organizations deploy multifunctional team to make a high value sale and to carry the relationship forward.

## VALUE PROPOSITION

The aim of all businesses is to create a value proposition for customers, be it implicit or explicit, which is superior to and more profitable than those of competitors. In specific usage, a 'value proposition' is the offer defined in terms of the target customers, the benefits offered to those customers, and the price charged relative to the competition. Value propositions explain the relationship between the performance of the product, the fulfilment of the customer's needs and the total cost to the customer over the customer relationship life cycle (from acquisition of the product through to usage and ownership, and eventual disposal). As every customer is different and has changing needs, it is crucial that the value proposition for each customer is clearly and individually articulated, and cognizant of the customer's lifetime value.

The checklist furnished here can be used to determine whether a superior value proposition has really been developed (Payne 2005).

1. Is the target customer clearly defined?
2. Are the customer benefits explicit, specific, measurable and distinctive?
3. Is the price, relative to competition, explicitly stated?
4. Is the value proposition clearly superior for the target customer (superior benefits, lower price or both)?
5. Do we have, or can we build, the skills to deliver it?
6. Can we deliver it at a cost that permits an adequate profit?
7. Is it viable and sustainable in the light of competitors and their capabilities?
8. Is it the best of several value propositions considered?
9. Are there any impending discontinuities (in technology, customer habits, regulation, market growth, etc.) that could change company position?
10. Is the value proposition clear and simple?

# CUSTOMER VALUE CHAIN

Supplementing the strategy of value proposition, 'value chain concept' (Porter 1985) is introduced to leverage benefits of the competitive advantage. Every activity performed by the firm creates some value, which reflects finally in the firm's product offer, and that these activities are linked into a chain. It is called the firm's *value chain*. In any marketing situation, one can discern four distinct steps in the value providing process:

- Value selection
- Value creation/delivery
- Value communication
- Value enhancement

Marketing planning, buyer analysis, market segmentation, etc. are concerned with **value selection**; product development, manufacturing, testing, packaging, service planning, and pricing are concerned with **value creation/delivery**. All the components of Marketing Communications mix, e.g. Advertising, Sales Promotions, etc. are concerned with **value communication**. Finally, the firm's conscious and continuous endeavour to improve upon the offered value to maintain customer satisfaction, having an edge over competitor, is concerned with **value enhancement**. This process is done through feedback, and customer survey exercises.

While value chain is basically a tool for identifying ways in which a firm can enhance the value it creates and delivers, firms can also use the concept for analyzing their competitors and for assessing their own competitive position within the industry.

In using 'value chain' approach in the competitor analysis, the firm examines competitors' value chains in addition to its own value chain. It examines the costs and performance in its value chain—in the total value chain as well as in each link in the chain. It also examines the costs and performance of the value chains of its competitors—of the total value chain as well as of each link in the chain. It compares and contrasts its value chain—the total value chain as well as each link in the chain with those of the competitors. This exercise will finally help the first target a position of superiority/distinction relative to the competitors.

While analyzing the value chain of the competitor, the firm actually identifies the strengths and weaknesses of the competitor; it also gets useful insights into the strategy followed by the competitor. Those insights help the firm to make the right assumptions about competitors, while formulating its own competitive strategy.

The basic ideas in the value chain approach are as follows (illustrated in Figure 4.1):

- Every firm is a collection of activities and can be desegregated in terms of the activities.
- There are nine distinct activities that create value in any firm; they would, of course, create cost as well.
- The nine are made up of five primary activities and four support activities.

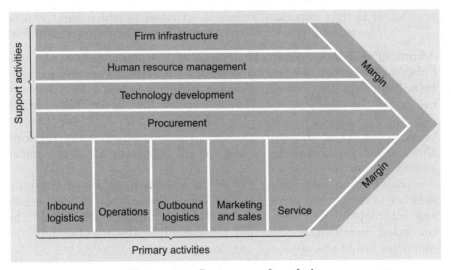

**Figure 4.1  Customer value chain.**

*Source:* Professor Michael Eugene Porter (1985), used with permission.

- The five primary activities consist of:
  - ➤ Inbound logistics (inward materials movement to business)
  - ➤ Operations (design, production)
  - ➤ Outbound logistics (outward movement of finished products)
  - ➤ Marketing and sales
  - ➤ Service
- The four support activities consist of:
  - ➤ Firm's infrastructure
  - ➤ Human resources
  - ➤ Technology development
  - ➤ Procurement

- The four support activities occur through all the five primary activities. For example, technology development, a support activity, occurs in every one of the primary activities of the firm. Thus, the primary and support activities together generate a vast matrix of value-creating activities in the firm.

- The matrix of value-creating activities along with their interacting effects constitutes the value chain of the firm.

- Business process is basically a value-creating and value-delivering process. Buyers patronize the firm that offers the highest value delivered to them.

- It is thus important to locate activities in which value can be created and create maximum possible value in each of them.

According to Sergio Zyman, Former Chief Marketing Officer of Coca-Cola, 'consumers are not just one link in a value chain that also includes manufacturing, distribution, planning, purchasing and sales. They are not 'one of the things' that marketers have to think about. They are not even the first among equals on the list of things that marketers have to think about. They are, quite possibly, the only thing worth thinking about. Everything else—including the all-important strategy—comes second to your consumers.

Relationship Marketing should be viewed in terms of the total network system perspective (Lee and Vida). Since all the channel actors are interdependent, one unsuccessful relationship affects all the connected, neighbouring channel relationships. The supplier and the consumer need to be allied not only for their mutual benefits but also for the greater social well-being. Thus, future investigation of Relationship Marketing research should take a larger, more multifarious perspective. This larger perspective would not only enhance the efficiency of channel system but would also contribute to relationship building efforts between the supplier (e.g. manufacturers and retailers) and the consumer.

In this context, a new emerging strategic approach in the consumer goods sector, known as *Collaborative Customer Relationship Management* (CCRM), has found much importance and the concept is bordered upon 'value chain contribution'. In the past, collaboration between a supplier and a retailer started with category management and soon proved to generate a mutual benefit for both parties and for the consumer as well (creating a win-win situation). Now, CCRM represents a quantum leap in the joint effort of both partners to meet and actually exceed customer expectations. First movers in implementing the new strategic concept, like Procter & Gamble, report increased sales and a significant higher customer retention rate. Besides enhanced sales, it also helps to exploit cost saving potentials in the value chain. The concept supports target-oriented-marketing-efforts and makes marketing investments of suppliers and retailers more efficient (Kracklauer et al. 2001).

| *Case Study:* Growth through Value Creation |

Reliance Industries Ltd (RIL) is gearing up to revolutionize the retailing industry in India. Towards this end, RIL is aggressively working on introducing a pan-India network of retail outlets in multiple formats. A world class shopping environment, state-of-the-art technology, a seamless supply chain infrastructure, a host of unique value-added services and, above all, unmatched customer experience, is what this initiative is all about.

The retail initiative of Reliance will be without a parallel in size and spread and make India proud. Ensuring better returns to Indian farmers and manufacturers and greater value for the Indian consumer, both in quality and quantity, will be an integral feature of this project. By creating value at all levels, Reliance will actively endeavour to contribute to India's growth. The project will boast of a seamless supply chain infrastructure, unprecedented even by world standards. Through multiple formats and a wide range of categories, Reliance is aiming to touch almost every Indian customer and supplier. One such ambitious project of RIL is Reliance Fresh.

**Reliance Fresh** is the retail chain division of RIL headed by Mukesh Ambani. Reliance has entered in this segment by opening new retail stores in almost every metropolitan and regional area of India. Reliance plans to invest Rs. 25,000 crores in the next 4 years in their retail division and plans to begin retail stores in 784 cities across the country and eventually have a pan-India footprint by year 2011. The super marts will sell fresh fruits and vegetables, staples, groceries, fresh juice bars and dairy products and also will sport a separate enclosure and supply-chain for non-vegetarian products. Besides, the stores would provide direct employment to 5 lakh young Indians and indirect job opportunities to a million people, according to the company. The company also has plans to train students and housewives in customer care and quality services for part-time jobs.

In 2007, **Reliance Fresh** opened several "Fresh" outlets in Chennai, New Delhi, Hyderabad, Jaipur, Mumbai, Chandigarh, Ludhiana increasing its total store count to 40. Reliance is still testing its retail concepts by controlled entry beginning in the southern states.

According to *Deccan Herald*, the company is planning on opening new stores with store-size varying from 1,500 sq ft to 3,000 sq ft, which will stock fresh fruits and vegetables, staples, FMCG products and dairy products. Each store is said to be within a radius of 1–2 km of each other, in relation to the concept of a neighbour store. However, this is only the entry roll-out that the company has planned.

In a dramatic change due to circumstances prevailing in UP, West Bengal and Orissa, it was mentioned recently in *News Dailies* that, Reliance Retail is moving out stocking. Reliance Retail has decided to minimize its exposure in the fruit and vegetable business and position

Reliance Fresh as a pure play supermarket focusing on categories like food, FMCG, home, consumer durables, IT, wellness and auto accessories, with food accounting for the bulk of the business. The company may not stock fruit and vegetables in some states, Orissa being one of them. Though Reliance Fresh is not exiting the fruit and vegetable business altogether, it has decided not to compete with local vendors partly due to political reasons, and partly due to its inability to create a robust supply chain. This is quite different from what the firm had originally planned. When the first Reliance Fresh store opened in Hyderabad, not only did the company said the store's main focus would be fresh produce like fruits and vegetables at a much lower price, but also spoke at length about its "farm-to-fork" theory. The idea the company spoke about was to source from farmers and sell directly to the consumer removing middlemen out of the way.

Reliance Fresh, Reliance Mart, Reliance Digital, Reliance Trendz, Reliance Footprint, Reliance Wellness, Reliance Jewels, Reliance Timeout and Reliance Super are various formats that Reliance has rolled out. In addition, Reliance Retail has entered into an alliance with Apple for setting up a chain of Apple Specialty Stores branded as iStore, starting with Bangalore.

*Source:* www.ril.com

## VALUE PROFIT CHAIN

According to value profit chain concepts (Heskett et al. 2002), organizations need to focus on providing what their employees, customers, investors, suppliers, and others value most. Focusing on value will bring about necessary organizational change, and tying the organization to the most valued needs of its customers will make it more responsive to the markets. In addition, giving employees what they appreciate in an organization will make them more productive and decrease the costs of employee turnover. Such value approach can result in greater organizational effectiveness and profitability.

The value profit chain model acknowledges the importance of the behaviours of a company's three key constituents:

- Customers or clients
- Employees
- Investors

The framework stresses the importance of the interrelationship of these three groups. Their behaviours can each be broken down into three areas:

- Retention
- Related sales
- Referrals

## Customers

Everyone wants the good customers to come back. This is a behaviour that is referred to as *retention*. Retention can be measured by calculating the revenue associated with keeping customers. Not only do we want our customers to stay with us, but we also want them to buy more from us. We want a higher share of their wallet in terms of the things they purchase. The third behaviour that companies look for, involves referrals. We want customers to feel so good about us, that they will go out and recommend our products or services to other people. Thus, getting customers to stay with a company (retention), buy more (related sales), and tell others (referrals) are crucial behaviours. These behaviours cause long-term profitability and growth for the company.

## Employees

Profit and growth cannot be expected merely by focusing on the customers. It is important to take a look at the employees. It is crucial for the company to look at the same behaviours that they evaluate for their customers and see how to apply them to their employees. Obviously, organizations want to retain the good employees; and want them to care about the company as well as behave as if they were owners. It is important to leverage more of their mental energy, something one calls 'share of mind', and make them feel so good about working for the organization that they will go out and tell their family and friends that this is a great place to work.

## Investors

There is a mirror effect between the behaviour that companies want to see in their customers and their employees. These behaviours are: (a) To retain employees with the same spirit as retaining the customers; (b) The objective of having a large share of customer wallet would be same while taking share of the employee's energy. It is beneficial that both customers and employees seek to gain from this exchange; and (c) Grooming the aspirations of the company to be referred by both employees and customers. Companies need to aim for retaining the employees just as retaining the customers.

If a company does this well, then investors will repeat the three behaviours. In other words, the company elicits greater interest from the investors who reck on that acquiring bigger share of the company's equity or ownership will result in higher return on investment, and they will go out and tell their families and friends that this is a great place to invest.

## ENHANCING CUSTOMER VALUE

Companies can gain competitive advantage by using the following methods for value enhancement with respect to various products and services offered to their clients (Mukherjee 2007):

- **Innovative features**—Gillette innovations in razors, namely Super Excel, Mach 3 Turbo, etc.
- **Complete solution**—End-to-end solution. Large IT companies provide such solution starting from consultancy, hardware and networking equipment supply and installation, software development, implementation and maintenance.
- **Value at lesser cost**—Nano of Tata Motors.
- **Removing pain points**—It is related to efficient delivery of service. One such example is home delivery of food, 24 hours service offered by some banks.
- **Technology**—iPod of Apple that offered enhanced value to music players.

## RELATIONSHIP MARKETING AND LIFETIME VALUE

Calculating Life Time Value (LTV) assists a company in a variety of applications for product development and marketing (Bose & Bansal 2000). LTV is a value added component to marketing return when marketing strategy is executed through relationship mode instead of conventional product marketing mode.

It can be illustrated through the general recognition and acceptance won by those who embraced the direct marketing concepts years ago. By logical extension, therefore, the more sales a company makes to its original customers, the profit a company makes from its continued sales to its own customer base is consistently higher than the profit made on the original sale. Each of the customers then delivers an income stream, and the stream of profit far exceeds the value of the original purchase. Income streams contribute cash flows in terms of years for any single product.

Hence, it is important that organizations use appropriate measures to assess their customers' value. It is general approximation that the top 20 per cent customers produce 80 per cent of the sales in the organization. Therefore, it becomes evident that specific customers need to be identified and retained as best as possible.

However, it should not be assumed that companies would wish to retain all their customers. Some customers may cost too much money to service, or have such high acquisition costs in relation to their profitability, that they will never prove to be worthwhile and profitable.

Clearly, it would be inadvisable to invest further in such customer segments. It is likely that within a given portfolio of customers, there may be some segments that are profitable, some that are at break-even point and some that are unprofitable. Thus, increasing customer retention does not always yield increases in customer profitability. It should be recognized, however, that unprofitable customers may be valuable in their contribution towards fixed costs and considerable caution needs to be placed in the allocation of fixed and variable costs to ensure that customers who make a contribution are not discarded. Research has highlighted the need for managers to adopt a stronger focus on customer retention and measuring LTV.

## RFM MODEL—CUSTOMER RESPONSE, RETENTION AND VALUATION CONCEPTS

Using RFM model it is possible to rank the customers relative to each other (Novo 2004).

It is like referring customer list as a "file"? Before computers, catalog companies used to keep all their customer information on 3 × 5 cards.

One rifles through this deck of cards to select customers for each mailing, and when a customer placed an order, one would write it on the customer's card. These file cards as a group became known as *the customer file*, and even after everything became computerized, the name stuck. It happens that while going through these cards by hand, and writing down orders, the catalog folks began to see patterns emerge. There was an exchange taking place, and the data was speaking. It spoke of three things:

1. Customers who purchased **recently** were more likely to buy again versus customers who had not purchased over a period of time.

2. Customers who purchased **frequently** were more likely to buy again versus customers who had made just one or two purchases.

3. Customers who had **spent the most money** in total were more likely to buy again. The most valuable customers tended to continue to become even more valuable.

With the results, the customers were ranked on these three attributes, sorting their customer records so that customers who had bought most **recently**, most **frequently**, and had spent the most **money** were at the top. These customers were labelled "A" (Excellent).

Customers who had not purchased for a while, had made few purchases, and had spent little money were at the bottom of the list, and these were labelled "B" (Poor).

Then they mailed their catalogs to all the customers, just like they usually do, and tracked how the group of people who ranked highest in the three categories above, that is, 'A' responded to their mailings, and compared this response to the group of people who ranked lowest, that is, 'B'. They found a huge difference in response and sales between excellent and poor customers. Repeating this test over and over, they found it worked every time!

The group who ranked "A" in the three categories above always had higher response rates than the group who ranked "B". It worked so well they cut back on mailing to people who ranked "B", and **spent the money saved on mailing more often to the group who ranked "A".** And their sales exploded, while their costs remained the same or went down. They were increasing their marketing efficiency and effectiveness by targeting the most responsive, highest future value customers.

The **recency, frequency, monetary value (RFM)** model works everywhere, in virtually every high activity business. And it works for just about any kind of "action-oriented" behaviour you are trying to get a customer to repeat, whether it is purchases, visits, sign-ups, surveys, games or anything else.

A customer who has visited your site recently (R) and frequently (F) and created a lot of monetary value (M) through purchases is much more likely to visit and buy again. And, a high recency/frequency/ monetary value (RFM) customer who **stops visiting** is a customer who is finding alternatives to your site.

Customers who have not visited or purchased in a while are less interested in you than customers who have done one of these things recently. Put recency, frequency, and monetary value together and you have a pretty good indicator of interest in your site at the customer level. This is valuable information for a business to have.

## RFM Implementation

Customers are ranked based on their R, F, and M characteristics, and assigned a "score" representing this rank. Assuming the behaviour being ranked (purchase, visit) using RFM has economic value, the higher the **RFM score**, the more profitable the customer is to the business now and in the future. High RFM customers are most likely to continue to purchase and visit, and they are most likely to respond to marketing promotions. The opposite is true for low RFM score customers; they are the least likely to purchase or visit again and the least likely to respond to promotions.

For these reasons, RFM is closely related to another customer marketing LTV—which is the expected net profit a customer will contribute to your business over the life cycle, the period of time a customer remains a customer. Because of the linkage to LTV and the life cycle, RFM techniques can be used as a proxy for the future profitability of a business.

High RFM customers represent future business potential because the customers are willing and interested in doing business with you, and have high LTV.

Low RFM customers represent dwindling business opportunity and have low LTV.

Scoring customers using RFM, it will be possible to:

- decide who to promote to and predict the response rate,
- optimize promotional discounting by maximizing response rate while reducing overall discount costs, and
- determine which parts of the site or activities attract high value customers and focus on them to increase customer loyalty and profitay.

# MEASUREMENT OF CUSTOMER LIFETIME VALUE (CLV)

Before getting into the measurement process, the following dimensions of customer lifetime value need to be understood (Kumar 2007):

- Duration of the customer lifetime
- What portions of the customer's purchases in the firm's offering categories that are captured by the firm as opposed to its competitors.
- Frequency of up- and cross-selling to its customers so as to increase the levels and monetary value of their purchases over time.
- Cost of acquiring, serving and retaining the customers.

## Calculating Value

*Process 1:*

CLV = Average transaction value × Frequency of purchase × Customer life expectancy

The relation between the customer retention rate and the average customer life is as follows:

Average customer lifetime (years) = 1/(1−retention rate)

If the customer retention rate is 90 per cent per annum (meaning that we lose 10 per cent of our existing customer base each year), then the average customer lifetime will be 10 years.

*Process 2:*

By segmenting customers across both dimensions, namely, current profitability and lifetime potential, financial firms, in particular, can better align marketing, sales, service resources and expenditures to optimize long-term customer value and, ultimately, organization profitability. There are various iterations of the CLV formula. As shown here, it is not a trivial calculation but a simplified formula. CLV incorporates some figures that are straightforward calculations based on historical data with other figures that are more difficult to predict or allocate a numeric value, e.g. reference potential, reduced price sensibility, etc.

### Customer Lifetime Value (Burelli and Dunn 2003)

$$CLV = \sum_{t=1}^{n} D[R_t - C_t) + R_f(A_c - A_{cr})]/(1 + r)^t - A_c$$

where

$t$ = Year
$R_f$ = Number of referrals generated by customer each year
$n$ = Length of customer relationship
$A_c$ = Full acquisition costs (for new customers)
$D$ = Customer retention rate
$A_{cr}$ = Reduced acquisition costs (for existing customers)
$R_t$ = Revenues earned from customer in year $t$
$r$ = Discount rate
$C_t$ = Cost of servicing customer in year $t$

Here variables, such as revenues earned and acquisition costs are based on historical data and these are calculable and absolute. The average number of referrals generated each year is less definite and those need to be estimated.

## CUSTOMER LIFE CYCLE AND LTV

There are two kinds of lifetime value measurement—absolute and relative. The first is very difficult to calculate; the second, very easy to calculate and in many ways more powerful than the first. The most difficult part of calculating LTV is deciding what a "lifetime" is. Lifetime value is the value of the customer over the life cycle. But what is a life cycle? The customer in the aggregate tends to follow similar behavioural patterns, and when any single customer deviates from the norm, this can be a sign of trouble (or opportunity) ahead. For example, if the average new cellphone customer calls customer service 60 days after they start, and an individual customer calls customer service 5 days after they start, this customer is exhibiting behaviour far outside the norm. There can be potential problem or opportunity—it can be likely that the customer is having difficulty in understanding how to use advanced services on the phone or inquiring about adding on more service. There is no "average customer", and a business will have many different customers groups, each exhibiting their own kind of "normal" behaviour. In the cellphone case, cited before, the measurement of

Latency (number of days until customer service call), serves as the "trip wire", raising a hand by the customer to say the marketer "I am different, Pay attention to me", and triggers the marketing behaviourist to determine the next course of action. Metrics like Latency provide the framework for setting up the capability to recognize the opportunity for increasing customer value. This raising of the hand by customers, and the reaction by marketers, is the feedback loop at the centre of relationship or life cycle-based marketing. It is a repeating action-reaction-feedback cycle. At the core of a life cycle-based marketing approach is customer behaviour. Customers tend to behave in certain ways unique to one's business and products, and if one can discover these patterns, these can be used to predict customer behaviour. Particularly when you can predict the likelihood of an average customer to turn into a best customer, and you successfully encourage this behaviour, or you can reverse a customer defection before it happens, then there are tremendously profitable longer-term implications for the bottom line. These opportunities are discovered by understanding behaviour and setting up "trip wires" to alert you to deviations from normal behaviour by a customer (Novo 2002).

## Advantages of CLV

One of the key advantages of CLV is segmenting customer groups according to their characteristics. This enables prioritization and thus the company can prepare its marketing budget to address the current and future needs. Until you identify and understand exactly how much combined profit a client represents to your business, for the life of the relationship, you cannot begin to know how much time, effort and other expenses you can afford to invest to acquire that client in the first place (Abraham, 2001). This information also helps an organization to segregate the customer using Pareto principle of 80–20, that is, 20% customers are responsible for 80% revenue of the firm. By calculating CLV, the marketer is then able to allocate funds to marketing more accurately, ensuring that the customers most likely to bring the greatest returns receive the greatest attention.

## VALUE ENHANCEMENT THROUGH CO-BRANDING

One of the popular strategies embraced by organizations for product or service value enhancement is co-branding, which is a happening thing in today's marketing circles, with different companies coming together and sharing their competencies to get the maximum revenues. For example, a credit card that is bearing the name of Jet Airways and Citibank, or logo of Intel on the Compaq or IBM PCs (Mehta 2002). The philosophy behind co-branding is to generate additional market share (and ultimately increase revenue streams) through customer awareness by forming alliances with one or more brands. Co-branding in the hospitality industry has existed in one form or another since the 1930s. But it was not until the 1980s, when Red Lobster opened two restaurants in Holiday Inn properties in Charlottesville, Virginia and Texarkana, Arkansas, that this idea became popular. To put it in the word of Intrabrand definition, co-branding is a form of cooperation between two or more brands with significant customer recognition, in which all the participants' brand names are retained.

According to an article written by Juliette Boone (1998) about co-branding, at least five reasons exist for forming an alliance:

1. To create financial benefits;
2. To provide customers with greater value;
3. To improve on a property's overall image;
4. To strengthen an operation's competitive position; and
5. To create operational advantages.

It is believed that performance may be enhanced when one company compensates for another firm's weak points; by forming a partnership, both companies can benefit. Such cooperation between the brands is of medium to long-term duration. Co-branding is, however, different from other forms of marketing alliances like joint promotions and joint ventures, in terms of duration and strength of relationship and the additional value created by sharing each other's strengths.

Joint promotion is cooperation for a shorter duration with a low additional value creation and is a temporary exercise, while a joint venture is a longer duration high value creating alliance of a stable nature involving the synergies of more than marketing only.

Co-branding lies between the two extreme points of marketing alliances. It is of medium-to long-term duration and its shared value potential is not as low as of a temporary nature nor it is as high to justify the culmination into joint venture.

On the basis of strength of relationship and shared value creation, there exist different forms of co-branding with subtle differences between the different layers of the hierarchy. Generally saying, co-branding has four layers in the hierarchy:

1. *Reach and awareness co-branding.* This is the lowest level of shared cooperation in a co-branding exercise and its objective is to rapidly increase the awareness of the sharing brands through each other's strength in the respective domain. The examples for this type of co-branding are found in the credit cards.

In fact, co-branding of this type finds the maximum utility of co-branding. In the Indian context, we have already observed a spate of co-branded credit cards between Citibank and Jet Airways, Standard

Chartered Bank and Indian Railways, Indian Oil and Citibank, and Citibank and *The Times of India.*

The benefit of co-branded cards to the cardholder is that he gets points whenever he uses it and he can get these points redeemed for additional products or services for free. Thus, it builds loyalty to the brand or service in use by the customer. This is a sort of affiliate marketing between three brands, viz a payment service franchiser (Mastercard, VISA), a bank and a product or service.

2. *Value endorsement co-branding.* This is the second level in the co-branding hierarchy wherein the shared value creation and the strength of relationship is such as to have endorsement of one brand values to the other with a strong affinity towards the other. The most appropriate example here would be of the companies getting involved with a cause with some non-government organization, e.g., the co-branding exercise between P&G and National Association of Blind in the form of Project Drishti where one rupee per pack of Whisper purchased by the customer was diverted towards the cause of a blind female child.

Thus, here one of the brands gives a small proportion of its transaction revenue to charity and the brand comes to be associated in the public mind with a worthy cause and with a good citizen brand values. The essence of this type of branding is that the two participants cooperate because they have, or want to achieve an alignment of their brand values in the customer's mind. Some of the other examples in two commercial brands coming together would include endorsement of Ariel by Vimal.

3. *Ingredient co-branding.* Intel Inside on a Compaq personal computer explains the basis of ingredient co-branding. In this form, there is a physical identifiable ingredient brand which has a high brand value for the customer and with it the value of the final product greatly increases. Here, one of the strong brands is an ingredient to another strong brand adding value to the final product. The potential of value created in this cooperation is tremendous and without it the value of the product will be diminished significantly.

4. *Complementary competence co-branding.* This is the highest layer in the hierarchy of co-branding. In terms of value creation, it is just next to joint ventures. Here, the two powerful and complementary brands come together and combine for a product or service that is more than sum of its parts and it relies on each partner committing a selection of its core skills and competencies to a product. The examples for this type would be Coke at McDonalds or tie-up of retail brands like Ebony and Crosswords or Planet M and Shoppers' Stop.

Thus, in the later case, tie-up with Shoppers' Stop provides Planet M more purchases and it adds value significantly to the Shoppers' stop positioning of 'one stop' shopping experience.

The success of such a co-branding exercise, however, relies on both parties contributing a high proportion of their competencies and operational advantages to it on an ongoing basis and not just in designing and launching the concept. The value creation in this type is also very high.

This co-branding requires increase in the **shared value creation**, which has to be more than the individual values created by the two brands. But also, there is a word of caution in terms of synergies of the two brands, which they bring together. If the two brands are such that the brand values are difficult to be shared, the success of a co-branding exercise between two such brands becomes a remote possibility.

## Choosing the Right Partner

Selecting the ideal partner is a strategy in itself, whether the alliance is between companies whose sizes are similar or significantly different. The selection process requires several steps: identifying the positioning strategy; contacting intermediaries to assist in the formation of partnerships; defining what is wanted; meeting with the principles involved; performing analyses to determine the feasibility of the partnership; getting the top executive's decision in moving forward with the alliance; and finally, negotiating the contract. Goals and objectives that each company brings to the alliance should enhance each other's ultimate partnership strategies. Partnerships composed of large and small companies would appear to result in a power imbalance between the partners; however, the important element in the alliance is that the products complement each other. The exercise of power does not necessarily depend only on the size of the partners; it also depends on each product's existing market share and recognition. Communication is vital from the beginning; if communication fails, alliances can easily crumble—a situation that can affect the bottom line for both parties.

## Advantages

From the perspective of both the client and the partner, the ability to access a broader customer base and form new relationships with clients is one of the more important and beneficial advantages. The revenue generated by the partnership can outweigh the expense of forming the alliance; as a result, budgeted expenditures can be concentrated in other areas. In addition, co-branding enhances the credibility of one's brand by borrowing credibility from other brands. Furthermore, the idea of receiving "more value for their money" when staying at a certain property is a critical factor for guests when choosing a hotel product.

## Challenges

Taking cue from the hospitality industry, it is observed that co-branding can also be difficult and complicated. The idea of introducing new variables that can complicate day-to-day operations is one of the major drawbacks. Hotel management teams have to be sure that partnering with a branded food and beverage outlet, for example, will not result in direct competition with the hotel's existing in-house food and beverage services; rather, the alliance should complement the hotel's established amenities. Other challenges include, but are not limited to: negotiating monetary commitment and initial investment fees between the two parties; the fear of losing brand reputation and recognition or of experiencing a decrease in quality levels during the term of the alliance; and the concern of partnering with the wrong brand. Many instances of unsuccessful partnerships have been the result of miscommunication between the partners.

# CROSS-PROMOTION

"Walk Your Talk" is when two or more groups (businesses, government agencies, or non-profit agencies) with shared values and markets act together to reach their shared markets more memorably, efficiently, frequently, and credibly. They "walk their talk" by thinking about the customer first, rather than the product, and looking for other ways the customer would gain convenience, savings, awareness, or other benefits through the joint efforts of multiple vendors reaching out to them. Cross-promotion has the potential for a big marketing payoff because partners can successfully expand through each other's customer base. They can gain an inexpensive and credible introduction to more of their kind of customer more effectively than with the traditional "solo" methods of networking, advertising, or public relations. Even the most time-pressed business owner can attract more customers with less effort through the right cross-promotions. Why? Because when you join forces with other credible people who also reach your market you can reach your customers more efficiently, credibly and memorably with the right offers and services (Anderson 2007).

## Strategies for Cross-Promotion

1. **Target your specific market.** Pick a niche market you want to reach better, more, differently, memorably, or credibly consider beginning with entrepreneurs and "Walk Your Talk" to reach out to them.

2. **Who is on your common ground?** Brainstorm to consider other owners/managers who also want to reach your "mutual market." Other than your niche market, the universally most helpful partners—the "Most Valuable Cross-Promotional Players (MVPs)"—are the main kinds of businesses most people visit at least once a month: banks, for example, shopping malls, etc.

3. **Start safely and successfully.** Choose a "quick-start," low-risk first action to propose to a potential cross-promotional partner.

4. **Jump-start.** Propose partnership to someone you know already or who has a very strong mutual interest in the same market. Demonstrate goodwill and commitment to partnering by making the first cross-promotional action even more beneficial to your partner than to you.

5. **One plus one plus one can equal five.** When you gain agreement with your partner to carry out your first action, ask your new partner to consider approaching a third partner to join you. With the right third partner, you increase the credibility, quality, and quantity of your visibility—and lower each partner's costs.

6. **Get concrete.** Be very specific with your partners about what each of you will contribute (including time, money, products or services, employees' participation, store space) and how you will benefit. Then write a simple agreement for all partners to read and approve.

7. **Just do it!** Carry out your first cross-promotional action with as much forethought, care, and fun as you might any newly valued venture or friendship—which it might be.

8. **Plentiful praise.** Thank your partner(s), employees, guests, vendors, and any others who even remotely helped to make the action happen. Also, praise them to each other.

9. **De-brief immediately.** Immediately after the action, compare notes about the level of success, needed improvements, and—if considered mutually successful—the next cross-promotional action on which to embark.

## Benefits of Cross-Promotion

The following are the benefits of cross-promotion:

1. **Broadens your customer base.** When two more companies team up, more customers can be reached. The team effort will broaden the chances of gaining more customers. Cross-promotion can also be referred to as networking. Thus, marketers can stand out by providing more credible, valuable, and eye-catching offers through their partner in ways and places where competition is not even in sight. One can gain memorability because promotions are more unique and eye-catching than the usual advertisement or public relations. Thus marketers reach people more often because the exposure at least doubles with just one partner—the cross-promotion appears in front of both customer bases. It

is possible to reach more potential guests by working with partners who are reaching the same kinds of people, but they may not be your customers yet.

2. **Time saving device.** Cross-promotion amounts to saving time. Since both businesses are putting in a lot of effort to promote each other and themselves, more people are reached at a quicker pace. In cross promotion, the workload gets distributed among the two or more businesses, and thus the people assigned to carry out marketing tasks can finish them in the assigned time limit.

3. **Saves money.** Cross-promotion saves quite a bit of money. Both businesses enjoy more profit, as more income is generated. The expenses and responsibilities are shared between the businesses. When there is a combination of two or more businesses in marketing, it proves to be more beneficial. Cost sharing is a major factor that should be taken into consideration. Money saved is money earned. Split costs of a common "offer" or promotion card, or trade free gifts of your services with products of your partners—to offer each other's customers. Furthermore, partners can help each other through "slow times" and leverage opportunities during "busy times."

4. **Building trust.** Cross-promotion facilitates reliability and credibility. One can gain credibility as partner(s) tout the services or products.

When another company does your marketing for you, it has the effect of enhancing your business' reputation and helps to build trust among customers. It is equivalent to another company putting in a good word for yours.

5. **Making news.** You become more newsworthy when you carry out unusual cross-promotions, especially with unlikely partners or nonprofit and/or government partners.

6. **Generate more reasons to buy—and buy more.** You offer your customers more reasons to buy and more reasons to visit more frequently, when you involve ideas and resources from partner(s).

7. **Increasing the advertising exposure.** As we all know, advertising plays a very important part in increasing business; and cross-promotion enables both businesses involved to gain more exposure. It is like killing two birds with one stone; each business individually advertises for both of the businesses.

8. **Enhanced creative thinking.** Cross-promotion increases creativity. Like the saying "two heads are better than one", the

combined efforts of the creative teams of two companies can come up with innovative ads, promotional products, and special offers. You can mix and match them—coming up with exciting, new and effective ways to reach out to new customers. Creative advertisements are usually very eye-catching and are easy for prospective customers to remember. They always stand out in the crowd of other advertisements. The fact is, creativity never goes unnoticed.

Marketers can punch up their marketing strategy through cross-promotion and reach out to new prospective customers that they have not been able to reach before, but will also forge new, effective (and profitable!) business relationships.

## KEIRETSU AFFILIATION—RELATIONSHIP SUBCONTRACTING

The Japanese automakers successfully increased their share of global automobile production from 3.6 per cent to 25.5 per cent between 1969 and 1985. What was the cause for this phenomenal success? Japanese-built cars were extremely reliable, had superior quality, and were very competitively priced and an excellent value for the growing number of middle-class buyers all over the world. Since the 1970s, some of these models became permanent fixtures on the top ten lists compiled by rating agencies such as J.D. Powers & Associates and Consumer Reports.

Prior research has indicated two broad reasons for this success: (a) the flexible production system pioneered by Toyota, and (b) the "Keiretsu" style automobile parts contracting system unique to the Japanese automobile and electronics manufacturing industries (Dyer 1996). "Keiretsu" is a distinguishing characteristic of the modern Japanese corporate system manifested in a unique inter-group network of firms (Fruin 1992). These business groups account for 24 per cent of Japan's sales and 10 per cent of the entire workforce (Orru et al. 1989). There are two types of Keiretsu: (i) horizontal Keiretsu and (ii) vertical Keiretsu. The 'horizontal Keiretsu' consists of a large network of firms operating in many industries competing across groups, but not within them. It is generally formed around an industrial conglomerate (like Mitsubishi, Mitsui, etc.) and is anchored by a premier bank or financial institution. In contrast, a 'vertical Keiretsu' consists of a core or parent firm with several affiliate firms that generally operate in one industry. In turn, many of these 'vertical Keiretsu' are part of a 'horizontal Keiretsu' (Orru et al. 1989). Vertical Keiretsu members coordinate their activities, both financial and non-financial, with each other creating a "stable collective structure of coordinated action".

The Japanese automobile industry is organized as a vertical Keiretsu, characterized by a large core firm and several affiliate firms.

The major automakers, such as Toyota, Honda, Nissan, Mitsubishi, etc. are the core firms and each of them has numerous affiliate firms as their suppliers. There is some cross-ownership of equity besides non-financial relationships between these firms. The Keiretsu member firms also emphasize close cooperation between them to coordinate production, and are situated in close geographical proximity to each other (Dyer 1996). A major goal of the member firms is to create a mutually beneficial, self-sufficient structure for their own benefit (Orru et al. 1989).

The suppliers in the Japanese automobile industry are hierarchically organized. They are divided into three tiers based on the type of product/service they provide (Asanuma 1985). At the top of the hierarchy are the first-tier suppliers, who supply finished components or sub-assemblies, such as completed seats, control panels, and so forth. These suppliers deal directly with the automakers. Below the first-tier suppliers are the second- and third-tier suppliers, which supply various components used in semi-finished products. The second- and third-tier suppliers, for the most part, deal with the level of suppliers just above them and rarely have very little commercial contacts with the automaker assembler itself (Mitsubishi Research Institute, 1987). On the basis of their relationship with the automakers, first-tier suppliers are divided into two broad categories: "group" firms and "independent" firms (Odaka et al. 1988).

The suppliers who have close ties with a specific automaker, often through exchange of personnel, technology, information, and capital, are known as "group firms." Many of these firms start off as divisions of the automaker, and later spin off as supplier firms. In many cases, the automaker helps the supplier to develop lean production methods to reduce cost and improve profitability. The "group firms" usually supply value-added key items that are closely associated with a particular model or car design (Mitsubishi Research Institute, 1987). Independent suppliers are those firms that are most affiliated with a particular automaker, even though it may do business with several other automakers simultaneously. There is a dependence relationship between automakers (core firms) and their first-tier suppliers (affiliate firms), which includes both "group" and "independent" firms (Banerji & Sambharya 2006).

A few studies have examined the operational and relational aspects of buyer-supplier relationship in the Japanese automobile industry. The major Japanese auto firms continuously monitor and grade the performance of their suppliers in terms of product quality, prices, delivery, and engineering. Those firms that received consistently better grades were given more responsibilities and long-term commitments, whereas those with poor grades were given a chance to improve. If discernible improvements were not made, suppliers firms were either discharged or forced to become lower-tier supplier serving higher-tier suppliers.

In the Japanese automobile industry, supplier subcontracting has four key features (Mitsubishi Research Institute, 1987). They are: (i) low ratio of in-house manufacturing by the automakers themselves; (ii) direct supply by a fewer number of supplier manufacturers; (iii) long-term supply contracts between suppliers and automakers; and (iv) affiliation of suppliers established by each of the automaker. These four key features help create long-term linkages between the automaker and the supplier.

According to the Ministry of International Trade and Industry (MITI), the "Japanese manufacturing industry owes its competitive advantage and strength to its subcontracting structure". Dore (1983) coined the phrase "Relational Subcontracting" to describe this unique nature of the buyer-supplier relationship in the Japanese automobile industry. The importance of this unique partnership between Japanese automakers and their first-tier suppliers cannot be overemphasized in a system where more than 70 per cent of the parts in a car are manufactured by ancillary manufacturers (Mitsubishi Research Institute, 1987). The excellent quality and low cost of Japanese cars could not have been achieved without the support of their suppliers.

The success of this unique partnership had an isomorphic effect on the American automobile industry. In the 1990s, leading manufacturers such as Chrysler successfully re-organized their supplier network on Japanese lines (Dyer 1996). During the same period, Japanese transplants in the United States, such as Honda, have also built up their Keiretsu networks in the United States. This has helped them to achieve productivity and quality levels similar to plants in Japan.

## GLOBAL VALUE CHAIN

Global value chain configuration increases the competitive leverage by helping company access global resources and capabilities. In a multi-domestic strategy, each subsidiary's competitive position is determined locally. Global companies, by taking an integrated view of their worldwide activities, are better equipped to cut costs and create more value. A truly global company configures its value chain activities across different countries to maximize efficiency and effectiveness. Efficiency can be understood as 'doing things right' and effectiveness as 'doing the right things'. Efficiency can be maximized by shifting activities to regions with low wages, low taxes and government incentives. But, along with cost, strategic benefits should also be considered for maximizing effectiveness. For example, location of research activities may be more influenced by the skills of the locally available manpower than the wage rates. In this context, exchange rates can be a major driver in the relocation of manufacturing facilities, which can direct a producer to shift its base from one country to another where gain would be higher.

Flexibility is another important consideration. A global network allows production to be shifted from one site to another, taking into account the changes in the environment. Think of the shirt brand, Arrow. Its makers began sourcing from Japan in the 1950s. As wages and real estate costs in Japan increased, the production moved to Hong Kong, then to Taiwan and then to South Korea. During the 1970s and 1980s, countries such as China, Indonesia, Malaysia and Bangladesh became key production bases.

While managing their value chain, global companies must combine both comparative and strategic advantages to put in place a globally leveraged strategy. Comparative advantages help in cutting costs in the short run, strategic advantages help in adding value in the long run.

Comparative advantages can be realized by locating value chain activities in cheaper locations. For example, global companies such as General Electric (GE), and Citigroup have located bulk of their back office operations in India. IBM has significantly ramped up its presence in India in the past four years to cut costs. The astounding growth of BPO operations in India highlights the benefits of comparative advantage—one billion population of India now does not sound as a threat but rather turning out into a boon in disguise to complement the concept of comparative advantage. India is a country with a huge repository of English-speaking people in the world.

Beyond a point, an obsession with comparative advantage may be counter-productive. By focusing too much on costs, opportunities to add value may be lost. Most global companies give equal, if not more, importance to strategic advantages while deciding where to perform their value chain activities.

The US is a strategically important market for products such as software, financial services, pharmaceuticals and automobiles. France is an important country for cosmetics and perfumes. Japan is the world leader in consumer electronics. Switzerland is a strategically important country for wealth management, Finland for wireless telecom and Germany for precision machinery. These are not the cheapest locations in the world but a presence in these is important not only to keep abreast of innovations but also to be in touch with highly sophisticated customer and tap local talent. One way to reap advantages is to be part of such cluster. For example, Silicon Valley in California is reputed for its cluster of computer hardware and software companies. Similarly, London and New York are financial hubs where academics, companies, deal makers and traders come together to drive financial services innovations.

Porter (1985, 1998) describes clusters as geographical concentration of interconnected companies and institutions in a particular business. Clusters include supplier of components, machinery, services and institutions, which provide specialized infrastructure. Sophisticated, demanding customers who keep companies on their toes can also be considered a part of the cluster. So can the local government, universities, research centres and think tanks that play a vital role in encouraging innovation and creating suitable conditions for more efficient value addition.

Both comparative and strategic advantages are important considerations. If a company is following a cost leadership strategy, comparative advantages are more important. If it is following a differentiation strategy, strategic advantages become more relevant. Global companies cannot overlook the importance of local advantages and a truly global firm needs to follow a flexible approach that allows value chain activities to be relocated quickly in response to shifts in strategic and comparative advantages (Vedpuriswar 2008).

> **Keywords**: *User Value, Customer Value Chain, Customer Life Cycle, Trip Wire, Lifetime Value, RFM Model, Keiretsu, Cross-promotion.*

## CONCLUSION

An organization's products and services are linked into a value chain in which value is created in each of the components of the chain. This approach is also used for competition analysis. Lifetime value (LTV) is one of the striking features of Relationship Marketing differentiating its core strength from conventional marketing. RFM model is used to rank the lifetime value and likelihood of customers' response relative to each other. Based on the scores of the RFM rankings, customer/prospect categorization is done and as a result, it is possible for a partner to identify which customers should be promoted in terms of discounts or other incentives. There are various processes for measurement of LTV. Co-branding is another technique of value creation process where there is a form of cooperation between two or more brands. The mechanisms used are: reach and awareness co-branding, value endorsement co-branding, ingredient co-branding and complementary competence co-branding. There are also instances where partners jointly take up promotional activities to reach wider audience enriching value of the services. Auto industries of Japan practice 'Keiretsu', that is, Relationship Subcontracting for value creation. Global value chain configuration increases the competitive leverage by helping the company access global resources and capabilities. Global companies, by taking an integrated view of their worldwide activities, are better equipped to cut costs and create more value. A truly global company configures its value chain activities across different countries to maximize efficiency and effectiveness.

### *Exercises*

1. What is the relevance of user value in the client-partner relationship?

2. What are the strategies a company can adopt to enhance customer value? Justify your explanation with examples from the Indian business scenario.

3. What are the client-partner's mutual benefits in the long-term relationship?

4. You run a travel agency and you want to promote a section of your clients with some discounts or benefits. What should be your approach?

5. How do you relate LTV with RFM?

6. Discuss with a specific example of an Indian MNC on the success accomplished by it by implementing strategies underlying global value chain.

7. Give three examples of co-branding in the banking and financial sectors and discuss how the partners are leveraging benefits out of this strategy.

8. What is the difference between vertical and horizontal Keiretsu? What can be the possible 'Keiretsu' arrangement one can envisage in personal products like soaps and detergents?

9. What are the benefits of cross promotion? How can such cross promotion facilitate value additions in the services/products?

Fill in the blanks:

10. The five primary activities in the value chain consist of:
    (a)_____, (b)_____,
    (c)_____, (d)_____,
    (e)_____ .

11. A firm's conscious and continuous endeavour to improve upon the offered value to maintain customer satisfaction, having an edge over competitor, is concerned with _____ and this process is done through _____, _____.

12. RFM means, customers who purchased _____ were more likely to buy again versus customers who had not purchased over a period of time customers who purchased _____ were more likely to buy again versus customers who had made just one or two purchases and customers who had _____ in total were more likely to buy again.

# References

Abraham, Jay, 2001. Getting everything you can out of all you have got, St Martin's Griffing, New York.

Anderson, Kare, 2007. Attract More Customers Through Cross-Promotion, Cross-Promotion Can Expand Your Customer Base, www.morebusiness.com

Asanuma, B., 1985. 'Nihon ni okeru buhin torihiki no jittai—jidousha sangyou to denkii kiki sanyou o chuushin ni [A report of the Japanese parts transactions—focusing on the automobile and electrical appliances industries]', Kousei Torihiki [*Fair Trade*], Vol. 416, June, pp. 32–37.

Banerji, Kunal and Sambharya, Rakesh B., 2007. The effect of Keiretsu affiliation and resource dependencies on supplier firm performance in the Japanese automobile industry, *Management International Review.* Gabler-Verlag, Vol. 46, No. 1, pp. 7–37.

Boone, Juliette M., 1998. Hotel-Restaurant Co-branding—A Preliminary Study, *Journal of Travel Research*, Vol. 36, p. 90.

Bose, Kallol and Bansal, S. Harvir, 2000. Regain Management: Issues and Strategies, in *Customer Relationship Management, Emerging Concepts, Tools and Applications*, Jagdish N. Sheth, Atul Parvatiyar and G. Sainesh (Eds.), Tata McGraw Hill, New Delhi, pp. 64–65.

Brendl, M., Markman, Aurther, B., and Messner, Claude, 2003. The Devaluation Effect: Activating a Need Devalues Unrelated Objects, *Journal of Consumer Research*, Vol. 29, pp. 463–473.

Burelli, Francesco and Dunn, Edgar, 2003. CRM: Organisational Challenges and Effective Client Management (working paper) www.cincom.com, Cincinnati, USA.

Chaudhuri, Arjun, 2006. *Perspectives on Value, "Emotion and Reason in Consumer Behaviour"*, Butterworth-Heinemann, Burlington, USA.

Dore, R., 1983. Goodwill and the Spirit of Market Capitalism, *British Journal of Sociology*, Vol. 34, pp. 67–77.

Dyer, J.H., 1996. How Chrysler created an American Keiretsu. *Harvard Business Review*, July-August, pp. 42–43, 46–47, 50–56.

Ford, D., 1980. The Development of Buyer-Seller Relationship in Industrial Markets, *European Journal of Marketing*, Vol. 14 (516), pp. 339–353.

Fruin, W.M., 1992. *The Japanese Enterprise System, Competitive Strategies and Cooperative Structures*, Oxford University Press, Oxford.

Hamouda, O.F., 1993. *John R Hicks: The economist's economist*, Blackwell, MA, Cambridge.

Heskett, James. L., Sasser, E.W. and Schlessinger, L.A. 2002. The Value Profit Chain, Treat Employees like customers and Custromers like Employees, Free Press, New York.

Hicks, John R., 1939. *Value and Capital.* Clarendon Press, Oxford.

Hicks, John R., 1973. *Capital and Time: A New Austrian Theory*, Clarendon Press, Oxford.

Kracklauer, Alexander, Passenheim, Olaf and Seifert, Dirk, 2001. Mutual Customer Approach: How Industry and Trade are Executing Collaborative Customer Relationship Management, *International Journal of Retail & Distribution Management*, MCB UP Ltd., Vol. 29, No. 12, pp. 515–519.

Kumar, Alok, Sinha, Chabi and Sharma, Rakesh, 2007. *Customer Relationship Management: Concepts and Application*, Biztantra, New Delhi, pp. 84–86.

Mukherjee, Kaushik, 2007. *CRM—A Strategic Approach to Marketing*, Prentice-Hall of India, New Delhi, pp. 31–32.

Novo, Jim, 2004. Drilling down-turning customer data into profits with a spreadsheet, Booklocker.com Inc., Saint Petersberg, Florida.

Orru, Marco, Hamilton, Gary, G. and Suzuki, Mariko, 1989. Patterns of Inter-firm Control in Japanese Business, *Organization Studies*, Vol. 10, No. 4, pp. 549–574.

Odaka, K., Ono, K. and Adachi, F., 1988. *The Automobile Industry in Japan, A Study of Ancillary Firm Development*, Kinokuniya/Oxford University Press, Tokyo.

Payne, A., 2005. *Handbook of CRM: Achieving excellence in customer management*, Butterworth-Heinemann, Oxford, p. 128.

Porter, Michael E., 1985. *Competitive Advantage*, Free Press, New York, p. 37.

Porter, Michael E., 1998. Clusters and New Economics of Competition, *Harvard Business Review*, Nov/Dec, Vol. 76, issue 6, p. 77.

Vedpuriswar, A.V., 2008. Riding the Global Value Chain, *Indian Management*, Vol. 47, No. 4, A *Business Standard* Publication.

Zyman, Sergio, 1999. The End of Marketing As We Know It, *Harper Business*, IBD, Delhi.

Websites

www.wikipedia.com
www.ril.com
www.jimnovo.com
www.cinmon.com
www.morebusiness.com
www.cincom.com.

# CHAPTER 5

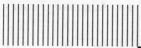

# Customer Equity

❖ Introduction
❖ Components of Customer Equity
❖ Customer Equity Model
❖ Implementing Customer Equity in the Organization
❖ Brand Equity and Customer Equity

## INTRODUCTION

It is a convention with most of the enterprises to measure the success of a marketing programme using brand equity as one of the tools. This has drawn continued focus on brand building and other product-centred programmes. Present-day customers have been taking an increasingly higher profile in marketing decision-making and thus they are accepted as a financial asset that companies should measure, manage and maximize just like any other asset. Customer equity management is a dynamic, integrated marketing system that uses financial valuation techniques and data about customers to optimize acquisition, retention and opportunities to sell additional products and services to a firm's customers. Although many of the concepts that underlay customer equity management, such as customer retention marketing and customer lifetime value measurement, are not new; the way that a true customer equity approach unifies and moves beyond them, is innovative. Chapter 4 has discussed the significance of value and its measures in the gamut of Relationship Marketing. This chapter discusses in detail customer equity concept, which is a recent emergence that has enriched the flavour of Relationship Marketing, and various techniques adopted for its implementation across the organization. This chapter also describes how customer equity can strengthen and enhance lifetime value.

# COMPONENTS OF CUSTOMER EQUITY

The concept of customer equity, which unifies customer value management, brand management and relationship/retention management, has recently emerged from the work of Professors Ronald Rust of University of Maryland, Valarie Zeithaml, University of North Carolina and Kay Lemon, Boston College (Rust et al. 2002). They view customer equity as the basis for new strategic framework from which to build more powerful, customer-centred marketing programmes that are financially accountable and measurable. Quantitatively speaking, a firm's customer equity is the total of the discounted lifetime value of all customers. Customer equity has three drivers:

1. **Value equity:** The customer's objective assessment of the utility of a brand based on the perceptions of what is given up for what is received.

2. **Brand equity:** The customer's subjective and intangible assessment of the brand, above and beyond its objectively perceived value. It must be remembered that the interpretation of brand equity in terms of customer value is different from the conventional meaning of brand equity.

3. **Retention equity:** The tendency of the customer to stick with the brand, above and beyond the customer's objective and subjective assessments.

The customer equity model enables marketers to determine which of the three drivers—value, brand or retention equity—are most critical to driving customer equity in their industry and firm. Using this approach allows marketers to quantify the financial benefit from improving one or more of the drivers (Clancy and Krieg, 2007; Clancy 2002).

In technology's modern incarnation, the individual customer analysis looks beyond the computation of a single year's profitability to the forecasting of the stream of profits attributable to the customer and the computing of discounted present value. Customers come to be viewed as assets (Rust, et al. 2001) or equity of the firm and a measurement literature for this is developing.

Hand in hand with the measurement literature, a prescriptive literature is growing (e.g. Peppers and Rogers) that generally advocates allocation of resources away from low-value customers and towards those of highest value to the firm.

Customer equity management is a dynamic, integrative marketing system that uses financial valuations techniques and data about customers to optimize the acquisition, retention, and selling of additional products to a firms' customers and that maximizes the value to the company of the customer relationship throughout its life cycle.

Customer equity management is more than just a method for calculating the asset value of customer relationships. It is a total marketing system. It requires integrative business strategies. Firms will need to develop strategies that simultaneously manage products and customers throughout the customer life cycle and that reframe brand and product strategies within the context of their effects on customer equity. In addition, the customer equity framework changes the way a business allocates resources and efforts. Today, most marketing functions allocate resources by product line. With a customer orientation, customer life cycle determines how managers distribute resources.

## CUSTOMER EQUITY MODEL

Customer equity management is different from "marketing" as most companies practise it.

To summarily describe the customer equity model in Figure 5.1, acquisition is affected by the number of prospects, the acquisition

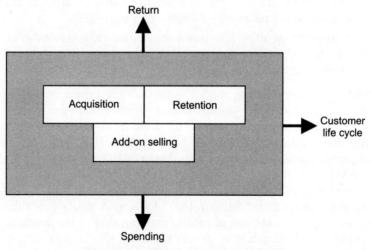

**Figure 5.1 Customer equity model.**

probability of a prospect and the acquisition spending per prospect. Retention is influenced by the retention rate and retention spending level. Add-on spending is a function of efficiency of add-on selling and number of add-on selling offers given to existing customers (Kotler & Keller 2006). Based on this customer equity model, the following marketing strategies can be envisaged:

1. Marketing strategy, tactics and execution become customer-centric, not product-centric.

2.  The firm manages a customer life cycle. The marketing mix varies by stage in the customer life cycle.

3.  The firm manages a portfolio of customers balanced across acquisition, retention, and add-on selling stages.

4.  The marketing output of the firm is quantifiable. Marketing is managed using the appropriate customer equity measures, and costs are balanced against financial returns.

5.  The firm communicates changes in the asset value of its customers through customer equity flow statements. The firm measures its customer assets through lifetime value.

6.  The firm organizes around customer acquisition, retention, and add-on selling.

## IMPLEMENTING CUSTOMER EQUITY IN THE ORGANIZATION

Customer equity management is now possible because of intersecting advances in four areas: affordable information technology, low-cost communications, sophisticated statistical modelling, and flexible fulfilment.

Customer equity depends to a great extent on technology because it requires the ability to build and use databases of customer purchases. Computing costs are continuing to decline to the point at which small businesses can have computing power sufficient to manage large databases at a fraction of what it would have cost in the 1980s. The ability to work with large, sophisticated databases is improving; software to manage customer relationships now exists, and its capabilities are expanding.

As managers seek to embrace the customer equity philosophy and implement it within their own organization, they will be faced with several challenges. In formulating a way ahead for customer equity management, the following seven action items are proposed (Bell et al. 2002):

1.  **Assemble individual-level, industry-wide consumer data:** Those firms that must accumulate customer data to perform their order fulfilment, such as direct marketers, subscription service providers, vendors offering warranties or insurance, extenders of credit card issuer banks and membership organizations, have led the migration to customer equity management. The trailing firms are those that have to incur special-purpose costs to assemble end-customer data, a group that includes manufacturers who sell through supermarkets and other retail stores; providers of casual services like entertainment and fast-food shops and in general those who serve a broad, shallow customer base with little potential for repeat business.

2. **Track marketing's effects on the balance sheet, not just the income statement:** Customers are assets, acquired at a cost that is justified or not by a flow of income into the future, just as the fixed assets of the firm. If that cost is routinely expensed through the income statement in the period in which it was incurred, there is a risk that firms will underinvest in customer acquisition. But the appraisal of customer assets has no place for in contemporary accounting practice. In that respect, brand assets have an advantage.

Customer asset metrics (Customer Lifetime Value [CLV] and customer equity) are clearly related to commonly applied financial measures, such as economic value analysis (EVA) and return on investment (RoI). Given this, it makes sense to draw on their heritage and to use them as a starting point (Gupta et al. 2004). CLV is the value of the customer relationship to the firm in monetary terms. CLV depends on assumptions about the future stream of income from a customer, the appropriate allocation of costs to customers, the discount factor, the expected "life" of a customer, and the probability that the customer is "alive" at a particular point in time.

3. **Model future revenues appropriately:** It is unlikely that research on CLV appraisal will converge on a single model to capture the timing and probability of revenue flows, yet to date there is no good typology of revenue generation models. The early work in direct marketing assumed that the appropriate model depended on the characteristics of the transactions.

4. **Maximize (don't just measure) CLV:** The measurement of CLV is necessary, but certainly not sufficient. Managers need to implement marketing initiatives (such as loyalty programmes, customer reactivations, cross-selling, and programme to anticipate and forestall defection) that maximize the value of the customer franchisee.

Models of lifetime value must account for the impact of the competitive environment. Although most organizations have access to information on their own customers, not all have access to information about the behaviour of competitors with respect to their customers. Yet, without such information, there is no way to estimate a model of the effect of marketing actions on CLV.

5. **Align organization with customer management activities:** When a firm adopts a brand or product management structure, it typically organizes the enterprise so as to facilitate broadcast marketing functions like advertising and new product development. Firms with a large customer base often supplement the brand or product line focus with a major accounts focus, often imposing a matrix relationship between the two in which a creative political tension is cultivated between the demands of product rationalization and customer demands

of customization and integration across products. The matrix organization falls far short of the radical customer management focus found in some organizations. Some firms in the industries that pioneered the application of customer asset management have aligned their organizations to focus on customer management functions.

6. **Respect the sensitivity of customer information:** The notion of a consumer's entitlement top privacy is in a flux, and rules and conventions that have acquired stability through testing over generations in the practice of traditional marketing are being challenged and re-examined in customer-centric data environments.

7. **Evolve CRM from an efficiency tool to a service improvement tool:** Industry studies constantly associate "successful" CRM implementations with comprehensive efforts to re-evaluate and refine all customer-facing business processes; to develop, motivate, and reculture customer-facing as well as back-office service and support personnel; and to select and tailor appropriate CRM-enabling technologies.

# BRAND EQUITY AND CUSTOMER EQUITY

Viewing customers as assets also differs significantly from treating brand equity as the primary marketing asset. Although the two are not mutually exclusive, they have different objectives. Brand orientation provides a clear goal for marketing activities: to maximize a brand's total revenues and extract the greatest possible return from brand investment. The customer asset orientation focuses on the firm's entire future income stream across brands and services. It does not view the customer only through aperture of the brand (Blattberg, et al. 2001).

Table 5.1 illustrates companies that take a customer asset approach to do things differently than their brand equity-based counterparts do.

Brand-oriented companies focus on product quality and customer service as a means to build the brand's perceived value. They advertise to position the brand and worry that promotions will dilute its value. In many brand-oriented companies, product development focuses online extension meant to leverage the brand name into new arenas. These companies pay substantial attention to how a strong brand can provide power in a battle against competitors within a multilevel distribution system.

In a customer equity-oriented company, these same elements work much differently. Quality and service act as customer retention tools. Advertising messages serve to build affinity between the customer and the company, and promotions function as strategic events designed to

**Table 5.1** Brand equity and customer equity

| Marketing activity | Brand equity | Customer equity |
|---|---|---|
| Product and service quality | Create strong customer preference | Create high customer retention rates |
| Advertising | Create brand image and position | Create customer affinity |
| Promotions | Deplete brand equity | Create repeat buying and enhance lifetime value |
| Product development | Use brand name to create flankers and related products | Acquire products to sell to the installed customer base |
| Segmentation | Customer characteristics and benefit segmentations | Behavioural segmentation based on customer database |
| Channels of distribution | Multistage distribution system | Direct distribution to customer |
| Customer service | Enhance brand image | Create customer affinity |

drive repeat buying and increase lifetime relationship value. New products present opportunities to cross-sell existing customers. Whether the company sells directly to customers or uses a multilayer channel system, direct knowledge of individual customers and their buying behaviour is its lifeblood.

## Relationship Equity

In this context, the recent concept of Relationship Equity that has emerged out of researches in Relationship Marketing can also be referred here for elaborating of customer equity. **Relationship Equity** is defined as "the wealth-creating potential that resides in the firm's relationships with its stakeholders" (Haugstetter 2005). Relationship Equity is the customer's tendency to "stick" with your store, beyond customer's objective and subjective assessment (Newell 2003). Think of Relationship Equity as the firm's social connection or glue with the customer—built up over time through the interactions the customer has with the firm. The action steps to strengthen Relationship Equity are: loyalty programmes (with both soft and hard benefits), community building-up programmes and knowledge building programmes. Figure 5.2 shows the factors that drive customer equity.

## Three Factors that Drive Customer Equity

First and foremost, the firm must determine what is the most important driver to customers in their future purchasing decisions—Brand Equity? Value Equity or Relationship Equity? The role of Relationship Equity for

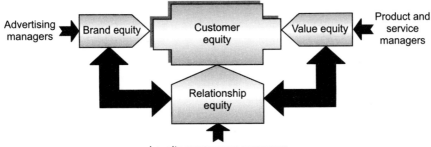

**Figure 5.2  Factors that drive customer equity.**

*Source:*  Hilary Haugstetter (2005), adopted with permission.

better customer equity has been described in Figure 5.2. Figure 5.3 illustrates the mechanism for improving customer equity in the pathways laid out in brand, value and relationship equity.

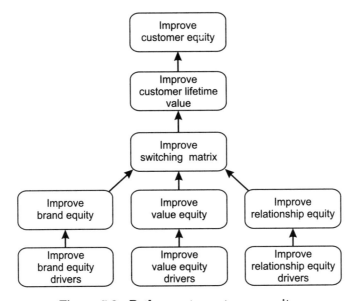

**Figure 5.3  Pathways to customer equity.**

*Source:*  Hilary Haugstetter (2005), adopted with permission.

## Drivers of Value Equity

A company is competitive when it is able to create and deliver value for its customers. Key drivers of value equity are, namely, price, quality and convenience. Value drivers are things that are important to customers adding significant value to them (Walters 2002). Value drivers are building blocks of the complex term 'value'. There are several approaches to describe the content of value and reveal its internal elements. There are four approaches that are, to some extent, similar, but in other aspects complementary in nature (Gelei 2005). These are as follows:

1. Sources of competitiveness (Chikán & Demeter ed.; 1999)
2. Value dimensions on the transaction, partnership and network level (Mandják & Durrieu, 2000)
3. Direct and indirect value dimensions (Walter et al. 2001)
4. Efficiency, effectiveness and network dimensions of customer value (Möller & Törrönen 2003)

Walter et al. (2001) have identified the following value drivers or value functions in a business relationship from the perspective of the supplier:

1. **Direct-Value Functions of Customer**
   - *Profit function:* It refers to the relative direct revenue from a customer.
   - *Volume function:* It refers to the volume of business generated by a customer.
   - *Safeguard function:* It refers to the possibility of guaranteeing a level of business and revenue through contractual arrangements with a specific customer.

2. **Indirect-Value Functions of Customer**
   - *Innovation function:* It refers to the possibility of product and process innovation with a particular customer.
   - *Market function:* It refers to the possibility of acquiring new customers/distributors through the reference impact of a particular customer.
   - *Scout function:* It refers to the market and other information that can be acquired from the working environment through a particular customer.
   - *Access function:* It refers to gaining access to relevant other actors in the working environment through a particular customer.

Walter et al. (2001) have determined the innovation function as indirect. This interpretation means that the realization of innovation—and its value—is a function of not only two cooperative partners but of other connected network members too. According to the experience of interviews made with the automotive suppliers, this description is relevant for the *strategic innovations*, which represents significant progress in product or technology. This description, on the other hand, is not relevant for those *incremental innovations* which represent a slow progress, usually achieved with the cooperation of the customer and its supplier firm.

## Drivers of Brand Equity

The following are the five major drivers of Brand Equity:

1. **Name awareness:** Share of mind
2. **Perceived quality:** Seen as better/best fit for me (functionality, trust, long lasting)
3. **Brand loyalty:** Enduring preference
4. **Positive associations:** Sponsorships, admired people using the product, corporate citizenship
5. **Other assets:** Trademarks, exclusive channels, merchandising systems.

First while these five are generic drivers of value as equity levers, each brand has its own specific set. In the case of professional service organizations, culture/people are the main drivers.

## Drivers of Relationship Equity

Great brand equity and value equity may not be enough to hold the customer. What is needed is a way to glue the customers to the firm, enhancing the stickiness of the relationship. Relationship equity represents this glue. Specifically, relationship equity is defined as the tendency of the customer to stick with the brand, above and beyond the customer's objective and subjective assessments of the brand. The key levers, under the firm's control, that may enhance relationship equity may be denoted as the drivers of relationship equity, which are, namely:

- Loyalty programmes
- Special recognition and treatment
- Affinity programmes
- Community building programmes
- Knowledge-building programmes.

Loyalty programmes include actions that reward customers for specific behaviours with tangible benefits. From airlines to liquor stores, from Citigroup to Music World, the loyalty programme has become a staple of many firms' marketing strategy.

Special recognition and treatment refers to actions that recognize customers for specific behaviour with intangible benefits. For example, US Airways' "Chairman Preferred" status customers receive complimentary membership in the US Airways' Club.

Affinity programmes seek to create strong emotional connections with customers, linking the customer's relationship with the firm to other important aspects of the customer's life. Consider the wide array of affinity Visa and MasterCard choices offered by First USA to encourage increased use and higher retention.

Community-building programmes seek to cement the customer-firm relationship by linking the customer to a larger community of like customers. In the United Kingdom, for example, soft drink manufacturer Tango has created a website that has built a virtual community with its key segment, the nation's youth.

Finally, knowledge-building programmes increase relationship equity by creating structural bonds between the customer and the firm, making the customer less willing to recreate a relationship with an alternative provider. The most often cited example of this is amazon.com, but learning relationships are not limited to cyberspace. Firms such as British Airways have developed programmes to track customer food and drink preferences, thereby creating bonds with the customer while simultaneously reducing costs (Rust et al. 2001).

---

### Case Study: Charles Schwab

---

A North American investment brokerage firm, Charles Schwab, offers an excellent example. In its early days, Schwab focused on customer acquisition by providing self-reliant investors with a value-priced alternative to full-service brokerage houses. The company invested little in understanding its customers' needs and wants at anything beyond the aggregate level. Its competitors used to know more about Schwab's customers than Schwab did. Later, in response to competitive pressures, Schwab began to apply the two other levers of customer equity: add-on selling and retention. It expanded its offerings to develop multiple relationships with customers who stay longer with Schwab. Schwab's OneSource mutual fund marketplace provided a multi-branded alternative that appealed to more investors than did the single-branded mutual fund offerings of brokerage houses and investment companies. Schwab outflanked the competition by creating a "best of breed marketplace" that gave unbiased access to the funds of multiple providers. The firm captured a higher share of customers' investment assets and raised retention rate.

---

### Case Study: Customer Equity and Lifetime Management Solution at Finnair

---

The Customer Equity and Lifetime Management (CELM) solution is based on a decision-support system that offers marketing managers a scientific framework for the optimal planning and budgeting of targeted marketing campaigns to maximize return on marketing investments. CELM technology can be used to simulate the financial impact of a given marketing policy using Monte Carlo simulation. This allows marketing managers to simulate several targeting scenarios to assess budget requirements and the expected impact of a given marketing policy. The benefits of the solution are illustrated with the Finnair case study, where CELM has been used to optimize marketing planning and budgeting for Finnair's frequent-flyer programme (FFP).

Finnair, a leading European airline, has offered an FFP called Finnair Plus for many years. As part of its FFP, Finnair conducts numerous marketing campaigns targeting more than 700,000 customers. Each customer is exposed to dozens of campaigns per year. These campaigns have different goals, such as cross- and up-selling, minimizing attrition, points accrual and redemption, and tier upgrade, and are delivered through various channels, such as mailings, in-cabin brochures, the Internet, and magazines. The driving business objective of Finnair was to reduce the costs of the FFP adequately while maximizing the lifetime value of its members.

To achieve these objectives, a team of Finnair marketing managers joined forces with IBM researchers and consultants to define a business transformation process. This included redesigning the marketing strategy around Finnair's FFP and implementing change management processes at several marketing functions, such as campaign management, marketing planning, and multichannel communication. The entire project, which was carried out from February 2003 to March 2005, was executed in three phases:

1. Gain deeper customer insight by deriving finer loyalty and value metrics and more homogeneous and customer profiles.

2. Better understanding of customer behaviours at various phases of the relationship and the underlying levers that Finnair could act upon at every customer contact.

3. Optimize marketing resource allocation to the FFP by focusing on processes where both cost and revenue can be optimized simultaneously.

Finnair's long-term relationship with IBM took a new turn with the deployment of mathematical modelling and optimization algorithms designed by researchers from IBM's Zurich Research Lab. Processing frequent-flier data has a potential impact of reducing marketing costs by 20 per cent while improving marketing response rates by as much as 10 per cent. And that means big money—in increased revenues and in savings.

IBM's Customer Equity Management solution already has an 80 per cent accuracy rate for predicting the eventual value a customer represents. By forecasting a frequent flier's future travel decisions, it has also helped improve the airline's customer satisfaction rate by 10 per cent (Tirenni et al. 2007).

## Measurement of Customer Equity

The specific RoI (Return on Investment) from building stronger customer relationships is very difficult to measure. David Taylor, Research Director with Jupiter Media Matrix, advocates creating a new "return on relationship metric "that measures whether or not relationships result in direct or indirect returns to a company". Jupiter believes that such a metric "will help business managers determine the value the Internet brings to the table for sales and marketing initiatives".

Until such a measure is developed, companies are measuring brand perception and preference qualitatively by conducting focus groups with consumers before and after the start of their customer equity marketing programmes.

Companies can also examine the "churn rate" (or the rate of customer defection) before and after instituting customer equity marketing programmes. Credit card and telephone companies traditionally used the churn rate to measure the success of marketing programmes. CRM consulting firm Peppers and Rogers notes, "A high churn rate implies customer disloyalty."

Another potentially useful metric for customer equity marketing programmes is "potential customer value". Puleo and Wheeler 2001 urged companies to consider not just profits generated from current customers but also potential customer value, defined as "the profit that can be captured in future periods from the same set of customers by increasing share of customer for those needs you are currently serving and also by expanding the set of needs addressed." Enterprises that survives and prosper during shifting economic cycles will be those that establish and maintain a dialogue with the customer and prove their ability to match products and services to the customers's demands (Maoz 2001).

## Benefits of Customer Equity

Customer equity marketing programmes offer companies the following critical benefits:

**Satisfied customers:** A customer equity marketing programme that features fresh, informative, valued, and persuasive content reinforces motivated customers' affinity and keeps them coming back.

**Committed relationship:** Satisfied customers who develop a dependency on your site's content interact with your brand on a regular basis, thereby raising level of commitment and decreasing the likelihood of defection.

**Halo effect:** Customers shift positive feelings about a site's content to the company behind it, and to the company's products. Over time, this halo effect translates into increased loyalty and respect, greater credibility for your company, and increased sales.

**Customers as evangelists:** Loyal customers who have invested in brand become inspired evangelists for partner's products, making recommendations to others.

**Less expensive recurring sales:** Customers who are loyal and committed not only do not defect, they become repeat buyers with minimal additional investment by the company.

**Valuable customer data:** Through membership registration, online surveys, and customer feedback mechanisms, companies generate essential data about their most valued customers. Companies that offer customer equity marketing programmes entice customers to submit their data, which in turn ensures that their long-term needs are met through product development.

Furthermore, organizations that use customer equity as a marketing system benefit because they can do the following:

> ➤ Compute the asset value of customers to make informed decisions regaining investment in acquisition, retention and add-on selling.

> ➤ Adjust marketing investment levels as customer relationships move through their dynamic life cycles.

> ➤ Organize processes and structures around acquisition, retention, and add-on selling to maximize the profitability of each over the customer life cycle.

> ➤ Address the "whole customer", who buys and uses a broad range of services and products.

> ➤ Utilize customer interactions to reinforce relationships and acquire new customers.

Managing the customer as an asset is more critical to a firm's success than ever before for three reasons. First, marketers who take an asset-based view of the customer make better decisions than those who limit themselves to product, brand, or transaction views. Second, today's computing technology makes precise customer asset management possible. Companies can now efficiently obtain and process the information they need to understand customer equity. Finally, changes in market conditions, driven by advances in information systems, communications, and production, will help companies that understand and manage the value of each individual customer to overtake and then displace mass marketers.

The rapid growth of the Internet as a medium for targeted communication allows firms to reach and communicate with customers at less than one-hundredth of the cost of more traditional techniques. Communication through the Internet to customers equipped with e-mail is virtually free, and the speed of transmission allows customers to retrieve communications almost instantaneously. Firms have access to their preferred customers at costs that early direct marketers could only dream about, combined with unprecedented ability to tailor messages to individual recipients and provide electronic coupons to selected prospects. Furthermore, software is being created using artificial intelligence to develop automated two-way communications with customers based on their specific responses to queries.

In addition, technologies ranging from checkout scanning to Internet cookies are making it increasingly possible to track customers' buying behaviours. Now companies can predict future consumer behaviour using the best possible indicator: current behaviour. Instead of relying on focus groups and surveys to ask customers what they want (or think they want), firms can examine actual purchase histories. As more and more online customers grant companies permission to use their personal data in return for anticipating needs, this trend towards greater availability of behavioural data should only accelerate.

Companies must use advanced analytical tools to turn these data into insights. Techniques such as collaborative filtering track customer buying patterns and make recommendations about which types of books, movies, or other products the customer might want to purchase. Modelling methods for determining customers' sensitivity to price and responsiveness to offers, central to improving the efficiency of marketing offers, have become both more sophisticated and more available.

## CONCLUSION

The concept of customer equity unifies customer value management, brand management and relationship or retention management. It has become apparent that brand equity alone cannot act as the only tool as a measure and evaluate marketing efforts. Consisting of add-on sales, acquisition retention, the customer equity model provides a basis for projecting the RoI of any strategic investment. Customer equity comprised the following: Brand Equity, Value Equity and Retention Equity. It appears that in terms of its interpretation, retention equity is converging more towards relationship equity. There are seven principles of implementing the customer equity in an organization. For this purpose, organizations need to devise their marketing strategy, make appropriate plans for its implementation, which would consequently enable them to reap immense benefits in terms of customer retention, repeat sales, maximizing customer life time value, etc.

**Keywords:** *Customer Value Management, Customer Equity Management, Value Equity, Brand Equity, Retention Equity, Relationship Equity, Halo Effect, Customer Lifetime Value*

## Exercises

1. Take any product of your choice. Using each of the marketing activities listed in Table 5.1, what are the action points you would undertake to promote customer equity?

2. What are the differences between brand equity and customer equity?

3. Your client is a producer of aerated water. You are the Relationship Manager for the IT services rendered by your organization to your client. What are the strategic initiatives you would adopt to enhance customer equity, given the fact that your client's business growth is 5% as compared with 8% in the industry?

4. Select a company in the banking sector and explain how it is enhancing the customer value equity.

5. What are the key benefits of customer equity?

6. What should be the focus of equity for organizations providing courier services?

7. What are the various measures of customer equity? Which measure you think is appropriate in the manufacturing sector, e.g. automobile?

Fill in the blank:

8. Indirect value functions of a customer are as follows: (a)_____ _____, (b)_____, (c)_____, (d)_____.

## References

Bell, David, Deighton, John, Reinartz J.W., Rust, T. Ronald and Swattz, Gordon, 2002. "Seven Barriers to Customer Equity Management", *Journal of Service Research*, Sage Publications, Vol. 5, No. 1, Aug., pp. 77–86.

Blattberg, Robert C., Getz, Gary and Thomas S., Jacquelyn, 2001. *"Managing Customers an Asset", Customer Equity: Building and Managing Relationships as Valuable Assets*, Harvard Business School Press, Boston, Masschusetts, pp. 4–12.

Chikán, A. and Demeter, K. (Eds.), 1999. The Management of Value-Creating Processes, Aula Publisher, Budapest, pp. 4–14, 24–36.

Clancy, J. Kevin, 2002. Beyond Brand Equity: Customer Equity as the Next Frontier, Boston University Distinguished Speaker series (Boston, MA), March 2002.

Clancy, J. Kevin and Krieg, P., 2007. *Your Gut is Still Not Smarter Than Your Head*, John Wiley & Sons, Hoboken, New Jersey.

Gelei, Andrea, 2005. Competitiveness: A match between value drivers and competencies in the Hungarian automotive supply chain, Research Paper, Budapest University of Economic Sciences and Public Administration, Hungary.

Gupta, Sunil, Lehmann, Donald R. and Sturat, Jennifer Ames, 2004. "Valuing Customers", Research and Application in Marketing, Vol. 19, No. 2, Grenable Cedex, France.

Haugstetter, Hilary, 2005. Managing Relationship Equity, Deptt of Maritime Business, www.amc.edu.au/mlm/papers/relnship.equity. sept.2005.ppt

"Itol Glossary," Peppers and Rogers Web Site (www.itol.com)

Jupiter Media Metrix Press Release, July 21, 2001, New York.

Kotler, Philip and Keller, Kevin, 2006. *Marketing Management*, 12th ed., Chapter 5, Prentice-Hall, New Jersey, pp. 139–171.

Mandják, T. and Durrieu, Fl., 2000. Understanding the non-economic value of business relationships; 16th Annual IMP Conference, Proceedings, CD Rom, Bath, pp. 1–16.

Maoz, M., 2001. "Relationship Value is Measured by Mutual Advantage", Gartner Group, March, 26.

Mishra, Randhir, 2000. "A Generalized Model for the Structure of Business Relationship—A Meta Analysis of Relationship Literature' in *Customer Relationship Management, Emerging Concepts, Tools and Applications*, Jagdish N. Sheth, Atul Parvatiyar and G. Sainesh (Eds.), Tata McGraw Hill, New Delhi, pp. 52–55.

Möller, K. and Törrönen, P., 2003. Business suppliers' value creation potential. A capability-based analysis in Industrial Marketing Management, Vol. 32, pp. 109–118.

Newell, Fredrick, 2003. *Why CRM does not work: How to win by letting customer manage the relationship*, Bloomberg Press, New Jersey, 189.

Paula, Puleo and Wheeler, Abigail, 2001. "How Much Are Your Customers Worth?" *Itol Magazine*, Sept.

Peppers, Don and Rogers, Martha, 1993. The one-to-one future, New York, Doubleday, a division of Bantane Doubleday Dell Publishing group, New York.

Rust, Roland., Katherine, Lemon and Zeithaml, Valarie, 2002. "Increasing Marketing Effectiveness: A Decision Support System for Building Consumer Equity", working paper, Robert H. Smith School of Business, University of Maryland, College Park, Maryland.

Rust, Roland, Katherine, Lemon and Zeithaml, Valarie, 2001. *Marketing Management,* Spring, American Marketing Association, Vol. 10, No. 1, pp. 20–25.

Tirenni, Giuliano, Labbi Abderrahim, Berrospi, Cesar, Elisseeff, André, Bhose, Timir, Pauro, Kari and Pöyhönen, Seppo, 2007. Customer Equity and Lifetime Management (CELM). Finnair Case Study, *Marketing Science,* Vol. 26, No. 4, July-August, pp. 553–565.

Walters, D. 2002: *Operations Strategy.* Palgrave Macmillan, Hampshire, UK.

Walter, A., Ritter, T. and Gemünden, H.G., 2001. Value-creation in buyer–seller relationships; theoretical considerations and empirical results from a supplier's perspective; *Industrial Marketing Management,* Vol. 30, pp. 365–377.


Websites

www.iimm.org/knowledge_bank (Value Drivers)
www.itol.com
www.copernicusmarketing.com
www.knowledgenetworks.com (Brand Equity Drivers)

# CHAPTER 6

# Strategies and Techniques of Cross-Selling and Up-Selling

| | |
|---|---|
| ❖ Introduction | ❖ Up-Selling Online |
| ❖ Conceptual Background | ❖ Other Strategies |
| ❖ Definitions of Cross-Sell and Up-Sell | ❖ Emotion Factors in Cross-Selling and Up-Selling |
| ❖ Cross-Selling Online | ❖ Building Profit Improvement |
| ❖ Rules for Cross-Selling | ❖ Critical Success Factors |

## INTRODUCTION

The success of Relationship Marketing is envisaged in the organization's potential in wooing the client in embracing the related products in a varied price range that are higher or lower than the price of the lead product. Cross-selling and up-selling of products and services summarily relate to such activity. There are certain prerequisites behind cross-selling and up-selling activities, which originate chiefly from the success of appropriate relationship strategies and techniques. Normally, clients recognize the opportunity for huge savings and pay the higher price. Such single merchandizing technique brings into business lots of revenue in increased sales each year. This chapter discusses the concepts and definitions of cross-selling and up-selling and their various rules and critical success factors.

## CONCEPTUAL BACKGROUND

Cross-selling is offering a similar product to what a shopper is looking at either an alternative model or accessories that go with the product (add-ons). Cross-selling strategy is likely to result in (Wilson 2007):

1. Customers finding exactly what they are looking for, thus increasing the rate of order completion, and/or

2. Customers adding accessories to their original selection, thus increasing the order total.

In addition to related products, many merchants use cross-selling capabilities to display popular items and high margin products throughout the store. A customer may just see the item and buy it on impulse along with his original selection.

Up-selling is offering a better and more expensive product. If the shopper exhibits behaviours of going to a product page or placing an item in the shopping cart, one can be pretty sure he has an interest in that product. If he selects the good model, he would also be open for purchasing the better and best models.

A vital component of retaining and growing high-value customers is to implement and execute optimal cross-selling and up-selling initiatives. Otherwise, diminished customer value and increased expense can result from presenting irrelevant and non-specific offers to customers. Customers increasingly expect organizations to understand their needs and be presented with cross- and up-sell offers that match their needs. When irrelevant offers are presented—or presented at the wrong time—the customer relationship can be diminished, along with customer loyalty.

Effective cross-selling also requires a multi-faceted approach that steers clear of common generalizations. One common assumption is that the depth of a customer's loyalty is highly correlated with the number of products or services that has been sold to them. There are actually many other critical factors to consider, such as the customer's need for the specific product one is selling.

Many companies do track a customer's level of satisfaction with a particular product or service and also monitor the perceived value and utilization of the offering. However, companies must also, as accurately as possible, rethink what incremental products and services they are selling to their customers, how they are sold, and how these campaigns are most likely to impact customer loyalty and financial results.

# DEFINITIONS OF CROSS-SELL AND UP-SELL

- *A cross-sell is an effort to encourage the committed buyer to add auxiliary items to the purchase, such as accessories or related items.*

- *An up-sell is simply convincing the buyer that he or she should purchase a more expensive (and higher quality or more versatile) product than the one under consideration.*

In a fast food restaurant, the chances are, the person taking the order will ask these two questions:

- *"Do you want fish fries with bread?" This is an example of a cross-sell. Everyone knows that fries go well with bread and butter.*

- *"Do you want a bigger size than that?" This is an example of an up-sell. The order taker is not asking to buy additional items, but is encouraging you to buy a bigger and more expensive version of something already ordered.*

## CROSS-SELLING ONLINE

Cross-selling from e-commerce sites has been quite effective, raising sale percentages by a satisfying amount for many online merchants. While one might initially hesitate, thinking that customers will exit quickly if they feel they are getting the hard sell, online customers tend to see cross-selling proposals as added value.

An excellent example of cross-selling is the Barnes & Noble website. For each book listing in the database, the buyer immediately sees a list of five books under the heading, "B&N Customers Who Bought This Book Also Bought." The list might include other works by the same author or a few works by that author and others of a similar genre.

Most products and services lend themselves well to cross-selling if one sells or provides multiple items. Complementary items are great to offer, and the customer will appreciate bringing his attention to the availability of these products. For example, a customer looking at a pair of red shoes might appreciate seeing thumbnails for matching handbags or belts. Or, a customer buying a garment bag might be glad to see a matching duffel and carry-on bag.

The items need not match. They can be related products. If the customer is buying an iron, he might like to look at ironing boards or stands that clip onto the board to keep the iron out of the way. A client taking out an ad for a garage sale might be glad to pay an additional fee for a small map to locate his home.

Accessories do well in cross-selling. Electronics may have optional power supplies, USB cables and rechargeable batteries that one can sell at the same time. In fact, some vendors do well selling batteries by inviting the buyer to "add all the batteries needed for this product." Customers looking at cutlery sets may wish to add on the matching service pieces. While selling appliances or electronics, it is important to consider cross-selling warranties. Banking, accounting and web design vendors can cross-sell an array of auxiliary services.

# RULES FOR CROSS-SELLING

Experienced online cross-sellers know that selecting the items that are to appear alongside each product is a huge, time-consuming job.

The selection and placement of cross-sell items should be part of the web design, so designers need some guidelines for the designing. These rules should also serve the buyers who will be selecting the items for the product page. One can set whatever rules one wants, but here are some samples of rules:

- Display a maximum of three cross-sell items.
- All items should be in stock.
- The items should not be sale items.
- Each cross-sell item should be less expensive than the main item.
- The items should be familiar and not require descriptions and explanations.
- The items should have no options (size or colour choice, for example).
- The images of the cross-sell items should be of a specific size (larger than thumbnail, but smaller than the main item, and tiled along the right margin).

The database of items provided for sell may be organized with an "affinity" link that identifies them as possible cross-sell items for another product. If there are thousands of items, creating these figures is bound to take a long time, although one can well decide to cross-sell on just the best-sellers or major items. If it is decided to display three cross-sell items per page, one should identify five or six compatible items in the database to ensure that offered items are not temporarily out of stock.

Here is a good hint for identifying cross-sell items. One large retailer identified a team of particularly perceptive floor salespersons and invited them to select the cross-sell items for their website. This worked well, as these persons knew exactly what customers tended to buy along with major purchases when they were in the store.

# UP-SELLING ONLINE

Up-selling from e-commerce website is a bit riskier than cross-selling. It is a matter of chance that the buyer will see the offer as a hard sell if it is not done smoothly. One should carefully monitor the buyer's behaviours when presenting up-sell items.

Recall that up-selling encourages the buyer to consider an alternate, more expensive item. The item may have additional features, more power, more options or higher quality. In fact, the alternative item may be just what the buyer is looking for, and the display should look very much like an effort to show the buyer what is there in stock that he otherwise might not find.

The buyer must see the added value in the more expensive item. In fact, it should be quite explicit about the added value, and it is necessary to create the value. For example, suppose a customer is pursuing dress shirts and has clicked on a thumbnail for a rupees 700 shirt. One can present a rupees 1000 shirt that comes with free cufflinks or a free tie. If the customer sees the free item as having a value close to the rupees 300 difference, he will choose the more expensive item.

---

**Case Study:** ICICI Bank

---

ICICI Bank undertook data warehouse installation that focused on building a single customer view in the first phase. In the second phase, the objective was to use the information in understanding the customer using suitable tools. The system helped the bank to generate over 242,975 leads resulting in cross-selling leads as well. These leads have resulted in 24% of the bank's sales. Business analytics have also been of use to banks managing their credit card customer. Prior to using analytics, ICICI Bank offered all customers the same credit limit. Using analytics, the bank differentiated between customers based on the low and medium risk profile of customers, the credit limits were suitably increased resulting in better matching of market averages. During the first year of usage of the analytics, ICICI Bank had run over 40 cross-sell, up-sell and retention campaigns. The cross-selling campaigns enabled generating about 18–20% of the business from credit cards using analytics

*Source:* www.icicibank.com.

## Rules for Up-Selling

It is important to identify some guidelines for up-selling, just as one should for cross-selling. Here are some suggestions:

- Offer the alternative before the customer has added the item to his shopping cart.

- Use text that is brief but makes it clear exactly what features the up-sell item has that are lacking in the main item.

- List more expensive items with the same brand name, or higher quality but similar items in other brands.

- The up-sell item should always be more expensive than the main item.

- Decide whether to offer sale items when up-selling. If so, select items whose sale price is higher than the main item. (*Note:* One can decide to use up-selling to move older inventory, but beware of bargain basement sales that reduce the income.)
- Use the opportunity to offer new releases or new inventory. Clearly label the photograph of the up-sell item with "Just released!" or "New item."
- When the buyer clicks on the picture of the up-sell item, display the item's catalogue page rather than adding the item to the shopping cart right away.

This advice by experts bears repeating: make sure the customer is clear about the advantages of buying the up-sell item. The offer should be seen as good customer care rather than a hard sell.

*Source:* www.buydomains.com.

## OTHER STRATEGIES

Variations on the up-sell and cross-sell are numerous. Consider having a few small items for sale in the checkout area, much as grocery stores and department stores do. This is how they sell magazines, gum and candy—keeping customers in shopping mode while they are waiting to check out.

Seasonal items can attract many customers. Offering gift items before any festival may work well to purchase related—for example, a free tee shirt may persuade the customer to buy casual wear trouser.

One might as well identify a few "loss leaders." These are sale items that can be sold at a slight loss, just to get buyers to the website. When the buyer comes in for a visit, have cross-selling and up-selling items ready to display.

Surveys show that most buyers appreciate being told about additional products or services that might better meet their needs or about new items that were not offered in the past. It is a way of demonstrating awareness of customers' needs and care about their satisfaction. Here are some ideas to help in improving cross-selling/up-selling success:

- **Stay relevant:** Overloading customers with too many unrelated cross-selling suggestions, may blow it. Offering socks with shoes is certainly a good fit. But any attempt to cross-sell or up-sell items that are not closely related to the original purchase, are far less likely to succeed.
- **Post expert recommendations:** One way to facilitate cross-selling and up-selling success is to state specific recommendations from professionals, experts or other customers. This could

be a chef's recommendation on a menu, a doctor's recommendation on a mailer, or lists of related items that other customers have purchased on a website. When one buys a book at Amazon.com, for example, the site automatically lists other related books purchased by people who bought the same book just ordered.

- **Train employees in cross-selling techniques:** The approach must be built around serving the customer, not just selling more stuff. For example, one might describe how the additional products or services would complement the original purchase and further solve the customer's problem.

- **Timing is important:** Cross-selling and up-selling can occur at different times, depending on the products and services one is selling. In some cases, the best time is while a customer is trying something out. If they are looking at a low priced digital camera, for example, but seem disappointed by lack of features or performance, they may really want a higher priced model. Or, it is better to suggest a belt to go with a pair of pants while the customer is trying them on. Other items are more appropriately offered once the initial buying decision has been made, such as extended warranty.

- **Leverage the cross-selling potential of the website:** Position cross-sell and up-sell items throughout the site in places where they can help educate shoppers on the depth and variety of what business offers. Try mixing and matching different items to see what works best.

- **Offer a range of prices:** If one suggests three items to complement a product, try to offer a mix of price points. The lowest cost items are most likely to be picked up as impulse buys. But other items that meet the customer's needs can also sell at higher levels.

- **Try product or service bundles:** Bundling has long been used as a way to entice shoppers to buy not just a single item, but an entire group of items that go together. Offering a price break on package deals will help close the sale.

*Source:* www.startupnation.com

## EMOTION FACTORS IN CROSS-SELLING AND UP-SELLING

Figure 6.1 would illustrate how the transition from rational buying motive to emotional buying motive facilitates cross-selling or up-selling of subsequent products.

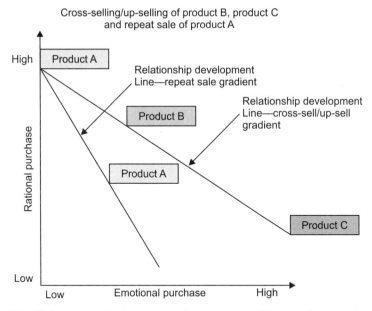

Cross-selling/up-selling of product B, product C
and repeat sale of product A

**Figure 6.1   Role of emotion in cross-selling and up-selling products and services.**

Figure 6.1 indicates the client's first time purchase decision of a product (Product A) depends highly on product performance and other related factors that endorse the product's credibility. This is an example of rational purchase where emotion has very little or no role to play in the buying process. Subsequent interactions with the partner develop relationship resulting in faith and confidence in the client. All these factors taken together normally lead to emotional relationship with the partner. It is because the 'pleasant experience' works at the top of the client's mind: 'I know those guys for a long time—they cannot do a bad job for us'. The success of Product A coupled with emotional relationship causes cross-sell/up-sell gradient's (referred in Chapter 2 as relationship development line) downward slope towards emotional purchase leading to smooth execution of cross-sell or up-sell of Product B and Product C, as well as repeat sale of Product A.

Based on the satisfaction of the first product, the repeat sale gradient has a greater slope towards emotional buying than the cross- and up-sell gradient. It is because, the first product has already established its credibility and customers would be ready to renew the order without much ado. But for cross-sell and up-sell, the confidence level of the customer is not going to be as high as the one of repeat sale. Although Product B depends on a lesser rational motive than it was for Product A, the downward or emotion-ward slope of the gradient has been justified by the client's positive emotional experience.

There are certain assumptions on this concept. Products and services that fall into this category are high value computer software, appliances, and financial services involving high investments where, excepting personal rapport, advertisement or other impulse oriented experience does not count much on the buying decision.

Figure 6.1 can be reconstructed and categorized according to the value of the product. In the reconstructed figure (Figure 6.2), it is obvious that intensity of reasoning and evaluation process underlying in rational buying process reduces, when relationship constructs start playing its role in the client interactions. For subsequent sale of high value product or service, it is relationship constructs that play a crucial role. Low value product purchase is mainly led by 'impulse' buying. Promotional schemes can have a temporary relationship effect but certainly for a short term. Once withdrawn, the sale collapses.

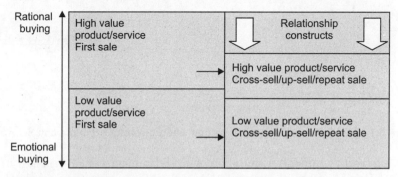

**Figure 6.2  Rational and emotional buying decision process.**

# BUILDING PROFIT IMPROVEMENT

In seeking to further increase in profitability, companies need to develop integrated programmes that address customer acquisition, customer retention and other related activities that can improve customer lifetime value. One framework for reviewing such profit opportunities is the ACURA model shown in Figure 6.3.

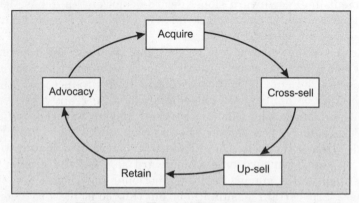

**Figure 6.3  The ACURA framework.**

*Source:*  Prof. Adrian Payne (2001) adopted with permission.

ACURA is an acronym for acquisition, cross-sell, up-sell, retention and advocacy. Rarely do companies systematically build CRM strategies that focus on all elements within the ACURA framework. While companies seek to improve customer acquisition and customer retention, they also need to exploit cross-selling and up-selling and advocacy opportunities (Payne, 2001). The ACURA model is used in the American Express to enhance the value delivered to the customer. It is a cyclic process that triggers off with cross-selling when a customer approaches for credit card facility. The bank offers traveller facilities, which implies more value. The next step is up-selling where the customer moves a level up from Gold to Platinum, etc. All these initiatives convert a customer into an advocate and thus new opportunities of acquiring new business are enhanced.

## CRITICAL SUCCESS FACTORS

The following are the critical success factors associated with successful cross-selling and up-selling:

**Sell the right products to the customers**. For customer value to be optimized, products must be linked to individual customer needs and preferences. Products must also be sold at an appropriate price point to achieve both profitability and customer satisfaction.

**Personalize customer communications**. Cross-selling and up-selling are optimized when customers are communicated with the right frequency intervals. Over-communication or irrelevant communication diminishes the impact of ongoing messaging and contributes to churn. By ensuring that, offers are targeted to specific customers, cross- and up-sell effectiveness and customer loyalty are increased. Identifying appropriate channels of communication based on customer preference is critical, as well as ensuring that messages are highly relevant to the specific audience being targeted.

**Measure cross-selling and up-selling in relation to the totality of the customer experience**. It is critical to understand the RoI and payback of cross-sell campaigns. It is important to project response rates and even consider other product lines that may be cannibalized by each campaign. Further, increases or decreases in churn must also be measured.

## CONCLUSION

Cross-sell and up-sell initiatives are adopted for retaining and growing high value customers. Effective cross-selling and up-selling requires multi-faceted approach that steers clear of common generalizations. Many companies track customer level of satisfaction with a particular product or service and also monitor the perceived value. There are certain rules and norms for cross-selling and up-selling products. For example, display of maximum of three cross-sell items and those items should be in stock. The items should also be relevant to the primary items sold. There are certain other tips for improving cross-sell and up-sell, such as stay relevant, post expert recommendations, train employees on the techniques of cross- and up-selling, timing of the sale, range of products in different prices and their bundling. Depending on the category of business, various strategies and mechanisms for cross-selling and up-selling can be adopted. There is a role of emotion in such selling process, which can be leveraged. Cross-selling and up-selling should be a continuous process that contributes to profit improvement of the organization. Critical success factors of cross-selling and up-selling are as follows: Choose the right product for the right customer, personalize customer communications, and establish a measurement standard for cross- and up-selling in terms of RoI.

> **Keywords:** *Cross-selling, Up-selling, Critical success factors.*

# Exercises

1. Take an example of a bookstore and list four items each for cross-selling and up-selling.

2. Why is timing is important for cross-selling and up-selling? Justify your views with an appropriate example.

3. What is the relevance of cross-selling and up-selling with customer relationship?

4. What are the critical success factors envisaged in the cross-selling and up-selling exercise?

Fill in the blanks:

5. _____ is simply convincing the buyer that he should purchase a more expensive (and higher quality or more versatile) product than the one under consideration whereas _____ is an effort to encourage the committed buyer to add auxiliary items to the purchase, such as accessories or related items.

6. ACURA is an acronym for _____, _____, _____, _____ and _____.

# References

Payne, A., 2001. The Value Creation Process in Customer Relationship Management, White Paper.

Wilson, Ralph F., 2007. E-Commerce Cross-Selling and Up-Selling, Web Marketing Today, Rocklin, CA, www.wilsonweb.com.

Websites

www.startupnation.com
www.wilsonweb.com
www.buydomains.com/business-resources/articles/cross-selling-upselling.jsp
www.icicibank.com

# CHAPTER 7

|||||||||||||||||||||

# Temperament of Business Relations

## INTRODUCTION

This chapter offers an overview of relationship temperament and signals, which are likely to prevail in business negotiations between the client and the partner from relation formative stages to execution. The purpose of this chapter is to explore different relationship signals that deepen and broaden the business relationship enabling continuity of client-partner enterprise expansion in a B2B scenario through cross-sell and up-sell. The analysis fits by and large into service providing sectors. This chapter gives some insights into various dimensions of business co-operations and conflicts since the texture and flavour of the relationship signalling and temperament depend on the presence or absence of conflict in the relation. An analysis has been done by construction of relationship temperament matrix showing different relationship temperament zones where relationship categories are mapped with different zones of that matrix. This chapter is concluded through exploring relationship signals and mapping different types of signals with relationship category, temperament zone and key constructs presenting a wholesome picture of a wide band of signals in terms of opportunities or threats in business development.

## RELATIONSHIP SIGNALS

In a client-partner business (B2B) scenario, relationship temperament, from business inception to product/service stabilization stage, is the driving force to set the rhythm, pace and mood of the business. It is another manifestation of business relationship coupled with presence or absence of stress generated through business negotiations. There is always an essence of stress in any business planning, operation and execution.

Business stress originates when there is a demand by the client and there is a gap in the perceived resources of the partner to meet that demand in a given timeline. This gap causes undesirable business conflict and strains the relationship, leading a project to challenged state. In view of growing uncertainties and 'shock factors' in socio-economic, political, and business environment, the stress is taken as an unavoidable component of business transactions.

In such a context, relationship signals are of fundamental importance as they embody body language, gestures, opinions, and expressions of the client in different communications channels conveying satisfaction or dissatisfaction right from the start. The understanding and anticipation of those signals helps in deepening and broadening relationship, averting any possible conflict and strain leading to termination of the business. The signals have much to do with the temperament. Favourable signals are marked by cooperation and cordiality in client-partner operations. This is a healthy sign for mutual business growth. The cohesiveness in their mode of operations projects an integrated client-partner image.

There are also examples of business managers spending much of their time in resolving conflict more often than required. This results in unwanted delay in evolving creative solutions for the clients. The irony is, both the parties accept such disturbed relationship as 'part of the game' till the same reaches the point of no return.

Some business managers feel that at the outset, it is important for both the client and the partner to assess whether the future business transaction between them would bring happiness or distress in their respective business domains. Looking at the six-stage model of business transactions (contact, involvement, intimacy, deterioration, repair and dissolution), the exit possibility is provided in any of these stages (De Vito, Joseph, A. 1993), which is certainly the least preferred option for any business partner.

The rationale behind such undesirable exit can be many. The client and the partner may have their own organization culture driven by their code of conduct, corporate philosophy, management style and similar other variances. At times it is very difficult to align them to accomplish mission critical business goals. Thus, in an identical line of business, the mindset and outlook of different clients are different. The client-partner may feel comfortable in one environment, while in the similar line of business, the other client may have a frustrating experience despite differential product offering.

Besides, there are some organizations that venture to accept mission critical job, where availability of their expertise and resources do not meet the demands of the client at that instant. There is an essence of adventurism and confidence that tempt the business manager to take such a plunge that results in unforeseen and unpredictable consequences.

However, under all circumstances, 'Business Exit' plan is always taken as the last resort.

Business conflicts start with signals that convey a feeling of organization discomfort or irritation from both sides. When discomfort and irritation intensify, relationship slips into a disturbing state. If the same is neglected further, it culminates into crisis, with a high probability of client attrition. A study of temperament would give an insight into how the business signals are emitted.

## TREND OF BUSINESS TEMPERAMENT FROM SUSPECT/PROSPECT

It is desirable to understand, anticipate and monitor the trend of relationship temperament right from the inception stage. This is further followed by its monitoring during transactions. But is there any set procedure or methodology for carrying out that assessment which could help arrive at certain decisions?

The answer depends on the experience and judgment of the relationship managers, shouldering the responsibility of navigating the business. In the prospecting stage, both client and partners, through interactive sessions, should rip open the facts and figures to the best possible extent and analyze those, to decide whether to 'exit' or begin 'entrance', whether the client is a terrorist or likely to become a terrorist or an all time precious advocate.

During the prospecting period, however strong each other's brand equity may be, both treat each other with fair amount of apprehension. The scale and degree of apprehension depends on the volume of business under negotiations. If this apprehension continues and turns more and more critical with time, then the trend is not a healthy one. On the contrary, the apprehension should be converted into a 'hand holding' or 'hand shaking' stage pre-empting trust and confidence in each other's relationship.

Thus, before entering into an agreement, there seems to be a need to evaluate and monitor the psychological comfort level of the interacting groups/organizations from time to time. This would act as a pointer to show how things would transpire when business would be in full swing. This is especially relevant when it is a matter of enormous investment, a battery of people is involved, and numerous processes come into place. Then the business manager must think many times before taking a decision. When there is a stiff sales target, they are tempted to take up anything and everything that comes on the way. But such risk might bring disaster with the obvious consequence—the client turns enemy or terrorist not only spoiling existing business but spread bad news about the partner.

This certainly does not point to the fact such problems do not happen with the experienced organization. Prior exposure of the organization to similar problems develops a sense of anticipation. As a consequence, they have the advantage to tackle them effectively or prevent such situation from happening.

However, assessment and analysis of relationship temperament and signals do not lead to achieve a straightjacket one-point solution to solve all the business problems. It reveals the causes and results of proactive and reactive approach and how they look like.

## EFFECT OF CLIENT CATEGORIES ON BRAND EQUITY

Given the fact that a typical enterprise has a broad spectrum of clients (Bansal and Gupta 2000), right from "terrorist" (extremely dissatisfied/ alienated customers that are likely to damage brand equity) to "advocates" (delighted customers who actively work to strengthen the market presence of enterprise), it should be appropriate to handle and manage the customer type accordingly. However, a brief description of different categories of client is given below (Griffin 2002).

**Suspect**: A suspect is anyone who might possibly buy your product or service. We call them suspects because we believe, or "suspect," they might buy, but we do not know enough yet to be sure.

**Prospect:** A prospect is someone who has a need for your product or service and is able to buy. Although a prospect has not yet purchased from you, he or she may have heard about you, read about you, or had someone recommend you to her. Prospects may know who you are, where you are, and what you sell, but they still have not bought from you.

**Disqualified prospects**: Disqualified prospects are those prospects about whom you have learnt enough to know that they do not need, or do not have the ability to buy your products.

**First time customer**: A first time customer is one who has purchased from you one time. The person can be a customer of yours and a customer of your competitor as well.

**Repeat customer**: Repeat customers are people who have purchased from you two or more times. They may have brought the same product twice or bought two different products or services on two or more occasions.

**Client:** A client buys everything you have to sell that he can possibly use. This person purchases regularly. You have a strong, ongoing relationship that makes him immune to the pull of the competition.

**Advocate:** Like a client, an advocate buys everything you have to sell that he or she can possibly use and purchases regularly. In addition, however, an advocate encourages others to buy from you, talks about you doing the marketing for you and brings customers to you.

**Lost customer:** A lost customer or client is someone who was once a customer or client but has not bought from you in at least one normal purchase cycle.

Without entering into a futile debate "why A is not like B", it is important that one of the objectives of managing customers experience for an enterprise should be to convert key customers to advocates and address the issues of "terrorist" and "rejecters" to minimize the negative impact on brand equity. Reworking this concept, it is possible to arrive at a picture as in Figure 7.1, where the thrust should be to turn the 'terrorist' to 'advocate'.

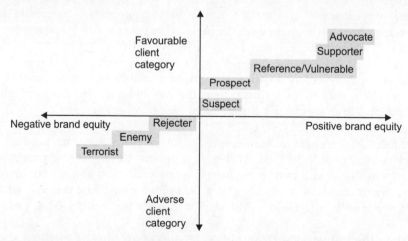

**Figure 7.1 Client categories and their effects on brand equity.**
*Source:* Adapted from Bansal and Gupta 2000.

Forward-looking organizations endeavour to possess the temperament of sustaining the stress and pressure of conflict. Even at the point of extreme crisis, situations may take a U-turn and both the parties regain confidence and cooperation of each other. This might be possible by realignment of the relationship where some key persons on both sides act as arbiters and nurturing those relationship constructs, as described in Table 7.1 (Mishra 2000) which are relatively weaker. The role of an arbiter is played by the relationship manager through well-balanced global/local approach that effectively reconciles the tensions that exist between self-interest and that of both the client and the employer (Millman & Wilson 2000). Of the constructs described in the table, trust and commitment are the ones having greatest impact on customer relationship.

**Table 7.1** Relationship Constructs

| Construct | Explanation |
|---|---|
| Trust | Confidence in an exchange partner's reliability and integrity |
| Commitment | An enduring desire to maintain a valued relationship |
| Adaptation | Need-based resource tailoring |
| Communications | Information and knowledge sharing |
| Collaboration | Coordinated action to align with the objective of the relationship |
| Conflict resolution | Collaboration to resolve disagreement |
| Ownership | Sense of belonging in the partnership |
| Interdependence | Scale and extent of dependence |
| Past satisfaction | Satisfaction level on the basic elements of business |
| Power equation | Ability of one partner to evoke change in other |

Trust is the key variable in the establishment of a relationship and is the main antecedent to commitment. Trust is defined as "confidence in an exchange partner's reliability and integrity" (Morgan & Hunt 1994). Given the intangible nature of a service and the fact that a service is consumed as it is purchased, it can be argued that a high degree of trust in the product and/or supplier required to encourage purchase and repeat purchase. Trust is also defined as the "perceived credibility and benevolence of a target of trust" (Doney & Cannon 1997). Relationships that are characterized as high trust are highly valued by exchange participants (Bennet et al. 2000).

Relationship commitment is defined as "an enduring desire to maintain a valued relationship" (Morgan & Hunt 1994). Essentially, commitment captures the buyer's desire to maintain a relationship with a particular vendor and reflects the strength the buyer has with the buyer's representative. Arguably, the relationship with the consultant is more important than the relationship with the company as a measure of commitment, as the consultant is viewed as the public face of the company.

# RELATIONSHIP TEMPERAMENT MATRIX

The client-partner relationship is promoted primarily on quick solutions for different requirements. Relationship signals depend on the temperament developed between the client and the partner from the initial stage of Business Development to Business Maturity, followed by the stage of Business Conclusion. Here the term 'conclusion' implies an end of one phase of business and optimistically beginning of a new phase, depending on the business generation potential of the client and execution potential of the partner. Various temperament stages that both the client/partner organization experience in the business transaction is categorized into four zones. It is possible to design a matrix on different Relationship Temperament Zones pre-empting a client-partner relationship (Figure 7.2). The conflict and stress that may prevail under different circumstances have been mapped in those zones.

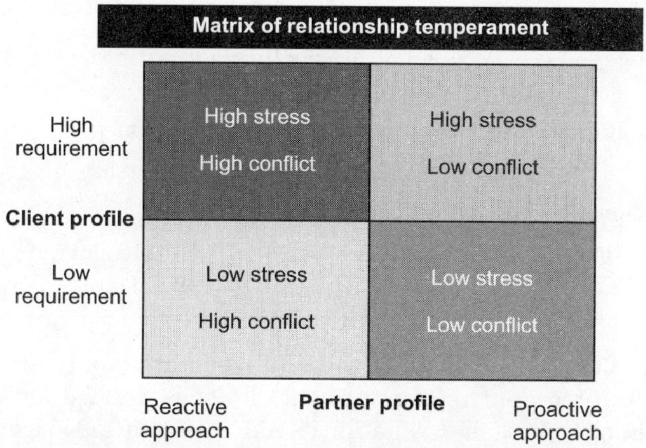

**Figure 7.2 Relationship temperament matrix.**

There are certain assumptions made during the development of the matrix. Those are as follows:

1. Clients have been categorized into two distinct groups. One group represents high requirement. These clients are of a demanding nature because of the nature of business they transact. The other group does not have high or fast changing requirement across a given time horizon. These clients are sometimes critical about the delivery, but generally contented with the partner unless there is serious indifference of the partner.

2. Similarly, partners are also categorized into two groups. One group is proactive enough to match or surpass the needs of clients. The other is complacent and reactive to the client's requirements.

3.  The matrix examines outcome of possible combinations of requirements of clients and approach of the partners.

The matrix is divided into four distinct temperament zones based on the partner's approach and client's requirements.

## High Conflict High Stress

The high conflict high stress zone can also be seen as a highly irritant zone to both the partner and the client. It becomes a normal practice for clients to shoot complaint letters. If it is a too demanding one, then strongly worded letter/mail every alternate day, may be very common routine. When there is a review meeting, it may start with complaints, onslaughts. All these could be enough to destabilize the relationship temperament of the partner. There is every possibility of crisis in this stage, but a proactive partner takes adequate care to ensure that the same does not turn dangerous.

High conflict high stress is a dangerous and business explosive zone. The partner must introspect and explore the ways to contain the problems. From the contact stage onwards, requirements may proliferate in the form of chain reaction, implying one requirement triggering off to multiple of others and so on until the process finally reaches a steady state by proactive delivery by the partner. If the partner understands the client's business domain, then resolution of issues becomes easy. But generally speaking, this may not be the ideal situation; the partner may take time to get into the heart of the client requirement. In future, a partner must stretch his thinking to transform the approach from reactive to proactive, to cater to those requirements. This would enable the partner to shift to the safer zone (high stress low conflict).

To accomplish this, the partner must work for serious adjustment, tactful negotiations, and often stretch much beyond normal working mode. If situations are not properly handled at this stage, stressed relationship temperament might culminate into highly adverse business signals. The relationship manager has a very critical role to play at this stage. He has to understand the client organization psyche and tune his organization to respond to that wavelength. Of course, such adjustments for the partner would be worthwhile if the client is very lucrative and profitable.

## Low Stress High Conflict

Low stress high conflict is not as the critical as previous zone, but this can transform into a high stress high conflict zone through indifference. In this zone, the client's requirements are not very pressing on the partner; at the same time, the reactive partner shows no interest or understanding towards the client. Somehow or the other, there is delivery. This gets more often rejected than accepted. But the sense of becoming alert or problem analysis takes a back seat in the partner's operations philosophy. As a result, the partner starts losing the confidence of the client and there is always a sense of discontent with the client who tries to switch over to alternative partner who could care for the client better.

## Low Conflict Low Stress

Low conflict low stress zone asserts the positive attitude and approach of the partner. This is not a high stress area, but the proactive partner promptly gets seasoned with that little stress and starts winning confidence level of the client. There are still some conflicts during negotiations, meetings. The partner, through hard work and meticulous client handling, is able to convince the fact regarding the product's position in the client organization, the 'more-than-expected' values the client has accrued out of it.

This helps cross-selling and expansion of the partner's business. Summarily speaking, the conflicts and differences come gradually under the control of both the groups. It is a step towards mutual acceptance from the inner self of both organizations. Once this stage is arrived, there is no looking back for both the client and the partner as the client has found benefits and real value in the product or service offered by the partner.

## Low Conflict High Stress

In low conflict high stress zone, the proactive partner successfully handles enormous requirement of the client. In fact, it takes one phone call to reach the partner and solve the problem. A TARP (Technical Assistance Research Programmes study conducted among the 800-number customers of 460 companies found that the number of customers reporting satisfaction after one call was dramatically higher than when two or more phone calls were made.

Low conflict high stress zone signifies an approach of business partner who responds spontaneously to customer call. This approach helps both the groups to succeed in finding space beyond conflicts for themselves—they come to understanding, think of each other's betterment, further improvements in the processes adopted in business implementation. This is the result of delivering excellent product and services. The team in the partner's group works harder to sustain and improve this level of performance. The little conflict that remains does not have a bad odour. It can also be noted here that during the pre-emptive stages, it is more of **permission marketing** that enables the partner to penetrate into client environment. In later stages, with growing satisfaction of the client, the power equation starts developing. Subsequently, a time comes when the partner acts as a business mentor of the client, leveraging the **power equation**.

# RELATIONSHIP TEMPERAMENT MATRIX AND RELATIONSHIP SIGNALS

Table 7.2 depicts the categories of business outcome in terms of relationship signals generated with respect to the business temperament prevailing in each business zone. Here, the key constructs, namely, adaptations, commitments, communications, collaboration, conflict resolution, ownership, power equations, past satisfaction, and trust are used as cross-references to relate the temperament with signals (Mishra 2000). The major objective of this table is to identify the areas where further effort can be exerted to build up strong customer loyalty, where situations can become grave enough leading to business loss, and what are the major signals for those situations.

**Table 7.2** Interconnectivity of Temperament Zone, Key Relationship Construct and Relationship Signals

| Relationship temperament zone | Key relationship construct | Relationship singals |
|---|---|---|
| High conflict high stress | Reactive partner—by and large indifferent to relationship constructs | Signals are very unfavourable and detrimental to business relations. |
| High conflict low stress | Superficial adoption of relationship constructs by the partners | Signals are discouraging. It is little overt and not as pronounced as in high stress high conflict zone. |
| Low conflict low stress | Adaptations<br>Commitments<br>Communications<br>Conflict resolution<br>Ownership<br>Past satisfaction<br>Power equations<br>Trust | Signals are very positive and encouraging for future business. High chances of materializing cross-selling and up-selling in the shortest possible time through persistent follow-up |
| Low conflict high stress | High tolerance<br>Pronounced interdependence<br>Deeper understanding<br>Collaborative approach<br>Proven past satisfaction<br>Effective power equations | Signals of repeat relation conveyed through different business interactions. This is the ideal zone where business partner leverages the constructs to broaden and deepen relationship. Clients acknowledge great service through appreciation letters, awards, etc. |

## Signals in High Stress High Conflict Zone

Signals are seemingly unfavourable in this zone. Common signals are disbelief in the partner's commitment, escalation of issues to the partner's top management for each and every thing. The situation starts getting so critical that it affects the client's psyche. For any problem, all the fingers get pointed to the partner. Client does not want to wait longer and watch situation over a given time horizon. The inevitable outcome is business separation if client service is not properly and strongly monitored and acted upon. Often litigation/penalty/liquidity damage/black listing, etc. are the acts being exercised by the client. In the high stress high conflict zone, the partner fails or is reluctant to exhibit any of the relationship constructs to develop rapport with the client transacting business under tremendous market pressure. The partner is either unaware of those constructs or not being briefed by the management team responsible for customer relationship.

## Signals in Low Stress High Conflict Zone

The client has unarticulated or low requirements. He comes to the partner in phases for requirement and that may turn off the partner. The partner is reactive and shows utmost reluctance towards the client's requirements. With persuasions from the client, the delivery is managed. A reactive partner manages to sustain the business temporarily. Due to budget or specific constraint, the client is forced to stick to such reactive partner. But given an option, the client is ready to get rid of the partner. In a situation like this, the partner's day with the client starts with conflict and stinkers from the client.

## Signals in Low Stress Low Conflict Zone

There is always a running but low stress for both the sides. Since the requirement is low and unarticulated, the proactive partner exerts all efforts to get deep into the client's requirements, anticipate issues and resolve them. In the process, the partner starts receiving signals of the client's confidence by surpassing far beyond the client's expectation. The partner learns to become proactive to retrieve the needs and shows utmost concern towards the client's requirements. Delivery is managed with the client's satisfaction. The partner manages to sustain the confidence of the client. This starts deepening of relationship and paves the way to repeat order.

## Signals in High Stress and Low Conflict Zone

The high stress and low conflict zone is the ideal zone to be aspired by any partner. For a proactive partner, business transactions are not devoid of conflict; initially it could be little disturbing, but later it is transformed into affective nature. There is visible effort from the partner to align with the client's requirements, leveraging the constructs —e.g. adaptations to client requirements, commitment of delivery and communicating what, when and how to deliver meeting quality and timeline.

Gradually, the client starts liking and trusting the partner. The partner becomes the client's mentor and counsellor. In the process, the client becomes the partner's supporter-cum-advocate. The partner nurtures all the constructs that are responsible for deepening and broadening the relationship. All these attributes elevate the comfort level of the client, and lead to a final level where power equations in both client and partner organizations assume one unique identity benefiting both the parties for business growth and expansion.

To wrap it up all, signals need to be comprehended and for that matter, all the senses are not enough to read them. By and large, today's accounting systems are designed to show short-term gains and losses and do not help to track the benefits of maintaining a relationship with the customer over a period of time. Expected cash flows over a loyal customer's lifetime cannot be evaluated using current systems. Yet it is clear that a satisfied, loyal customer can contribute a great deal to the financial bottom line of any company (Griffin 2002).

---

*Case Study:* **Business Temperament Consultancy**

---

Synergy Leaders is the global provider of consulting, training, and coaching solutions utilizing Keirsey Temperament Theory™. For more than 50 years, Keirsey Temperament Theory has been utilized by the world's leading organizations. The US government and military, the world's finest academic institutions, two-thirds of the Fortune 500, and prestigious global consulting firms use Keirsey Solutions™. Synergy Leaders help their clients to identify the temperament of their customer segment. They assess whether an organization's products/services, its brand image, and its messaging are actually connecting with its audience. Synergy Leaders also help product designers, marketing strategists, and creative teams gain clarity on who their customer target is, and how to become customer centred, which ultimately lead to success. Synergy leaders train the sales professionals, understand their own temperament, and how that shapes their persuasion tactics and proposals, helping them to understand how temperament plays a key role in the buying patterns of a customer.

*Source:* www.keirsey.com

---

*Case Study:* **Relationship Constructs Showing Commitment to Customer's Interest—Withdrawing a Candidate on Bad References—Magna Services India**

---

One client in Africa, was expanding their business and looking for a professional as Country Head. Magna Services' one of the professionals, who was in Africa earlier and was with another client of Magna, came back to India to take part in his family business. However, things did not work well in India, hence he was considering a return. Magna had known this person in the past as a customer and had known that he enjoyed good reputation with his previous employer in Africa. As expected, this gentleman got selected without any problem and it was sure for him to have flying colour references from his previous employer but it happened to be very subdued. This made Magna team think that everything was not okay. Despite two repeated attempts, his previous employer refused to open his mouth more than what was already told. It was felt there was something amiss and decided to check his entire career, right from start. After contacting about 14 people, who happened to be across the globe, it was revealed that 14 years ago he was told to leave the first job due to some integrity issue. The client, the new employer, was so enamoured with the person at that time that they wanted to ignore the reference check reports.

Magna Services called the gentleman and the appointment letter was withdrawn. Though no recruitment took place and the organization ended up spending almost a month with no gains, the pleasant surprise was when Magna Services found US$ 10000 cheque towards the efforts to safeguard the client's interest.

*Source:* http://www.magnaservicesindia.com/CaseHistories.asp

## CONCLUSION

Understanding of relationship temperament and relationship signals right from the business negotiation stage enables an organization for appropriate relationship strategy planning. Different categories of business relationships that transpire in future depend on the type of interaction between the client and the partner with special reference to relationship constructs. The relationship temperament matrix can illustrate the emergence of various types of client relationship zones due to business approach differences. The signals are mapped with each of those zones exploring the client's temperament and attitude for the partner.

> *Keywords:* Relationship temperament, Relationship signals, Relationship constructs, Relationship temperament matrix, Permission marketing, Power equation.

## Exercises

1. Why should you consider relationship signals significant in business transactions?

2. "Stress would always be there in today's business environment"— What would be your approach towards handling business stress with your client, when you are under tremendous delivery pressure?

3. Discuss the signals in high stress low conflict zone and explain its relevance in business environment.

4. Match the following:

| | |
|---|---|
| (a) Adaptation | (a) Reliability and integrity |
| (b) Trust | (b) Enduring desire to maintain relationship |
| (c) Commitment | (c) Need-based resource tailoring |
| (d) Communications | (d) Alignment with relationship objective |
| (e) Collaboration | (e) Information and knowledge sharing |
| (f) Conflict resolution | (f) Sense of belonging in the partnership |
| (g) Ownership | (g) Act together to resolve disagreement |
| (h) Power equation | (h) Scale and extent of dependence |
| (i) Interdependence | (i) Satisfaction level on the basic elements of business |
| (j) Past satisfaction | (j) Ability of one partner to evoke change in other |

Fill in the blank:

5. The understanding and anticipation of relationship signals help in _____ and _____ relationship, averting any possible _____ and _____ leading to _____ of the business.

## References

Bansal, Sharat and Gupta, Gagan, 2000. "Building Customer Loyalty Business-to-Business Commerce" in *Customer Relationship Management, Emerging Concepts, Tools and Applications*, Jagdish N. Sheth, Atul Parvatiyar and G. Sainesh (Eds.), Tata McGraw Hill, New Delhi, p. 229.

Bennett, Rebekah, McColl-Kennedy, Janet and Coote, V. Leonard, 2000. "Trust, Commitment and Attitudinal Brand Loyalty: Key Constructs in Business-to-Business Relationships", ANZMAC (Australia and New Zealand Marketing Academy Conference),

Visionary Marketing for the 21st Century: Facing the Challenge, p. 89.

De Vito, Joseph A., 1993. *Messages: Building Interpersonal Communication Skills*, HarperCollins College Publishers, New York, p. 260.

Doney, Patricia M. and Cannon, Joseph P., 1997. "An Examination of the Nature of Trust in Buyer–Seller Relationships," *Journal of Marketing*, Vol. 61, April, pp. 35–51.

Griffin, Jill, 2002. *Customer Loyalty—How to Earn it, How to Keep it, Jossey-Bass*, a Wiley Imprint, San Francisco, p. 35.

Mishra, Randhir, 2000. "A Generalized Model for the Structure of Business Relationship—A Meta Analysis of Relationship Literature," in *Customer Relationship Management, Emerging Concepts, Tools and Applications*, Jagdish N. Sheth, Atul Parvatiyar and G. Sainesh (Eds.), Tata Mcgraw Hill, New Delhi, pp. 52–55.

Millmen, A.F. and Wilson, K.J., 2000. "Career Development of Global Account Managers: The Dilemma of the Political Entrepreneur", Paper Presented at the Sixteenth Annual Industrial Marketing and Purchasing (IMP) Conference, University of Bath, United Kingdom, September.

Morgan, R.M. and Hunt, S.D., 1994. "The Commitment-Trust Theory of Relationship Marketing," *Journal of Marketing*, Vol. 58, July, pp. 20–38.

Technical Assistance Research Programmes (TARP), SOCAP (Society of Consumer Affairs Professionals International, Virginia, USA, www.socap.org) 800 Number Study: A 1992 Profile of 800 Numbers for Customer Service," June 1993, p. 30.

Websites

http://www.magnaservicesindia.com/CaseHistories.asp
www.keirsey.com

Temperament of Business Relations was first published in *Indian Management*, January 2007 under the title 'Creating a win-win dialogue—How can you take the stress out of business negotiations'. The author acknowledges the guidance and review from Dr Jagdish N Sheth, Charles H Kelistadt, Professor of Marketing, and Dr Atul Parvatiyar, President, ICRM and Adjunct Associate Professor of Marketing at Goizueta Business School.

# CHAPTER 8

# Managing Customer Satisfaction through Quality

## INTRODUCTION

Another major force driving the adoption of relationship marketing is the total quality movement that recently revolutionized industry's perspectives regarding cost and quality. Through the design and implementation of a formal organization system, quality becomes integral to the organization's activities. In customer value creation, we have noted that product development is not a 'one touch event'. This is especially relevant for a large enterprise having numerous complexities in the production process. Such processes comprise a large grid of events, involving multifunctional and multidimensional activities, supported by a pool of experts and professionals. Each event requires control and monitoring through proper quality assurance. The objective of this exercise is apparent—customer's acceptance of the product and services, which, in turn, leads to their satisfaction, protects and promotes mutual business interest without any alarming signals in relationship. It is evident, that the purpose of relationship is totally defeated if a defective product is delivered or a product delivered beyond schedule. In this context, organizations following well defined processes and standards rarely face the wrath of customer dissatisfaction. Therefore, it is important for the organizations to understand and practise accepted quality standards to leverage customer delight. This chapter discusses historical frameworks and best practices of quality, across manufacturing and IT industries.

## CUSTOMER SATISFACTION AND QUALITY

The common belief that generally prevails in the mindset of the marketers is: use relationship marketing when you have a good or better product. If you have the best product, then you need not bother about relationship marketing. Relationship cannot always defend an inferior product—by the term 'inferior', it may not point at a bad or defective product or service, rather there is the likelihood of implying a 'less competitive product'. Again, in a competitive scenario, the best product without relationship cannot sustain 'as the best', because relationship feedback benchmarks its performance from time to time. Hence, the awareness and attention towards quality is mandatory while thinking of success in relationship marketing.

---

*Case Study:* **Accenture Study Finds Expectations Increased most in Emerging Economies—Customer Service Quality Falling Short of Rising Expectations across the Globe**

---

### ABOUT ACCENTURE

Accenture is a global management consulting, technology services and outsourcing company. Combining unparalleled experience, comprehensive capabilities across all industries and business functions, and extensive research on the world's most successful companies, Accenture collaborates with clients to help them become high-performance businesses and governments. With more than 175,000 people in 49 countries, the company generated net revenues of US$19.70 billion for the fiscal year ended Aug. 31, 2007.

### STUDY REPORT

Companies are not keeping pace with consumers' rising expectations for service, especially in emerging economies, according to the results of a global study released by Accenture (NYSE: ACN).

The findings are outlined in a new report, "Customer Satisfaction in the Multi-Polar World: Accenture 2007 Global Customer Service Satisfaction Survey Report," the third in a series of annual studies designed to examine consumer attitudes towards customer service. While the studies in 2005 and 2006 focused on the United States and the United Kingdom, the 2007 report expanded the geographic scope to also include Australia, Brazil, Canada, China and France.

#### Consumer Service Expectations Increasing

More than one-half (52 per cent) of the more than 3,500 consumer respondents surveyed this year across five continents reported that their expectations for better service have increased over the past five years. Additionally, one-third (33 per cent) said they have higher service expectations today than they did just last year.

Expectations increased the most among consumers in emerging economies. More than nine out of 10 consumers in China (93 per cent) said their expectations for better service had increased over the past five years, and 75 per cent said their expectations are higher than they were a year ago. In Brazil, nearly half (48 per cent) of the respondents said that their expectations had increased since last year.

The findings indicate that increases in customer service expectations continue to outpace efforts made by companies to improve service. Globally, nearly one-half (47 per cent) of survey respondents said their expectations were met only "sometimes," "rarely" or "never." The highest level of dissatisfaction was found among Brazilian consumers, with two-thirds (67 per cent) of those respondents reporting that their expectations are met only "sometimes," "rarely" or "never."

Even in developed economies, where companies have spent billions on customer service capabilities, dissatisfaction with service remains high. For instance, more than half (52 per cent) of U.K. consumers said the frequency with which their customer service expectations are met is "sometimes," "rarely" or "never."

### Gap between Service and Consumer Expectations Contributing to "Churn"

The gap between service expectations and the services consumers receive translates into lost business. A majority (59 per cent) of consumers in developed and emerging economies reported that they quit doing business with a company due to poor service; the figures were significantly higher for consumers in the emerging economies of China and Brazil—85 per cent and 75 per cent, respectively. Additionally, the findings found an increase in the number of U.K. consumers who reported a significant increase in switching service providers due to poor service—58 per cent, up from 50 per cent in 2005.

"Consumers are empowered with more knowledge and choices than ever—driving a seismic shift in the balance of power to the consumer and adding to the complexities multinational corporations face," said Woody Driggs, managing director of Accenture's Customer Relationship Management practice globally. "Consumers in developed and emerging economies alike have shown their willingness to stop shopping at companies that can't meet their service expectations."

The study found that customer churn resulting from poor service remained prevalent across industries. Retailers, banks and Internet service providers were the industries most frequently identified by consumers as those where poor service had led them to take business elsewhere—selected by 21 per cent, 21 per cent and 20 per cent of all respondents, respectively.

### Knowledge of Diverse Consumer Preferences must Underpin Service Delivery

To begin to address the service issues identified in the findings, the Accenture report recommends that organizations incorporate the customer's perspective, values and actions into their business and operations strategy, and into their capability development and execution. For instance, 43 per cent of consumers surveyed identified the ability to resolve an issue with a single call rather than speaking with multiple service representatives as one of the most important aspects of a satisfying customer service experience. By contrast, only 22 per cent identified the speed of the response.

"To differentiate themselves, rebuild loyalty and fend off competition for valued consumers, leading companies respond by consistently delivering an experience that is tailored to the customer," said Robert Wollan, managing director of Accenture's CRM Service Transformation Management Consulting practice. "Competing in multiple countries has made this an even more complex challenge, and companies are finding that a 'one size fits all' experience—even an improved one—won't be enough to drive growth around the corner, let alone around the world."

More than four out of 10 (41 per cent) of all respondents reported that the overall quality of service they receive is "poor/terrible" to "fair." French consumers rendered the most severe evaluation of quality, with 60 per cent of them saying that the service they receive tends to be "poor/terrible" to "fair." Although satisfaction with service was highest in the United States, only 7 per cent of US respondents rated it "excellent," and 28 per cent said it was "poor/terrible" to "fair."

Additionally, when asked if they expect better service in exchange for spending or purchasing more frequently from a company, 71 per cent of respondents said they expect "much" or "somewhat" better service. The expectation for "much better service" when spending more was particularly strong among Chinese and Brazilian consumers, at 83 per cent and 63 per cent, respectively. Expectations of consumers in developed countries were a bit lower: 35 per cent in the United Kingdom, 38 per cent in Canada and 39 per cent in the United States. Country by country, the mix of factors that determine whether an experience is satisfying or frustrating varies, as do consumers' responses to poor service. For instance:

- Consumers in the United Kingdom were more likely than those in China to report being frustrated when left on hold too long while speaking with customer service representatives (81 per cent versus 59 per cent).

- The ability to interact with just a single customer service representative is more important for respondents in France,

Brazil and Canada—selected by 39 per cent, 34 per cent and 32 per cent of respondents in those countries, respectively—than it is for Chinese consumers (12 per cent).

- Brazilian consumers were the most inclined to identify lack of personalized solutions from companies as a service frustration—cited by 63 per cent of respondents in Brazil—while it was considerably less important to US and UK consumers, cited by only 37 per cent of respondents in each of those countries.

This report highlights the frustrations consumers face and the need for companies to implement customer-focused programmes that can improve services.

"To keep pace with rising customer expectations, enterprises must continue to reinvest in their customer-facing capabilities," said Matthew Goldman, Gartner Research vice-president. "Through use of internal or external capabilities, successful enterprises will develop or enhance their understanding of changing customer preferences and how to deliver on those needs."

## Methodology

The Web-based survey of 3,552 consumers in Australia, Brazil, Canada, China, France, the United Kingdom and the United States was fielded in July and August 2007. The findings served as the basis for the new white paper, "Customer Satisfaction in the Multi Polar World: Accenture 2007 Global customer Service Satisfaction Survey Report." In 2005 and 2006, Accenture conducted similar studies in the United States and the United Kingdom.

*Source:* newsroom.accenture.com, www.accenture.com

Quality control in its traditional costume epitomizes the hazard of approaching a phenomenon on a substantive and narrow basis, not seeing it in the context of total management. It was not until quality management was expanded to encompass all activities in the company that TQM emerged and became a driver in the New Economy. TQM is not only a revolution in quality management but also a *strengthening of marketing orientation.* In marketing management, quality had regressed to a hollow cliché, which was routinely appended to advertising copy and sales-talk, and without further elaboration was mentioned as "important" in marketing textbooks. Today, quality is interpreted as *customer perceived quality,* meaning that it is marketing-oriented and focused on customer satisfaction. The most conspicuous contribution from TQM to relationship marketing is the creation of a link between the internally and technically oriented operations management and the externally oriented marketing and sales function. That quality has moved from the shop floor to the management of the whole corporation becomes evident in the now widespread quality awards for which The Malcolm Baldrige National Quality Award initially became a role model. The European Quality Award, with a different structure than the Baldrige, has become a driver for a holistic and customer-oriented view on management among corporations and governments in Europe. The awards have increasingly added aspects of relationships to its criteria and explanatory notes. Here are excerpts from the Malcolm Baldrige Award (1997) that underscore dimensions of market, mega and nano relationships:

- "Describe how the company determines and enhances the satisfaction of its customers to strengthen relationships ... [and] ... explain how the company ensures that complaints are resolved effectively and promptly ..." (p. 9)

- "Examples of approaches that might be part of listening and learning strategies are: ... relationship building, including close integration with customers ... interviewing lost customers to determine the factors they use in their purchase decisions ... won/lost analysis relative to competitors ... post-transaction follow-up ..." (pp. 22–23)

- "Relationship enhancement provides a potentially important means for companies to understand and manage customer expectations. Also, frontline employees may provide vital information to build partnerships and other longer term relationships with customers." (p. 23)

- "... analysis and priority setting for improvement projects based upon potential cost impact of complaints, taking into account customer retention related to resolution effectiveness." (p. 23)

- "For many companies, key suppliers and partners are an increasingly important part of achieving not only high performance and lower-cost objectives, but also of strategic objectives ... improving your own procurement and supplier management processes (including seeking feedback from suppliers and 'internal customers'), joint planning, rapid information and data exchanges, use of benchmarking and comparative information, customer-supplier teams, training, long-term agreements ..." (p. 29)

- "The item addresses current levels and trends in key measures and/or indicators of supplier and partner performance." (p. 30)

- "Internal partnerships might include labour-management cooperation, such as agreements with unions ... [and] ... network relationships among company units to improve flexibility, responsiveness, and knowledge sharing ... External partnerships might be with customers, suppliers, and education organizations ... An increasingly important kind of external partnership is the strategic partnership or alliance ... [which] ... might offer a company entry into new markets or a basis for new products or services ... blending of company's core competencies or leadership capabilities ... thereby enhancing overall capability, including speed and flexibility." (p. 41)

The concept of *relationship quality* was introduced in the Ericsson Quality program in 1985 (Gummesson 2002). The purpose was to call attention to the fact that relationships are part of customer perceived quality. This quality concept is a long way from the traditional engineer's logic of quality inspection and statistical process control of mechanical components manufacturing. Relationship quality now stands out as a pivotal issue in relationship marketing (Storbacka et al. 1994; Holmlund 1997).

Improving quality has a few positive side effects, too. First, it relieves some of the pressure from a customer service department. With better product quality and fewer complaints, a company can redirect resources away from things like repairs, returns, and replacements, and invest them in the emotional Es, the product itself, or the bottom line. Second, more than any other product dimension, quality can have a profound impact on equity. Reliably constructed products and impeccably delivered services result in a strong halo effect for a brand. Poor quality is a fast ticket to a negative brand reputation and stories of customer disappointment that may never go away.

Besides, when companies embraced Total Quality Management (TQM) to improve quality and reduce costs, it became necessary to involve suppliers and customers in implementing the programme at all levels of the value chain. This needed close working relationships with customers, suppliers and other members of the marketing infrastructure. Thus, several companies, such as Motorola, IBM, Xerox, Ford, AT&T, Toyota, etc. formed partnering relationships with suppliers and customers in order to practice TQM. Other programmes such as Just-in-Time (JIT) supply and Material Resource Planning (MRP) also made use of the interdependent relationships between suppliers and customers (Frazier et al. 1988).

Furthermore, managing satisfaction, being one of the primary tasks of the organization, once the product, processes and people are standardized to customers' requirements, is achieved automatically without much ado. The formal regulations/institutions of the marketing equilibrium are partly found in the law based relationship having one of the objectives as Quality Assurance through prevention. Law for preventive purposes, during negotiations and contracts, is used to avoid potential misunderstanding and install a certain protection against a party that does not fulfil its obligations. The work of legislators and lawyers then is quality assurance. As in all quality work, prevention should be maximized (Gummesson 2002).

There are international standards of quality and generally, the customers are aware of those standards. But before going for discussions on those standards, it is important to understand the essence of quality, what is its significance and meaning in business, and how organizations view customer satisfaction through quality.

Think of durable goods that last longer, smaller commodities that do not break apart, food that tastes better, or services that are more reliable. Quality can also be extended to packaging (making it extra durable or innovative) or to service (making it excellent or offering an extended warranty).

According to Kotler (1999), 'Monitor your current customers' level of satisfaction with your product and services; don't take them for granted; do something special for them from time to time; encourage their feedback.' Some companies also view this satisfaction as their greatest asset. For example, Roberto C. Goitzueta, ex-President of Coca-Cola, had mentioned, consumer satisfaction is Coca-Cola's "most valuable asset (but) the truly successful company creates something beyond simple satisfaction. It creates an emotional bond between its products and consumers." Indeed, coke is the most well known and admired brand both in the United Sates and outside. The best-managed companies use quality to do what they do best—create value. These companies devote significant efforts towards achieving the highest levels of quality. Each of the best-managed companies possesses process quality certifications.

'Zero defect' in relationship quality is a very common term, which, in other words, is interpreted as zero defection in relationship. This may not always be true as it differs from case to case. The important point is: Aim for the best, if not better—but never make it a bad experience and here shows up the factor of quality which is the holy grail of client relationship. The power equation, which enables the partner to drive the client, can only work out if the client perceives and is convinced of enormous value in every deliverable of the partner.

At ICICI Bank, increasing customer grievances and service lapses made the management set up an Organizational Excellence Group (OEG) in 2002. Its aim was to engage in building, sustaining and institutionalizing quality in the bank by facilitating development of skills and capabilities in various quality frameworks.

In the industrial products sectors, L&T's Heavy Engineering Division is focusing on improving manufacturing operations through automation, Six Sigma and IT enabled re-engineering. Tata Steel's focus on quality led it to launch the ASPIRE programme, incorporating initiatives such as TOC (Theory of Constraints), TQM (Total Quality Management) and technology. Unrelenting commitment to quality, which is a defining feature of each of the best-managed companies, creates that all-important value among stakeholders—trust (*Business Today 2008*).

# QUALITY SYSTEM

A quality system is the means by which an organization manages its quality aspects in a systematic, organized manner and provides a framework for planning, implementing, and assessing work performed by an organization and for carrying out required quality assurance and quality control activities (www.epa.gov). It encompasses a variety of technical and administrative elements, including:

- Policies and objectives
- Organizational authority
- Responsibilities
- Accountability
- Procedures and practices.

In other words, it lays down the complete procedure to ensure highest standards of quality meeting the business goals. From consumers' viewpoint, products compete on the following eight dimensions of quality (Garvin 1987):

1. *Performance.* The best example is the sound and picture colour of the TV or cruising speed and comfort of riding a car. With these factors, the performance of the product is assessed.

2. *Features.* Free drinks while on board in the aircraft—these are the bells and whistles of product and services.

3. *Reliability.* This dimension reflects the probability of a product malfunctioning or failing within a specified time period. The measures are: (a) mean time to first failure (b) mean time between failures and (c) failure rate/unit time. This is important, as downtime and maintenance have become expensive.

4. *Conformance.* Degree to which a product's design and operating characteristics meet established standard.

5. *Durability.* Amount of use one gets from the product before it deteriorates and becomes unfit for use.

6. *Serviceability.* For support services, this is the most important as it indicates the speed, courtesy, competence and ease of repair in case of any fault or breakdown.

7. *Aesthetics.* The factors leading to product aesthetics are, for example, the look and feel of the product, its taste and smell, packaging, etc. The ambiance of the reception of a hotel leaves an impression of its quality.

8. *Perceived quality.* Images, advertising, and brand names lead to perceived quality of the product.

Aesthetics and perceived quality are the subjective dimensions highlighting how the product is viewed by its users/consumers.

The components of quality system are the ones that make a product to occupy the topmost slot in the customer's mind. The punchline of 'Head and Shoulders' shampoo was "You never get a second chance to make a first impression". Impeccable service, too, cannot save you if you do not deliver a good quality product each and every time. This is true especially for restaurants, where the food served has to be of the same quality across the customers. Here, quality is conveyed via word-of-mouth. One bad experience is enough to ruin the impression forever.

Another good way of assuring customers value with respect to the quality of the product is through endorsement by external agency or celebrity brand ambassador. For instance, DishTV endorsement by Shah Rukh Khan persuading the viewers not to remain complacent with poor picture quality, Colgate Toothpaste continually reminds the customer that it is endorsed by IDA, the Indian Dental Association and it is the brand trusted by most dentists, HLL gets customers to talk about their "Pond's Age Miracle" range of cosmetics and Dove soaps in their television ads, to endorse the quality of their products. That is also the psyche behind prompting a customer to try out the product. If a Vim Bar is a good dishwashing bar for Mrs. X, a housewife, it has to be good for you too! If others say that your product is good, it is going to be good!

## DIFFERENCE BETWEEN QUALITY CONTROL (QC) AND QUALITY ASSURANCE (QA)

Quality control is an activity that verifies whether or not the product produced meets standards. Quality assurance is an activity that establishes and evaluates the processes that produce the products. If there is no process, there is no role for QA. Assurance would determine the need for, and acquire or help install methodologies and processes. Once installed, QA would measure them to find weaknesses in the process and then correct those weaknesses to continually improve the process. The following statements help differentiate QC from QA (CSQA CBOK 2006):

### Quality Control

➤ Relates to specific product or service.

➤ Verifies whether particular attributes exist, or do not exist, in a specific product or service.

➤ Identifies defects for the primary purpose of correcting defects.

➤ Is the responsibility of the worker.

**Quality Assurance**

> ➤ Helps establish processes.

> ➤ Sets up measurement programmes to evaluate processes.

> ➤ Identifies weaknesses in processes and improves them.

> ➤ Is a management responsibility, frequently performed by a staff function.

> ➤ Evaluates whether or not quality control is working for the primary purpose of determining whether or not there is a weakness in the process.

> ➤ Is concerned with all of the products that will ever be produced by a process.

> ➤ Is sometimes called quality control over quality control because it evaluates whether quality is working.

In the marketing context, quality control is more of product or production-centric activity whereas quality assurance is a customer-centric activity that involves cross-functional team across the organization.

# TOTAL QUALITY MANAGEMENT (TQM)

The TQM or Total Quality Management concept can be of use in quality assurance in services. The principal elements of TQM are: people, appropriate technology, quality control through problems solving tools/ procedures and a resolve for continuous improvement. All these elements are equally applicable to quality assurance in service marketing.

There is a Japanese word named **'Kiesin'** that has no equivalent in English language. It roughly translates as **'constant and never ending improvement'**. The Japanese philosophy is to do a thousand things one per cent better not one thing a thousand per cent better. This means that everybody that works with organization—every supplier/partner, every employee, and every manager, everybody in the customer satisfaction value chain—should be constantly required to innovate to improve things and suggest ideas. Coming up with the ways to improve how things are done, should almost become a mandatory part of any job.

Quality management in its modern form fortifies the relationship between operations management and marketing management. In Figure 8.1, the characteristic features of the internal and external orientations are listed with TQM as the bridge. The quality concept has succeeded in doing what marketing has strived to do for decades—unite production orientation with marketing orientation. From having been based on technical data and 'rational' and 'objective' statistics, quality management has moved to regard customer perceptions and the value for the customer as its touchstone (Gummesson 2002).

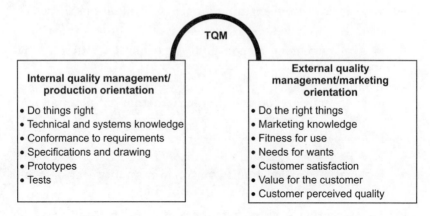

**Figure 8.1** **Total quality management forging a relationship between marketing functions and technical funictions.**

*Source:* Prof Evert Gummesson (2002), adopted with permission.

The external part of TQM starts with customer perceived quality and market needs. The most comprehensive contributions are found in the marketing literature, often expressed in terms of needs, need satisfaction, and satisfied—and today even delighted—customers. Within market research, there is a long tradition of studying consumer satisfaction, consumer behaviour, organizational buying behaviour and customer relationships to brands, but this literature almost exclusively deals with goods, not services. The quality concept from service is above all externally oriented, towards customers and revenue.

Three techniques to design models for facilitating the technology-market link will be described here. The first is quality function deployment (QFD). Its purpose is to unite customer requirements with the properties of goods and services. It is also referred to as 'the quality house' after the house-like form of its matrices. What customers want is found out in detail and linked with how the supplier shall achieve this technically in order to design an offering. The connections between the whats and hows are established and analyzed, technical conflicts between properties are listed, and finally a specification is established (Hauser & Clausing 1988).

The second technique is based on process descriptions of services in service encounters concentrating on the interaction between the customer and the provider's front staff, and the interactions between front staff, support staff and management. The vantage point is the 'customer's path', that is, the customer's way of moving from considering to buy a service and to getting the service produced and delivered (Gummesson 1993).

The third technique consists of the quality awards and certifications, which demand integration between technical aspects, internal aspects and customers. The quality standard ISO 9000 with its recent and more demanding upgrade ISO 9000:2000 requires, among other things, a clear documentation of processes. In the subsequent sections, ISO and other standards have been discussed.

# BUSINESS QUALITY STANDARDS

## International Organization for Standardization

The ISO 9000 series of documents was created by the International Organization for Standardization to set international requirements for quality management systems. Now adopted by over 80 countries, use of the series of standards has become commonplace in the business world.

The previous ISO 9000 family of standards contained some 20 standards and documents. In the year 2000, ISO 9000 family of standards consists of four primary standards supported by a number of technical reports. The four primary standards are:

- ISO 9000: Quality Management Systems—Concepts and Vocabulary
- ISO 9001: Quality Management Systems—Requirements
- ISO 9004: Quality Management Systems—Guidelines
- ISO 10011: Guidelines for Auditing Quality Systems

## ISO 9000 and ISO 14000 in Plain Language

Both "ISO 9000" and "ISO 14000" consist of standards and guidelines relating to management systems, and related supporting standards on terminology and specific tools, such as auditing (the process of checking that the management system conforms to the standard).

*ISO 9000* is primarily concerned with "quality management". In a plain language, the standardized definition of "quality" in ISO 9000 refers to all those features of a product (or service) which are required by the customer. "Quality management" means what the organization does to ensure that its products conform to the customer's requirements.

*ISO 14000* is primarily concerned with "environmental management", meaning what the organization does to minimize harmful effects on the environment caused by its activities.

Both ISO 9000 and ISO 14000 concern the way an organization goes about its work, and not directly the result of this work. In other words, they both concern processes, and not products—at least, not directly. Nevertheless, the way in which the organization manages its processes is obviously going to affect its final product. In the case of ISO

9000, it is going to affect whether or not everything has been done to ensure that the product meets the customer's requirements. In the case of ISO 14000, it is going to affect whether or not everything has been done to ensure a product will have the least harmful impact on the environment, either during production or disposal, either by pollution or by depleting natural resources.

## DNV Standard

Established in 1864, DNV is an independent foundation with the objective of safeguarding life, property and the environment and is a leading international provider of services for managing risk. DNV is a knowledge-based organization with prime assets as creativity, knowledge and expertise of the employees. DNV is an international company with 300 offices in 100 different countries. Headquartered in Oslo, Norway, DNV's global network is linked by efficient information technology to create value for customers in a coherent and consistent manner worldwide.

The following are DNV's areas of operations:

- Quality Management System certification to ISO 9001 and other industry specific quality standards.
- Environmental Management System certification to ISO 14001 and EMAS.
- Occupational Health and Safety Management System certification to OHSAS 18001. Safeguard the health and safety of employees and the environment.
- Information Security Management System certification to BS 7799 (now ISO 27002). Protect company information and reduce leaks.
- eBusiness Management System certification. Convey trust and confidence that your website is a safe place to shop.
- Combined Certification of two or more management systems. Benefit from a comprehensive approach to certify all your management systems in one go.

DNV offers certification worldwide, and holds a wide range of national accreditation. With global network of local resources, DNV provides one with the certification most suitable to the needs, type of business, and company location.

## BVQI—Bureau Veritas Quality International

BVQI certified its first client in India, Sundaram Fasteners back in 1990. Companies certified by BQVI are some of India's most quality conscious organizations like Alstom, BHEL, Larsen & Toubro, Lucas TVS and Sundaram Group. Such organizations dominate not just in India, but in the international market as well.

BVQI runs with a team of over 37 highly trained and competent auditors all over India, who bring with them the experience, technical skills and knowledge they have acquired while working for the parent organization, Bureau Veritas, a large multinational organization involved in inspection, classification and certification in the marine, industrial, construction, aeronautical, food, textile and chemical fields.

## National Institute of Standards and Technology (NIST)— Malcolm Baldrige National Quality Award

Founded in 1901, NIST is a non-regulatory federal agency within the US. NIST's mission is to develop and promote measurement, standards, and technology to enhance productivity, facilitate trade, and improve the quality of life. NIST carries out its mission in four cooperative programmes, one of which is the Malcolm Baldrige National Quality Programme. This programme promotes performance excellence among US manufacturers, service companies, educational institutions, and health care providers; conducts outreach programmes and manages the annual Malcolm Baldrige National Quality Award, which recognizes performance excellence and quality achievement.

The award is named after Malcolm Baldrige, who served as Secretary of Commerce from 1981 until his tragic death in an accident in 1987. His managerial excellence contributed to long-term improvement in efficiency and effectiveness of government. The Baldrige performance excellence criteria are a framework that any organization can use to improve overall performance. Seven categories make up the award criteria:

- **Leadership**. How senior executives guide the organization and how the organization addresses its responsibilities to the public and practices good citizenship.

- **Strategic planning**. How the organization sets strategic directions and how it determines key action plans.

- **Customer and market focus**. How the organization determines requirements and expectations of customers and markets.

- **Information and analysis**. Examines the management, effective use, and analysis of data and information to support key organization processes and the organization's performance management system.

- **Human resource focus**. How the organization enables its workforce to develop its full potential and how the workforce is aligned with the organization's objectives.

- **Process management**. Examines aspects of how key production/delivery and support processes are designed, managed, and improved.

- **Business results**. Examines the organization's performance and improvement in its key business areas: customer satisfaction, financial and marketplace performance, human resources, supplier and partner performance, and operational performance. The category also examines how the organization performs relative to competitors.

The criteria are used by thousands of organizations of all kinds for self-assessment and training and as a tool to develop performance and business processes. Approximately 2 million copies have been distributed since the first edition in 1988, and heavy reproduction and electronic access multiply that number many times.

For many organizations, using the criteria results in better employee relations, higher productivity, greater customer satisfaction, increased market share, and improved profitability. According to a report by the Conference Board, a business membership organization, "A majority of large US firms have used the criteria of the Malcolm Baldrige National Quality Award for self-improvement, and the evidence suggests a long-term link between use of the Baldrige criteria and improved business performance."

## Difference between Baldrige Award and ISO 9000

The purpose, content, and focus of the Baldrige Award and ISO 9000 are very different. The Baldrige Award was created by Congress in 1987 to enhance US competitiveness. The award program promotes quality awareness, recognizes quality achievements of US organizations, and provides a vehicle for sharing successful strategies. The Baldrige Award criteria focus on results and continuous improvement. They provide a framework for designing, implementing, and assessing a process for managing all business operations.

ISO 9000 is a series of five international standards published in 1987 by the International Organization for Standardization (ISO), Geneva, Switzerland. Companies can use the standards to help determine what is needed to maintain an efficient quality conformance system. For example, the standards describe the need for an effective quality system, for ensuring that measuring and testing equipment is calibrated regularly and for maintaining an adequate record-keeping system.

## Baldrige Award and Japan's Deming Award

The basic purposes of both awards are the same: to promote recognition of quality achievements and to raise awareness of the importance and techniques of quality improvement. However, the Baldrige award:

- Focuses more on results and service,
- Relies upon the involvement of many different professional and trade groups,
- Provides special credits for innovative approaches to quality,
- Includes a strong customer and human resource focus, and
- Stresses the importance of sharing information.

During the 1980s, the management consultant **W. Edwards Deming** (1900–1993) gained international fame as a scathing critic of American business and a tireless advocate for the methods of statistical quality control. The source of Deming's reputation—and his very credibility as a tutor to American industry—was the widespread belief that he was personally responsible for introducing quality control to Japan in the early 1950s. According to the popular wisdom, Deming took to Japanese industry the powerful concept of quality, a concept which found more fertile soil across the Pacific than at home, which spurred the post-war renaissance of Japanese manufacturing, and led ultimately to the collapse of America's dominance in international competitiveness. As "the genius who revitalized Japanese industry," Deming was revered in the United States as the very incarnation of Yankee know-how and a prophet of management acumen (Tsutsui 1996).

# INDIAN STANDARDS—BUREAU OF INDIAN STANDARDS

## Purpose

During the pre-independence period, standardization activity was sporadic and confined mainly to a few government purchasing organizations. However, immediately after independence, economic development through coordinated utilization of resources was called for and the government recognized the role for standardization in gearing industry to competitive efficiency and quality production. The Indian Standards Institution (ISI) was, therefore, set up in 1947 as a registered society, under a Government of India resolution.

The Indian Standards Institution gave the nation the standards it needed for nationalization, orderly industrial and commercial growth, quality production and competitive efficiency. However, in 1986, the government recognized the need for strengthening this National Standards Body due to fast changing socio-economic scenario and according it a statutory status. Thus came the Bureau of Indian Standards Act 1986 and on 1 April, 1987, newly formed BIS took over staff assets, liabilities and functions of erstwhile ISI. Through this change over, the Government envisaged building of the climate of quality culture and consciousness and greater participation of consumers in formulation and implementation of National Standards.

## Objectives

The following were the objectives of BIS:

- Harmonious development of standardization, marking and quality certification
- To provide new thrust to standardization and quality control
- To evolve a national strategy for according recognition to standards and integrating them with growth and development of production and exports

## Quality Policy

The Bureau of Indian Standards (BIS), the National Standards Body of India, resolves to be the leader in all matters concerning Standardization, Certification and Quality. In order to attain this, the Bureau would strive to:

- Provide efficient timely service.
- Satisfy the customers' needs for quality of goods and services.
- Work and act in such a way that each task, performed as individuals or as corporate entity, leads to excellence and enhances the credibility and image of the organization.

BIS would achieve these objectives by working in close cooperation with all concerned organizations and by adopting appropriate management systems, motivating and ensuring active participation of all the employees.

## QUALITY STANDARDS IN INFORMATION TECHNOLOGY INDUSTRY

In IT Industry, ISO standards are also used. But there are other standards, which have found more prominence. Those are namely:

1. SEI-CMM levels
2. Tick IT
3. Six sigma

## Capability Maturity Model (SEI CMM)

Back in the past in the US, there was a need to distinguish between the competing bids for software development. As such, the US Department of Defence (DOD) was the world's largest software customer, spending over $30 billion per year on software during the 1980s. During that period, the software projects constantly slipped into crisis situations and were frequently responsible for delays and overruns. To address this crisis, on a national scale, the DOD funded the development of the Software Engineering Institute (SEI), a federally funded research and development centre at Carnegie Mellon University in Pittsburgh, PA. Incidentally, Watts Humphrey and his colleagues in IBM developed original concept for Software Process Maturity framework in the early 1980s. In his 27 years at IBM, Humphrey noticed that the quality of a software product was directly related to the quality of the process used to develop it. Having observed the success of total quality management in other parts of industry, Humphrey wanted to instal a Shewart-Deming improvement cycle (Plan-Do-Check-Act) into a software organization as a way to continually improve its development processes. He brought this concept to the SEI in 1986 where he founded its software process program. The process maturity framework evolved into Capability Maturity Model. In 1991, CMM version I was released.

The Capability Maturity Model for Software describes the principles and practices underlying software process maturity and is intended to help software organizations improve the maturity of their software processes in terms of an evolutionary path from ad hoc, chaotic processes to mature, disciplined software processes. The CMM is organized into five maturity levels:

1. **Initial.** The software process is characterized as ad hoc, and occasionally even chaotic. Few processes are defined, and success depends on individual effort and heroics.

2. **Repeatable.** Basic project management processes are established to track cost, schedule, and functionality. The necessary process discipline is in place to repeat earlier successes on projects with similar applications.

3. **Defined.** The software process for both management and engineering activities is documented, standardized, and integrated into a standard software process for the organization. All projects use an approved, tailored version of the organization's standard software process for developing and maintaining software.

4. **Managed.** Detailed measures of the software process and product quality are collected. Both the software process and products are quantitatively understood and controlled.

5. **Optimizing.** Continuous process improvement is enabled by quantitative feedback from the process and from piloting innovative ideas and technologies.

Predictability, effectiveness, and control of an organization's software processes are believed to improve as the organization moves up these five levels. While not rigorous, the empirical evidence to date supports this belief.

## People Capability Maturity Model

The People Capability Maturity Model (People CMM) is a framework that helps organizations to successfully address their critical people issues. Based on the best current practices in fields such as human resources, knowledge management, and organizational development, the People CMM guides organizations in improving their processes for managing and developing their workforces. The People CMM helps organizations characterize the maturity of their workforce practices, establish a programme of continuous workforce development, set priorities for improvement actions, integrate workforce development with process improvement, and establish a culture of excellence. Since its release in 1995, thousands of copies of the People CMM have been distributed, and it is used worldwide by organizations, small and large.

The People CMM was first published in 1995 by Bill Curtis, and has successfully guided workforce improvement programmes in companies. The People CMM consists of five maturity levels that establish successive foundations for continuously improving individual competencies, developing effective teams, motivating improved performance, and shaping the workforce the organization needs to accomplish its future business plans.

### Structure of People CMM

The People CMM document describes the key practices that constitute each of its maturity levels, and information on how to apply it in guiding organizational improvements. It describes an organization's capability for developing its workforce at each maturity level. It describes how the People CMM can be applied as a standard for assessing workforce practices and as a guide in planning and implementing improvement activities.

PCMM leads to organizational practices that contribute to maturing workforce capability. These practices describe an evolutionary improvement path from ad hoc, inconsistently performed practices, to a mature, disciplined development of workforce competencies, just as the CMM for Software describes an evolutionary improvement path for the software processes within an organization.

### Integrated CMM—CMMi

In 1997, the Federal Aviation Administration (FAA) developed the FAA integrated Capability Maturity Model to guide improvement of its engineering, management, and acquisition processes in an integrated, effective, and efficient way.

### CMMi Level Summary

Like CMM, the following levels of CMMi are defined and explained here:

**Level 0: Incomplete**
There is no goal and there are no generic practices at this level

**Level 1: Initial**
Goal: The process achieves the goals of the process area.
Generic practices: Identify work scope, perform the process

**Level 2: Managed**
Goal: The process is institutionalized as a managed (planned and tracked) process.
Generic practices: Establish organizational policy, document the process, plan the process, provide adequate resources, assign responsibility, ensure skill and knowledge, establish work product requirements, consistently use and manage the process, manage work products, objectively assess process compliance, objectively verify work products, measure process performance, review performance with higher-level management, take corrective action, coordinate with participants and stakeholders.

**Level 3: Defined**
Goal: The process is institutionalized as a defined process.
Generic practices: Standardize the process, establish and use a defined process, improve processes.

**Level 4: Quantitatively managed**
Goal: The process is institutionalized as a quantitatively managed process.
Generic practice: Stabilize process performance.

**Level 5: Optimizing**
Goal: The process is institutionalized as an optimizing process.
Generic practice: Pursue process optimization.

## *Difference between ISO and CMM*

ISO 9001 is part of the ISO 9000 family of standards. The new ISO 9001:2000 designation comprises the ISO 9001, ISO 9002, and ISO 9003 standards. ISO 9001 targets the manufacturing process, although it also includes manufacturing services and software development.

CMM offers a model for judging the software processes of an organization and for identifying key practices required to increase the maturity of these processes. It establishes a successful means for modelling, defining, and measuring the maturity of the processes used by software professionals.

ISO started out as a European standard. If the company did not have ISO 9000 certification, it was not permitted to bid on a proposal, in particular, many European telecom companies require ISO 9000. ISO

9000 shows customers and potential customers that you have a basic quality system in place to produce a consistent product.

The United States, however, is not as stringent about ISO certification. While some American companies require ISO certification, many others do not; it is found that CMM has higher preference than ISO in the IT companies. US companies use ISO in order to sell in Europe.

## TickIT

TickIT is about improving the quality of software and its application. Almost every business depends on the correct manipulation of information by computer systems. Software is the key to the successful operation of these systems—poor quality software can severely affect efficiency and competitiveness. To meet customers' quality expectations, software suppliers, including in-house developers, need to define and implement a quality system, which covers all the essential business processes in the product life cycle. TickIT guides the developer to achieve this objective within the framework of ISO 9000.

### *Objectives*

An important purpose of TickIT, which is supported by the UK and Swedish software industries, has been to stimulate software system developers to think about:

- What quality really is in the context of the processes of software development.
- How quality may be achieved.
- How quality management systems may be continuously improved.

Although certification of compliance to ISO 9001 is a contractual requirement for software suppliers in certain market areas, it should be a by-product of the more fundamental aims of quality achievement and improvement, and the delivery of customer satisfaction.

With regard to certification itself, the objectives are to:

- Improve market confidence in third party quality management system certification through accredited certification bodies for the software sector.
- Improve professional practice amongst quality management system auditors in the software sector.
- Publish authoritative guidance material (the TickIT Guide) for all stakeholders.

# Six Sigma—Historical Background

If practice makes perfect, then practicing the precepts of Six Sigma leads to virtual perfection. Six Sigma is a concept for now and well into the next century: It focuses on the customer, not the product! And while philosopher's debate and cynics doubt whether anything can be truly flawless, the Six Sigma programme developed by Motorola Corporation is winning converts because it works. It brings about a cultural change in a company, a paradigm shift towards expecting the highest quality, which then drives a passion for continuous improvement by all players.

The Six Sigma concept matured during 1985 to 1986, growing out of various quality initiatives at Motorola. The company's Land Mobile Products Sector first established a single matrix for quality known as total defects per unit, which dramatically changed the way management measured and compared quality improvement rates for all divisions. Because all operations used the same measurement, the goal for defect reduction could be uniformly applied to all activities. For the first time, everyone spoke the same language.

In 1986, Bill Smith, a senior engineer and scientist at Motorola, introduced the concept of Six Sigma to standardize the way defects are counted. Six Sigma provided Motorola the key to addressing quality concerns throughout the organization, from manufacturing to support functions. The application of Six Sigma also contributed to Motorola winning the Malcolm Baldrige National Quality award in 1988.

Since then, the impact of the Six Sigma process on improving business performance has been dramatic and well documented by other leading global organizations, such as General Electric, Allied Signal, and Citibank. That is why investing in Six Sigma programmes is increasingly considered a mission-critical best practice, even among mid-sized and smaller firms. Today, Motorola continues to implement Six Sigma throughout its own enterprise, and extends the benefit of its Six Sigma expertise to other organizations worldwide through Motorola University.

Six Sigma is a measure of quality that strives for near perfection. The Six Sigma process uses data and rigorous statistical analysis to identify "defects" in a process or product, reduce variability, and achieve as close to zero defects as possible. Using a universal measurement scale, Six Sigma defines and estimates the opportunities for error and calculates defects in the same way every time, thus offering a means for measuring improvement. In fact, Six Sigma takes its name from the Greek letter "sigma," which is used in statistics to indicate standard deviation and "Sigma" is a statistical expression indicating how much variation there is in a product.

The Six Sigma methodology incorporates this data and statistical analysis into a project-based workflow that allows businesses to make intelligent decisions about where and how to incorporate improvements.

A performance level of Six Sigma equates to 3.4 defects per 1 million opportunities—not perfect, but pretty close. A defect is defined as anything that causes customer dissatisfaction. A unit is any unit of work—an hour of labour or a circuit board, or even a keystroke.

For example, the number of units processed is multiplied by the number of potential defects per unit; the answer is divided into the number of defects actually occurring and then is multiplied by 1 million. The result is the number of defects per million operations. A conversion table translates that number into sigma:

6 sigma = 3.4 defects per million

5 sigma = 230 defects per million

4 sigma = 6,210 defects per million

3 sigma = 66,800 defects per million

2 sigma = 308,000 defects per million

1 sigma = 690,000 defects per million

Six Sigma is achieved through a process, which is tracked using simple tools such as the Pareto chart. This bar chart is widely used as a data display tool in Six Sigma because it identifies which problems occur with the greatest frequency or incur the highest cost. Hence, it provides direct evidence about what should be corrected first. Italian economist Vilfredo Pareto, after whom the chart is named, theorized that 20 per cent of possible causes are responsible for 80 per cent of any problem.

## Six Sigma Successes

After examining how various financial companies pursue quality, Citibank, the international financial division of Citicorp, undertook the Six Sigma method in the spring of 1997. Its goal: to reduce defects within its various divisions by a factor of 10 during the first three years. The corporation already has seen reductions ranging from five to 10 times.

"Six Sigma appealed because it's pretty straightforward," comments James Bailey, Citicorp's executive vice-president and corporate quality officer. "It also seemed like a programe that would involve everyone." Previously, various businesses and divisions within Citibank had tried different quality programmes, but the company had never instituted a universal quality language or method.

"Continuous improvement is our goal," maintains Bailey. "We started training senior management in April 1997, and so far we've trained about 2,000 people around the world." Besides the defect reductions, the company has recorded a decreased response time for credit card applications and fewer errors in customer statements.

Six Sigma requires more than a monetary investment, Erwin points out. "You must have a plan, necessary resources, the commitment of everyone and uncompromising matrixes," he says. "Then you set aggressive goals along the path and hold people accountable."

## The DMAIC Model

At the heart of Six Sigma is a systematic method for analyzing and improving business process called DMAIC. The DMAIC model includes five phases:

- Define opportunities
- Measure performance
- Analyze opportunity
- Improve performance
- Control performance

Six Sigma, a highly disciplined methodology and practice that provides the tools to achieve consistent, high-performance, results from the products and processes. By increasing performance and decreasing variation, Six Sigma allows organizations to make customer-focused, data-driven decisions that ultimately yield a reduction in product defects, increased profits and employee morale, and high-quality products—a win-win situation for everyone involved.

| *Case Study:* General Electric (GE) Initiatives in Six Sigma |
| --- |

GE began moving towards a focus on quality in the late '80s. Work-Out®, the start of the journey, opened the culture to ideas from everyone, everywhere, decimated the bureaucracy and made boundaryless behaviour a reflexive, natural part of GE culture, thereby creating the learning environment that led to Six Sigma. Now, Six Sigma, in turn, is embedding quality thinking—process thinking—across every level and in every operation of GE around the globe.

Globalization and instant access to information, products and services have changed the way customers conduct business—old business models no longer work. Today's competitive environment leaves no room for error. There is an urgency to delight customers and relentlessly look for new ways to exceed their expectations. This is why Six Sigma Quality has become a part of GE's culture.

First, what it is not. It is not a secret society, a slogan or a cliché. Six Sigma is a highly disciplined process that helps us focus on developing and delivering near-perfect products and services. Why "Sigma"? The word is a statistical term that measures how far a given process deviates from perfection.

The central idea behind Six Sigma is that if you can measure how many "defects" you have in a process, you can systematically figure out how to eliminate them and get as close to "zero defects" as possible. Six Sigma has changed the DNA of GE—it is now the way we work—in everything we do and in every product we design.

The three major components of Six Sigma are:

- Customer
- Process
- People

### Customer—Delighting Customers

Customers are the centre of GE's universe: they define quality. They expect performance, reliability, competitive prices, on-time delivery, service, clear and correct transaction processing and more. In every attribute that influences customer perception, we know that just being good is not enough. Delighting our customers is a necessity. Because if we don't do it, someone else will!

### Process—Outside-in Thinking

Quality requires us to look at our business from the customer's perspective, not ours. In other words, we must look at our processes from the outside-in. By understanding the transaction lifecycle from the customer's needs and processes, we can discover what they are seeing and feeling. With this knowledge, we can identify areas where we can add significant value or improvement from their perspective.

### People—Leadership Commitment

People create results. Involving all employees is essential to GE's quality approach. GE is committed to providing opportunities and incentives for employees to focus their talents and energies on satisfying customers.

All GE employees are trained in the strategy, statistical tools and techniques of Six Sigma quality. Training courses are offered at various levels:

- Quality overview seminars: Basic Six Sigma awareness.
- Team training: Basic tool introduction to equip employees to participate on Six Sigma teams.
- Master black belt, black belt and green belt training: In-depth quality training that includes high-level statistical tools, basic quality control tools, change acceleration process and flow technology tools.
- Design for Six Sigma (DFSS) training: Prepares teams for the use of statistical tools to design it right the first time.

Quality is the responsibility of every employee. Every employee must be involved, motivated and knowledgeable if we are to succeed.

*Source:*  www.ge.com/sixsigma/makingcustomers.html

# CONCLUSION

To manage customer satisfaction, the deliverables in terms of product and services should meet excellent quality standards. Earlier, industries used to operate on the concept of quality control that was but a post-audit of quality of products and services. Now there is a shift in the paradigm, and each organization has its quality policy that lays down the standard and guidelines all the activities in the business process should adhere to while developing product and services for customers. There are various standards being followed by the organizations worldwide. One of the widely accepted standards of quality across the industry is International Standard Organization or ISO. ISO standards are applicable for manufacturing and service as well as IT industries. Apart from ISO, there are other standards of quality practised by the IT industries, such as SEI CMM and CMMi, Tick IT, and Six Sigma. These standards have considerable significance with regard to software export.

> **Keywords:** *Quality system, Client-partner business cycle, Quality standards, Malcolm Baldrige, ISO, BIS, SEI CMM, PCMM, Six Sigma, Tick IT, DNV, BVQ.*

## *Exercises*

1. Describe the relevance of quality of product and services in Relationship Marketing.

2. Describe eight dimensions of quality with respect to a washing machine.

3. List the quality standards used in the manufacturing industry. Can Six Sigma be used in the manufacturing industry? What are its touch points in Relationship Marketing?

4. What do you understand by 'Total Quality Management'? How does it act as a bridge between marketing and technical functions?

5. What is the purpose of quality function deployment? Describe with suitable examples.

6. What do you understand by the term 'zero defect' in relationship quality?

Fill in the blanks:

7. _____ is a management or oversight function; it deals with setting policy and running an administrative system of management controls that cover planning, implementation, and review of data collection activities and the use of data in decision making. _____ is a technical function that includes all the scientific precautions, such as calibrations and duplications that are needed to acquire data of known and adequate quality.

8. The five maturity levels of CMMi are as follows:
   (a)_____, (b)_____, (c)_____,
   (d)_____, and (e)_____.

9. The Six Sigma concept matured during _____ to _____,
   growing out of various quality initiatives at _____.

10. Six Sigma allows organizations to make _____,
    _____ decisions that ultimately yield a _____ in product
    defects, increased _____ and employee _____, and
    _____ products leading to a _____ situation for
    everyone involved.

## References

Frazier, G.L., Spekman, R.E. and O'Neal, C.R., 1988. Just-in-Time Exchange Relationship in Industrial Markets, *Journal of Marketing*, Vol. 52, October, pp. 52–67.

Garvin, D.A., 1987. *Total Quality Management*, IFS (Publications)/ Springer-Verlag, UK.

*Guide to the CSQA Common Body of Knowledge*, Version 6.1, 2006, Quality Assurance Institute, Orlando.

Gummesson, Evert., 1987. Using Internal Marketing to Develop a New Culture—the case of Ericsson Quality, *Journal of Business and Industrial Marketing*, Vol. 2, No. 3 (Summer), Georgia, Atlanta, pp. 23–28.

Gummesson, Evert., 1993. *Quality Management in Service Organizations*, New York: ISQA, 1993.

Gummesson, Evert., 2002. Marketing in the New Economy, *Journal of Relationship Marketing*, Vol. I, No. 1, The Haworth Press, Pennsylvania, pp. 41–44.

*Ibid.,* p. 131.

Holmlund, Maria, 1997. Perceived Quality in Business Relationship, Doctoral Thesis no. 66, The Swedish School of Economics and Business Administration, Helsinki.

Hauser, J.R. and Clausing, D., 1988. The House of Quality. *Harvard Business Review*, No. 3, May–June.

India's Best Managed Companies, A Business Today–Ernst & Young Study, *Business Today*, March 2008, p. 58.

Kotler, Philip, 1999. Kotler on Marketing: How to create, Win and Dominate Markets, 'Acquiring, Retaining and Growing Customers', *The Free Press*, New York.

Lyon, Barbara, 2008. Customer Service Quality Falling Short of Rising Expectations Across the Globe, Accenture Study.

Storbacka, Kaj, Strandvik, Tore and Grönroos, Christian, 1994. Managing Customer Relationships for Profit: The Dynamics of Relationship Quality. *Service Industry Management*, Vol. 5, No. 5, pp. 21–38.

Tsutsui, William M., 1996. Creating Quality: The Japanese QC Movement and the Legend of W. Edwards Deming, White Paper, Session 162, Association of Asian Studies.

Websites:

www.epa.gov/quality

www.ge.com/sixsigma/makingcustomers.html

www.tickit.org

www.iso.org

www.bvi.org

www.aasianst.org/absts/1996abst/japan/j162.htm

www.sei.cmu.edu/cmm-p/

www.bis.org.on

mu.motorola.com/history.shtml

www.nist.gov/public_affairs/factsheet/baldfaqs.htm

www.faa.gov/aio/common/documents/iCMM/FAAiCMMv2.htm

www.zdnet.com.au/builder/manage/business/story/

www.accenture.com

# CHAPTER 9

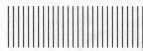

# Customer Loyalty

## INTRODUCTION

We are living in a time when loyalty does not seem to have much of an impact on any of the groups—investors, employees and customers. US Corporations lose half their customers in five years, half their employees in four and half their investors in less than one. In India's BPO Sector, the scenario is not as intense as in the US—but it is true there is a decline in the loyalty feeling. The attrition rate in IT companies in India is good enough to keep the HR preoccupied round the clock to explore unique incentives to attract and retain talents. Has the time really come to abandon hope and enter the world of fast-money speculators, job-surfing careerists, disposable employees, and fickle customers? Even more important, can companies succeed by embracing opportunism as a way of life? The answer is no, not if they care about long-term growth and profits. Businesses that concentrate on finding and keeping good customers, productive employees, and supportive investors continue to generate superior results. Loyalty is by no means dead. It remains one of the great engines of business success. In fact, the principles of loyalty —and the business strategy we call loyalty-based management—are alive and well at the heart of every company with an enduring record of high productivity, solid profits and steady expansion. This chapter discusses different dimensions of loyalty in business transactions as well as some of the approaches of its measurements.

# HISTORICAL FRAMEWORK OF CUSTOMER LOYALTY

During the late 1980s through the early 1990s, executives believed that reducing costs was the answer to increased global competition. Businesses downsized, de-layered, re-engineered and restructured and flattened their organizations. While this was probably necessary to cut the fat out of organizations, it was not a formula for long-term success. Today, the focus is on delivering more value and increasing customer loyalty.

Loyalty means customers returning again and again to do business with you, even when you do not have the best product (note the difference between good product and best product), the lowest price, or fastest delivery. How do you explain such seemingly irrational behaviour? Good relationship is the sum total of all customer interactions over time to deliver value above and beyond what customers pay for. The total value proposition is the combination of what a customer receives and how they receive it. Companies that do both well invariably become industry leaders in market share and profitability.

Frederick Reichheld developed the importance of building customer commitment in his 1996 book *The Loyalty Effect*. He focused on the cost of customer defection and set the stage for the problem by claiming "many major corporations now lose and have to replace half their customers in five years [...]". The term *customer loyalty* is used to describe the behaviour of repeat customers, as well as those that offer good ratings, reviews, or testimonials. Some customers do a particular company a great service by offering favorable word of mouth publicity regarding a product, telling friends and family, thus adding them to the number of loyal customers. However, customer loyalty includes much more. It is a process, a programme, or a group of programmes geared towards keeping a client happy so that he will provide more business.

Using examples from financial service companies, advertising agencies, and manufacturing firms, Reichheld claimed that even small improvements in customer retention can as much as double company profits. This is because:

- It costs less to serve long-term customers.
- Loyal customers will pay a price
- Loyal customers will generate word-of-mouth referrals to other prospective customers.

Given that customers buy value, it makes perfect sense that improving the customer experience will increase loyalty, which means better customer retention. Reichheld in *The Loyalty Effect* reported that a multi-industry study found raising customer retention rates by five percentage points could increase the value of an average customer by 25 to 100 per cent. Of course, the trick is finding and keeping the right customers. Reichheld advises that loyalty-focused companies should attract and keep customers in one of the following groups:

- Customers that are inherently more loyal because they prefer long-term relationships.

- Customers that are more profitable because they spend more, require less service and pay their bills on time.

- Customers that find your products and services more valuable and a better fit than those of your competitors.

Before discussing the strategic models, we shall paraphrase various definitions proposed by the thought leaders.

## DEFINITIONS OF LOYALTY

Customer loyalty is the "behavioural outcome of a customer's preference for a particular brand or a selection of similar brands, over a period of time that is the result of an evaluative decision making process" (Jacoby & Kyner 1973). Dick & Basu (1994) define customer loyalty as 'the strength of the relationship between an individual's relative attitude and their repeat patronage". The customer attitude toward potential moderators of repeat patronage relationship is based on social norms and situational factors. Oliver (1997) summarized the word of customer loyalty to include cognition, affect and behavioural intentions. This recognized the key issues of commitment and preference and consistency while acknowledging the dynamic nature of marketing environment and situational influences. Building on the three-phase model (Jacoby & Kyner 1974) and later work by Dick & Basu (1994), Oliver (1997) identified a fourth loyalty phase. The first three phases lead to a deeply held commitment, predicting that the consumer become loyal first in a cognitive (knowing and perceiving) sense, then later in affective (emotional) sense and third a conative (desire to act) manner. These three states may not be in synchrony or linearly related. The fourth phase is related to action loyalty, which Oliver suggests the missing link. This involves commitment to overcome situational constraints that may intervene in a purchase decision (Gilmore 2003).

However, when Reinartz and Kumar (2002) redefined loyalty, their results supported the loyalty effect. Their original definition specified only the behavioural dimension of loyalty—that is, repeat purchase within a specified time frame. They included customer attitudes such as whether they felt loyal to the company, whether they were satisfied and whether they had an interest in switching brands or service providers, the loyalty effect emerged. They called this "thought and deed loyalty." For example, grocery customers who had strong thought and deed loyalty were 120 per cent more profitable than those that were repeat purchasers. In the corporate services company, thought and deed customers were 50 per cent more profitable than customers defined just by purchase frequency or recency. The facilitating effect of loyalty on achieving the marketing outcomes of higher market share and premium pricing was confirmed in another recent study.

Chaudhuri and Holbrook (2001) measured consumers' attitudes towards 107 brands in 41 different product categories (86). They differentiated between a consumer's purchase loyalty ("I will buy this brand again") and attitudinal loyalty ("I am committed to this brand"). These attitudes were averaged over the survey responses to develop brand level data (that is, the brand was the unit of observation). The results showed that purchase loyalty was positively related to market share but not relative price of brand. That is, brands that had higher ratings on statements such as "I will buy this brand again" had higher market shares but were not the premium price brand in the market. Conversely, attitudinal loyalty was related to relative price but not market share. That is, brands that had higher ratings on statements such as "I am committed to this brand" were able to charge higher prices than those brands that received lower ratings on attitudinal loyalty.

Loyalty is the result of building past positive experiences with an individual. However, the following models are considered with respect to understanding the essence of loyalty.

## LOYALTY MODELS—SERVICE QUALITY MODEL

A model by Kay Storbacka, Tore Strandvik, and Christian Grönroos (1994), the service quality model, is more detailed than the basic loyalty business model, but arrives at the same conclusion. In it, customer satisfaction is first based on a recent experience of the product or service. This assessment depends on prior expectations of overall quality compared to the actual performance received. If the recent experience exceeds prior expectations, customer satisfaction is likely to be high. Customer satisfaction can also be high even with mediocre performance quality if the customer's expectations are low, or if the performance provides value (that is, it is priced low to reflect the mediocre quality). Likewise, a customer can be dissatisfied with the service encounter and still perceive the overall quality to be good. This occurs when a quality service is priced very high and the transaction provides little value.

The service quality model then looks at the strength of the business relationship; it proposes that this strength is determined by the level of satisfaction with recent experience, overall perceptions of quality, customer commitment to the relationship, and bonds between the parties. Customers are said to have a "zone of tolerance" corresponding to a range of service quality between "barely adequate" and "exceptional." A single disappointing experience may not significantly reduce the strength of the business relationship if the customer's overall perceptions of quality remains high, if switching costs are high, if there are few satisfactory alternatives, if they are committed to the relationship, and if there are bonds keeping them in the relationship. The existence of these bonds acts as an exit barrier. There are several types of bonds, including: legal bonds (contracts), technological bonds (shared technology), economic bonds (dependence), knowledge bonds, social bonds, cultural or ethnic bonds, ideological bonds, psychological bonds, geographical bonds, time bonds, and planning bonds.

This model then examines the link between relationship strength and customer loyalty. Customer loyalty is determined by three factors: relationship strength, perceived alternatives and critical episodes. The relationship can terminate if:

- Customer moves away from the company's service area.
- Customer no longer has a need for the company's products or services.
- More suitable alternative providers become available.
- Relationship strength has weakened.
- Company handles a critical episode poorly.
- Unexplainable change of price of the service provided.

The final link in the model is the effect of customer loyalty on profitability. The fundamental assumption of all the loyalty models is that keeping existing customers is less expensive than acquiring new ones. It is claimed by Reichheld and Sasser (1990) that a 5 per cent improvement in customer retention can cause an increase in profitability between 25 per cent and 85 per cent (in terms of net present value) depending upon the industry. However, Carrol and Reichheld (1992) dispute these calculations, claiming that they result from faulty cross-sectional analysis.

## EXPANDED MODEL

Schlesinger and Heskett (1991) added employee loyalty to the basic customer loyalty model. They developed the concepts of "cycle of success" and "cycle of failure". In the cycle of success, an investment in your employees' ability to provide superior service to customers can be seen as a virtuous circle. Effort spent in selecting and training employees and creating a corporate culture in which they are empowered can lead to increased employee satisfaction and employee competence. This is likely to result in superior service delivery and customer satisfaction. This, in turn, will create customer loyalty, improved sales levels, and higher profit margins. Some of these profits can be reinvested in employee development thereby initiating another iteration of a virtuous cycle (Figure 9.1).

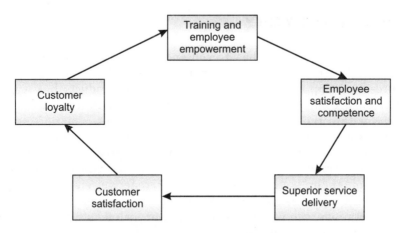

**Figure 9.1  Virtuous circle.**

*Source:*  Prof. Leonard Schlesinger & James Heskett (1991), adopted with permission.

Fredrick Reichheld (1996) expanded the loyalty business model beyond customers and employees. He looked at the benefits of obtaining the loyalty of suppliers, employees, bankers, customers, distributors, shareholders, and the board of directors.

In any case, organizations need to thoughtfully measure if actions actually move a customer to buy more, select other items from your company and tell their friends about you. In Janice Anderson's views, the keys to building loyal relationships are:

- **Target:** Identify customer segments specially the high-value customers. Determine the products and services they want.
- **Focus:** What is your value? What are you really selling? It is not just a list of products. You need to focus on what you are trying to be to your customers.
- **Service:** Consistent service is great service. If you consistently deliver on promises you are fulfilling your brand
- **Cost:** Keeping costs low is part of the business model in almost every industry now. If you keep operating as if you are getting Rs. 2 crores a trade when you are getting Rs. 2 lakhs a trade, you are going out of business fast (Source: www.businessweek.com).

When you are running a small boutique, you have the institutional memory to do all this intuitively. Larger and more sophisticated operations need a set of Relationship Management tools to take real-time care of customers and consistently provide a personalized experience.

# MEASURING LOYALTY

Virtually, every company has to contend with scarce resources (time, money, staff, and facilities) as an everyday fact of life. How those resources are applied to improving services and products has a major impact on a company's capacity to retain customers and increase its position within the marketplace.

Satisfaction is less reliable as an indicator of customer loyalty because it often tends to be more passive than proactive. Product and service performance measurements can also provide little direction because of their tactical, general, and reactive viewpoint. Many measurement systems fail because they do not consider customer needs and expectations, the value of a customer, or include staff as customers in the measurement process.

Proactive loyalty and retention measurement systems overcome these deficiencies and recognize that customers make trade-offs in every service, product, and supplier selection decision. As a result, customer needs, expectations, problems, and complaints must be identified and assessed on a systematic, continuous basis.

## Quantifying Customer Loyalty—Examples from Loyalty Builder

US Based company named Loyalty Builder presents its product for measuring Customer loyalty. Most business people know it costs more to acquire a new customer than to serve one already on the books. They also understand that loyalty is affected by product quality, customer service, price, and other brand values. But most business people continue to struggle with how to retain customers. Part of the problem lies in the fact that many businesses fail to understand the critical difference between loyalty and satisfaction. Satisfaction, while a component of loyalty, is transitory and ephemeral, while loyalty is stable and tends to endure. Satisfaction is transaction-based and product-focused while loyalty is relationship-based and focused on the overall customer experience. But even business people who "get it" find that customer loyalty has been impossible to measure reliably.

## The Measurement Problem

Business, today, has no quantitative way to measure whether or not the time, money and energy spent on "loyalty" and CRM programmes are really making a difference. It's true that each customer's revenue can be measured. But measuring only revenue hides important factors. For example, it tends to undervalue the smaller but loyal customer who makes regular purchases, and overvalue the customer who makes a single large purchase. Nor does measuring revenue suggest what a customer is likely to buy next, or indicate which customers' loyalty is growing and which is declining. And qualitative surveys of customer intent are unreliable because customers usually don't act as they say they will. If a company cannot measure loyalty reliably, it can spend forever on advertising, marketing, and customer service, and never know which effort, if any, is affecting loyalty.

## Loyalty Builder to the Rescue

Most companies know when they have a loyalty problem. But there is no way they can understand the problem, and devise a strategy for fixing it, without a reliable way to measure customers' loyalty behaviour. Loyalty Builder has developed new, proprietary mathematical models that for the first time enable any company with transaction data to quantify loyalty. The Loyalty Builder's methodology examines the totality of a customer's purchase experience. It enables the marketer to rank customers by loyalty score, and segment them into groups based on their behavior as customers. These rankings reveal trends, uncover purchase patterns, and help predict customer revenue. Loyalty Builder's data can also identify the customers whose loyalty is slipping and customers whose loyalty is growing. And, equally important, the data can help suggest the most effective way to serve the customer who shows up in the showroom, website, or call centre.

## Behaviour-based Segmentation

The notion of personalization and 1:1 marketing has become very popular as the technology to support has matured. It is no surprise that any customer appreciates being treated individually and likes the fact that you know his name and have a history of his purchases at hand. But while customers are each individual, they usually have common needs. In fact, if you are not able to segment your customer base in terms of characteristics they share, you have virtually no hope of creating a marketing plan you can afford and execute. Segmentation has traditionally meant dividing a population into separate "buckets" based on demographics and attitudes. Demographic segmentation works when customer needs are based on age, income, zip code, marital status, or other easy-to-obtain objective data. Attitudinal segmentation works only when people act on the intentions they express, which happens all too rarely. In contrast, Loyalty Builder's methodology segments customers by behaviour and generates quantitative measures of loyalty based on that behaviour.

This approach has important advantages. First, it is based on actual purchases, rather than on age, zip code, gender, ethnicity or other demographic. Second, it is based on data that already exists in order entry or accounting systems, so results are available in real time. Third, every transaction adds to the data set so learning is continuous. Fourth, the parameters of loyalty in the Loyalty Builder's model (size of purchase, frequency, recency, duration, product categories) create a holistic picture of the customer and produce segmentation that illuminates behaviour patterns, which may otherwise go unnoticed.

### A Tool for the New Economy

Today, business rightly values relationship over product. It has never been more important then to understand customers and act accordingly. The new economy dictates that a company must market, measure, analyze, and adjust in an accelerated time frame. "Street smarts" certainly have a role in this volatile environment. But quantitative knowledge of customer behaviour gives a company huge competitive advantage.

### Limitations

The ideas that coalesced and became the Loyalty Builders model are the result of the many missteps we made as we used common sense and accepted wisdom in the search for loyalty measurement. As we began to measure customer behaviour, the following facts surfaced:

- No single loyalty parameter (amount of purchase, frequency, etc.) is a reliable measure of a particular customer's loyalty.

- Segmentation based on attitudes does not reflect or predict customer behaviour.

- Segmentation based on quantitative loyalty measurement reveals startling and previously unrecognized patterns of customer behaviour, as well as uniquely useful information about the company as whole.

*Source:*   Quantifying Customer Loyalty, http://www.loyaltybuilders.com/ howtouse.html.

# HOW TO CHOOSE A LOYALTY INDEX—THE MATHEMATICS OF LOYALTY ANALYSIS

There is, in general, a high degree of correlation within a purchase data set. Long-time accounts tend to make more purchases, spend more, and buy a wider selection of products, and place orders more frequently. Accordingly, any of the traditional loyalty indices—total amount, number of purchases, number of products, retention (duration of customer relationship), or recency (time since last purchase)—will tend to identify the most favourable and least favourable customers. However, these indices will not, in general, provide a consistent evaluation of the middle 75–80 per cent of a firm's customers. A tool with a broader scope than provided by the traditional measures should evaluate the customers who are not at the extremes on the traditional measurements. Such a tool will, for example, recognize that a customer with a consistent record of small purchases may be more loyal, hence with a greater potential for the firm, than one who made a single large purchase last quarter.

A successful loyalty measurement tool must, when faced with an inconsistent purchase record, be capable of a meaningful tradeoff that recognizes the important relationships within a firm's customer purchase records.

## Characteristics of a Loyalty Measurement Tool

There are many alternative measurement indices that can stratify a customer population into groups related to what we can call "customer loyalty". Given this situation, what characteristics of a customer segmentation might we use to evaluate or, hopefully, to select the "best" of the available measurements? If we assign customers to loyalty groups based on their ranking by a "loyalty index", then we expect that:

1. The groups agree with the traditional measures in the statistical sense or, individually, in the "all else equal" sense. Statistically, those groups ranking higher on the loyalty scale should, in the aggregate, have means and medians that agree with the usual concept of customer loyalty. That is, customers in these higher groups have made more purchases, spent more money, purchased a wider variety of products, etc.

2. The loyalty index should be comparable over time. It is important that the loyalty segmentation provide a base for the assessment of future performance—both at the level of the individual customer and the aggregated customer base.

3. The loyalty index should decline due to inactivity. Regardless of a customer's previous loyalty ranking, an atypical prolonged period of account inactivity should be recognized as a possible decline in loyalty that suggests the need for remedial action.

## LOYALTY ANALYSIS

Most companies know that it costs from five to ten times more to acquire a new customer than it does to make another sale to an existing customer, so a lot of lip service is given to the idea of building customer loyalty. It is complex and difficult for an organization to measure customer loyalty in numeric terms and have no effective way to see if they are even moving in a direction to increase it. They are usually limited to looking at total revenues or revenues from individual customers. The very best and unfavourable customers are easy to spot, but quantifying the loyalty and value of the huge majority of customers has previously been impossible.

Typically, managers have two main objectives. First, they want to understand the behaviour of their customers as a whole, so they can sharpen their messages and refine their product offerings. Second, they want to drill down to the account level to produce groups of customers to whom they can direct specific marketing campaigns. There are eight techniques they use to meet those objectives.

1. **Find out who are the best, middling and poor customers, and why.** Loyalty analysis reveals the most loyal customers, helps you retain them and build a more profitable relationship with them.

2. **Use an early warning system that reveals eroding customer loyalty.** Purchase deficit is another measure available to clients. This parameter reports the number of purchases that a customer should have made since his previous purchase.

3. **Reveal purchase patterns that can help build loyalty.** Methods to track the progression of purchases through a company's product set.

4. **Discover marketing opportunities and spend marketing money more efficiently.** Combining the measures described above enables a company to more intelligently target its marketing promotions. The probability of next purchase is calculated for each customer. Based on their previous purchase, the company knows what their most likely next purchase will be, and when it will likely happen. The company can tailor a promotion to groups of customers, bundling not only what they expect that customer to buy, but also other products that the company wants to sell at an attractive combination price. At just the time the customer is thinking of making a purchase, they can receive an offer for just what they were thinking of buying, along with some other products. This practice puts more items in the 'shopping cart'.

5. **Spotlight your best dealers and support them more effectively.** Whenever individual customers are uniquely associated with particular dealers, customer scoring can be used as the basis for dealer evaluation.

6. **Predict future revenues more accurately.** Besides measuring the probability of future purchases of a customer, a loyalty analysis can be the basis for forecasting company revenues. Customer growth is measured, as are contributions from both new and existing accounts. When this data is combined with probability of future purchase, and summed over the entire customer population, it is possible to predict future revenue from both new and existing accounts for one or two purchasing cycles into the future.

Of course, major external events such as wars or large stock market fluctuations can disrupt these predictions, but in a 'business as usual' environment, the loyalty analysis data may be the best predictor a company has. It is especially valuable when forecasting revenues for mature product lines moving towards the end of their life cycle or for newer products in a rapid growth phase.

7. **Get a sharper picture of your company.** Just as dealer organizations can be gauged on their associated customers, the company can also get a picture of itself and its customer population as a whole.

8. **Manage customer relationships to build loyalty.** Ultimately, customer loyalty is about the relationship between a customer and the company, and this relationship needs to be nurtured and managed. All customer-facing employees should have detailed data about the customer with whom they are interacting. Whether it is a sales person wondering whether or not to offer a discount or a customer service representative solving a customer problem, knowing the value of the customer should be a part of the decision making process.

Proactive relationship management absolutely requires loyalty analysis. Good customers know they are good customers, and like to be recognized. Identifying them through a loyalty analysis and then contacting them to thank them for their business is very important. Making a relationship call to high-value customers whose purchase deficit is growing can rescue that customer before a competitor steps in.

## SOCIAL BONDING AND LOYALTY

Based on study and observations, there is a strong relation between the social bonding and loyalty (Cann & Sumrall 1997). The social bond is an outgrowth of personal relationships that develop between the parties involved from both the buyer and the seller organization. The better the "personal fit" between the parties, the stronger the social bonds. Wilson (1995) explains that studies that have been done on social bonding reveal that if a strong personal relationship develops between the buyer and the seller, both parties will be more interested in continuing the relationship.

Social bonding can be seen as a mechanism that adds value to the relationship between the salesperson and the customer by addressing the needs that the customer has for a close personal relationship with the service provider. Social bonding between the salesperson and the customer can be an important precursor to customer loyalty and can produce a more indulgent and forgiving atmosphere between the seller and the buyer, especially when there is differentiation between competitive services (Berry 1995). Wilson (1995) talks about how added value is a shared creation between the buyer and the seller that serves to enhance the relationship so that they each can gain more benefit from the relationship. Wilson (1995) further advises that value creation brings the two closer and that the outcome of this closeness is that the parties are less able to find a suitable replacement. Bonds are part of the process of relationship development (Wilson 1995). Social bonding, in particular, is discussed as an important step in relationship building (Berry 1995; Dwyer et al. 1987; Sheth 1994; Wilson 1995). As Berry (1995) states, "relationship marketers capitalize on the reality that many service encounters also are social encounters". Focus groups that were undertaken by Berry & Parasuraman (1991) emphasize the importance of a strong personal link between the vendor firm and the customer, and the desire that many customers have to form close relationships with the service provider.

A close social relationship between the customer and the salesperson should lead to more open, two-way communication, which, according to Morgan & Hunt (1994) and Wilson (1995), will lead to more trust between the two parties involved. Trust can lead to commitment, which can lead to long-term cooperation between the two parties involved in a relationship (Morgan and Hunt 1994). Social bonding is an important antecedent to trust in the service encounter. Trust is in the area of services marketing (Berry & Parasuraman 1991). As an example, selling activities that involve building high-profile credibility have been found to characterize sales jobs in health care services. Trust will lead to greater commitment in the relationship. Wilson (1995) suggests that once commitment is reached, there is a strong desire on the part of both parties to continue the relationship for the long-term.

## ATTACHMENT AND LOYALTY

The attachment a customer feels toward a product is presented in two dimensions representing (a) the degree of preference (the extent of the customer's conviction about the product or service) and (b) the degree of perceived product differentiation (how significantly the customer distinguishes the product or service from alternatives). If these two factors are cross-classified, four attachment possibilities emerge, as shown in Figure 9.2 (Griffin 2002).

| Product differentiation | | | |
|---|---|---|---|
| | | No | Yes |
| Buyer preference | Strong | Low attachment | Highest attachment |
| | Weak | Lowest attachment | High attachment |

**Figure 9.2  Four relative attachments.**

*Source:*   Jill Griffin (2002), adopted with permission.

1. **Highest attachment and strong preference.**   Attachment is highest when the customer has a strong preference for a product or service and clearly differentiates it from the competitive products. This kind of attachment is found in the professional services rendered by some specialist. For example, some doctors may be staying quite far away from the patient's locations—but because of the quality of treatment and behaviour of the doctor—the patient takes the pains to visit the doctor in spite of paying more in the travel cost and similar physicians available nearby.

2. **High attachment and weak preference.**   An attitude that is weak towards a company's product or service but differentiates it from competitors' offerings translates to high attachment and may in turn contribute to loyalty. An individual's attitude toward his auto mechanic may be mildly positive but much more so compared with that toward other mechanics. Therefore, these circumstances contribute to loyalty.

3. **Low attachment and strong preference.**   In contrast, a strong preference combined with the little perceived differentiation may lead to multiproduct loyalty. This is particularly true in fast-moving consumer goods. Sometimes a consumer chooses Coke, other times Pepsi. The customer has a set of two or three favourites, and situational factors such as shelf positioning and in-store promotion drive a particular purchase.

4. **Low attachment and weak preference.**   Finally, a positive but weak preference associated with no perceived differentiation leads to lowest attachment, with repeat purchase less frequent and varying from one occasion to the next. For example, a homeowner who has her carpets cleaned sporadically may consult the telephone directory and call a different carpet cleaning service each time.

# FOUR TYPES OF LOYALTY

After attachment, the second factor that determines a customer's loyalty towards a product or service is repeat patronage. Four distinct types of loyalty emerge if low and high attachments are cross-classified with high and low repeat purchase patterns (Figure 9.3) (Griffin 2002).

| Repeat purchase | | | |
|---|---|---|---|
| | | High | Low |
| Relative attachment | High | Premium loyalty | Latent loyalty |
| | Low | Inertia loyalty | No loyalty |

**Figure 9.3   Types of loyalty.**

*Source:*   Jill Griffin (2002), adopted with permission.

## No Loyalty

For varying reasons, some customers do not develop loyalty to certain products or services. For example, a manager of travel agency who goes anywhere in town to get a haircut as long it cost him less than Rs. 15 and he does not have to wait. He rarely goes to the same place two consecutive times. To him, a haircut is a haircut regardless of where he receives it. His low attachment toward haircut services combined with low repeat patronage signifies an absence of loyalty. Generally speaking, businesses should avoid targeting no-loyalty buyers because they will never be loyal customers. The challenge is to avoid targeting as many of these people as possible in favour of customers whose loyalty can be developed.

## Inertia Loyalty

A low level of attachment coupled with high repeat purchase produces inertia loyalty. This customer buys out of habit. It is the "because we have always used it" or "because it is convenient" type of purchase. In other words, non-attitudinal situational factors are the primary reason for buying. This buyer feels some degree of satisfaction with the company, or at least no real dissatisfaction. This loyalty is most typical for frequently bought products. It is exemplified by the customer who does dry cleaning from the store down the block and shoe repair from the nearby cobbler. This buyer is ripe for a competitor's product that can demonstrate a visible benefit to the switching. It is possible to turn inertia loyalty into a higher form of loyalty by activity courting the customer and increasing the positive differentiation he or she perceives about your product or service compared to others available. For example, a dry cleaner that offers home delivery or extended hours could make its customers aware of this fact as a way to differentiate its service quality from that of its competitors.

## Latent Loyalty

A high relative attitude combined with low repeat purchase signifies latent loyalty. If a customer has latent loyalty, situational effects rather than attitudinal influences determine repeat purchase. I am a big fan of Chinese food and have a favourite Chinese restaurant in my neighbourhood. My wife, however, is less fond of Chinese food, and so despite my loyalty I patronize the Chinese restaurant only on occasion and we go instead to restaurants that we both enjoy. By understanding situational factors that contribute to latent loyalty, a business can devise a strategy to combat them. The Chinese restaurant might consider adding a few North Indian dishes to its menu to pacify reluctant patrons who favour such food habits.

## Premium Loyalty

Premium loyalty, the most leverageable of the four types, prevails when a high level of attachment and repeat patronage coexist. This is the preferred type of loyalty for all customers of any business. At the highest level of preference, people are proud of discovering and using the product and take pleasure in sharing their knowledge with peers and family. This is particularly observed in the service industry, for example, among the mobile service users. Airtel users tell their friends about the benefits of lifetime free incoming calls, credit limits, etc. These customers become vocal advocates for the product or service and constantly refer others to it.

## RELATIONSHIP LADDER OF CUSTOMER LOYALTY

Relationship marketers speak of the "relationship ladder of customer loyalty". It groups types of customers according to their level of loyalty. The ladder's first rung consists of "prospects", that is, people that have not purchased yet but are likely to in the future. This is followed by the successive rungs of "customer", "client", "supporter", "advocate", and "partner" (Chapter 7—Temperament of Business Relations, Client Categories). The relationship marketer's objective is to "help" customers get as high up the ladder as possible. This usually involves providing more personalized service and providing service quality that exceeds expectations at each step.

# RETENTION STRATEGY

Customer retention efforts involve considerations such as the following:

1. **Customer valuation.** Gordon (1999) describes how to value customers and categorize them according to their financial and strategic value so that companies can decide where to invest for deeper relationships and which relationships need to be served differently or even terminated.

2. **Customer retention measurement.** Dawkins and Reichheld (1990) calculated a company's "customer retention rate". This is simply the percentage of customers at the beginning of the year that is still customers by the end of the year. In accordance with this statistic, an increase in retention rate from 80 per cent to 90 per cent is associated with a doubling of the average life of a customer relationship from 5 to 10 years. This ratio can be used to make comparisons between products, between market segments, and over time.

3. **Determine reasons for defection.** Look for the root causes, not mere symptoms. This involves probing for details when talking to former customers. Other techniques include the analysis of customers' complaints and competitive benchmarking.

4. **Develop and implement a corrective plan.** This could involve actions to improve employee practices, using benchmarking to determine best corrective practices, visible endorsement of top management, adjustments to the company's reward and recognition systems, and the use of "recovery teams" to eliminate the causes of defections.

A technique to calculate the value to a firm of a sustained customer relationship has been developed. This calculation is typically called customer lifetime value (discussed in Chapter 4).

Retention strategies also build barriers to customer switching. This can be done by product bundling (combining several products or services into one "package" and offering them at a single price), cross-selling (selling related products to current customers), cross-promotions (giving discounts or other promotional incentives to purchasers of related products), loyalty programmes (giving incentives for frequent purchases), increasing switching costs (adding termination costs, such as mortgage termination fees), and integrating computer systems of multiple organizations (primarily in industrial marketing).

Many relationship marketers use a team-based approach. The rationale is that the more points of contact between the organization and customer, the stronger will be the bond, and the more secure the relationship.

# LOYALTY PROGRAMMES IMPLEMENTATION

In order to implement the loyalty programme in an organization, one needs to follow five steps listed here (Sahoo & Vyas 2007):

## Step 1: Observation

This is the stage of accumulating all information possible about customers from many disparate sources, including:

- Purchase records and history
- Costs associated with servicing each customer
- Demographic information
- The share-of-wallet or of spending that each customer gives.

The demographic information varies from B2B to B2C as described in Table 9.1.

**Table 9.1** Useful Demographic Information

| *For* B2B *customers* | *For* B2C *customers* |
|---|---|
| Customer's years in business | Customer's age |
| Customer's gross revenue | Customer's household income |
| Number of locations a customer has | Customer's household size |
| Customer's Dun & Bradstreet rating | Customer's activity (has he/she contacted our customer service centre? complained? complimented? Give us a referral?) |
| Customer's decision making process: centralized/decentralized | Customer's receptivity to deals/offers |
| Number of executives involved in customer's decision making unit | Customer's geodemographic code |
| How we interact with customer: impersonally/personally | Customer's credit rating |
| Number of competitors with whom customer does business | |
| Customer's complaint/returns activity | |

*Source:* Sahoo and Vyas, (2007), adopted with permission.

## Step 2: Calculating Inertial CLV (customer lifetime value)

Determining contribution to profit from each customer (projected purchases minus anticipated costs of serving). It is called inertial CLV as the figure represents the current status. At the same time, it provides a convenient metric by which customers can be segmented for the next step.

## Step 3: Selection

After using the inertial CLV, the customers are differentiated into three customer types like the desired customers, breakeven customers and costly customers. The ratio of costly customer should not be more than 15 per cent in the organization; otherwise, it may affect the bottom line. So, there has to be a good balance between these three categories of customers to maintain a good financial health of the organization.

## Step 4: Prioritization

In this stage, the company's should divide each of these three customer groups into pairs like *low share of spending* and *high share of spending* and determine which customers to focus for developmental efforts after knowing their share of current spending. The strategies followed in this stage are:

- Improving the company's financial gains by reducing servicing cost for *low-share costly customers* and moving them to the status of *low-share break-even customers*.

- Improving financial condition of the company by increasing *low-share costly customer's* share of spending and by advancing them to *high-share break-even customers*.

- Improving financial condition of the company by controlling offers for *low-share break-even customers*, reducing servicing costs and moving them to *low-share desired customers*.

- Improving financial condition of the company by increasing share-of-spending and controlling servicing cost of *low-share break-even customers* and advancing them to *high-share desired customers*.

- Improving financial condition of the company by increasing the share of spending of *low-share desired customers* and evolving them into *high-share desired customers*.

- Divest the *low-share costly customers* and *low-share break-even customers* whose purchasing behaviour cannot be improved.

## Step 5: Leveraging

In leveraging, each strategy requires moving as many customers as possible from one status to another, but still there are some leveraging tools, which must be taken into consideration like brand equity, value equity, relationship equity and satisfaction. Attitudes of customers towards brand, its communications, its associations with community events, etc. constitute brand equity. Similarly, perceptions about quality, price and convenience constitute value equity. Various types of loyalty programmes comprise relationship equity and satisfaction with the brand make up satisfaction—these are the leveraging tools. The company needs to find the deficits vis-a-vis its competitor to determine how to leverage each of the equity in its favour (Keiningham et al. 2006).

## LOYALTY APPROACH—PHARMACEUTICAL INDUSTRY

The concept in the context of pharmaceutical industry has a twixt since the customer (the doctor) is not the actual consumer (the patient) of the product (Lal 2000). Thus, there are ethical issues involved in rewarding points in return for prescriptions. One cannot have a reward programme based on redemption of these points.

One approach would be to set the whole programme based on the classification into which the doctor falls. Thus, the lowest rung would be restricted to the basic activities. The number and level of activities would increase as the importance of the doctor grows. A branded programme can be started for the most important doctors. It is important that it is clearly defined at the onset what will be the objective of the programme and, more importantly, convey the exclusivity of the programme. The doctor has to be made to realize that he is the 'chosen one'. All activities and inputs should only reinforce this communication. The success of such a programme hinges on masking the doctor-coveted membership to the programme. Thus a continuous monitoring is required of the returns generated from the doctor. In view of the sensitivity of the profession, such programmes should be handled with utmost care without hampering the ethics of the trade.

| *Case Study:* Loyalty Programme of Jet Airways |
| --- |

Jet Airways (India) Ltd., operating with a fleet of 85 aircraft, in its endeavour to further promote customer loyalty, relaunched its frequent flier programme under the 'Jet Privilege' name in the year 1999. Jet Privilege works on the upgraded version of the earlier programme.

According to the company, Jet Privilege (JP) consumers would not be required to pay a membership fee unlike the other loyalty programmes in the market. A passenger would start earning free JP miles (points) the moment he or she takes the first flight.

Depending on the number of miles accrued or the flights flown, the new programme offers 5 different levels of privileges:

- JP Blue
- JP Blue Plus
- JP Silver
- JP Gold
- JP Platinum

All other loyalty programmes in the market offer equal benefits to all their members. Members belonging to the higher category, for example, Silver, Gold and Platinum would be eligible for the airport lounge facilities after check-in, gold and platinum would have priorities in baggage collection on landing.

To enrich the offerings of Jet Privilege and to strengthen its competitiveness in terms of robust exit barrier and entry barriers, Jet Airways has diversified its partnership programmes with various organizations, offering multitudes of facilities to its loyal customers. Some of the examples are mentioned here.

### Airline Partner

American Airlines is the largest domestic US airline and American Eagle is the largest regional airline in the world. American Airlines and its regional airline partner American Eagle serve over 250 cities around the world, and operate more than 3,600 daily flights. In addition to their extensive domestic service, they also serve numerous destinations in Europe, Asia, the Caribbean, Canada, Mexico, and Latin America. Other airline partners are as follows: Air Canada, Lufthansa, Northwest Airlines, Qantas, South African Airways, SWISS, and Virgin Atlantic.

### Hotel Partner

Mandarin Oriental is the award-winning owner and operator of some of the world's most prestigious hotels and resorts. The Group now operates, or has under development over 10,000 rooms in 23 countries across four continents—Asia, America, Europe and Africa. Inter Continental Hotels Group, one of the world's largest hotel groups by number of rooms, owns, manages, leases and franchises almost 4,000 hotels and more than 585,000 guest rooms in nearly 100 countries around the world. Other hotel partners are as follows:

**Domestic**: ITC-Welcomegroup, Leela Palaces and Resorts, Oberoi Hotels and Resorts, Radisson Hotels and Resorts, The Park Hotels.

**International**: Hyatt Hotels and Resorts®, Hilton Family Hotels, Meritus Hotels and Resorts, Marriott International, Raffles Hotels and Resorts Shangri-La Hotels and Resorts., Swissôtel Hotels and Resorts, WORLDHOTELS.

Jet Privilege members can now earn JPMiles during their stay at the Group's 18 select premier properties across Asia, Europe and America. Jet Privilege members who are also members of the Priority Club Rewards programme can earn 500 JPMiles per eligible stay at the participating brands—InterContinental Hotels and Resorts, Crowne Plaza Hotels and Resorts, Holiday Inn Hotels and Resorts, Holiday Inn Express, Staybridge Suites, Candlewood Suites and Hotel Indigo.

### Conversion Partners

**SBI Card:** SBI Card offers Indian consumers an extensive access to a wide range of world-class, value-added payment products and services. Members can convert Power Points on SBI Platinum Card, SBI Gold Card, SBI International and SBI Domestic cards to JPMiles in the ratio of 3 Power Points for 1 JPMile, after accumulating a minimum of 400 Power Points.

**Tata Card:** Jet Privilege members holding Tata Empower Card and Tata Credit Cards can now earn JPMiles by converting their Empower Points into JPMiles in the ratio of 2 Empower Points for 1 JPMile.

Jet Privilege members would also continue to enjoy the benefit of exchanging their miles for free flights on the international network of British Airways, KLM and Northwest. Members can redeem their miles when they have earned at least 10,000 miles or have flown 10 flights.

Citibank and Master Cards are a co-brand partner for the Jet Airways Citibank Credit Card. JPMiles are also earned on spends on this card.

Jet Airways regularly analyses the customer inputs obtained from their regular 'Service Trackers'. The frequent flier members are administered a different type of 'Service Tracker' so as to have a regular update of the community of their ever increasing loyal members. The success of any loyalty programme is determined by the prevalence of single brand loyalty towards Jet Airways. All these initiatives not only improved the overall business of Jet Airways, but also enjoyed the status of most respected airlines in India.

*Source:* www.jetairways.com

---

*Case Study:* **Bharat Petroleum Corporation Ltd's Petrobonus Programme**

---

On September 29, 1999, Bharat Petroleum Corporation Limited (BPCL) launched the PetroBonus TM programme, which was the first of its kind in India. With the launch of this programme, BPCL ushered in a new age of convenience for customers. PetroBonus programme continues to offer customers the convenience and security of paying through an electronic purse, with the added opportunity to collect exciting rewards and exclusive benefits!

On enrolling into the programme, the user receives a personalized stored value smart card—the Petro Card (Figure 9.4). The user can load money at the Bharat Petroleum PetroBonus Outlets and use the Petro Card to purchase fuel, lubricants, and all items sold in the In&Out Stores. It simply means convenience, security, speedy transactions and opportunities to earn gifts and benefits when shopping at a PetroBonus outlet. And that's just the beginning—Petro Card also opens up

**Figure 9.4  BPCL's Petro Card.**

opportunities for huge savings at restaurants, stores and many other merchant establishments across the country.

PetroBonus is one of the largest in the country with about 2 million members for the fuel card program. The Petro Card is accepted across 67 cities in over 2,804 petrol pumps in India.

The Petro Card is a plastic card, with a microprocessor chip embedded on it. Membership to PetroBonus enables the users to make purchases from a PetroBonus outlet using the electronic cash stored on the microprocessor chip that is embedded on the Petro Card. It accepts stores and sends information. It can hold as much as 80 times more data than magnetic-stripe cards (a normal Credit Card). The basic benefits that these cards provide are convenience, speed and security of transaction at the PetroBonus Outlets. There is no transaction fee levied on any of the transactions with Petro Card. The Petro Card is not associated with a bank and functions independently. Thus, there is no fee attached for doing any transaction from a Petro Card. In fact, one can earn points called Petromiles for loadings as well as transacting through the Petro Card. Petromiles are the points earned when making a transaction through the Petro Card. One earns Petromiles when one loads money on Petro Card as well as when one buys using the Petro Card.

Each time using the Petro Card to make payments, the user would earn Loyalty Points called Petromiles, which can be redeemed for Gifts and Rewards. The Loyalty Points are stored on the card, which also has advanced security features.

Along with Reward Points, it offers other benefits through its alliance partners. It rewards for all purchases at the Bharat Petroleum PetroBonus Outlets. PetroBonus offers the convenience and security of paying through electronic purse, with the added opportunity to earn valuable rewards and enjoy exclusive benefits, when you consolidate all your fuel and convenience store purchases at Bharat Petroleum's PetroBonus Outlets—currently there are 14,085 outlets for PetroBonus.

The PetroBonus membership is valid for a period of 3 years. If one continues to use Petro Card regularly, the membership will be extended at the end of this period.

*Source:* www.petrobonus.com

| *Case Study:* Tata AIG DIREM Loyalty Programme |
| --- |

DIREM and Tata AIG used a loyalty programme and its twin pillars of recognition and rewards, to motivate a sales force to measurably improve performance.

### The Background

Tata AIG General Insurance Company has a Partner Recognition Programme 'Giant Steps' for their channel members, the 'Producers'. Members earn points based on business generated. Based on performance, they are allocated different tiers with specific benefits and privileges. Tata AIG employees who interact with the Producers on behalf of the Company and are responsible for their growth are called Developers. Each Producer is linked to a single Developer who is responsible for driving his growth.

### Market Situation

An analysis of members at each tier level showed that there were some producers who were at the threshold of their respective tiers (Silver, Gold or Platinum). An opportunity was spotted to motivate them to increase sales and move up to a higher tier.

### Objective

To encourage the Producer-Developer team to boost sales and thus achieve a tier upgrade for the member Producer.

### The Challenge
- Highlight the role of the Developer as a 'coach' in his relationship with his Producers.
- Create and sustain a sense of urgency over a full quarter.

### The Target Audience
- X member Producers who are fence sitters; just short of the qualifying threshold for the next tier
- Y Developers associated with these X producers

### The Medium

Direct mailer

### Customer Insight
- **Producer:** Personalized communication with clearly defined month-on-month targets helps motivate the individual.

- **Developer:** Developers do not like to be seen just as sales drivers. They are coaches and trainers and the producers' performance is to a large extent dependent on their push and encouragement.

## Creative Idea

In keeping with the thought of the coach, the creative idea was based on the analogy of sports. Visually appealing, with a strong competitive feel and the use of motivational quotes—it proved a strong incentive for performance.

## The Campaign

The campaign was rolled out in three stages:

- Announcement mailer with personalized targets (targeted to Producers and Developers)
- Mid campaign reminders through personalized mailers (targeted to Producers only)
- Winner letters (targeted to Producers and Developers)

## Offer

For producers: Giant Step points leading to upgrades.
For developers: Cash prizes.

## Timing

This was a time-bound campaign done for a period of 3 months, i.e. from 1st July to 30th September, 2005.

## Results

1. 22 per cent of the producers successfully upgraded to higher tiers corresponding to 58 per cent of the developers who helped them achieve higher sales.
2. The producers who upgraded with the help of this campaign achieved a 22 per cent growth in Gross Premium Written.

*Source:* www.direm.com/direxion/casestudies/tata-aig.as.

---

| Case Study: Maruti Auto Card |
| --- |

## Company Background

Maruti Suzuki is one of the India's leading automobile manufacturers and the market leaders in the car segment, both in terms of volume of vehicles sold and revenue earned. Until recently, 18.28 per cent of the company was owned by the Indian government, and 54.2 per cent by

Suzuki of Japan. The Indian government held an initial public offering of 25 per cent of the company in June 2003. As of May 10, 2007, Government of India sold its complete share to Indian financial institutions. With this, Government of India no longer has stake in Maruti Udyog.

Maruti Udyog Limited (MUL) was established in February 1981, though the actual production commenced in 1983. Through 2004, Maruti has produced over 5 million vehicles. **Marutis** are sold in India and several other countries, depending upon export orders. Cars similar to Marutis (but not manufactured by Maruti Udyog) are sold by Suzuki in Pakistan and other South Asian countries.

To benefit existing and new Maruti Suzuki customers, Maruti rolled out a first of its kind 'Loyalty cum Rewards Programme' in early 2006.

Through this programme, Maruti car owners can easily earn as many as 20,000 Autopoints in four years. One Autopoint is valued at one rupee. The customer, while purchasing the next Maruti car, can use this Rs 20,000 for additional discount.

Alternatively, customers can instantly redeem the accumulated points when they get their car serviced at Maruti workshops or while purchasing a Maruti Genuine Accessory worth equivalent amount.

### Autocard Advantages

- No membership fee
- Worldwide acceptance
- Cashless transactions
- Valuable autopoints for the next car
- International ATM access

The programme is quite unique in terms of the focus on Maruti Suzuki car customers, and the technology deployed to offer flexibility to customers. The loyalty cum rewards programme will be operated through a Maruti Suzuki Autocard, which will be offered to Maruti Suzuki car owners who choose to enroll in the programme. A combination of chip based card technology, state-of-the-art Point of Sale Swipe Terminal and IT hardware has been used to make the programme user-friendly.

Maruti Suzuki partners in this initiative are Citibank, part of Citigroup, the world's largest and most diversified provider of Financial Services and Indian Oil Corporation, the largest commercial enterprise in the country and a leader in the petroleum retailing business in India. The programme rewards Maruti Suzuki car owners for all their spends at Maruti outlets, Indian Oil fuel outlets and for lifestyle spend as the Maruti Suzuki Autocard can be used as an international credit card. Besides expenditure on car maintenance, even a Sunday night meal out or a shopping trip can contribute to making the customer's next Maruti Suzuki car a whole lot cheaper.

The customer has the option to carryover the points for redemption against exchange (trade-in) of his car for a new Maruti Suzuki car. In addition to autopoints earned by customers, Maruti and its dealers will provide attractive exchange loyalty bonus based on regular servicing and age of car at the time of exchange.

### Results

Maruti Suzuki India Ltd. has created a new record by selling 764,942 vehicles in 2007–2008, the highest ever in its history, marking a 13.3 per cent growth over the previous year. However, the entry level Maruti-800, the popular people's car, recorded a dip of 12.2 per cent in its sales over 2006–2007, according to a company statement. The latest baby to roll out of the Maruti stable, Dzire, was launched and sold 5,658 units within just six days. Alto, the model currently popular among the middle-class, continued to be the country's top selling car, notching sales of 227,173 units last year. This is the second consecutive year that Alto sales have crossed the 200,000 mark.

The total Maruti sales figure of 764,942 includes export of 53,024 vehicles, again the highest since it started production in 1983 and marked a growth of 34.90 per cent in its exports.

Buoyed by these developments and terming last year as 'the best ever for the company so far', Maruti said it has strengthened its leadership in the A2 segment with Alto, Zen, WagonR, Swift models while attaining leadership in the A3 segment with Baleno, Dzire, Esteem, SX4.

*Source:* www.marutiautocard.com

## ENTRY AND EXIT BARRIER—STRATEGIES TO INTENSIFY LOYALTY

### Entry Barrier

Barriers to market entry include a number of different factors that restrict the ability of new competitors to enter and begin operating in a given industry. For example, an industry may require new entrants to make large investments in capital equipment, or existing firms may have earned strong customer loyalties that may be difficult for new entrants to overcome. The ease of entry into an industry in just one aspect of an industry analysis; the others include the power held by suppliers and buyers, the existing competitors and the nature of competition, and the degree to which similar products or services can act as substitutes for those provided by the industry. It is important for small business owners to understand all of these critical industry factors in order to compete effectively and make good strategic decisions.

Porter (1980) identified six major sources of barriers to market entry:

1. **Economies of scale.** Economies of scale occur when the unit cost of a product declines as production volume increases. When existing competitors in an industry have achieved economies of scale, it acts as a barrier by forcing new entrants to either compete on a large scale or accept a cost disadvantage in order to compete on a small scale. There are also a number of other cost advantages held by existing competitors that act as barriers to market entry when they cannot be duplicated by new entrants—such as proprietary technology, favourable locations, government subsidies, good access to raw materials, and experience and learning curves.

2. **Product differentiation.** In many markets and industries, established competitors have gained customer loyalty and brand identification through their long-standing advertising and customer service efforts. This creates a barrier to market entry by forcing new entrants to spend time and money to differentiate their products in the marketplace and overcome these loyalties.

3. **Capital requirements.** Another type of barrier to market entry occurs when new entrants are required to invest large financial resources in order to compete in an industry. For example, certain industries may require capital investments in inventories or production facilities. Capital requirements form a particularly strong barrier when the capital is required for risky investments like research and development.

4. **Switching costs.** A switching cost refers to a one-time cost that is incurred by a buyer as a result of switching from one supplier's product to another's. Some examples of switching costs include retraining employees, purchasing support equipment, enlisting technical assistance, and redesigning products. High switching costs form an effective entry barrier by forcing new entrants to provide potential customers with incentives to adopt their products.

5. **Access to channels of distribution.** In many industries, established competitors control the logical channels of distribution through long-standing relationships. In order to persuade distribution channels to accept a new product, new entrants often must provide incentives in the form of price discounts, promotions, and cooperative advertising. Such expenditures act as a barrier by reducing the profitability of new entrants.

6. **Government policy**. Government policies can limit or prevent new competitors from entering industries through licensing requirements, limits on access to raw materials, pollution standards, product testing regulations, etc.

It is important to note that barriers to market entry can change over time, as an industry matures, or as a result of strategic decisions made by existing competitors. In addition, entry barriers should never be considered insurmountable obstacles. Some small businesses are likely to possess the resources and skills that will allow them to overcome entry barriers more easily and cheaply than others. "Low entry and exit barriers reduce the risk in entering a new market, and may make the opportunity more attractive financially." (Urban and Star 1991). But "in many cases, we would be better off selecting market opportunities with high entry barriers (despite the greater risk and investment required) so that we can enjoy the advantage of fewer potential entrants."

## Exit Barrier

Building a barrier to prevent customers from leaving their relationship with you or creating an artificial cost to switch to your competition sounds pejorative. However, exit barriers and switching costs are healthy elements of any customer relationship. Indeed, best practice suggests that customer exit barriers and switching costs should be built into every element of the customer relationship. Leading businesses use the following nine exit barriers, either alone or in combination, to deliver value to the customer relationship (Roche 2005).

1. **Customer learning curve.** If a customer has taken time to learn how to work with and become familiar with you, the chances of his staying improve. Provide customers with knowledge about a particular domain, tied to your company's products and processes. eBay extensively educates its customers in the art of the auction—or at least, the auction in eBay's world.

2. **Process integration.** Becoming tightly integrated with a customer's business can make it expensive, inefficient, or painful for that customer to sever a relationship. If a home banking customer has invested the time to set up his account for online or phone-based bill payment, it will be disruptive to do this again with another bank should the customer consider switching banks for other reasons. B2B organizations can build exit barriers through shared equipment and contractual commitments like volume purchase agreements.

3. **Personalization.** Consumers expect, and respond well to, personalized marketing. Using customer-specific information to

customize the interaction can enhance the buying experience and overall relationship. Companies need to collect and analyze customer information that includes transactions, as well as interactions (e.g. click streams, buying behaviour, and preferences).

4. **Mass customization.** Marketers can prevent customers from looking elsewhere by offering the ability to customize or personalize standard products to meet unique needs. Lands' End, for example, offers mass customization of its men's and women's dress shirts—as well as chinos and blue jeans—all without having to specify every detailed measurement.

5. **Risk reduction and trust.** Safe is better than good. Marketers can build loyalty by reducing the perceived risk of a company's products or services and generating trust through accumulated service history and support. Companies that adopt this exit barrier use psychological strategies to make switching appear to be too risky, even in the face of more attractive solutions.

6. **Loyalty programmes.** Delivering incentives or benefits for frequency-of-usage or increased patronage create tangible motivation for customers to come back. Frequent flier miles have been a marketing mainstay for years. CRM technology just makes them better and easier to weave into the sales, marketing, and service processes.

7. **Brand affinity.** Marketers can build loyalty by establishing a brand's "psychic" value through positive affinity or affiliation with a community. Linking your e-commerce site to destination sites like iVillage.com and WebMD.com creates brand affinity by aggregating products and editorial content specific to a particular interest or lifestyle.

8. **Customer collaboration.** Keep the customer's attention by maintaining an ongoing, value-added dialogue with the company, supply chain partners, and/or other customers. AOL and Priceline effectively use collaboration to retain customers, even though their core services are no longer leading edge.

9. **Become a standard.** Being the only choice is still a good way to keep customers. This involves dictating industry standards, either proprietary ones in a closed environment or industry standards in an open environment. The classic example is Microsoft, which has been using this winning strategy in operating systems and browsers. Restraint-of-trade issues aside, organizations can build this exit barrier through electronic channels by supplying freeware.

## POINTS TO PONDER IN LOYALTY PROGRAMMES

The companies launching their frequent-buyer or customer loyalty programmes, suggest that these schemes are expected to achieve a variety of objectives. The most common objective for new category buyers is to entice them to buy the brand with the (best) loyalty scheme. The more common outcomes expected from programmes for existing customers are to:

- Maintain sales levels, margins and profits (a defensive outcome to protect the existing customer base).

- Increase the loyalty and potential value of existing customers (an offensive outcome to provide incremental increases in sales, margins and profits).

- Induce cross-product buying by existing customers (this may be defensive or offensive).

Usually these desired outcomes refer to specific target segments; for instance, heavy buyers, or high-net-worth customers. The underlying belief is that a small percentage of customers generate most of a company's sales, and that these customers can be "locked-in forever". The "80/20 Law" is often invoked in support of this viewpoint. The 80/20 Law says that typically about 80 per cent of revenue comes from just 20 per cent of customers. With such a skewed distribution of customers, it appears to make sense to concentrate most marketing resources on this 20 per cent. The problem with this law for loyalty programmes is that the "best" 20 per cent are not necessarily loyal buyers, especially in the sense of exclusive loyalty. There is reliable empirical evidence to suggest that many/most heavy users will be multi-brand loyal for a wide range of products and services. That is, your most profitable customers will most probably be the most profitable customers of your competitors as well (Dowling 1997).

To sum it up, achieving profitable, organic growth is never simple. Today, however, attracting and keeping profitable customer relationship seems even harder. New industry dynamics, changing customer demographics and outmoded marketing practices present considerable challenges to establishing the loyal customer relationships that are the foundations of growth. In sharp contrast with transaction marketing, the fact that a customer has bought a product does not forecast the possibility of new purchase, not even if a series of purchases have been made. A customer may repeatedly use the same supplier because of high switching costs, but without feeling committed to the supplier or wanting to enter a closer relationship. Transactions lack history and memory and they do not get sentimental. In Relationship Marketing, loyalty—especially customer loyalty—is emphasized. In the loyalty ladder, the lowest rung is the prospect who hopefully turns into a customer and a first purchase. Recurrent customers are clients' who come back and forge ahead a long-term relationship. In the next stages, the client becomes supporter and finally an advocate for the supplier (Gummesson 2002).

## CONCLUSION

The term 'customer loyalty' is used to describe the behaviour of repeat customers, as well as those that offer good ratings, reviews, or testimonials. These also include customer attitudes such as whether they feel loyal to the company, whether they are satisfied and whether they have an interest in switching brands or service providers through which the loyalty effect can emerge. In Relationship Marketing, loyalty—especially customer loyalty—is emphasized. To elaborate cross-functional relationship across loyalty, quality, customer satisfaction, various models are proposed and one such model is Service Quality Model. It is more detailed than the basic loyalty business model. In it, customer satisfaction is first based on a recent experience of the product or service. Another model considered employee loyalty to the basic customer loyalty model. They developed the concepts of "cycle of success" and "cycle of failure". In the cycle of success, an investment in the employee's ability to provide superior service to customers can be seen as a virtuous circle. There are tools for measuring loyalty and the effective tool should be able to identify a customer satisfying appropriate loyalty trend, for example, consistent record of small purchases. Because they may be more loyal, hence with a greater potential for the firm, than one who made a single large purchase in the past. Apart from this, there are eight techniques of loyalty analysis. Numeric data can be used to define loyalty index although loyalty measurement has its own limitations. There is always a social bonding and attachment related to customer loyalty. There are four relative attachments leading to four different types of loyalty, namely, No loyalty, Inertia Loyalty, Latent Loyalty and Premium Loyalty. To strengthen loyalty, organizations need to develop exit barrier through brand, customer learning curve, process integration, brand affinity, etc. which are nothing but some special values that the client enjoy from the association with the partner, and are not available elsewhere. There are organizations in India that carries out loyalty programmes to promote relationships. Still there are issues and concerns in the findings of loyalty analysis, for example, 80/20 rules for identifying and nurturing loyal customers. Future researches on the loyalty programmes need to address such areas of customer loyalty.

**Keywords:** *Loyalty index, Social bonding, Premium loyalty, Inertia loyalty, Latent loyalty.*

## Exercises

1. What is the importance of social bonding in customer relationship?

2. Give two examples of premium loyalty from your personal experience.

3. You are a channel partner of laptop computer. Over a period of last two months, you observed that three of your ten existing clients switched over to your competitor. What would be your strategy to address such defection?

4. Discuss the stages involved in loyalty programme implementation.

5. Describe various retention strategies which are used to build barriers to customer switching.

6. What are the differences between 'exit barrier' and 'entry barrier'?

Fill in the blanks:

7. The term _____ _____is used to describe the behaviour of repeat customers, as well as those that offer good ratings, reviews, or testimonials.

8. _____ _____ model then looks at the _____ of the business relationship; it proposes that this strength is determined by the level of _____ with recent _____, overall perceptions of _____, customer _____to the _____, and _____ between the parties.

## References

Berry, Leonard L., 1995. Relationship Marketing of Services—Growing Interest, Emerging Perspectives, *Journal of the Academy of Marketing Science*, Vol. 23 (Fall), pp. 236–245.

Berry, Leonard L. and Parasuraman, A., 1991. *Marketing Services*. The Free Press, New York.

Cann, Cynthia W. and Sumrall, Delia A., 1997. University of Scranton, Services Relationship Marketing: Social Bonding in the Service Encounter, white paper.

Carrol, P. and Reichheld, F., 1992. The Fallacy of Customer Retention, *Journal of Retail Banking*, Vol. 13, No. 4, pp. 15–20.

Chaudhuri, A. and Holbrook, M., 2001. The Chain of Effects from Brand Trust and Brand Affect to Brand Performance: The Role of Brand Loyalty. *Journal of Marketing*, Vol. 65, pp. 81–93.

Dawkins, P. and Reichheld, F., 1990. Customer Retention as a Competitive Weapon, *Directors and Boards*, Vol. 14, No. 4, pp. 42–47.

Dick, A.S. and Basu, K., 1994. Customer Loyalty: Toward an Integrated Conceptual Framework, *Journal of Academy of Marketing Science*, Vol. 22, (Winter), pp. 99–113.

Dowling, Grahame R., 1997. Do Customer Loyalty Programmes Really Work?, Research Brief, The Australian Graduate School of Management, School of Marketing, University of New South Wales, Sydney, Australia.

Dwyer, F. Robert, Schurr, Paul H. and Sejo, Oh., 1987. Developing Buyer–Seller Relationship, *Journal of Marketing*, Vol. 51, April, pp. 11–27.

Gilmore, A., 2003. *Services Marketing and Management*, Sage Publications, New Delhi, pp. 24–25.

Gordon, Ian., 1999. *Relationship Marketing: New Strategies, Techniques and Technologies to Win the Customers You Want and Keep Them Forever*. John Wiley and Sons Publishers, p. 336.

Griffin, Jill, 2002. *"Customer Loyalty—How to earn it, How to keep it"*, Jossey-Bass, A Wiley Imprint, San Francisco, pp. 20–23.

Gummesson, Evert, 2002. *Total Relationship Marketing, Marketing Management, Relationship and Strategy and CRM Approaches for the Network Economy*, Butterworth-Heinemann, UK, p. 17.

Jacocby, J. and Kyner, B., 1973. Brand Loyalty versus Repeat Purchasing Behaviour, *Journal of Marketing Research*, Feb, pp. 1–9.

Keiningham, Timothy L., Vavra, Terry G., Lerzan, Aksoy and Wallard, Henri, 2006. Loyalty Myths: Hyped Strategies that will put you out of business and proven tactics that really work, John Wiley and Sons, Hoboken, New Jersey. pp. 172–176.

Lal, Sameer, 2000. Building Relationships with Doctors for Effective Marketing: The Case of the Pharmaceutical Industry, in *Customer Relationship Management, Emerging Concepts, Tools and Applications*, Eds. Jagdish N. Sheth, Atul Parvatiyar and G. Sainesh (Eds.), Tata McGraw Hill, New Delhi, p. 211.

Levitt, Theodore, 1983. Relationship Management, *Harvard Business Review*, September-October, pp. 87–93.

Morgan, Robert M. and Hunt, Shelby D., 1994. The Commitment–Trust Theory of Relationship Marketing, *Journal of Marketing*, Vol. 58, July, pp. 20–38.

Oliver, R., 1997. *Loyalty and Profit: Long-term Effects of Satisfaction, A Behavioural Perspective on the Consumer*, McGraw Hill, New York.

Porter, Michael E., 1980. *Competitive Strategy: Techniques for Analyzing Industries and Competitors*, Free Press, New York.

Reichheld, F., 1996. *The Loyalty Effect*, Harvard Business School Press, Boston.

Reichheld, F. and Sasser, W., 1990. Zero Defects: Quality Comes to Services, *Harvard Business Review*, Sept-Oct., pp. 105–111.

Reinartz, Werner and Kumar, V., 2002. The Mismanagement of Customer Loyalty. *Harvard Business Review,* Vol. 80, pp. 86–97.

Roche, Elizabeth, 2005. *Vice President and Research Lead, Technology Research Services, How to Strengthen Customer Exit Barriers,* www.destinationcrm.com

Sahoo, Debjani and Vyas, Preeta, 2007. Loyalty Programme Applications in Indian Service Industry, Research Project, IIM Ahmedabad.

Schlesinger, L. and Heskett, J., 1991. "Breaking the Cycle of Failure in Service, *Sloan Management Review*, Spring, pp. 17–28.

Sheth, Jagdish N., 1994, "Relationship Marketing: A customer perspective," in Proceedings of the 2nd Annual Relationship Marketing Conference. Atlanta, GA: Center for Relationship Marketing, Emory University, 1–7.

Storbacka, K., Strandvik, T. and Grönroos, C., 1994. Managing Customer Relationships for Profit, *International Journal of Service Industry Management*, Vol. 5, No. 5, pp. 21–28.

Urban, Glen L. and Star, Steven H., 1991. *Advanced Marketing Strategy*, Prentice Hall, Englewood Cliffs, New Jersey.

Wilson, David T., 1995. An Integrated Model of Buyer–Seller Relationships, *Journal of the Academy of Marketing Science*, Vol. 23, (Fall), pp. 335–345.

Websites:

www.businessweek.com/adsections/care/relationship/crm_author.htm

Quantifying Customer Loyalty, http://www.loyaltybuilders.com/howtouse.html

www.wisegeek.com for customer loyalty terminology

www.expressindia.com (Jet Privilege)

www.destinationcrm.com (Exit Barrier)

en.wikipedia.org/wiki/Loyalty_business_model

www.petrobonus.com

www.direm.com/direxion/casestudies/tata-aig.asp

www.marutiautocard.com

www.jetairways.com

# CHAPTER 10

||||||||||||||||||||||

# Measuring Relationship Effectiveness

## INTRODUCTION

The conventional way of measuring impacts of business relations is interpreted in the analytical studies indicating the growth of market share and net profit. For both consumer and industrial products and services, it is true that the growth of market share of its products, including the extent of cross-sell, up-sell and repeat sale, vouches for relationship orientation of the organization. For measuring effectiveness of relationship, some cardinal points may be taken into consideration on conceptual basis, for example clients' views on products or services, evaluation of client orientation within the organization, etc.

It is through market offering that a firm extends the benefits to the customer. The customer assigns different weightings for the benefits that he seeks from the offer and makes a mental note of the total value provided by the offer. The total weight he assigns to a product reflects the value he perceives in it. The customer has to pay a cost for acquiring this value. This cost includes the price of the product plus other elements of cost to him, economic and non-economic. The customer is delighted when the value exceeds the cost he incurs. And, he gets satisfaction when on using the product, he finds that the value he actually receives matches the value that he assumed. The larger is the value-cost gap, the greater is his satisfaction. The customer compares the value-cost gaps of competing offers and selects the one that gives him the best trade-off.

Business firms have to arrive at the best and ideal configuration of benefit-value-cost-satisfaction, which is a challenging exercise. Now, whatever is the measurement methodology, there should be an alignment in the measurement factors and its weightings from both ends—customer as well as his partner—then only will there be a meaningful approach. This chapter describes some of the methodologies applied for measuring relationship effectiveness.

## MEASUREMENT PARAMETERS

For measuring the effectiveness of relationship, the following points need to be addressed and focused:

1. **Identify and differentiate between the successful and unsuccessful products.** Some products may have very high RoI whereas some others may not be showing that result. There could be several reasons of such a difference. For example, take the failure of the product. The possible causes could be:

   (a) Inferior product

   (b) Obsolete product

   (c) Product look not satisfying the users

   (d) Poor packaging of the product

   (e) Price not competitive

   (f) Poor channel of distribution

   (g) Absence of awareness because of weak promotion

   (h) Wrong client/customer handling.

   Likewise, there could be several reasons that could be attributed behind the success of a product. As long as there is success, organizations seem to be complacent and there is little urge for probing into the causes of success. Rather, there is a trend to replicate the model for related other products. However, it all happens when there is a failure—the product, process and person are subject to microscopic evaluation.

But it is equally important to note and make an in-depth analysis of the causes of success keeping in mind the improvements that are anticipated and likely to be demanded in future. The simplest form of carrying out the starting point of the exercise is, by using the following worksheet (Figure 10.1).

| Successful acts | Unsuccessful acts |
|---|---|
| Actions/decisions:<br><br>Results:<br><br><br>Improved action | Actions/decisions:<br><br>Results:<br><br><br>Improved action |

**Figure 10.1  Basic worksheet for relationship quality measurement.**

2. **Evaluate the quality of relationship in all the cases.** There can be a number of measurement parameters which would be analyzed by carrying out survey among the clients—starting from the channel partners to end user, as well as within the organization to have a better insight about the success and failures of the product.

3. **Mapping those relationship with successes/failures of the product.** This is more pertinent as it reveals the vital finding, if anything has gone wrong with relationship process or else what is the contribution of relationship management, if it is a success. This analysis can be done mapping the points scored against each product and from there it is possible to make a forecast on the feasibility of further opportunities in the form of cross-sell or up-sell.

To augment the process, it is necessary to take inputs from the users/clients on a periodic basis. This is essential and to some extent it may require the data inputs from market research, but it gives signals in advance about any impending danger so that adequate measures are taken for preventive action.

Some of the survey questions related to the products or services can be put forward directly to the client or end-users. The outcome of their answers reveal the relationship quality.

## RELATIONSHIP QUALITY SURVEY

### Feedback from the Client

Instead of going through the traditional approach of customer satisfaction survey, the following feedback about client servicing, covering their feelings on vital areas of product and relationship, presents a fair idea about the satisfaction level of the client, and the client's overall perception as regards how effective is the relationship. The feedback from the client can be collected on monthly basis or half yearly basis as jointly decided by the client and partner on the following two areas:

1. Product related inputs
2. Relationship related inputs

## Product Related Inputs

The responses can be framed on a 7-point rating scale.

1. How the wholesalers, retailers, dealers, distributors rate the product quality, product availability, promotion?
2. What are the views of the end-users on the product? Are they satisfied with the benefits they are accruing out of it?
3. Are they happy with the value of the money paying for it?
4. Are the customers aware of competitors? How do they rate their product?
5. Have they ever enjoyed any incentive for being a long-term user of the product?

## Relationship Related Inputs

This would be placed before the clients for their inputs. But this pertains more to service or B2B sphere.

1. What is the comfort level by using the product?
2. What makes them feel comfortable with the product?
3. What makes the client think of the product when the need arises?
4. What is the best thing the client likes in the partner's organization?
5. What is the major weakness the client feels present in the partner's organization?
6. What is the client's perception of positive attitude of the partner with respect to the complaints made?
7. What is the client's perception of the partner's concern with respect to the complaints made?
8. What is the rating of the acceptance of the partner by different departments of the client's organization?
9. Does the client feel that the partner's team has become a major part of client's organization?
10. How do the client rate different communications processes, channels open with the partner in terms of its effectiveness?
11. How do the client rate different decision-making processes in the partner's organization concerning their transactions?
12. How does the client view the long-term relations with the partner?

## Feedback within the Partner's Organization

Feedback within the partner's organization is important with respect to the outlook or orientation of the organization that determines whether the organization is in continuous endeavour to nurture relationship or not, to promote strategies for relationship building, attention to client, etc. This feedback can be taken from everyone in the organization and the scores reflect the overall outlook of the organization towards client relationship. This can be conducted every month on the following key areas:

- Client servicing
- Managerial role
- Synergy and integration
- Person skill orientation
- Operations

### *Client Servicing*

1. There is a top priority in taking customer care and this is accepted as more important than cost or expense.

2. Whenever clients call up, their views are listened with utmost concern and the company promptly acts on that information.

3. The organization has formal process to register its requirements and the client is periodically updated about actions being taken.

4. In the case of lost business, the reason is explored. The company makes all-out efforts to regain the client.

5. There is always an attention to ensure that daily activities are in line with the client servicing and satisfaction.

6. There is a periodic survey process in client satisfaction and it is adhered to very strictly.

### *Managerial Role*

1. Managers encourage team spirit to service clients—there is no existence of inter-person or inter-group rivalry. The group shares achievements, and competition implies some other company not anyone from the group.

2. Managers are transparent and inspiring about sharing knowledge on matters related to customer care.

3. Managers risk positive action to ensure client satisfaction.

4. Managers enable the subordinates to ensure proper customer servicing.

5. Managers promote the sense of client-partner relationship among the team members within the company.

## Synergy and Integration

1. The organization encourages group decision than individual decision-making process.
2. There is a seamless integration of action processes when staff and managers of different groups work together.
3. There is sufficient clarity of role and responsibilities defined in the system.
4. There are clear measures for evaluating the client satisfaction.
5. There is a periodic review to share among the team about progress of the work.
6. People can identify themselves with the goals set by the organization and those goals are clear and achievable.

## Person Skill Orientation

1. People work in an open environment—staff, executives and managers enjoy the same facilities in the workplace.
2. There is positive empowerment of the people—they are made to feel important in their activities.
3. The client servicing team is well conversant with the concerns of the clients and they are masters in solving those problems.
4. All the procedures for tackling clients concerns are well documented and standardized.
5. The service team is geared to rise to the occasion when the client needs something extra.

## Operations

1. The focus is given more on preventive maintenance than rectifying problems on almost regular basis.
2. There is adequate attention on analysis and evaluation of cost of waste, additional resource utilization for fire-fighting and anything that add up to undesirable service quality.
3. The focus is given on exceptional customer care than cost reduction for adding to margin of profit.

Scores and interpretation summing up the feedback from the customer and within the organization are given in Table 10.1 (assuming 7-point rating scale).

**Table 10.1** Measurement Score Interpretation Table

| Scores | Explanation |
|---|---|
| 170 and above (80% and above) | Organization culture is highly client-oriented, market leader, excellent supplier |
| 130–169 | Individual commitment to excellence is present—the system needs to be streamlined with such commitment. Client servicing is adequate but still needs attention for further improvement |
| 100–129 | Individual commitment to customer is present—organization goals need to have such orientation |
| Below 100 (below 50%) | Lack of concern from both individual and organization towards the customer. Serious cause for concern. The company may almost certainly be losing market |

According to Heskett et al. (1997), an average rating of 9 out of 10 (90 per cent) is required on most of the key issues that drive the buying decision. If suppliers fail to achieve such high ratings, customers show indifference and will shop elsewhere. Capricious consumers are at risk of being wooed by competitors, readily switching suppliers in the search for higher standards. This concept of the zone of loyalty, zone of indifference and zone of defection as suggested by the three Harvard Professors is illustrated in Figure 10.2.

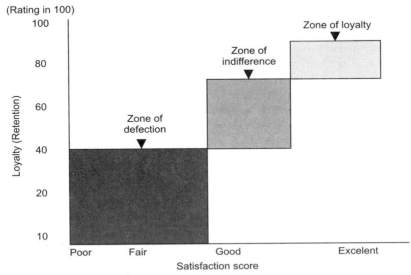

**Figure 10.2 Loyalty (retention) versus satisfaction score.**

*Source:* Professor James Heskett, W. Sasser & Loenard Schlesinger (1997), adopted with permission.

## CUSTOMER SATISFACTION INDEX—A USEFUL TOOL FOR FINDING CUSTOMER'S EVALUATION OF VALUE DELIVERY

What ultimately matters in marketing is, customer's satisfaction on using the product. After using the product, does the customer feel that the product has actually delivered the value he had perceived? In other words, does the product satisfy him that he originally expected? This is the ultimate test in the value delivery process. Marketers use several tools to assess customer satisfaction level. Customer Satisfaction Index (CSI) is one such tool and an indicator of customer satisfaction level. With CSI, the marketer is able to understand the perceived value of his offer.

> *Case Study:* **Customer Satisfaction Index from J.D. Power and Associates**

Established in 1968, J.D. Power and Associates is a global marketing information firm that conducts independent and unbiased surveys of customer satisfaction, product quality and buyer behaviour. The firm's services include industry-wide syndicated studies; proprietary (commissioned) tracking studies; media studies; forecasting; and training services, as well as business operations analyses, and consultancies on customer satisfaction trends. According to the J.D. Power Asia Pacific 2007 India Customer Satisfaction Index (CSI) Study[SM] for the eighth consecutive year, Maruti Suzuki ranks highest in customer satisfaction with authorized dealership service.

The study, measures the overall satisfaction of vehicle owners who visited their authorized dealer/service centre for maintenance or repair work during the first 12 to 18 months of ownership. Overall satisfaction is determined by utilizing seven measures. They are (in order of importance): problems experienced; service quality; user-friendly service; service advisor; service initiation; service delivery; and in-service experience.

The 2007 India Customer Satisfaction Index (CSI) study is based on responses from more than 5,300 owners of nearly 40 different vehicle models. The study was fielded from May to August 2007 and includes customers who serviced their vehicles at authorized service facilities between November 2006 to August 2007.

Recording only a single-point increase since 2006, overall satisfaction in the industry remains stable. Maruti Suzuki leads the industry in customer satisfaction with a CSI score of 838 points on a 1,000-point scale and continues to set the industry benchmark in all measures of the CSI. While ranking below the industry average, the remaining eight nameplates included in the study have improved since 2006. Honda, Skoda and Hyundai, respectively, demonstrate the greatest improvement.

"The steady improvement in industry-wide CSI performance during the previous three years reflects the success that many manufacturers have had in enhancing the customer experience at their dealerships," said Mohit Arora, senior director at J.D. Power Asia Pacific, Singapore. "The improvement in performance is especially encouraging, given the sharp increase in the service volumes for most dealer networks."

The study finds that vehicle pick-up and delivery before and after service has a strong impact on customer satisfaction. In particular, customers who say that their vehicle was picked up from their doorstep before service and delivered to the same point after service are notably more delighted with their after-sales service experience, compared with customers who do not receive this service. Although this value-added service is utilized more frequently over the past two years, fewer than one of 10 customers report receiving it.

"Picking up and delivering vehicles provides greater convenience to customers, who travel an average of nine kilometers each way to reach their authorized service centre," said Arora. "With increasing traffic congestion in cities and consumer preference of delivering their vehicle for service during peak morning hours, it is not unexpected that customers are delighted with this gesture from their dealerships."

The study also finds that customers who service their vehicles only at authorized service centres report higher overall service satisfaction, compared with those who have also used non-authorized service centres in the past. In 2007, just 13 per cent of customers report visiting a non-authorized service centre, a figure that has steadily declined in the past two years.

"Most customers who use a non-authorized service centre do so for routine maintenance or repairs—both of which are revenue-generating opportunities for dealerships," said Arora. "Customers use the services of a non-authorized service facility mostly due to its convenient location or speedy service. Automakers can benefit by optimizing their network reach and providing quicker service to maximize revenues for their after-sales network."

The study also examines the cost of operating new vehicles, both in terms of actual costs and owner satisfaction with those costs. The overall cost of operation is an aggregation of three components: fuel; repair and maintenance; and tyre expenses. With lower fuel prices in 2007, the cost of new-vehicle operation has decreased since the 2006 study—down 7 per cent for petrol vehicles and 2 per cent for diesel vehicles. This year, diesel models such as the Ford Fiesta, Chevrolet Tavera, Tata Indica and Tata Indigo/Marina post strong performances in the diesel segment in terms of cost of operation. Maruti models continue to lead the petrol segment, both in terms of actual costs and overall satisfaction with the cost of operation.

*Source:* www.jdpower.com/corporate/news/releases/pressrelease.asp

---

| *Case Study:*  **Freddie Award for Frequent Flyer Programme** |

Sir Freddie Laker, who in 1978 was knighted by Queen Elizabeth II for his contribution to commercial aviation and the British economy, inspired the Freddies. Known for his pioneering marketing ideas within the travel industry in the 1970s, Laker founded Britain's first all-jet air carrier, Laker Airways Limited. He also founded the "SKYTRAIN" service, which revolutionized the airline industry by offering no-reservation, low-cost air service.

Voting for all regions begins from January 15 and continues through the entire month of February. Travellers who wish to speak their minds may access the ballot by visiting freddieawards.com and clicking on the "Ballot" button.

Each person who votes for the Freddies is also asked to rate their choice from 1–10. This allows travellers to not only choose the best programme in nine different categories, but also rate their choices with 10 equating the highest score possible. Freddie winners are then chosen from those who score the highest average in delivering membership benefits and value. This is a change from the popular vote, which was used in the first nine years of the presentation of the Freddie Awards. With the return of Value Voting, it will once again focus on quality and not quantity. How many votes a programme receives do not matter, but the overall merits of what each programme has to offer will determine the winners.

Freddie Award winners are announced to the public at an annual awards ceremony. Freddie Award winner information is also released to the media the day the winners are announced.

For 19 years, frequent travellers have been asked to make their picks for the best frequent travel programmes via the Freddie Awards. Introduced by *InsideFlyer* magazine publisher Randy Petersen in 1988, the Freddies allow members to rank airline and hotel programmes from their point of view. The awards have grown in stature and importance and are the most prestigious member-generated awards in the industry. Frequent guest and frequent flyer programmes from around the world compete in nine Freddie Award categories, culminating in the highly coveted Programme of the Year award.

Individual categories are:

- Best Award
- Best Bonus
- Best Affinity Credit Card
- Best Newsletter/Member Communications
- Best Website
- Best Customer Service
- Best Award Redemption

- Best Elite Level
- Programme of the Year

Freddie voting focuses on quality, not quantity. Winners are determined not by how many votes a programme receives, but by the overall merits of each programme as reflected in "Value Voting." Value Voting asks voters to assign a number between 1 and 10 for each programme in addition to simply ranking programmes according to the voter's preference. The programme receiving the highest average Value Vote with at least 1 per cent of the overall popular vote in a category wins that category. In some categories, results are so close that Value Votes have to be tallied to four decimal numbers.

Jet Airways' JetPrivilege programme won top Honours at the 20th Annual Freddie Awards 2007 held on April 24, 2008 bagging 7 of the 9 categories, including the most coveted 'Programme of the Year Award' for the second consecutive time.

The prestigious consumer-generated 'Freddie Awards' recognize the best frequent flyer programmes across the globe. JetPrivilege has been voted number one, in the Japan, Pacific, Asia and Australia region, for the following categories:

- Programme of the Year
- Best Customer Service
- Best Web Site
- Best Elite-Level Programme
- Best Affinity Credit Card
- Best Bonus Promotion
- Best Award

JetPrivilege has also finished second in the other 2 categories, namely, Best Member Communications and Best Award Redemption.

*Source:* www.jetairways.com

## EXAMPLE OF CUSTOMER SATISFACTION SURVEY PROCESS BY TECHNOLOGY SERVICES ORGANIZATION

If it is too big a form, the customer may not be interested in reading all the details and filling them up. Preferably it should be crisp and lean with each line carrying lots of weight, which can be useful to serve as feedback. This can be used in the 5-point rating scale, namely Not applicable (0), Poor (1), Satisfactory (2), Good (3), Very Good (4), and Excellent (5).

| Description of Service | Rating |
|---|---|
| Promptness in responding to grievances | ☐ |
| Capability to address the issues and concerns | ☐ |
| Competence in adhering to agreed time schedule | ☐ |
| Attitude and cooperations of support persons | ☐ |
| Availability of competent person | ☐ |
| Knowledge transfer process | ☐ |
| Availability of sufficient documentation to facilitate knowledge sharing process | ☐ |
| Effectiveness of escalation process | ☐ |
| Overall rating | ☐ |

In the above example, the first point shows the attitude and concern of the organization towards customer grievances. The rating here reflects the level of indifference or concern of the partner. Much of the problems are resolved when the service provider has high score in this point.

The feedback on capability and competence shows the skill level, and quality of work, quality of people deployed for the activities. The emotional content of relationship is touched in the attitude and co-operations of support persons who can come close to customer personnel to form cohesiveness in the operations.

Knowledge transfer process illustrates the openness of the organization to enable the customers to be on their own. Once this is successful, the next level of business comes through with lots of ease—because this builds trust and confidence in the customer. Take another example of escalation process. In case there is no such incident for escalation, the customer has the option to put '0' in the box. But in case the customer puts it 1, then there is a genuine problem with the senior management in handling customer complaints.

## THE SERVQUAL MODEL

The ServQual model, developed by Parasuraman et al. (1985) provides a reliable methodology for measuring customer satisfaction in service situation. It seeks to measure perceived service quality on the basis of five parameters as shown in Table 10.2.

**Table 10.2** Dimensions of Service Quality

| Parameter | Explanation |
|---|---|
| Tangibles | The appearance of the firm's physical facilities, equipment, personnel and communication material |
| Reliability | The firm's ability to provide the service dependably and accurately |
| Responsiveness | The firm's willingness to help customers and its ability to provide prompt service |
| Competence | Possession of required skills and knowledge to perform service |
| Empathy | The individual attention the firm provides to its customers, including access, communication and caring |

When there are gaps between expectations and perceptions of service quality, organizations can suitably tune the various parameters under the dimensions of service quality to bridge these gaps (Figure 10.3).

To summarize the model, it propounds that there are five kinds of gaps, which together contribute to the problem relating to service quality (Table 10.3).

**Table 10.3** Gaps in Service Quality

| Gaps | Explanation |
|---|---|
| GAP 1 | The difference between customer expectations of the service and the firm's perception of those expectations |
| GAP 2 | The difference between the firm's perception about customer expectation and the specifications the firm actually adopts |
| GAP 3 | The difference between the adopted specifications and the service quality actually delivered |
| GAP 4 | The difference between the service delivered and the promise made to the customer through communication/promotion |
| GAP 5 | The difference between the service level expected by the customer and the service level perceived by him |

The extent of each of these gaps in the given case is measured, using structured questionnaires. They are measured in terms of scores generated on the five parameters explained on a seven-point scale.

They are combined to arrive at a final score, which denotes the index of customer satisfaction. The individual scores help pinpoint the firm's shortcomings in specific parameters.

It can be seen that the parameters—except for reliability, which represents an outcome—deal with process. Often, firms ignore process

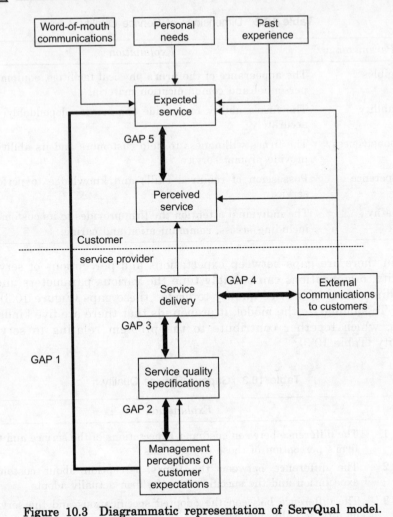

**Figure 10.3 Diagrammatic representation of ServQual model.**

*Source:* Professor A. "Parsu" Parasuraman et al. (1985), adopted with permission.

dimensions, leading to big gaps in customer satisfaction (Ramaswamy and Namakumari 2002).

# AMERICAN CUSTOMER SATISFACTION INDEX

The **American Customer Satisfaction Index (ACSI)** is an economic indicator that measures the satisfaction of consumers across the US economy. It is produced by the National Quality Research Center (NQRC) at the University of Michigan in Ann Arbor, Michigan.

The ACSI interviews about 80,000 Americans annually and asks about their satisfaction with the goods and services they have consumed.

Respondents are screened to cover a wide range of business-to-consumer products and services, including durable goods, services, non-durable goods, local government services, federal government agencies, and so forth. Results from data collection and analysis are released to the public each quarter. ACSI data is used by academic researchers, corporations and government agencies, market analysts and investors, industry trade associations, and consumers.

The ACSI was started in 1994 by NQRC researchers who worked with counterparts at the American Society for Quality in Milwaukee, Wisconsin, and CFI Group in Ann Arbor. The ACSI was based on a model originally implemented in 1989 in Sweden called the Swedish Customer Satisfaction Barometer (SCSB). Both the Swedish version and the ACSI were developed by Claes Fornell, now the Donald C. Cook, Professor of Business Administration at the University of Michigan, and chairman of CFI Group. Fornell remains the director of the NQRC, and the principal researcher behind the ACSI.

ACSI results provide both an economic indicator of the quality of economic output and information for business applications. It serves as a strategic business tool for gaining competitive advantage and creating shareholder value through investments in quality and customer satisfaction. It is a predictor of consumer spending and corporate earnings.

The ACSI model is a set of causal equations that link customer expectations, perceived quality, and perceived value to customer satisfaction. In turn, satisfaction is linked to consequences as defined by customer complaints and customer loyalty—measured by price tolerance and customer retention. For most companies, repeat customers are major contributors to profit.

Thus, customer retention is a key to financial performance. By combining it with certain financial data, ACSI corporate subscribers are able to calculate the net present value of their company's customer base as an asset over time.

1. **Customer expectations.** Expectations combine customers' experiences with a product or service and information about it via media, advertising, salespersons, and word-of-mouth from other customers. Customer expectations influence the evaluation of quality and forecast (from customers' pre-purchase perspective) how well the product or service will perform.

2. **Perceived quality.** Perceived quality is measured through three questions: overall quality, reliability, and the extent to which a product or service meets the customer's needs. Across all companies and industries measured in the ACSI, perceived quality proves to have the greatest impact on customer satisfaction.

3. **Perceived value.** Perceived value is a measure of quality relative to price paid. Although price (value for money) is often very important to the customer's first purchase, it usually has a somewhat smaller impact on satisfaction for repeat purchases. Perceived value is measured through two questions: overall price given in quality and overall quality given in price. In the ACSI model, perceived value influences ACSI directly, and is affected by expectations and perceived quality. Although perceived value is of great importance for the (first) purchase decision, it usually has somewhat less impact on satisfaction and repeat purchase.

4. **Customer complaints.** Customer complaint activity is measured as the percentage of respondents who reported a problem with the measured companies' product or service within a specified time frame. Satisfaction has an inverse relationship to customer complaints.

5. **Customer loyalty.** Customer loyalty is measured through questions on the likelihood to purchase a company's products or services at various price points. Customer satisfaction has a positive effect on loyalty, but the magnitude of that effect varies greatly across companies and industries.

## LOYALTY ACCOUNTING MATRIX

According to Johansen and Monthelie (1996), Loyalty Accounting Matrix (Figure 10.4) combines the attractiveness of a supplier ('brain appeal') and the strength of the relationship ('heart appeal'). The most satisfied customers are called *ambassadors*. They find the supplier highly attractive, have a strong relationship to the supplier, and recommend him to others. The next groups consist of loyal customers who are slightly less enthusiastic than the ambassadors. *The diagonal represents*

| Strength of relationship | | |
|---|---|---|
| Risk | Loyal | Ambassador |
| Searching | Risk | Loyal |
| Lost | Searching | Risk |

Figure 10.4  Loyalty accounting matrix.

risk customers who are easy prey for competitors. The last two groups are those who are actively searching for a new supplier and those who are already lost customers.

A study of one company showed the following pattern: ambassadors 32 per cent, loyal 30 per cent, risk 25 per cent, searching 9 per cent and lost 4 per cent. Ambassadors and loyal customers constituted almost two-thirds of the customers, a result that might or might not be satisfactory, depending on the type of business.

## FRAMEWORK OF BALANCED SCORECARD (BSC)

A clearly defined strategy for implementing Relationship Marketing is a key to building customer retention and loyalty. The balanced scorecard lends a strategic direction that facilitates the strategic marketing team to evolve with right perspective for relationship development, maintenance and growth.

Professors Kaplan and Norton (1992) first introduced the concept of the balanced scorecard in an article published in *Harvard Business Review*. The balanced scorecard is a means of linking a company's current actions to its long-term goals. Balanced scorecards are in widespread use among Fortune 1000 companies. The measures described in BSC are based upon the company's vision and strategy. The balanced scorecard has the following four sections (Kaplan and Norton 1996):

**Financial:** It describes the organization strategy for growth and profitability from the investors' perspective.

**Customer:** The strategy for creating value and differentiation from the customer perspective.

**Internal processes:** Priorities for value addition in the internal business process to leverage customer satisfaction

**Learning and growth:** Education and training, development programmes to accommodate the changes in the business climate.

It should be noted here that the balanced scorecard management process, derived from Deming's Total Quality Management, is a continuous cyclical process. It has neither a beginning nor end. Its task is not directly concerned about the mission of the organization, but rather with internal processes (diagnostic measures) and external outcomes (strategic measures). The system's control is based on performance metrics or "metadata" that are tracked continuously over time to look for trends, best and worst practices, and areas for improvement. It delivers information to managers for guiding their decisions, but these are self-assessments, not customer requirements or compliance data (Averson 1998).

## BALANCED SCORECARD FOR RELATIONSHIP MARKETING

Industry trend of being seduced to CRM technology for better customer relationship is well known. The adoption of CRM technology may not always yield favourable results if the framework of application is not in place.

*Harvard Business Review* article 'Avoid the four perils of CRM' explains the attributes for CRM failure (Rigby et al. 2002):

- Implementing CRM technology before creating a customer strategy
- Installing CRM technology before creating a customer-focused organization
- Assuming that more CRM is better
- Stalking not wooing customers

CRM growth is driven by the perennial necessity to achieve competitive parity. Some organizations are making progress in CRM, which puts competitive pressure on others to keep up with the leaders.

For the measurement of relationship marketing performance, a balanced scorecard that combines a variety of measures based on the defined purpose of each relationship marketing programme is recommended (Kaplan & Norton 1992). In other words, the performance evaluation measure for each relationship or relationship marketing programme should mirror the set of defined objectives for the programme (Sheth & Parvatiyar 2002). Therefore, strategy and implementation of balanced scorecard for effective Customer Relationship Management play a pivotal role in its success. The exercise may call for Business Process Management to Business Transformation or to the extent cultural change management to accomplish organization mission, vision and objectives. A generalized strategy with a focus on relationship elements can be proposed with a bottom up approach from learning and growth, elaboration of process perspective, followed by customer perspective, where thrust on customer relationship building automatically results in encouraging financial perspective of the organization. However, the best way to build strategy map is from the top down, starting with the destination and then charting the routes that will lead there (Kaplen & Norton 2000). With rapid changes in the business architecture, this exercise would be a continuous process. Adhering to the principles of balanced scorecard, this can be achieved through stages using subjective as well as objective measurement techniques of targets set and targets achieved.

Financial and customer perspectives can become unrealistic with indiscriminately high sales and revenue targets coupled with 'driving-the-customer' instead of 'driven-by-customer' practice through forceful and arrogant means. Such drive may not be fruitful in the long run as it focuses on profit only, not on the people who are going to generate the revenue and add customers.

For a reasonably balanced action, along with framing realistic goals under customer and financial perspectives, the focus and initiatives are required to be given on learning and process areas. This would educate organization team and establish successful and effective processes to ensure a robust customer relationship foundation.

It is imperative that those inputs drive the people towards growth and development, refinement and reinforcement of process than forcing them to look at these goals and measures as objects of threat instead of challenge. Ideally, stage-wise implementation of these processes would be most appropriate.

## STRATEGY AND IMPLEMENTATION

### Learning and Growth

Knowledge has become the key economic resource and perhaps the even only source of competitive advantage (Drucker 1995). Knowledge dissemination should be taken up with adequate importance with due focus on customer needs and requirements. In the first stage, customer orientation for each and every employee of the organization through training, seminars, workshops would be emphasized so that concern for customer becomes the second nature of the employees and organization as a whole. The training could be on any business related subject, like technology, soft skill but that should have a clear and direct bearing with the customer and prospect requirements. For example, IT service provider relationship manager has to understand the technology that the customer aspires to switch over. It is important whether the organization is in a ready state to offer it. There should be Key Performance Indicators (KPI) for measuring the learning and growth, which would be decided by the senior management in consultation with the bottom line team.

If an existing customer wants a change in technology for competing in business, the relationship manager needs to sense this information. In this perspective, the factors that would contribute in building relationship, are training of the relationship manager in relevant technology, broader and deeper interactions with technology partners, understanding the changing business perspectives and mapping the same with business goals. Accordingly, the scorecard would focus on relationship and technology training, duration of training, when and whether it has been undertaken and what is the performance of the relationship executive/manager of the training. Likewise, learning and growth initiatives for persons, other than the Relationship Managers, who act as customer touch points in business activities can also be planned, designed and implemented.

## Process Perspective

In the subsequent stage, the focus of Relationship Marketing team would be to contribute in acquiring, retaining and growth of the customer. For existing customers, growth would be measured in terms of cross-sell, up-sell, repeat sale or combination of all. For acquiring and retaining customer, there would be database of prospects. There should be strategic plan and process for addressing those areas. If we consider a financial services organization as an existing client and IT organization as its service provider, the following could be some of the measures that can be considered to address the process perspective.

1. If the existing customer wants to expand its line of business (for example, in terms of introduction of new product), what are processes ready for its development and deployment to support the customer?

2. In terms of knowledge and skill, what is the readiness of the relationship team to take the concept forward?

3. What are the long-term and short-term business benefits the organization would gain from promoting the existing relationship?

4. How can the organization achieve the business goals following the existing process?

5. What are the improvements required in the relationship maintenance processes?

6. In the new scenario, how is customer satisfaction objectively and subjectively interpreted?

7. What baseline should be adopted for measuring the above initiatives?

8. What are the initiatives to audit the processes put into operations?

9. What are the mechanisms to record and resolve customer issues?

Many more such points can be framed based on the outlook and policy of the organization to implement process perspective.

## Customer Perspective

Customer perspective is a significant and vital perspective for achieving the final result of meeting the financial perspective that is business and revenue goals. The success of customer perspective would automatically trigger revenue and business growth, stakeholders' confidence. Some of the strategic objectives in this perspective are to identify:

- Customer's past satisfaction

- Customer perception of value of product or service offered
- Customer confidence in the relationship
- Customer confidence in the people and processes.

Customer satisfaction survey would indicate customer faith in the relationship. Measures of customer confidence in the relationship would indicate likelihood of relationship continuity and finally confidence in the relationship manager would establish intimacy of relationship and the location of the power equation.

Major stakeholders considered for the development of customer perspective in the relationship plane are namely internal business team and external customers. A Business Unit (BU) strategy describes how BU intends to create products and services that offer a unique, differentiated mix of benefits called the customer value proposition to potential customer. If the value proposition is sufficiently attractive, the customer makes a series of purchases that create a value for the business unit (Kaplan and Norton, 2006).

While designing the scorecard for customer perspective, reconciliation of measures, target set, target achieved, action plans taking both stakeholders into confidence can contribute to the balanced scorecard's success in relationship growth. This can be illustrated in the block diagram (Figure 10.5) where the relationship manager reconciles various strategic objectives related to product, delivery, training and service in day-to-day interactions, conferencing with the customers and internal business unit leaders.

**Figure 10.5 Relationship manager reconciliation with internal business team and external customer.**

The relationship manager collects the feedback at appropriate time interval. Using the data, the deviations are examined and the root cause is analyzed. To address those deviations, an action plan is devised and implemented to bridge those gaps.

The areas of reconciliation with internal business team and external customers can be expressed in terms of agreement percentage and it is necessary to reduce the gap of disagreement through relationship workouts.

For example, if the internal team feels that customer satisfaction percentage is 90 and customer data shows it is 60, the relationship manager should probe the causes for 60 both with the customer and internal business unit leaders. On the other hand, if the customer expresses 80 and internal business unit leader feels it is 40, then there is something hidden under the customer's carpet that needs to be revealed and corrected.

The objective of the relationship manager is to bring 100 per cent agreement between the stakeholders on the relationship growth objectives and measures (Figure 10.5). Once this is achieved, cross-sell/ up-sell can take off in its own momentum. This leads to natural convergence from any disagreement to agreement culminating in seamless integration of customer and business unit leaders' goals and objectives in business development.

## Financial Perspective

The last and concluding perspective is financial perspective—success of this perspective would be totally dependent on the performance of the layer right underneath, that is, customer perspective. If the targets of customer perspective are met, its effects would automatically be reflected in the financial results and the organization's capability to achieve the targets of financial perspective, that is, meeting shareholders' expectation of financial performance in terms of growth of business, expansion of market share, growth of revenue, life time value of such relationship—all these would summarily establish the success of relationship.

## Balanced Scorecard Pyramid

The entire strategic objectives and processes can be illustrated with the help of a pyramid, as described in Figure 10.6.

In the pyramid, the perspectives have been grouped into two categories: action category and result category.

Learning and growth and process perspectives belong to the action category, primarily being the independent variables of the internal function and driven by the decisions of the organization.

The next upper layers, namely customer perspective and financial perspective focus on results achieved out of the actions of the organization.

Taking customer perspective as an example, the columns of the figure can be explained in the light of relationship aspects:

**Objective**: Improving customer confidence in relationship

**Measures**: Feedback on relationship constructs, namely, organization commitment, adaptability, trust, etc. on a seven-point scale

**Target**: Maximum points aggregated in the matrix

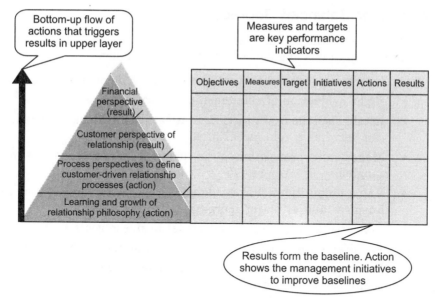

**Figure 10.6  View of balanced scorecard pyramid for relationship marketing.**

**Initiatives:** Self-driven initiatives and organization-level initiatives, for example, periodic review meeting proactively organized to explore areas of weaknesses identified from customer interactions

**Action:** Staff and management actions to improve customer confidence in relationship through training, and proper orientation of the customer interface personnel.

**Expected results:** Positive customer feedback

The iteration of the process and its consequential improvement would lead to **best practice** of that particular objective. Similarly, when the sum of all the components of customer perspective attains close to the target as acknowledged by the customer, the same would be treated as the best practice within the organization for that perspective.

The growth of the relationship would be numerically interpreted, that is, sum of points scored in all the perspectives versus sum of points arrived from the target.

The effect of implementing balanced scorecard for promoting customer relationship cannot be magical and deliver success overnight. Just like the philosophy of quality, this is one such focus area where continuous top management involvement and buying out organization wide support is vital for its successful implementation. Product and service quality goes hand in hand with customer relationship. Each one is complementary to the other.

## Benefits of Balanced Scorecard

Enriching effect of the balanced scorecard from the academic perspective of Relationship Marketing can be enumerated as follows:

- Provides foundation for continuous improvement of relationship.
- Right evaluation of relationship constructs
- Establishes the best practices in Relationship Marketing which can serve as a role model to other business units
- Makes value proposition to the customer more transparent and tangible
- Value propositions that would encourage customers to do more business and at better margins with the company
- Convergence of mutually beneficial business goals
- Facilitates smooth transformation to long-term relationship
- Innovation of processes leading to effective and successful relationship marketing
- The capabilities and alignment of employees and systems towards enhancing customer relationships to generate and sustain growth.

---

*Case Study:* **Turn It**

---

This case shows how a successful and fast-growing Swedish company, TurnIT (2000), has customized the scorecard and intellectual capital to its needs. TurnIT offers IT support to businesses in supplies, software, communication, consulting and outsourcing. Its sales in the year 2000 were $160 million (in 1996: $5 Million) and the number of employees were 1300 (in 1996: 16). The scorecard includes four types of intellectual capital: *business formula, human capital, organization-based structural capital* and *relationship-based structural capital.* Within the last category, there are three subcategories: network (the strengths of relationships to partners, suppliers, intermediaries and others), brand (brand equity in various target groups), and customers (size and breadth of customer base, loyalty, potential and so forth). Assessments of the indicators are made on scales through internal and external interviews and accounted for in the annual report, together with financial data. The assessments are made in three dimensions to grasp the dynamics of the present and the future rather than history: current position, efforts to improve and risks of deteriorating (Gummesson 2002).

## DEFECTION OF SATISFIED CUSTOMER

The gulf between satisfied customers and completely satisfied customers can swallow a business (Jones & Sasser 1995). The scene is familiar: the monthly management meeting attended by a company's senior officers and the general managers of its operating divisions. The company's eight divisions operate in diverse markets, including light manufacturing, wholesale distribution, and consumer services. All are feeling pressure from strong competitors, and the corporation has created a customer-satisfaction survey as one method of measuring the impact of its quality-improvement process.

After dispensing with several items on the agenda, the group turns to the third-quarter customer-satisfaction indices, and a transparency is placed on the overhead projector (Figure 10.7). The CEO proudly points out that 82% of the customers surveyed responded with an overall satisfaction rating of either 4 (satisfied) or 5 (completely satisfied). Everyone in the meeting agrees that the company must be doing pretty well because only 18% of its customers were less than satisfied.

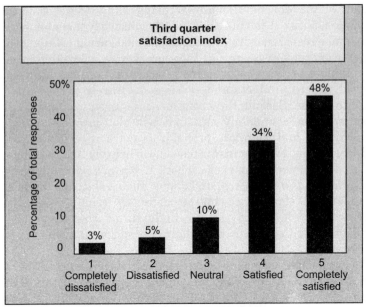

**Figure 10.7 Customer satisfaction index.**

There are three divisions with average ratings of 4.5 or higher. There is a general consensus that they have reached the point of diminishing returns and that further investing to increase customer satisfaction will not make good financial sense.

The group next examines the results of the division with the lowest average rating, a 2.7. This business unit manufactures bulk lubricants and sells to companies that repackage the product for sale to the retail channel. It is a highly competitive, commodity-type business and operates with very tight margins. The group concludes that the lubricant division's market is difficult and that its price-sensitive customers will never be satisfied. Moreover, the division's rating is equal to or above those of most competitors. There is a general consensus that its customers are a lost cause and that it does not pay to make additional investments to try to satisfy them.

Finally, the discussion turns to four business units whose customers generally are neutral or pleased but certainly not delighted. Two divisions manufacture large industrial machinery. Two other divisions provide after-market service for the products of both the company and its competitors. Each division has an average rating between 3.5 and 4.5, meaning that, although the majority of their customers are not dissatisfied or neutral, a significant number are. "Our battle plan is to find out what's making the least-satisfied customers mad and fix it!" the head of one industrial-machinery division says. The others nod in agreement.

Implicit in this discussion are a number of beliefs widely held by managers of the dozens of manufacturing and service companies we have studied. First, it is sufficient merely to satisfy a customer; as long as a customer responds with at least a satisfied rating (4), the company–customer relationship is strong. In other words, a level of satisfaction below complete or total satisfaction is acceptable. After all, this is the real world, where products and services are rarely perfect and people are hard to please. Second, the investment required to change customers from satisfied to completely satisfied will not provide an attractive financial return and therefore probably is not a wise use of resources. Indeed, there may even be instances—most notably, when competing in a cut-throat commodity market—where it doesn't pay to try to satisfy any customers. Finally, each division with a relatively high average rating (3.5 to 4.5) should focus on the customers in its lowest-satisfaction categories (1 to 2). Striving to understand the causes of their dissatisfaction and concentrating efforts on addressing them is the best use of resources.

The extensive research conducted on the relationship between customer satisfaction and customer loyalty, however, shows that these assumptions are deeply flawed. They either ignore or do not accord enough importance to the following aspects of the relationship: *Except in a few rare instances, complete customer satisfaction is the key to securing customer loyalty and generating superior long-term financial performance.* Most managers realize that the more competitive the market, the more important the level of customer satisfaction. What most people tend to overlook, however, is just how important the level of customer satisfaction is in markets where competition is intense, such as hard and soft durables, business equipment, financial services, and retailing. In markets like these, there is a tremendous difference between the loyalty of merely satisfied and completely satisfied customers. Automobile industry shows, completely satisfied customers are—to a surprising degree—much more loyal than satisfied customers.

To put it another way, any drop from total satisfaction results in a major drop in loyalty. The same applies to commodity businesses with thin profit margins; the potential returns on initiatives to increase satisfaction in such businesses can be as high as the return on initiatives in more profitable businesses. In fact, attempts to create complete customer satisfaction in commodity industries will often raise the product or service out of the commodity category. In most instances, totally satisfying the members of the targeted customer group should be a top priority.

## CONCLUSION

There are various measurement parameters for relationship effectiveness and the feedback comes primarily from the customer as well as from other stakeholders in the business. For measuring effectiveness of relationship, some cardinal points may be taken into considerations on conceptual basis, for example, client views on product or services, evaluation of client orientation within the organization, etc. Whatever is the measurement methodology, there should be an alignment in the measurement factors and its weightings from both ends—customer as well as his partner—and then only there will be a meaningful approach in arriving at the total value from these measurements. Measurement exercise is applicable irrespective of the success and failure of the products or services. This measurement process is termed *Relationship Quality Survey.* Inputs are gathered covering product and relationship dimensions from the client. There are organizations that have come up with satisfaction index serving as a standard to measure the effectiveness of client partner relationship. The Customer Satisfaction Index (CSI) is one such tool and an indicator of customer satisfaction level. With CSI, the marketer is able to understand the perceived value of his offer. The overall objective of this measurement is to examine strengths and weaknesses at a granular level so that remedial measures can be undertaken by the organization to forge the relationship for mutual benefits. The ServQual model provides a reliable methodology for measuring customer satisfaction in service situation. It seeks to measure perceived service quality on the basis of five parameters, namely, tangible, responsiveness, reliability, assurance, and empathy. Based on the inputs on these parameters, various gaps are identified in relationship. The American Customer Satisfaction Index covers the following input parameters, such as customer expectations, perceived quality, perceived values, customer complaints and customer loyalty. The balanced scorecard model measures organization effectiveness from four different perspectives and aims to integrate its operational control with long-term vision and strategy. The method has been endorsed by reputed organizations and it has been getting acceptance in many forward-looking corporate bodies worldwide. The application of balanced scorecard in relationship marketing has been explored and it is observed that a staged approach would be conducive for achieving favourable results. This has been illustrated in the form of a pyramid where the lowest layer is growth and learning for enabling the people within the organization and the top layer is the revenue perspective, which is the outcome of the effectiveness of the lower layers. Successful implementation of lower layers will result in revenue and business growth in the financial perspective. Measurement results are critical as those give significant insight on the quality of relationship, which helps management to strategize their business plans for client retention. Measurement objective should be to identify and focus on the customers who are other than the ones completely satisfied.

> **Keywords:** RoI, Client servicing synergy, Customer satisfaction index, ServQual model, ASCI.

## Exercises

1. How would you prepare the customer feedback form for satisfaction survey with respect to an Sales Training Course? What are the actions you propose to take if 30% of the participants give an overall rating of 'Satisfactory'?

2. From your past experience, list down at least two products that you had discontinued to purchase. What was your rationale for such discontinuance?

3. What is the importance of taking within the organization feedback regarding relationship outlook? What are the areas of feedback that top management needs to focus upon for improving the relationship outlook?

4. How is the concept of balance scorecard applied in improving customer relationships?

Fill in the blanks:

5. _____ is one such tool and an indicator of customer satisfaction level. With this, the marketer is able to understand the perceived value of his offer.

6. State at least five reasons for rejection of a product or service by a client:
   (a) _____
   (b) _____
   (c) _____
   (d) _____
   (e) _____

# References

Averson, Paul, 1998. http://www.balancedscorecard.org/basics/bsc1.html

Drucker, Peter F., 1995. *Managing in Time of Great Change*, Trueman, Talley Books, E.P. Dutton, New York.

Gummesson, Evert, 2002. *Do RM and CRM play? Total Relationship Marketing*, Butterworth-Heinemann, Oxford, UK, p. 241.

*Ibid.*, p. 230.

Heskett, James. L., Sasser, E.W. and Schlessinger, L.A., 1997. The Service Profit Chain, The Free Press, A division of Simon and Schuster Inc., New York.

Johansen, Jon Ivar and Monthelie, Caroline., 1996. Lojalitetsredovisning. Gothenburg: Infonet Scandinavia, p. 17.

Jones. T.O. and Sasser, E.A., 1995. Why satisfied customers defect, *Harvard Business Review*, Boston, 73(6), pp. 88–99.

Kaplan, Robert S. and Norton, David P., 1992. The Balanced Scorecard— Measures that Drive Perforamance, *Harvard Business Review*, Vol. 70, No. 1, Jan–Feb., pp. 71–79.

*Ibid.*, 14–18.

Kaplan, Robert S. and Norton, David P., 1996. *The Balanced Scorecard —Translating Strategy into Action*, Harvard Business School Press, Boston, p. 322.

Kaplan, R.S. and Norton, D.P., 2000. Having Trouble With Your Strategy? Then Map It, *Harvard Business Review*, September–October, pp. 167–176.

Kaplan, R.S. and Norton, D.P., 2006. *Alignment: Using the Balanced Scorecard to Create Corporate Synergies*", Harvard Business School Press, Boston, p. 4.

Parasuraman, A., Zeithaml, Valarie A. and Berry, Leonard L., 1985. A Conceptual Model of Service Quality and its Implications for Future Research', *Journal of Marketing*, Fall.

Ramaswamy, V.S. and Namakumari, S., 2002. *Marketing Management —Planning, Implementation and Control, Global Perspective Indian Context*, Macmillan India Ltd., Delhi, pp. 662–663.

Rigby, D.K., Reichheld, F.F., Schefter, Phil, 2002, Avoid the Four Perils of CRM', 2002, *Harvard Business Review*, Vol. 80, No. 2, pp. 101–109.

Roberts-Phelps, Graham, 2003. '*Customer Relationship Management—How to Turn a Good Business into a Great One*, Viva Books Private Ltd., Delhi.

Sheth, N. Jagdish and Parvatiyar, Atul., 2002. Performance Evaluation Process, in *The Handbook of Relationship Marketing*, Response Books, a division of Sage Publication, New Delhi, p. 25.

Websites

ASCI Source: www.theacsi.org/model.htm
www.jdpower.com/corporate/news/releases/pressrelease.asp
www.oph.fi/english/page.asp

# CHAPTER 11

# Relationship Manager

## INTRODUCTION

The importance of Relationship Marketing in the competitive business scenario has gained high level of acceptance from all cross-sections of business. Although it is recognized as an integral function of marketing, in practice it means a lot more as it envisages enormous coordination of network of activities that bridges all visible gaps between the client and the partner. The role of the relationship manager has attracted industry attention because there needs to be someone who would be dynamic and enterprising enough to understand and work upon to eliminate the gaps between the client and the partner. In accordance with such requirements, a position has been created to facilitate and ensure a smooth and long-lasting relationship with the client. Clients look at relationship managers for their business comfort and hence organizations empower them with proper authority and responsibility so that when they walk into the client's office, the client is relieved to see them because he feels related to them. To create delighted clients, a sense of ownership, commitment and dedication forms the kernel of the role of a relationship manager. Very often, the relationship manager is termed *client servicing manager*. This chapter discusses the rationale of having the position of relationship managers and their roles and responsibilities.

## IMPORTANCE OF RELATIONSHIP MANAGER

Customer relationships are the lifeblood of every good company. Relationships between a company and their customers, distributors, employees, referral sources, are vital to continued, sustained growth, and stability. Loyal relationships with these valued individuals make for a strong bottom line. The objective of having a relationship manager in the organization is to facilitate a process that would enable the partner to live inside the DNAs of the client. It should be noted here that without mention of the DNA, the function is as simple as that of a marketing manager. Hence, the first step in building a business unit partnership is to assign someone to lead and manage the relationship. It is impossible to conceive of an external consultant to manage a client relationship without identifying a relationship manager (Kaplan & Norton 2006). According to research, only 33 per cent of IT organizations and 43 per cent of HR organizations follow the practice of assigning relationship manager to the business (CIO Insight 2002).

A good relationship marketing programme takes into consideration both customer relationship marketing and customer. With well-planned relationship marketing efforts, the organization can impact retention—and that will impact the bottom line. The relationship manager is expected to meet the goals and objectives of business relationship, to provide the strategic marketing vision, management skills in order to direct relationship network team members and implement loyalty strategy.

In this context, it is also viewed that the skills of the project manager and the business manager can be merged into what may well become the most exciting new professional assignment in business in the years to come—the relationship manager. The relationship manager's role is almost of an orchestral conductor who will balance the activities of the business cycle with that of the project life cycle and beyond. Relationship management involves a wide range of tasks and responsibilities, which are as diverse as the needs of business (Daves et al. 2003).

## WHAT CLIENTS NOTICE

Every interaction with the client represents a "moment of truth". This is, each time the relationship manager interacts, the clients pay attention to everything he does and says. In most cases, they would not comment on what they see and hear. The sum total of all these interactions represents how they see him. It also represents how they are likely to describe the relationship manager to others (including all prospective clients). Generally speaking, the clients pay attention to the following traits (Po-Chedly 2007):

**Professionalism:** The relationship manager is required to speak clearly and appropriately to the situation (e.g, the client dislikes slang, jargon, acronyms). Their expectation is a positive attitude and they notice this.

**Communication:** The relationship manager's ability to ask question at the right time is critical to successful communication with the client. Also important is the relationship manager's ability to tell clients what they need to know at the right time.

**Availability and responsiveness:** The clients appreciate if the relationship manager is there when they need him. They also appreciate timely responses to their calls, questions, etc.

**Understanding expectations:** If the relationship manager takes the time to clearly understand their needs (i.e. around quality, value, timeliness, etc.), they will understand that he actually cares about them.

**Product/service knowledge:** The relationship manager's ability to speak intelligently about the products, services and organization affects the clients' confidence and ultimately their interest to work with him.

**Managing client problems:** If one can prevent most client problems from happening, one is well ahead in the game. Equally important, when problems do arise, one needs to be able to manage them in a way that shows the client that the relationship manager is well prepared to deal with difficult situation.

## MARKETING AND SALES PERSONNEL'S ROLE TRANSITION

Taking into account the expectations of the clients, there is a transition from the 'sales oriented' role to the 'relationship oriented' role of the customer interaction manager. As a consequence, the role of the relationship manager is a response to the move from a transactional focus to a relationship focus (Jackson 1994; Wortuba 1996; Weitz and Bradford 1999) coupled with the economic imperative of customer retention. Historically, the principles of personal selling have been viewed from a transaction orientation (Jackson 1994) with the sales people committed to customer acquisition; the thrust has been to obtain the order and get the sale, backed up by reward systems designed to focus on revenue generation (Wortuba 1996). Salespeople have considered their roles fulfilled when the sale is made (Corcoran et al. 1995). One of the largest barriers to relationship development is the organizational reward system, which encourages salespeople to sell, not manage relationships; while senior management talk about relationships, the relationship managers operate in a transactional mode (Wilson 1995). Revenue generation will need to change to satisfaction generation as the main responsibility of those in relationship management roles and selling as a persuasive act will diminish in importance as efforts focus on facilitating a relationship between the customer served and the company providing satisfaction (Wortuba 1996). Leading companies are beginning to measure salespersons success not only by units sold, but also by contribution to relationship quality through customer satisfaction (Biong and Selnes 1995, 1996).

## RELATIONSHIP MANAGER IN THE ORGANIZATION STRUCTURE

In this context, it may be mentioned that much of the hierarchical operational concepts of business have gone through reforms. The earlier models of commercial organization pre-empted after the Second World War that followed the structure templates in the government, police and military force, as it was the only available model before the enterprise. Today, most of the progressive organizations follow the flat organization structure than hierarchical, enabling easy information exchange between peers, superiors and subordinates. Today, the manager has to be much more of a facilitator than a policy executor. An example of the organization chart with the position of the relationship manager or client servicing manager, as denoted by and practised in the service industry, is illustrated in Figure 11.1.

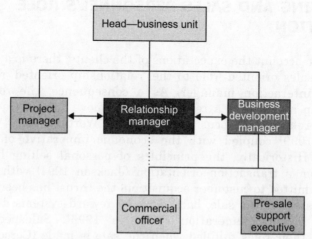

**Figure 11.1  Organization structure with relationship manager.**

Summarily, the pre-sale support executive is concerned with prospect identification through cold calls and other leads and initiates product presentations, preliminary discussions with the 'suspect' for converting into a potential prospect. The relationship manager collaborates with the pre-sale team and nurtures the prospect for transforming them into potential customer. Once the prospect transforms into a client, the relationship manager works hand in hand with the commercial officer for finalizing the commercial terms and conditions, agreement, etc. The commercial officer and the pre-sale support executive report to the business development manager, who is overall responsible and accountable for business acquisition along with the relationship manager. The business development manager can focus on multiple accounts for acquisition. The project manager is concerned with implementation activities, for example, project planning, product piloting, product roll out and maintenance, customer education and training. The role of the relationship manager is more of a coordination within the organization and outside, with the client at the focal point. Based on some defined missions, the functional responsibilities of the relationship manager are discussed here.

The following are the missions of the relationship manager:

- To ensure that excellent service is provided to that particular customer in all respects
- To ensure that the delivery of services to the customer is consistent with the goals of that customer.

The following are the roles of the relationship manager:

1. **To understand client's business requirements.** The relationship manager is not a salesperson who, having "sold" you, then passes you on to another unit (where the real work takes place). Instead, he or she works with the client and other business professionals and advisers to bring forward the tools the business needs.

   For example, in the banking industry, the relationship manager must have the knowledge and experience to fully marshal the bank's internal and external resources. As the lead consultant within and outside the bank, the relationship manager will work to understand the full spectrum of the customer's financial situation and needs. Through detailed and fully confidential planning, short-term and long-term personal goals and objectives will be carefully analyzed. The relationship manager will draw on various specialists within the bank to assemble a team tailored to meet specific goals. He will also work closely with the customer's team of professional advisors such as accountant, lawyer, and tax specialist, to insure that the client's entire financial plan is coordinated and meets objectives.

2. **To develop interpersonal relationship.** Show you care. The relationship manager needs to demonstrate the commitment to important relationships. For example, invite the best client to enjoy a sumptuous dinner and casual conversation at the end of the day. Choose an attractive, relaxed setting. Doing something pleasant and social together elevates the interaction from strictly business to a solid foundation of friendship.

When meeting the clients, make it a point to inquire about their personal interests, from golf to movies to family events. Take notes (if needed) and make an effort to ask about their pursuits. Learning more about them will give greater enjoyment in working together and will encourage to do even better work for them. Forming deeper relationships increases the likelihood that the clients will do more business and enthusiastically refer you to their friends.

Because an enterprise generally is valued on projected revenues rather than any given day's bottom line, the single most important indicator of an organization's value is the quality of its clients. A relationship manager is to continuously enhance client base. This boils down to developing long-term relationships and concentrating on customer satisfaction. Focus on nurturing the loyalty of those who hold the fate of business in their hands: for example, clients, prospects, referral sources, management team and staff and others in the marketplace. Keep in mind that the single most important reason clients leave an accounting firm is because they feel no one cares.

The following are the responsibilities of the relationship manager:

- Encouraging an atmosphere of trust, openness and communication and an attitude based on working together and shared objectives.
- Proactively looking for ways to improve the relationship wherever possible.
- Ensuring that all stakeholders in the arrangement feel that they are involved, that their views are important and that they are acted upon.
- Establish and manage a communication framework and ensure that it is used effectively.
- Establish and manage communication flows between customer and provider, and ensure that they are used.
- Ensuring that communications at all levels are peer-to-peer.
- Managing the dispute resolution process. Advising the customer of the responsibilities of the relationship manager

and explaining that any new projects, complaints, etc. should be directed to the relationship manager.

- Resolving 'soft' tensions between the customer and the provider, that is, situations where tension is felt or perceived but no formal issue has yet arisen.

- Managing upwards to ensure that senior management are informed about issues before they escalate, and can intervene as appropriate.

- Establishing regular reporting procedures, both formal and informal, and ensure that they are used.

- Organize forums, working groups, seminars, roadshows, training sessions, and other information-sharing activities involving staff from both the customer and the provider side.

- Promoting understanding of each other's business practices and common techniques.

- Developing a customer team so that the same staff and suppliers are consistently involved in work for the customer, and ensuring that the customer is aware of which staff undertakes the customer's work at any one time.

- Monitoring workflow from and to the customer, and ensuring that all work is undertaken by staff having the appropriate skill and experience.

- Monitoring work quality of its own and its suppliers.

- Holding regular meetings with the customer to discuss the handling of their affairs and particular matters, and what improvements can be made.

- Establishing a billing policy for the customer (after discussion with the customer), and monitoring billing to ensure that it is timely and in line with the billing policy.

- Seeking on a regular basis to identify areas or matters where it can assist the customer, especially by regular visits to the customer's premises, maintain a close interest in the customer's performance and where possible, suggesting ways in which this can be improved.

- Arranging regular social occasions, after taking care to decide what is likely to be the most appropriate and enjoyable kind of function.

*Source:* www.ogc.gov.uk

It is vital that the relationship manager has the authority to make or suggest changes to the arrangement—working practices, communication flows, the contract itself—to ensure that the relationship is safeguarded.

Here are some examples for basic requirements of relationship managers and their duties in the domain of banking:

### Example: Role of Relationship Manager—ABN AMRO NRI Services

ABN AMRO NRI Services brings to you a truly premium banking experience and a personalized service based on careful understanding of your diverse needs as a Non Resident Indian (NRI)—before you leave India, while you are abroad and when you plan to return to India.

As a customer of ABN AMRO NRI Services, you are not only assured the best of products and services, but also an unparalleled experience in relationship banking.

Our relationship managers are certified to provide you sound financial and wealth management advice. They will work with you personally to maximize your growth opportunities and enhance your wealth.

### How Your ABN AMRO Relationship Manager Empowers You

- Your relationship manager will personally handle all your transactions, so that you are assured of getting exactly what you want.
- Your relationship manager analyzes your profile thoroughly to anticipate your needs and recommend the best investment products, considering your preferences and requirements.
- You will get to know about the latest trends in the international financial market through your relationship manager, who will tell you how to leverage the opportunities to enhance your growth.

On your request, your relationship manager can also visit you in the comfort of your home or office to offer you our exclusive wealth management consultation.

*Source:* www.abnamro.co.in

## RECRUITING THE RELATIONSHIP MANAGERS

Some of the desired profile and personality attributes of relationship managers are:

- Flexibility
- Tolerance
- Ability to monitor and change behaviour on the basis of situational cues

- Empathy for customers
- Willingness to help others
- Mobility at a short notice
- Presentation skills.

---

**Case Study:** **Requirements of Relationship Manager at Gartner, Google and Royal Bank of Scotland**

---

### Relationship Manager at Gartner

**Summary:** Executive Programme (EXP) Public Sector Relationship Managers (RM) is the primary interface to Gartner for EXP Public Sector Premier Members. They are responsible for all aspects of EXP programme fulfilment and for retention. RMs are expected to deeply engage their clients and develop lasting, trusted relationships. They are also responsible for developing collaborative partnerships with sales colleagues and with other business units in support of growth and retention. RMs must work as well in teams as they do individually and they must be skilled communicators. They must have the ability to engage and influence at senior-levels and be able to actively set/manage expectations of clients and stakeholders. They need to possess or develop a strong working knowledge of business and IT trends, and the federal government structure and key federal processes and legislation impacting the role of the CIO and technology in business. The working environment for RMs is a dynamic, multi-tasking environment. Each RM manages up to 35 clients. Consequently, they must have excellent organization, time management and prioritization skills. To deliver fully on EXP Premier's preferential access/trusted partner value proposition, RMs must be highly responsive to member needs, they must develop and maintain a deep knowledge and inventory of member issues.

### Qualifications

- Strong interpersonal and relationship skills—must have an ability to develop and sustain executive-level relationships as well as internal organization relationships across a variety of roles and levels
- Superior written and oral communications skills (applied in both in person and phone interactions)
- Excellent presentation and facilitation skills (applied in both in person and phone interactions)
- Strong organizational, account management, and time management skills
- Managing multiple relationships and working in a highly multi-tasking environment

- Ability to interpret and understand CIO's key issues
- Ability to deliver (at the executive level) scenarios, interpret research, deliver presentations and address complex, cross-industry executive-level inquires
- Detail oriented
- Knowledge of general office systems.

**Desired Knowledge**

- Broad understanding of the technology industry (key trends in hardware, software, strategy, management)
- General knowledge of major business trends and executive management issues
- General knowledge of the role of the CIO
- Strong understanding of the Federal Government, including the various branches of government, as well as broad understanding of legislation that impacts the CIO and the IT organization
- Top security clearance desired.

*Source:* www.gartner.com/gartner_careers/asset_125977_1497.html

### Google: Agency Relationship Manager—Istanbul

**The Area: Sales**

At Google, we believe a salesperson's success depends on the customer's success—and we offer our clients technology solutions to help them grow their business and maximize their return on their marketing investment. This ability requires our sales team to have varied skills and talents, including thorough knowledge of the advertising business, understanding of complex technologies and the ability to sell effectively. We also have a keen eye for new opportunities and a skill for presenting them effectively to our clients.

**The Role: Agency Relationship Manager—Istanbul**

As a Google Agency Relationship Manager, you'll collaborate closely with agency representatives, serve as their ambassador within Google, evangelize new Google products and technologies throughout the agency, identify sales and business-development opportunities, and develop and manage strong relationships with agency influencers and decision-makers. You'll also collaborate with Google's Direct Sales teams to exchange knowledge regarding client needs in specific industry sectors. Among your many attributes, you are persuasive, gregarious, self-starting, a natural leader and skilled at solving problems and explaining complex issues.

## Responsibilities

- Evangelize Google within the advertising agency community
- Solidify executive relationships and drive revenue growth with targeted agencies
- Define and implement a national strategy for agencies in conjunction with the overall Google strategy
- Work consultatively with agencies, educate and train them on 3rd party strategy
- Prepare and attend customer meetings, presentations and contract negotiations.

## Requirements

- High-calibre University, MBA preferred
- Strong online sales and business-development experience
- Substantial experience in advertising sales/marketing
- Established relationships and presence within the agency marketplace
- Excellent written and oral communication skills
- Fluent in Turkish and English.

*Source:* www.google.com/support/jobs/bin/answer.py.

### Royal Bank of Scotland: Relationship Manager

The Royal Bank of Scotland operates across a global network, delivering world class banking and financial services to help customers make it happen. We are looking for relationship managers to be part of our Royal Preferred Banking Business in the United Arab Emirates.

### Role

To target high net-worth individuals (minimum liquid assets of USD 100,000). The job entails the core requirement of developing and enhancing relationships with high net-worth clients, providing financial advice/solutions and ongoing service, ensuring customer level profitability.

### Key Responsibilities

- Sale of all banking services and products including the bank's proprietary and third party funds, structured products, bonds, LIBOR notes, Regular Investment Plan, etc.
- Growth and retention of Consumer Banking liability book.
- Maintenance and servicing of accounts.

- Acquisition of new high net-worth customers, correct profiling of clients and maintaining ongoing updates on profile.
- Management and resolution of customer complaints.
- Preparation of credit and business proposals to meet specific client's needs.
- Maintain proper files and documentation
- Ensure compliance with the bank's policies and procedures, and Central Bank requirements.

**Requirements**

- MBA graduates with 3 to 4 years of total work experience and 2 years of relevant wealth management experience.
- Bachelor's degree in Commerce/equivalent with 5 to 6 years of work experience and 3 years of relevant wealth management experience.

*Source:* *The Times of India,* Ascent, Oct. 15, 2008.

## FUNCTIONAL CATEGORIES OF RELATIONSHIP MANAGERS

The functions of the relationship manager can be based on any of the following three categories:

1. Client/customer Assignment on the basis of product
2. Client assignment on the basis of geographic location
3. Selective client assignment

Each category has its own advantages as well as disadvantages. The business enterprise has to decide which one should be more suitable in view of its style of functioning, operations and business objectives.

### Assignment on the Basis of Product

The manager tackles all the clients who are users or deal with a single product or a couple of similar line of products in different parts of the country

### *Advantages*

- The product knowledge of the relationship manager helps the client to learn and understand all possible aspects of its usage and benefits. The client gets answer to any problem related to the product from the relationship manager.

- The relationship manager becomes the champion of that product and is able to win the confidence of any prospect, or new client on the very first impact.

## Disadvantages

- The relationship manager's skillset becomes limited to that particular or that very range of products. There may be a tendency on the part of the relationship manager to resist change in case there is any re-assignment to another product.
- Once the market rejects the product, the relationship manager's existence becomes redundant.
- Product tends to sit on the focal point pushing the client aside. As a result, the client loses organization attention and this becomes a grave danger for the organization and an opportunity for the competitors.

## Client Assignment on the Basis of Geographic Location

The relationship manager looks after the client activities with respect to a range of products or a specific product in a given territory.

## Advantages

- The relationship manager establishes the organization credibility in that geography which can fetch a lot of business from the clients across the geography.
- He develops the skill to handle different types of clients and becomes conversant with the varied customer psychology and behaviour.

## Disadvantages

- Covering too many customers at a time does not lead to high satisfaction of any of them. If there are a number of products along with the customers, then the relationship manager finds it difficult to master the products and the customers as well.
- Attending too many clients leads to a superficial relationship lacking genuine concern for the client.

## Selective Client Assignment

For large business clients, the relationship manager is assigned a few clients on a selective basis. Sometimes, this is done on discussions and concurrence of the clients.

## Advantages

- Client's acceptance helps partner to work in collaborative mode.
- A client gets maximum attention of the partner and hence improves relationship.

## Disadvantages

- The organization may lose the relationship manager to the client or to similar clients or competitor.
- It becomes difficult to withdraw the relationship manager from the client place for other assignment, that is, replacement becomes difficult once the client leverages comfort level out of the relationship manager. Once comfort level is achieved, the organization must focus on replacement/alternative development, otherwise organization may run into a risk of being driven by the irrational whims and fancies of the relationship manager or the client.

> **Case Study:** Brian Epstein—The Architect of The Beatles Relationship with the World

The Beatles, consisting of John Lennon, Paul McCartney, George Harrison and Ringo Starr, are one of the most commercially successful and critically acclaimed bands in the history of popular music, selling over a billion records internationally. In the United Kingdom, The Beatles released more than 40 different singles, albums, and EPs that reached number one, earning more number one albums (15) than any other group in UK chart history. This commercial success was repeated in many other countries; their record company, EMI, estimated that by 1985 they had sold over one billion records worldwide. Recording Industry Association of America (RIAA), Washington, DC—based on their universally recognized Gold®, Platinum®, Multi-Platinum™ and Diamond® Award program, which has tracked the careers of artists since 1958, recently announced its own "Artists of the Century" list. Thirty-five years after Beatlemania reached its crest, the Fab Four remain the most successful recording act of the 20th Century. According to the RIAA, The Beatles have sold more than 106 million albums in the US alone—more than any other artist in this century.

Leaving aside the Fab Four's inherent musical talent, much of the credit behind their astounding success goes to Brian Epstein (Figure 11.2), who was a manager of record department in North End Music Stores in Liverpool. In a TV interview, Brian recalled that somebody came in one day and asked for a record by the group he never heard of and he was the one who believed that "customer is always right and should get some

**Figure 11.2** Brian Epstein—the relationship architect of The Beatles.

service". He started enquiring the group and found out from the local magazine *Mersey Beat*, it was a group from Liverpool where he went down to cellar or a cabin and found The Beatles (Fig. 11.3).

**Figure 11.3** The Beatles—World's greatest entertainment legend (clockwise from top left—Paul, Ringo, John and George).

Epstein was persistent in trying to sign a record deal for The Beatles, even after being rejected by every major record label in UK, like Columbia, Philips, Oriole, Decca, and Pye. Epstein transferred a demo tape to disc with HMV technician Jim Foy, who liked the song and referred it to Parlophone's George Martin.

Brian groomed them up to rise to that spectacular height and became their Business Manager or 'Relationship Manager'. Having no experience at artist management, Epstein made the right steps by bringing serious improvements to their image. Detail-oriented and highly focused on maintaining their clean-cut image, Epstein called them "The Boys" and managed every aspect of their career, their everyday life, concert gigs, and media appearances. They switched from blue jeans and leather jackets to Pierre Cardin suits and cleaned up their stage act. He advised them not to smoke in public. Epstein directed the famous synchronized polite bow at the end of their shows. Their clothes, styles, and statements made them trend-setters, while their growing social awareness saw their influence extend into the social and cultural revolutions of the 1960s. Overall improvements to 'The Beatles' image made by Epstein transformed their appearance enough to get them accepted by the mainstream media and public of that time.

His personal friendship with George Martin was also important. By leaving the recording production and the repertoire work mainly in the professional care of Martin, Epstein made himself available for other artist management contracts.

He was intelligent enough to understand the potential of their music. Pop group music was not so popular before The Beatles and western pop/rock and light music scenario was primarily dominated by the US artists, namely, Elvis Priesley, Frank Sinatra, Pat Boone and others. But Brian successfully marketed their innovative songs made up of easy-to-sing rhythmic melodies with simple lyrics. Added to these, were their attire and unique hairstyle. Combination of all these drove the whole world into an amazing musical frenzy. The Beatles are recognized for leading the mid-1960s musical "British Invasion" into the United States.

Brian was a creative member of The Beatles, a multi-talented man with a good disposition, sharp memory, and an eye for details. Epstein could also manage the relationship within the group, because it was not a very pleasant one with the passage of time and the group ultimately disintegrated after Epstein's death in 1967. Allen Klein succeeded Brian as their manager for a short period. Allen Klein's records showed The Beatles earned £7.8 million between 6/62 and 12/68 not including songwriting. During the 19 months of Klein's involvement, The Beatles earned £9 million with £8 million coming from record royalties. The band finally broke up in 1970, all four members embarked upon solo careers.

"Now one of their best-loved recordings is to be beamed into the galaxy in an attempt to introduce the Fab Four's music to alien ears. NASA will broadcast the song, across the universe, through the transmitters of its deep space communications network on Monday—the 40th anniversary of its recordings at London's Abbey Road studios. The music will be converted into digital data and sent on a 431 light year-journey towards Polaris, the North Star, in a stunt that also commemorates the space agency's 50th anniversary" (*The Hindu*, Feb. 2008).

The Beatles and Elvis Presley revolutionized pop culture—reshaping music, fashion and society—in the 1950s and 1960s. In 2004, *Rolling Stone* magazine ranked The Beatles number one on its list of 100 Greatest Artists of All Time. According to that same magazine, The Beatles' innovative music and cultural impact helped define the 1960s, and their influence on pop culture is still evident today. In 2008, *Billboard* magazine released a list of top-selling Hot 100 artists to celebrate the chart's fiftieth anniversary; The Beatles reached #1 again.

Sir Paul McCartney once expressed that Brian was the 'Fifth Beatles'. With growing success, Brian's personal habits had become untenable and the cause of his untimely death. But the fact still remains that Brian Epstein is the chief architect of The Beatles' relationship with the music lovers of the world.

*Source:* www.riaa.com, www.wikipedia.com, www.imdb.com

## CONCLUSION

Considering the growth and expansion of one-to-one marketing, organizations are giving considerable emphasis on the importance as well as roles and responsibilities of the relationship manager. The relationship manager is the coupling between the client and the partner—which enables the client to enjoy maximum comfort level in working with the partner. For recruiting the relationship managers, the following skillset is required to be considered, namely, flexibility, tolerance, ability to monitor and change behaviour on the basis of situational cues, empathy for customers, willingness to help others, mobility at a short notice and presentation skills. Relationship managers are very much like business diplomats who independently operate to garner the client's confidence in bringing success to partner's business mission. Three functional categories of assignment of the relationship manager can be considered, such as, product-based, geographic location-based and selective client-based. Each category has its advantages and disadvantages.

> **Keywords:** *Project manager, Pre-sale support manager, Business development manager, Commercial officer.*

## *Exercises*

1. List down ten vital responsibilities of a relationship manager assigned to oversee the customer relation of a mobile phone services company.

2. What are the basic role differences between a business development manager and relationship manager?

3. What are the strategic points you would consider while assigning a relationship manager in a client location?

Fill in the blank:

4. The client notices the following while interacting with the relationship manager:

   (a) _____

   (b) _____

   (c) _____

   (d) _____

   (e) _____

# References

Biong, H. and Selnes, F., 1995. Relational Selling Behaviour and Skills in Long-term Industrial Buyer–Seller Relationships, *International Business Review*, Vol. 4, No. 4, pp. 483–498.

Biong, H. and Selnes, F., 1996. The Strategic Role of the Salesperson in Established Buyer–Seller Relationships, Working Paper 98–118, Marketing Science Institute (Dec.).

Corcoran, K.J., Patersen, L.L., Baitch, D.B. and Barrett, M.F., 1995. *High Performance Sales Organizations; Creating Competitive Advantage in the Global Marketplace*, McGraw-Hill, New York.

Daves, Tony and Richard Pharro, 2003. *The Relationship Manager—The Next Generation of Project Management*, Gower Publishing Ltd., London, pp. 14–15.

Epstein, Brian., 1964. A *Cellarful of Noise, Autobiography of the Man Who Made The Beatles*, Byron Preiss Multimedia Books, Paperback, New York.

Jackson, D.W. Jr., 1994. Relationship Selling: The Personalization of Relationship Marketing, *Asia-Australia Marketing Journal*, Vol. 2, No. 1, pp. 45–54.

Kaplan, R.S. and Norton, D.P., 2006. *Alignment: Using the Balanced Scorecard to Create Corporate Synergies*, Harvard Business School Press, Boston, p. 162.

New Age Communication, Beatles to Beam Across the Universe, *The Hindu*, Feb. 3, 2008, p. 18.

Po-Chedly, David A., 2007. *Client Relationship Management–How to Turn Client Relationships into a Competitive Advantage*, Jaico Publishing House, Mumbai, pp. 12–13.

Society of Human Resource Management (SHRM)/Balanced Scorecard Collaborative, Aligning HR with organization strategy, Survey Research Study 62-17052 (Alexandria, VA: Society for Human Resource Management, 2002); The Alignment Gap, *CIO Insight*, July 2002.

Weitz, B.A. and Bradford, K.D., 1999. Personal Selling and Sales Management: A Relationship Marketing Perspective, *Journal of the Academy of Marketing Science*, Vol. 27, No. 2, pp. 241–254.

Wilson, D., 1995. An Integrated Model of Buyer–Seller Relationships, *Journal of the Academy of Marketing Science*, Vol. 23, No. 4, pp. 335–345.

Wortuba, T.R., 1996. The Transformation of Industrial Selling: Causes and Consequences, *Industrial Marketing Management*, Vol. 25, No. 5, pp. 327–338.

Websites

www.ogc.gov.uk/stdoolkit/reference/roles/relmanager.html

www.abnamro.co.in

www.google.com/support/jobs/bin/answer.py

www.gartner.com/gartner_careers/asset_125977_1497.html

www.riaa.com

www.wikipedia.com

www.imdb.com

hdfcbankcareers.jobstreet.com/hdfcbank.htm

# CHAPTER 12

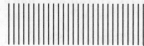

# Technology in Relationship Marketing

| | |
|---|---|
| ❖ Introduction | ❖ Knowledge Management |
| ❖ Major Considerations for Technology Deployment in Relationship Marketing | ❖ CRM Initiatives |
| | ❖ Self-Service Kiosks and Portals |
| ❖ Technology for Relationship Marketing | ❖ Self-Service Portal |
| ❖ Call Centre and Contact Centre | ❖ Web and Relationship Marketing |

## INTRODUCTION

Traditionally, technology offerings in the domain of Relationship Marketing used to be in the form of marketing information system that represented various findings and analysis from business transactions. This process is still in practice but its limits have been pushed further off. CRM technology has provided limbs to Relationship Marketing and Management for operations. Supplementing the CRM, the major technology enablers have been the Internet and enterprise-wide management information systems. The former allows businesses, for the first time, to get low cost interactions with customers. The latter allows a firm to generate a single view of a customer across all functional areas of a firm. For analytical purposes, Data Mining, Data Warehousing, and Data marts support the move to futuristic activities allowing the enterprise to use the huge repository of past and present data in order to have a clear view of future. This chapter gives a view of how benefits of technology are leveraged in the areas of Relationship Marketing.

## MAJOR CONSIDERATIONS FOR TECHNOLOGY DEPLOYMENT IN RELATIONSHIP MARKETING

- Meet customer needs better but also reduce costs of other means of communication—for example, timetable look-up, booking confirmation, perhaps best demonstrated by cinema seat booking.

- Harmonize your approach within traditional advertising and communication programmes. Ensure that the message and brand are delivered consistently across all media.

- Use the technology to allow the customer to find out the full range of what you offer and what you do—product, research, product development, loyalty programmes and promotions.

- Use the Internet to allow the customer to take control and provide or update information.

- Anticipate user constraints. Will customers be able to access your site quickly and conveniently? For example, using advanced graphics may waste customer time as it takes so long to download.

- Drive traffic—do not wait for visitors to find you, the portal should be fast enough to value customers' time.

- Keep your offering uptodate, topical and relevant to maintain interest, but ensure it follows a consistent pattern for your loyal audience.

- Use the best security and guard your customer's privacy.

- Resource and maintain your Internet site adequately.

- Measure everything including traffic volumes and patterns, user profile and satisfaction, ideally through independent auditing.

Apart from the above, some of the processes provided in Information Technology for controlling the activities in the sales and customer service are as follows:

- Facility for display list of customer contacts for each sales/service person everyday. The manager can follow up to be sure the list is called and review the results of the calls.

- "Every time we talk to a customer, we need to tell them about our specials." Availability of a promo list that can be used with each customer contact.

- "When customers call in for any reason, it is a great opportunity to up-sell and cross-sell." Information quickly available to know what they are buying, or have bought in the past, and links to companion or complimentary items that are appropriate to their buying patterns.

- "When we have a customer on the phone, we need to know if there are any open issues that need to be addressed, such as open quotes, outstanding receivables, backorders, shipping questions, short supply, etc."

- "We need to be able to respond to customers' questions with knowledge and authority." Seamless integration with appropriate software, there is a quick link to all the pertinent information. It is even possible to establish a link to catalogue file and display a picture of an item and the associated text on the screen so the employees can respond knowledgeably.

- "When a customer needs to be followed up, we need to do it on time." The reminder portion will record a reminder and display a message describing the action required on the proper day.

- "As the owner/manager, I need to know what is going on with my customers." Facility to track the chronology of conversations and events that surround each customer. Review is simple and easy.

## TECHNOLOGY FOR RELATIONSHIP MARKETING

There are diverse areas in Relationship Marketing where technology deployment is considered. The following are some of the examples of technology widely practised in promoting the objectives of Relationship Marketing:

- Call centre and contact centre
- Data warehousing
- Data mart
- Data mining
- Knowledge management
- Customer relationship management
- Self-service portals

A technology must be in place for supporting customer to overcome their problems, to address their needs on a one-to-one basis, and that is what a contact centre stands for. Very often, the contact centre is a representative component of CRM tool. Such interactions, in tandem with the past and present business transaction, lead to accumulation of vast information, and gathering, managing, analyzing and sharing of information facilitate deeper insights that can be used to make better business decisions. Technology embodying Business Intelligence turns information into intelligence, intelligence into knowledge, and knowledge into business wisdom. Combining advanced techniques such as data warehousing, data mining, and decision support, the technology should possess the ability to transform information into powerful customer relationship management systems that can help create stronger, more profitable relationships, identify new business opportunities—even anticipate customer demands. Starting with the contact centre, each area of technology has been described here.

## CALL CENTRE AND CONTACT CENTRE

Many people tend to think of a call centre as people neatly organized into rows, sitting beside their phones, answering customer calls. So, what is a *contact centre?*

Contact centrese are more than headset-wearing switchboard operators. The modern contact centre handles phone calls, e-mail, and online communication—including instant messaging.

Traditionally, contact centres have been called call centres. The newer name—contact centre—reflects the fact that more than just phone calls are being handled, particularly collective handling of letters, faxes and e-mails at one location is known as a **contact centre**. Many call centres have evolved over the years to do much more than just answer phones. A picture of a call centre is presented in Figure 12.1.

Figure 12.1 A busy contact centre.

Some companies choose to separate the handling of customer contacts by medium. For instance, a company may establish a department for inbound calls, one for outbound calls, and a group for e-mail. Some companies, especially smaller ones, opt to create "universal agents" who handle all contact types. Companies create universal contact agents for reasons of efficiency and service, and often because they find it easier to train agents in multiple communication methods than to train multiple agents in product or service information.

However, it is up to the customer to decide how they want to communicate with the company, and it is up to the company to respond appropriately through its contact centre. The following categories of contact centres are discussed here:

1. Inbound and outbound call centre
2. Self-service call centre
3. Transforming the call centre
4. Resources.

## Inbound and Outbound Call Centre

Contact centres communicate with customers in a number of ways, but who initiates the contact defines the type of contact centre. If the outside world initiates contact, then the contact centre is said to be an inbound contact centre. Conversely, if the contact centre itself is responsible for initiating contact, then the contact centre is said to be an outbound contact centre.

Customers contact inbound centres to buy things, such as airline tickets; to get technical assistance with their personal computer; to get answers to questions about their utility bill; to get emergency assistance when their car won't start; or for any number of other reasons for which they might need to talk to a company representative.

Increasingly, companies are looking to inbound call centres for proactive customer service that could be used for cross-selling and up-selling.

In outbound centres, representatives from the company initiate the call to customers. Companies might call to notify a customer that the product ordered is now available or because the customer has not paid a bill or to follow up on a problem the customer was having.

Outbound contact centres are, most often, very telephone-centric because of tradition and perception. It is not unusual for a company's representatives to call a customer on the phone, but it is more unusual for them to send an e-mail to a customer. If companies send out e-mail to customers, it is often done through some mass mailing effort, not as one-on-one contact. Perception enters into the picture because people are very quick to categorize unexpected e-mail as spam, but less likely to be upset by unexpected phone calls. Tata Indicom voice mail reminder of broadband expiry date to its customer is one such example of outbound contact centre.

## Self-service Call Centre

A new breed of inbound centres is starting to emerge—self-service centres. In traditional contact centres, all interaction between the customer and the centre is done with human agents. However, in self-service centres a good portion of the load is being shifted towards non-human systems, such as automated response or even speech-enabled.

This shift provides significant cost savings and faster response times to customer inquiries.

Automated response systems enable customers to use the keypad on their phone to answer questions by pushing buttons. Each button push brings them closer to the information they want. Automated response systems have been around for years, giving the customer access to simple (and common) information such as addresses, account balances, and procedural instructions. These systems can also be used to route calls to the most appropriate agent able to answer the call.

## Transforming Call Centre for More Efficiency

There are many ways to transform the call centre and gain efficiencies. Many companies are adding more channels of contact to create an enhanced experience with high customer satisfaction. Market research indicates that the new standard for contact centres is a combination of phone, e-mail, self-service, and web.

If the contact centre is running separate call-handling groups (customer service and collections, for example), then by merging these two groups one can take advantage of the economies of bigger contact centres. One can continue to have call handling groups logically separated, but with the ability for available agents in one area to handle overflow in the other area.

## Resources

A call centre is often operated through an extensive open workspace for call centre agents, with work stations that include a computer for each · agent, a telephone set/headset connected to a telecom switch, and one or more supervisor stations. It can be independently operated or networked with additional centres, often linked to a corporate computer network, including mainframes, microcomputers and LANs. Increasingly, the voice and data pathways into the centre are linked through a set of new technologies called computer telephony integration (CTI).

Call centres use a wide variety of different technologies to allow them to manage large volumes of work. These technologies facilitate queueing and processing of calls, maintaining consistent work flow for agents and creating other business cost savings. Such technologies include:

**Automatic Call Distributor (ACD)**, also known as **Automated Call Distribution**, is a device or system that distributes incoming calls to a specific group of terminals that agents use. It is often part of a computer telephony integration (CTI) system.

Routing incoming calls is the task of the ACD system. ACD systems are often found in offices that handle large volumes of incoming phone calls from callers who have no need to talk to a specific person but who require assistance from any of multiple persons (e.g. customer service representatives) at the earliest opportunity.

The key features of Automatic Call Distribution are as follows (Kumar et al. 2007):

1. *Call hold* allows an agent to place a call on hold, search the information and then resume the conversation.
2. *Call transfer* allows the call to be transferred to another agent or a supervisor or to another number.
3. *Call forward* allows redirecting all incoming calls to another number.
4. *Three-way calling* allows a third party on an outgoing call; it is very much like conferencing.
5. *Station hunting* is placed on individual telephone lines that make up a group, also known as a hunt group. Hunt groups are a series of lines organized in such a way that if the first line is busy the next line is hunted and so on until a free line is found.
6. *Call park* places a call on hold so that it can be retrieved from any other telephone. Once the call has been parked, your telephone line is available for reuse. Call park is useful for allowing a call to be handed off to another telephone line even when that telephone line is in use.

**Call recording software** or **call logging software** allows a party to record a telephone conversation (Figure 12.2).

**Figure 12.2 Call record list.**
*Source:* www.prettymay.com

**Computer telephony integration (CTI)** is technology that allows interactions on a telephone and a computer to be integrated or co-ordinated. As contact channels have expanded from voice to include e-mail, web, and fax, the definition of CTI has expanded to include the integration of all customer contact channels (voice, e-mail, web, fax, etc.) with computer systems.

**Issue tracking system** (also called **trouble ticket system** or **incident ticket system**) is a computer software package that manages and maintains lists of issues, as needed by an organization. Issue tracking systems are commonly used in an organization's customer support call centre to create, update, and resolve reported customer issues, or even issues reported by that organization's others employees.

**Outbound predictive dialler** is a computerized system that automatically dials batches of telephone numbers for connection to agents assigned to sales or other campaigns. Predictive diallers are widely used in call centres.

**Virtual queueing** is a concept that is used in inbound call centres. Call centres utilize an ACD to distribute incoming calls to specific resources (agents) in the centre. ACDs are capable of holding queued calls in First In First Out order until agents become available. From the caller's perspective, without virtual queueing he or she has only two choices when faced with a queue: wait until an agent resource becomes available, or abandon (hang up) and try to call again later. From the call centre's perspective, a long queue can result in many abandoned calls, repeat attempts, and customer dissatisfaction (Figure 12.3).

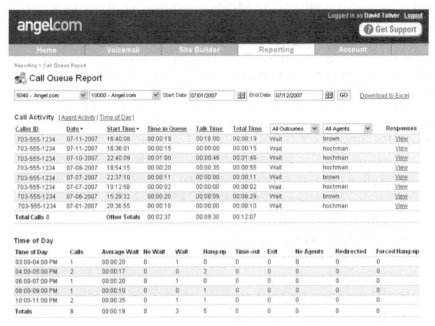

**Figure 12.3  Call queue report.**

*Source:* www.angel.com

Virtual queueing systems allow customers to receive callbacks instead of waiting in an ACD queue. This solution is analogous to the "fast lane" option used at amusement parks, which often have long queues to ride the various coasters and attractions. For an additional fee, a computerized system allows park visitors to secure their place in a "virtual queue" rather than waiting in a physical queue.

Call centre technology is subject to improvements and innovations. Some of these technologies include speech recognition and speech synthesis and software to allow computers to handle first level of customer support, text mining and natural language processing to allow better customer handling, agent training by automatic mining of best practices from past interactions, and many other technologies to improve agent productivity and customer satisfaction (Subramaniam 2008). Automatic lead selection or lead steering is also intended to improve efficiencies (US Patent), both for inbound and outbound campaigns, whereby inbound calls are intended to quickly land with the appropriate agent to handle the task, whilst minimizing wait times and long lists of irrelevant options for people calling in, as well as for outbound calls, where lead selection allows management to designate what type of leads go to which agent based on factors including skill, socio-economic factors and past performance and percentage likelihood of closing a sale per lead.

| Case Study: BSNL Call Centre |
| --- |

Call centres provide single window solution and convenience to customers. Data Infocom Ltd. is running an inbound call centre services for Bharat Sanchar Nigam Limited (BSNL), one of the largest public sector undertakings of India. Data Infocom is serving a 30-seater call centre round the clock attending almost 3000 calls a day related with broadband, dial up, mobile and basic telephone, providing help in the toll free numbers, attending queries, and solutions are provided for basic phone (complaints, transfer and shifting), mobile phones, WLL. BSNL call centre functions with the following features:

- Interactive voice response (IVR)
- Automatic call distribution (ACD)
- Access by telephone/FAX/Internet
- Call recording/barging/monitoring/coaching
- 3rd party switch integration
- Voice recording
- Inbound fax/e-mail
- Inbound service level alerts
- Internal and external call transfers

- Overflow agent group queueing
- Estimated wait time in queue
- CTI screen pops
- Call wrap-up information
- Call information history
- Skills-based routing
- Automatic operation via day and time project mapping
- Comprehensive inbound reporting
- Internal messaging.

*Source:* www.datainfocom.in.

## Data Warehousing

In a given enterprise, data is generated everyday in different forms and multiplies every year. The fact is, there is no dearth of data, rather the enterprise suffers from overabundance of data. The dilemma is that much of it is duplicate or redundant, unnecessary, inconsistent and difficult to access, manage and use effectively for decision-making process. Building separate data warehouses creates an environment tailored to decision-making and is the foundation for deploying an effective business intelligence solution. The process of collecting, correlating, reconciling, integrating, organizing, describing, enhancing and summarizing business information is what data warehousing is all about.

A data warehouse structures data in a way that makes it easier and more effective to manage, access and analyze. It is precisely known as databases that consist of cleansed, reconciled, and enhanced data integrated into logical business subject areas for the purpose of improving decision-making. Typically, they are enterprise scope in nature so that executives can readily understand company-wide sales or the complete business relationship with a given customer.

Data warehousing creates supporting structures for knowledge management and business intelligence. It contributes to solve very complex IT problems, such as developing an ABC costing model with profitability analysis of a:

- Client
- Region
- Marketing campaign.

Data warehouse systems belong to On-Line Analytical Processing (OLAP) world. They make you:

- Analyze situations and scenarios, giving decisional support
- Forecast developments and spot dangerous situations in advance

---

> **Case Study:** Data Warehousing System for Godrej Consumer Products Ltd.

Godrej Consumer Products Limited is the flagship company of the Mumbai-based Godrej Group. The company manufactures consumer products like soaps, detergents, and hair care solutions. The group has 18 factories and 120 locations all over India. A lot of ERP data in a standardized format was lying idle in the company's servers. It would be a good idea to use the data for other intelligent applications that can enhance business productivity. The company decided to implement data warehousing applications and functions to help extract maximum usefulness from the data. A range of data warehousing tools from Oracle was used to make this possible. The range of data warehousing products includes Oracle Express Server and the OLAP (On-Line Analytical Processing) client. The system serves as a decision support platform based on historical sales and cost pattern analysis. These tools are mostly used for analysis and trends that allow the company to create short- and long-term strategies and business problem solutions. For example, a particular product is manufactured in different factories of the company at different locations. Ordinary reports will give the amount of sales that the product has made (product-wise contribution) and the amount of profit that a particular customer has generated for the company (customer-wise contribution). Using DWH tools, the company now can perform a number of contribution analyzes, profit and loss analyzes, and sales breakup analyzes from the data in its warehouse. This has given it competitive advantage and the ability to manage resources better.

*Source:* Dasgupta, 2002.

## Data Mart

If data warehouses were to be viewed as actual retail warehouses, then data marts can be viewed as the showroom. A retail warehouse is packed full of items with the main consideration being well-organized storage with the ability to get items in and out. In contrast, the showroom's consideration is presentation, showing the value of the items, and taking care of overall customer satisfaction. The warehouse has to be suited to store items of all different uses, while the showroom will focus on items of a particular use.

The analogy works well for the data warehouse and data mart. The warehouse's job is to store large amounts of data with little or no concern as to exactly how the customer will view the data, while the data mart's concern is precisely the opposite. It focuses on ease of use for the customer, isolation of sensitive data, speed of reporting, and overall presentation of the data. The data mart is where the customers get their value and see their return on investment (RoI). Therefore, the data mart plays a crucial role in the success of the data warehouse.

A data mart is simply defined as a logically related subset of data from the complete data warehouse, normally meaning that the subset of data is related to a single business process or a group of related business processes. Data marts can be seen as the data from the data warehouse that meets certain criteria, such as all data relating to purchase orders that fall within the date range of the last three months, or all the data relating to shipping over the last two years. Therefore, sometimes data marts are considered to be subject areas of the data warehouse. This allows the data warehouse customer to only have to work with their business area data, and not be overwhelmed with the entire business data. This implies that there can be many data marts that get data from one central data warehouse.

However, the following are some of the many benefits from utilizing the data mart.

1. **Incremental development.** By adhering to the overall architecture of the data warehouse, data marts can be designed and built separately. The process can fit into an incremental development strategy where only one data mart at a time will be delivered, which will provide the customer with benefits from the warehouse before the entire warehouse is complete. Also, separate teams can build different data marts asynchronously. As long as each data mart conforms to the data warehouse architecture, the marts can be used in conjunction with each other.

   This has great advantages over attempting to complete the entire data warehouse as one single project: a project too large for even the most experienced development team.

2. **Customer understandability of data**. The data mart only supplying data that matters to a specific area of the business, there is less confusion for the customers. The customers do not need to sift through data that they are not interested in. The data mart ETL (Data Extract, Transform and Load) process does the filtering at the data mart level.

   Since the customers only have to work with data that pertains to their area of the business, they are already familiar with it. This familiarity allows them to focus more on how to use the data and less on understanding the data. Therefore, customers' requirements are easier to gather and development time is cut. Also, less training on the report generation is needed.

3. **Manageable pieces.** Data marts break down the complicated data design into small, manageable pieces, as already shown. This is helpful to the customer, but this is also helpful to the development teams. By the mart being simplistic in design, it is easy to communicate across teams and design customer applications, as well as maintain them.

4. **Manipulation of data in the mart.** Inside the data mart, the data can be aggregated, summarized, averaged, etc., to meet the specific needs of the business area. Since the mart is separate from the data warehouse as a whole, there is freedom to work with the numbers as the business chooses, without having to consider impact of the entire warehouse. As long as the lowest grain of data still exists in its original form in the data mart and the overall data warehouse architecture is complied with, the numbers can be used in any manner the business deems necessary, while the same base data could be used in other marts for other areas of the business.

5. **Better reporting performance.** By having only a subset of the data in the mart, the database system can manage the data faster and easier. Also, since the filtering has already been applied at the mart ETL, the reporting queries become much smaller. Smaller queries performing on a small subset of data are, of course, easier to tune. Therefore, the end customer will experience better reporting performance.

6. **Use of distributed technology.** Since the data marts are smaller, they can be placed on smaller distributed machines to allow data warehouse users to break away from massively powered machines and still handle processing of the reports.

7. **Microsoft data mart.** For many years, all systems that extracted production and other data from source systems and stored it in useful ways in a decision-support system were called *data warehouses*. Over the past few years, a distinction has been articulated between *data warehouses* and *data marts*. General industry discussions indicate that, as of January 1997, approximately 70 per cent to 80 per cent of all data warehouses currently in production are, in fact, data marts. Microsoft SQL Server on Windows NT is an especially popular platform for the deployment of data marts. The price/performance and capabilities of the Microsoft platform are a strong fit with the selection priorities of customers who are implementing data marts. With data marts, it is easier to identify a committed customer or sponsor within an organization. Compared to enterprise data warehouses, data marts are more limited in scope and more focused on a set of user needs. The key here is a focused challenge and a focused team.

*Source:* msdn2.microsoft.com

## Data Mining

Data is a set of facts about an event, object or any other thing. For example, 5 km, 300 grams, etc. provide no judgment or decision-making action. But information has been defined as 'endowed with relevance and purpose'. When we mention 5 km south of Eden Gardens of Kolkata, it points to some place or location. Information mining comprises text mining and data mining.

The general objective of the text mining system is to minimize the time a user spends in the steps leading to understanding the content of document or a collection of a documents. Text mining, therefore, involves two aspects: information retrieval and text analysis. The data mining utility provides Text Mining, Text Analysis tools. For example, using data and text mining allows the user to analyze at the same time the customers' personal data (age, gender, number of children) together with the full text information provided by their complaint letter, opinion survey entry fields, and business transaction related text and data. The business insights obtained from the combined mining of text and data are far more powerful than the ones obtained from data type alone.

The following are the major data mining operations:

**Proactive modelling:** Building a model of certain concept and to predict if a new model fits into that concept or not. Like building a model of loyal clients, and to find out whether the transactions with the new clients follow that model or not.

**Database segmentation or clustering:** Grouping similar records by their attributes. For example, information on places having largest rural wealthy males—this may be required for a new product launching.

**Link analysis:** Linking between individual records in a database— these links are called associations. The links between products and customers forecast the probability of repeat purchase, cross-sell and up-sell.

**Deviation detection:** To understand why certain values exhibit deviations from previously known expectations.

### Customer Profiling

- Enterprise-wide transactional and behavioural data (such as call centre).
- Third-party demographic data.

### Customer Modelling

- Predict customer responses to marketing and sales campaigns.
- Identify cross-sell and up-sell opportunities.
- Manage customer attrition.
- Perform customer valuations.

### Customer Scoring

- Identify top prospects for targeted marketing campaigns.
- Tailor call centre services and scripting.
- Increase efficiency of direct sales efforts by improving lead qualification.

It is also possible to define and select populations of customers, use data mining to build predictive models, and score customers based on relevant criteria. These predictive models are key in determining which:

- Customers are most likely to purchase products.
- Customer segments will maximize RoI on marketing campaigns.
- Personalized, targeted offers the call centre representatives should present.
- Customers are at risk of attrition.

Competitive business pressures and a desire to leverage existing information technology investments have led many firms to explore the benefits of data mining technology. This technology is designed to help businesses discover hidden patterns in their data—patterns that can help them understand the purchasing behaviour of their key customers, detect likely credit card or insurance claim fraud, predict probable changes in financial markets, and so on. Using data mining tool, the user can increasingly leverage the data warehouse and more quickly derive business value from that investment.

---

### Case Study: Data Mining

### Oracle Data Mining

Oracle Data Mining (ODM)—an option to Oracle Database 10*g* Enterprise Edition—enables the user to produce actionable predictive information and build integrated business intelligence applications. Using data mining functionality embedded in Oracle Database 10*g*, one can find patterns and insights hidden in the data. Application developers and integrators can quickly automate the distribution of new business intelligence—predictions, patterns and discoveries—throughout the organization.

Oracle Data Mining enables business decision makers, data analysts, integrators, and IT to extract greater value from corporate data resulting in better informed business decisions that address a wide range of business problems.

*Source:* www.oracle.com

## IBM Data Mining

IBM Data Mining Technology provides a simple and common data mining application through the analysis of sales data in retail environments; much of this is said to involve "market basket" analysis, as it requires understanding purchases made by a customer in a single transaction (or what items he/she placed in a shopping cart or market basket for purchase). Understanding customers' buying patterns is important, and retailers commonly seek to learn if and how sales promotions influence their customers' purchases. Such information can help retailers optimize their sales strategies and maximize their profits. It can also help them improve their responsiveness to changes in the market.

Source: www.ibm.com

## SPSS Text Mining Tool

SPSS Inc., a leading global provider of predictive analytics software and solutions, announced that Nucleus Research, a leading IT research analyst firm, found that text mining technology from SPSS can reduce customer churn by more than 50 per cent when properly implemented as part of an overall customer satisfaction strategy. Nucleus Research also found that text mining functionality increases analyst productivity by up to 50 per cent.

"We found SPSS text mining, either on its own or in conjunction with traditional transactional data mining, can help companies put customer insights in context, identify areas for improvement and better understand, predict and proactively manage customer interactions," said Rebecca Wettemann, vice-president of Nucleus Research. "Companies adopting text mining can leverage the growing content on the Web and in customer interactions for competitive advantage."

SPSS Text Mining for Clementine 12.0® software gives organizations a unique advantage to extract key concepts, sentiments and relationships in different languages from textual or "unstructured" data, such as e-mail, call centre notes, blogs, and surveys. Users can easily extract additional insight and predictive power from these channels to reduce customer churn, improve productivity, detect fraud and increase marketing campaign results.

*Source:* www.spss.com

# KNOWLEDGE MANAGEMENT

Market orientation (Jaworshi and Kohli 1993) requires organizations-wide dissemination of market intelligence pertaining to current and future customer needs, dissemination of the intelligence across department, and organization-wide responsiveness to it. The importance of customer information is quite obvious to most companies. McKeen and Smith (2005) conducted a study and found that 89 per cent of the companies felt that customer information was extremely important for business success.

After studying various aspects concerning knowledge management, they have created a conceptual framework that uses three components:

1. *Knowledge of customers*—Transactions of customers as well as basic data, such as demographic profile and contact numbers.

2. *Knowledge from customers*—Interactions with customers through focus group interviews, etc. to gain knowledge.

3. *Knowledge co-creation*—Customers are made a part of the knowledge development process like a partner. Computer software-makers offering beta version to the customer is an example of this method.

## Solution from Soffront

Soffront Knowledge Management is a fully web-based self-help, knowledge management software. The product provides:

- Knowledge base and self-help to customers, partners and employees.

- A knowledge management platform for employees and partners to build and share knowledge.

Users can leverage it for sales, marketing, customer support, employee support and defect tracking applications. Using Soffront Knowledge base for sales and marketing, the user can share key competitive information and best practices with the sales and marketing team. It also provides a self-help interface to customers/partners to find the right product. It assists users to leverage the knowledge base as a training tool for new recruits. All these features can enhance customer loyalty, increase conversions, and reduce costs for acquiring customers.

*Source:* www.soffront.com

## CRM INITIATIVES

Customer relationship management (CRM) is a multifaceted process, mediated by a set of information technologies that focuses on creating two-way exchanges with customers so that firms have an intimate knowledge of their needs, wants, and buying patterns. In this way, CRM helps companies understand, as well as anticipate, the needs of current and potential customers (Bateman & Snell 2007). Functions that support this business purpose include sales, marketing, customer service, training, professional development, performance management, human resource development and compensation. Many CRM initiatives have failed because implementation was limited to software installation without alignment to a customer-centric strategy (Rigby et al. 2002). Technologies for facilitating Collaborative, Operational and Analytical CRM activities are the visible limbs of CRM (Goodhue et al. 2002). Apart from these, Geographical CRM has also found immense importance for viewing these three CRMs from geographical dimensions.

## Operational CRM

Operational CRM provides support to "front office" business processes, including sales, marketing and service. Each interaction with a customer is generally added to a customer's contact history, and staff can retrieve information on customers from the database when necessary. One of the main benefits of this contact history is that customers can interact with different people or different contact *channels* in a company over time without having to describe the history of their interaction each time. Consequently, many call centres use some kind of CRM software to support their call centre agents.

Operational CRM processes customer data for a variety of purposes:

- Managing campaigns
- Enterprise marketing automation
- Sales force automation.

## Analytical CRM

Analytical CRM analyzes customer data for a variety of purposes:

- Design and execution of targeted marketing campaigns to optimize marketing effectiveness
- Design and execution of specific customer campaigns, including customer acquisition, cross-selling, up-selling, retention
- Analysis of customer behaviour to aid product and service decision making (e.g. pricing, new product development, etc.)
- Management decisions (e.g. financial forecasting and customer profitability analysis)
- Prediction of the probability of customer defection (churn analysis).

Analytical CRM generally makes heavy use of <u>data mining</u>.

## Collaborative CRM

The function of the Customer Interaction System or Collaborative Customer Relationship Management is to coordinate the multi-channel service and support given to the customer by providing the infrastructure for responsive and effective support to customer issues, questions, complaints, etc. Collaborative CRM aims to get various departments within a business, such as sales, technical support and marketing, to share the useful information that they collect from interactions with customers. Feedback from a technical support centre, for example, could be used to inform marketing staffers about specific services and features requested by customers. Collaborative CRM's ultimate goal is to use information collected from all departments to improve the quality of customer service.

## Geographic CRM

Geographic CRM (GCRM) is a customer relationship management information system which collaborates geographic information system and traditional CRM. GCRM combines data collected from route of movement, types of residence, ambient trading areas and other customer and marketing information which are matched with relevant road conditions, building formations, and a floating population. Such data are conformed with a map and are regionally analyzed with OLAP (On-Line Analytical Processing) for visualization. This enables a company to examine potential customers and manage existing customers in the region.

| *Case Study:* CRM Initiatives of Standard Chartered Bank |
| --- |

Standard Chartered Bank was looking for a tool that would help it analyze the huge volumes of data captured by its OLTP systems. The objective was to analyze new business opportunities, provide better customer service, and boost profitability.

Standard Chartered Bank (SCB) previously used On-Line Transaction Processing (OLTP) system, which facilitated and managed transaction-oriented applications. "The system was reliable but provided little scope for in-depth customer analysis, which is the key to survive in the fiercely competitive financial marketplace. It answered the financial queries and generated reports at a broad portfolio level, which included total earnings, debt situation, interest income, cost, fee income, and profits," said Sedjwick John Joseph, Head—Business Intelligence Unit, SCB.

The bank realized that it needed to go a step further and deploy a solution, which it can use to analyze the huge vol`umes of data captured by its OLTP systems. The idea was to search for crucial nuggets of information from the vast amounts of transactional data at its disposal to get the right information, to the right executive and at the right time. This information can help a bank take critical business decisions.

The bank's IT team looked at the business requirement in detail and deduced that the organization needed a data warehousing and analytical solution that would help analyze customer data to enable fact-based decision making in areas ranging from acquisition and risk management to cross-selling and portfolio management. After evaluating a number of vendor offerings, SCB decided to use a suite of products from SAS. It went for the SAS Customizable CRM Solutions.

## Varied Services

A better way to understand the bank's need would be to understand its customer base and the varied services it provides.

SCB has over 2.2 million retail customers and over 1.3 million credit card customers nationwide. It claims to be the first to launch initiatives like a Global Credit Card and a Photocard in India. Its products and services include cash management, custody, lending, foreign exchange, interest rate management, and debt capital markets for corporates. And credit cards, personal loans, mortgages, deposit taking activity, wealth management services to individuals and medium-sized businesses, and mutual funds to retail customers.

"Our customer base has grown three-fold in the last three years. Such a fervent pace needed to be supported by efficient management of the huge volumes of data generated and captured at each touch-point. After all it is absolutely essential to keep up the bank's unchallenged reputation of efficiency," said Sedjwick.

## Defining Benefits

The bank's vision was to champion fact-based strategic business decisions using best-in-class analytics. The objective was to enhance the organization's competitive advantage and boost profits. The bank was looking forward to the following broad benefits:

- The ability to exploit changing and widening markets.
- The ability to implement a customer-centric approach focused on optimizing the lifetime value of the customer.
- The ability to concentrate on financial budgeting, cost control, and risk management.
- To look for new ways to minimize costs, while increasing profitability and shareholder value by effectively managing consumer relationships.

### Solution Needs

It was clear that in order to achieve the desired benefits, the bank had to implement a data warehouse and analytical solution. Sedjwick said, "We wanted a solution that can perform analytics on the valuable customer data to answer queries across divisions. The answers would then enable us to proactively service customers and thereby ensure customer loyalty and retention. This exercise is a must for survival in a fiercely competitive environment."

Sedjwick continues, "Any bank today cannot ignore the risk: reward equation. Calculating it is a complex and challenging task that all bankers have to accomplish. It is the process of applying a variety of scoring techniques across product lines to arrive at the probable risk associated with each product sale and the possible rewards. Examples of products are credit cards, auto loans, and personal loans. We wanted the solution to leverage information on customer profiles and segments and enable us to spread our risks based on empirical data analysis."

"We also wanted the solution to be scalable. This was crucial as the solutions would be very critical to our business, and the volumes of data kept increasing exponentially."

### Evaluation

The bank created a team of 25 people in Bangalore and called it a Business Intelligence Unit. This unit was responsible for deriving and implementing strategies to analyze and exploit customer data.

"The company evaluated a number of solutions from Brio, Cognos, Business Objects, and SAS. SAS was chosen as the preferred solution partner and SCB today relies on SAS solutions across Asia for its customer analytics," said Sedjwick.

The SAS solutions reside on an IBM RS/6000 server running the AIX operating system. The SAS software accesses and integrates data from multiple sources and disparate systems across the enterprise. This data is then used for a variety of analyzes by the Business Intelligence Unit and is disseminated to all information consumers across the bank. The information consumers include sales managers, finance resources, credit resources, product heads and managers, and the head of consumer banking via the SCB Intranet. "As a result, analytics provide a key competitive edge and are used seamlessly for empowering business manager in their goals," said Sedjwick.

### Analytics' Benefit

The solution has helped the bank effectively manage and optimize profitability of all the products that constitute its retail portfolio.

Sedjwick said, "SAS's solutions forms a central part of the bank's CRM strategy. It is easier for us to run targeted campaigns and elicit substantially higher returns since we perform profit modelling for each account. This also enables micro-segmentation. Using analytics, and a test and learn culture we know the likelihood of customers to take a new product. We now know which card member is more likely to take an auto loan. This has resulted in more focused marketing campaigns and reduced costs with improved customer satisfaction."

The organization's marketing team is now empowered with information to increase cross holding, and can target its most valuable customers (not accounts within a product line) and also help in the next best product strategy for a customer.

## New Products

With the help of the Business Intelligence (BI) solutions, SCB was able to successfully launch DIVA. DIVA is a specially designed women's international credit card targeted at the Indian woman and bundled with several features. It includes discounts and zero interest rates on categories like jewellery, cosmetics, apparel, consumer durables, leather products, and mobile phones.

"This was possible due to an in-depth analysis of our customer data provided by the BI solutions. We realized that a significant proportion of our business came from the upwardly mobile Indian woman and was likely to grow substantially from this section in the coming months. This gave us an impetus to launch a product which catered to the needs of this segment and consolidate our position in the mind of the customer," said Sedjwick.

The bank also launched the aXcess plus savings account. Customers who have this account can access cash at over 1800 ATMs worldwide through the Visa network. Besides, they can use this account to shop for goods and services at over 25,000 outlets in India and at 10 million outlets worldwide. "This strategy was validated and facilitated by the information provided to us by the BI unit. We realized that by using this technique we could provide more value to our savings account customers and help increase customer loyalty," declared Sedjwick.

## Other Benefits

"We are successfully able to calculate our risk: reward equation," said Sedjwick. SCB uses SAS for scoring virtually all its products in the asset portfolio ranging from its 1.3 million credit card holders to its loan portfolio in excess of $ 860 million. "Information on customer profiles and segments forms the backbone of product strategy for us. It allows us to tailor our products across a diversified consumer base, enabling us to spread the risk across a much wider spectrum," explained Sedjwick.

SAS solutions are also used to carry out simulations that help the bank assess its overall profitability and balance its exposures across portfolios. The bank can carry out stress tests on its portfolios and learn about the best case and worst case scenarios. The working of the SAS library of advanced statistical techniques helps in achieving the results and arriving at an optimized risk-adjusted capital.

"The solution can scale to handle different sizes of data and takes much less time to analyze SAS data sets than it takes to analyze a standard relational database," said Sedjwick.

**Future Plans**

In future, SCB plans to embark on SAS' data mining technologies for various predictive modelling and advanced scoring initiatives to strengthen its risk management framework in the area of retail lending.

"Now that we know our customer well enough to provide effective customer service and maximize shareholder value, we will keep using information strategically so that it contributes in providing a cutting edge to our organization," said Sedjwick.

*Source:* www.networkmagazineindia.com.

---

**Case Study: CRM in HDFC Bank**

---

HDFC Bank, India's 12th largest bank (but one of the country's fastest growing), kicked off its CRM initiative about four years ago, when it had about 5 million customers. Rahul Bhagat, senior vice-president, Retail Banking at HDFC Bank, remarks that from the very beginning, customer data was already well structured to support analytical marketing and enterprise marketing automation technology. The bank deployed Unica's Affinium solutions to design, test, optimize, execute, and analyze all marketing programmes, including event-based and multistage communication initiatives. Affinium's Universal Dynamic Interconnect (UDI) technology allows the bank to simultaneously access its multiple data systems, resulting in a complete view of its customers across channels and products. Affinium enables marketing communications such as registration alerts and product cross-sell. It also supports models for activation propensity, response likelihood, and usage. Unica's Affinium Model solution has embedded algorithms to solve these tactical cross-sell and segmentation problems using the Unica file structure. Meanwhile, the bank is also using SAS for modelling needs that require significant data preparation as well as customization. Alongside the impressive growth in the bank's customer base, the bank currently already has grown to about 9 million customers, marketing velocity has significantly increased. The bank used to run about 120 campaigns in 2004. In 2005, this number had risen to approximately 700 campaigns, a dynamic mixture of campaigns across several channels and ranging in size from about 5,000 to 150,000 customers. The bank is currently working on a customer data model that covers over 6,000 fields, which should allow it to have one comprehensive and intelligent view of its customers. Also, as the bank's modelling capabilities mature, it will be running more event-based campaigns, quickly identifying when customers are at the point of making financial decisions.

With regard to operational CRM, HDFC Bank has brought online its RAP Computer Telephony Integration (CTI) initiative for the bank's 14 contact centres, which service as many as 650,000 actual calls per month (from the 2.5 million in-bound customer calls per month, most of which can be handled by interactive voice response). The system gives the bank's contact centre agents a view of data most often needed in standard customer interactions. The RAP CTI system pulls the select data from various screens in the host and makes it available as the agent picks up the call. HDFC Bank says that with the new system, the agent does not need to toggle between data sources any longer. "If the agent were to toggle, it would affect the customer experience and adds to the call time," remarked Rahul Bhagat, vice-president and head of direct banking channels at HDFC Bank. The agent is also able to see outstanding offers. The bank has populated the host system (updated at least once a month) with offers available for qualified customers. Lead generation over the bank's 1,350-strong ATM network (Diebold and NCR machines) has already started, based on CRM and predictive marketing and supported by locally developed ATM marketing software (Araneta 2006).

*Source:* http://www.oracle.com/corporate/analyst/reports/ent_apps/crm/resurgence-asia-2006.pdf.

---

| **Case Study:** Airtel's Customer Relationship Magic |
| --- |

CRM is the lifeline of Airtel, India's largest mobile service provider. From managing customer transactions to cross-selling, up-selling and preventive security, CRM does it all. And, at Airtel, executives struggle less as they fight customer churn, build loyalty and find new avenues to sell value.

### Don't Want Excuses

Wise maxims like 'The customer is king' and 'Customer service is critical' have created who want solutions pronto. But 'right-away' solutions were not always something Airtel could provide, admits Amrita Gangotra, Group Chief, IT Solution Engagement, Bharti Tele-ventures, who led the CRM initiative at the company.

As Airtel grew a national footprint, it cobbled together a number of local players, spreading into new circles and accumulating a number of different systems. In the resultant chaos, it was hard to service customers across circles, let alone implement an idea pan-Airtel. Delays in service, or worse a lack of it, were fraying the image Airtel's brand managers busy creating. In the time between a first call to the resolution of a query or a problem, Airtel's brand image grew clumsier. It was evident that without an integrated and a centralized CRM system, it would be impossible to process data and manage Airtel's homogenous customer base.

"When we created Airtel's macro vision of CRM, we aspired to provide a single-window of service throughout the country. Centralized and integrated were definitely two pillars we were looking for," Gangotra says. Today, integration and centralization distinguish Airtel's CRM from other run-of-the-mill deployments, adds Gangotra.

Manoj Kohli, President Mobility, Bharti Televentures, Airtel's holding company, believes CRM was not built merely as a tool but to be part of Airtel's culture. "It reflects Airtel's brand message: Think fresh, deliver more."

Delivering more was the driving force when Airtel made a call to deploy a composite tool that would serve millions of its customers. Anurag Parashar, Head of Customer Service Delivery, Bharti Televentures, says it was essential for them to have a standard platform. "Why shouldn't a person from Assam, holidaying in Kashmir, be able to make payments?" he asks rhetorically.

Airtel would make that possible and it would be among mobile telephony's pioneers to make it the norm. But before it could achieve this, it had to create a system that kept records of a customer's portfolio, profile, payment history, etc. Airtel also made a crucial decision at this stage. It chose to take an interest in the lives of its customers. And that, it found, made all the difference.

### Express Yourself

When a customer dials into Airtel's CRM, he set off a chain reaction that activated one of the CRM's two modules explains Gangotra Airtel's CRM consists of two parts: operational and analytical. The operational CRM makes sure everyday customer transactions hum along efficiently and the analytical module pieces together databased on customer habits that can help market a variety of services. The analytical module sits on a data warehouse, which contains customer profiles, usage patterns, demographics, revenue per customer, and other information. After Iyer's frantic call, for instance, Airtel offered to bump up his credit limit but also urged him to move to a talk plan that involved a higher monthly rental, cheaper talk time and smarter roaming rates.

In the main, however, CRM is associated with retaining and servicing customers. "Few people harness the potential of CRM to cross-sell and up-sell," says Gangotra. "Market analytics of a ready customer database can do wonders in converting prospective customers into real ones."

Understanding what a prospect is looking for is key. It was towards that end that Airtel sought to integrate all its processes across multiple functions with a centralized CRM.

Feeds from different areas within the company made sense, especially when business intelligence (BI) was applied to the data. Identifying prospective customers was made easier and BI ensured that whenever a customer interacted with one or multiple touch points, an auto alert was sent to a customer service representative who then made an up-sell or cross-sell bid.

And a customer relation has to make every contact count. Airtel's customer privacy policy forbids them to solicit a customer beyond a fixed number of times. Thanks to CRM, up-selling is now both more focused and accurate. "With such a narrow window, we have to make sure we score every time. We use CRM analytics to generate accurate leads from a customer database. If, for example, someone uses ten minutes worth of international dialling a month, we are going to try and capitalize on that information and make a cross-sell that will allow him to use the service more. It is win-win," says Parashar.

The CRM also serves to segment customers, thereby helping Airtel proactively identify the needs of its customers. "There are well-established events or stages in customer's lifecycle that clue us into his or her needs. For example, the aspirations of a corporate customer are very different from those of a retail customer. The former segment is attracted to our Blackberry offer and the latter can't get enough Hello tunes. One segment could be happier with an eBill, while another likes regular paper invoices. But we couldn't have differentiated one group from the other without CRM," Kohli says.

From the company's standpoint, it is also hard to overstate how far a little CRM can go in addressing an exchange of information between Airtel and its millions of customers. Its power to trigger off an SMS to large defined chunks of users is formidable—something even law enforcement agencies have picked up on.

Airtel receives thousands of queries everyday, many in the late hours of the night. Airtel's CRM system is closely linked to a host of other back-end systems. Once a customer is acquired, information to serve him better is available with the front-end (help desk)—the doorway to the CRM system. The people manning the doors have access to a customer's file, which makes it possible for them to field queries of varying natures.

If an agent is able to help a customer in the first go, it is called a 'first time resolution' and the call is closed. Calls that require specialized help are escalated by the CRM, to appropriate departments. Given that the CRM is centralized and supports workflows specific to queries, problems are fixed fast. But it has meant a lot of scripting on the CRM system.

"The beauty of this solution lies in the amount of automation that is built into the CRM system," says Parashar.

It is hard for Airtel's customers, both internal and external, to wrap their minds around the worth of the CRM. They envisage a morning when they awake without the CRM and stop dead in their tracks. That is because the CRM crunches millions of transactions, all of which generate data that has a specific place in the system. Some of the areas where the system has brought change include customized and simplified bill formats, payment collection centres, network deployments, and the activation process.

Now, it is just as hard to remember the days when customers agreed to wait or call back for an answer to their queries. Whether customers need to increase their credit limits or merely check the status of an additional offering like voice-mail, agents manning the call centres and hooked on the CRM react quicker because they have customer history and credentials ready.

Parashar, like his colleagues, cannot imagine life with the CRM. "Ultimately, it boils down to an ability to attend to millions of customers. Ninety-nine per cent of complaints that find their way into the CRM can be resolved in a first call," he says.

The CRM does not only reduce back-end traffic, but it also regulates it. Service requests, like issuing a duplicate bill, that are sent to the back-end now have a cut-off time. If a request is not attended to and breaches a pre-set time limit, it is automatically escalated to a superior authority. According to Parashar, neither networking issues nor problems related to coverage area are referred to the back-end anymore. Customers, of course, benefit the most.

"Customers moving between circles," reveals Gangotra, "best show up the advantages of CRM. Immaterial of where they are, they can dial a number and access the CRM or speak to a call centre agent who is logged on the system."

"We are trying to give the IVR more intelligence to make information available as a self-service. Some of our work includes speech recognition, which will enable the IVR to take on more natural languages," says Gangotra.

Airtel would like to offer its customers personalized services like never before. Especially clubbed with research—an example of which Parashar shares.

Personalized service, it is hoped, will also help the company retain more customers for a longer period. Unlike the hotel industry, which handles small numbers, it is tougher for Airtel to offer personalized services with 18.4 lakh subscribers in Delhi alone. Airtel aspires to provide personal service to crores of its customers through CRM analytics. "Without a CRM, we can't even think of attempting this," says Gangotra.

Thus, technology backed customer services, Airtel's customers can enjoy a host of rich features only with Airtel e-bill. The consumer can register free on 'My Airtel' section of its website and view the monthly bill with call details for last three months. The consumer can also sort their calls between personal and official or analyze the usage, at the click of a button. To change the tariff plan call by calling Airtel's IVR at 121 and leave a request, the consumer can also send in the requests through e-mail 121@airtelindia.com, logging into the request on My Airtel section of the website or SMS the change to 121. There are many other such features, namely:

- **Easy payment options. Anytime anywhere.** One can choose from a host of convenient payment options only with Airtel. Walking into any Airtel relationship centre one can make the payments by cash or credit card. Drop a cheque at any of the drop boxes for making payments or simply log on to My Airtel section and pay instantly through credit card.

- **Standing instructions.** Standing instructions to debit the credit card account for monthly Airtel bills. All one has to do is to fill the Standing Instruction Form and mail, fax or drop it at any of relationship centres.

- **Electronic clearing system.** Fill an ECS form and mail, fax or drop it at any of relationship centres to directly debit the bank account for monthly Airtel bill.

- **Credit limit.** One can pre-set credit limit mentioned on the monthly bill helps one keep the mobile charges in control, keeps track of usage and ensures that mobile phone is not misused. Should one exceed the credit limit, one will be informed via a voice or a non-voice message to make an interim payment and reduce the account balance below the credit limit. One may also choose to pay us an additional refundable deposit to enhance the credit limit or opt for convenient payment method of Credit Card Standing instruction. One can also make use of ECS facility.

- **Strong network coverage.** Enjoy complete clarity when calling with Airtel. It offers worldclass technology and unbreakable network coverage that spans over its circles across the country.

*Sources:* www.airtel.in, Rahul Nil Mani, www.cio.com

## SELF-SERVICE KIOSKS AND PORTALS

The self-service kiosks and self-service terminals are most definitely "in". From banking ATM service counters to checkout to railway enquiry kiosks, self-service is proving to be a very large benefit to business, and more importantly their customers.

### Self-service Kiosk

The following are the features of a self-service Kiosk.

- Self-service kiosks can provide higher service levels for the customers.
- More people get served quicker and better. The experience for the customer needs to be efficient, save time and be pleasant.

- Faster transactions.
- Self-service kiosks can better utilize the employees for more in-depth customer relations and service.

Let us take an example.

ClearSky Mobile Media, Inc., a leading cellular brand entertainment company and content publisher for cellular smart phones and camera phones in the USA, released its first integrated mobile downloads station (Figure 12.4). ClearSky's Mobile Download Station is the first

**Figure 12.4  A self-service Kiosk.**
*Source:*  www.clearskymobilemedia.com

fully integrated, fully functional download kiosk offering mobile users the opportunity to do the following:

- Browse and purchase ringtones, real tones, college logo wallpaper, and MP3 music files
- Download Java<sup>TM</sup> Games

- Instantly print camera-phone colour pictures via Bluetooth or USB
- Pay cellular phone bills
- Browse and print out mobile coupons
- Customize and download animated greetings card.

## Self-Service Portal

**Customer self-service portal** allows companies to provide self-service capabilities to customers and prospects for key marketing, sales and support activities. Customers can create cases, upload relevant information, search the knowledgebase, and track cases to resolution without ever having to pick up a phone. For railway enquiry, the following portal is illustrated (Figure 12.5).

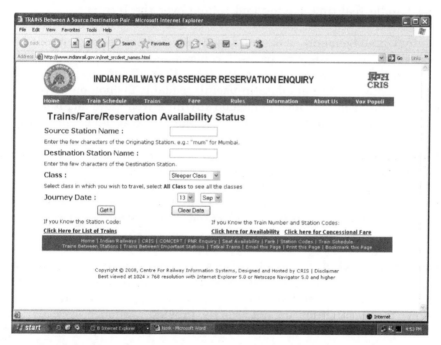

**Figure 12.5   Indian Railways self-service portal for passengers.**

*Source:*  http://www.indianrail.gov.in/inet_srcdest_names.html

## WEB AND RELATIONSHIP MARKETING

Back in the past, it was the trait with the IT people to think only about issues like how to efficiently handle monthly billing with respect to their clients in the banking, power, securities or other service-oriented business sectors. So, they designed the systems to deal with customers in bulk and to retain only the most essential information (Alsop 1999).

The Net has changed all that so dramatically that the systems must be redesigned. The key now is to put customer data at the centre of the IT infrastructure. The customer database is the hub; arrayed around it are five spokes with systems for processing transactions, managing content, acquiring new customers, providing customer service, and marketing to customers.

**Transaction processing:** Unlike the other spokes, which depend on software that has been created in the past three or four years, this one consists of traditional systems that run key functions of 'brick and mortar' companies: accounting, manufacturing, distribution, enterprise resource planning, and so forth. All these need to be integrated into programs for credit card transactions, auction management, and so on, that handle real-time buying and selling over the Internet.

**Content management:** For years, software for publishing content has focused on the design of pages for magazines, books, brochures, or presentations. Now, software is available that allows any company to display up-to-the-minute data in useful, readable fashion on a Website. Content has been redefined to include anything Web users might interact with, be it data, software, or classic content like text, audio, or video.

**Customer acquisition:** For many companies, this simply means buying applications that deliver ads to the customers they want to woo. But a new kind of Web software, called affiliate-management programs, can track the customer as he moves across the Web visiting other sites. If he buys something at a site he is affiliated with, he can get a cut of the purchase.

**Customer service:** Some of today's enterprise-software companies supply systems for customer service—those programs that manage the 1–800 call centres you dial into when you have a problem. But as we all know, these programs do not exactly provide customer service. Now there is software that serves customers via e-mail, telephone, fax, and chat rooms.

**Customer marketing:** This spoke is the most fascinating, because it has been completely reshaped by the Web—in fact, in its new form, it would not be possible without the Web. Think of it as 'one-to-one marketing' brought to life. The idea was introduced in a 1993 book by Don Peppers and Martha Rogers *The One to One Future: Building Relationships One Customer at a Time*. It proposed that technology could be used to customize marketing for millions of customers. At the time, the technology was not good enough to do that. But now the Internet has tied everybody together, and a small group of companies have developed tools to help companies market directly to individuals in volume. Customer-marketing software keeps track of customer preferences— learned either by watching transactions or by keeping track of online forms filled out by customers who reveal what they would like in the way of products and marketing.

## CONCLUSION

Technology is a tool to reinforce the foundations of Relationship Marketing. It is used in making predictive analysis regarding customer-behaviour on the short- and long-term basis. In general, the following areas of technology are widely embraced by Relationship Marketing for promoting its objectives, namely, Contact Centre, Data Warehousing, Data Mart, Data Mining, Customer Relationship Management (CRM), Knowledge Management, and Self-service kiosks and Portals. The information is collected from daily transaction over a time horizon from customer-orientated applications. With the help of this information and applying technology tool, data repository is built, namely data warehousing. Various exploratory analysis can be made using Data Mining and Business Intelligence tools. This information can be used further to help in building up the knowledge repository for the organization as well as the customer. CRM technology has been very useful in implementing various customer relationship-centric initiatives in terms of collaborative, analytical, operational and geographic CRMs. Customers can have greater independence of handling routine type of transactions and some organizations provide self-service kiosks and portals enabling the customers to handle their requirements.

> **Keywords:** *Data warehousing, Online Analytical Processing (OLAP), Data mart, Data mining, Text mining, Information mining, Proactive modelling, Clustering, Link analysis, Knowledge management.*

## Exercises

1. What are the major consideration for deployment of technology for promoting Relationship Marketing?

2. Give examples of two products or services where customer relationship has been greatly facilitated through portals.

3. You are advised to prepare contents of Knowledge Management Portal for a client in the banking sector. What would be your approach?

4. What are the four components that constitute the conceptual framework of Knowledge Management? Why are these important in the context of Relationship Marketing?

5. What do you understand by the terms 'customer profiling', 'customer modelling' and 'customer scoring'?

6. Station hunting is one of the key features of ACD (True/False).

7. If the outside world initiates contact, then the contact centre is said to be an outbound contact centre (True/False).

8. ATM counters are examples of self-service portal/self-service kiosk. (True/False).

Fill in the blanks:

9. The following are the major customer-centric operations of data mining:

    (a) _____

    (b) _____

    (c) _____

    (d) _____

    (e) _____

10. Technologies for facilitating _____, _____,

    _____ CRM activities are the visible limbs of CRM.

## References

Alsop, Steward, 1999. The Five New Rules of Web Technology, *Fortune Magazine*, June, New York.

Araneta, Michael, 2006. CRM Resurgence in Asia—Which Banks Lead the Change, *Financial Insights* (an IDC Company), white paper website: www.idc_fi.com, pp. 8–9.

Bateman, T. and Snell, S., 2007. *Management: Leading & Collaborating in a Competitive World,* McGraw-Hill Companies, Inc, New York.

Dasgupta, Soutiman, 2002. A Warehouse of Value, Case Study Special, Godrej's Data Warehousing Initiative, CRM initiatives of Standard Chartered Bank. www.networkmagazineindia.com

Goodhue, D.L., Wixom, B.H. and Watson, H.J., 2002. Realizing Business Benefits through CRM: Hitting the Right Target in the Right Way. *MIS Quarterly Executive*, Minnesota, Vol. 2, pp. 79–94.

Jaworski, B.J. and Kohli, A.K., 1993. Marketing Orientation: Antecedents and Consequences, *Journal of Marketing*, Chicago, Vol. 57, No. 3, p. 53.

Kumar, Alok, Sinha, Chabi and Sharma, Rakesh, 2007. *Customer Relationship Management: Concepts and Application*, Biztantra, New Delhi, pp. 110–112.

Nil Mani, Rahul, www.cio.com (Airtel Case Study).

Pappers, Don and Rogers, Martha, 1993. The One to One Future: Building Relationship one customer at a time, Bantam Donbleday Dell Publishing Group, Inc. Broadway, New York.

Rigby, Darrell, Reichheld, K. Frederick, F. and Schefter, Phil, 2002. Avoid the Four Perils of CRM, *Harvard Business Review,* Vol. 80, No. 2, pp. 101–109.

Smith, H.A. and McKeen, J.D., 2005. Development in Practice— Customer Knowledge Management: *Communications of AIS*, Vol. 16, pp. 745–755.

Venkata Subramaniam, L., 2008. Call Centres for the Future, White paper, February, pp. 48–51. (www.itmagz.com)

Websites

www.ibm.com
www.oracle.com
www.dell.com
msdn2.microsoft.com
www.soffront.com
www.allsands.com/History/Objects/historymicrosof_sax_gn.htm
www.networkmagazineindia.com
www.spss.com
www.cio.com
www.avaya.com
www.wikipedia.com
www.indianrail.gov.in/inet_srcdest_names.html
www.clearskymobilemedia.com
www.datainfocom.in

# CHAPTER 13
||||||||||||||||||||||

# Virtual Relationship Marketing

| | |
|---|---|
| ❖ Introduction | ❖ Real and Virtual Relationship |
| ❖ Relationship Marketing in the Virtual Space | ❖ Virtual Relationship Circle |
| | ❖ Virtual Value Chain |
| ❖ Effect of Technology | ❖ Implementation of Virtual Relationship |

## INTRODUCTION

The traditional model of 'Relationships' embodies physical presence of individual, group of persons, and their uninterrupted interactions to strengthen client-partner bondings. In view of the rapid growth of communications technology all over the world, manifested in the surging number of Internet connections, physical significance of relationship is somewhat reaching a challenged state. In the changed circumstances, similar interaction may not be ignored or discarded totally; nevertheless, such involvement need not be as intense as before, on the assumption that technology would take care of it. This has been accepted by business community the world over. It saves time, movement and can also lead to more effective business transactions. As it is evident now, business environment, resting on the platform of IT enabled virtual organization, has begun to talk more of Virtual Relationship with emphasis on meeting the changing needs and core competence in a networked environment. This chapter discusses the essence of Virtual Relationship Marketing and the shape it is going to take in future.

## RELATIONSHIP MARKETING IN THE VIRTUAL SPACE

There is a transformation about the look-and-feel of marketing in a world where distance has been reduced as it is within the reach of broadband, fiber-optic communications, Virtual Private Network, Intranet and Internet. Videoconferencing has successfully transformed the physical presence of an individual to virtual presence; on the site, meetings have now taken the shape of virtual meetings. The evolution of the virtual experience and the promise of cyberspace have recently begun to open doors to information, which were previously inaccessible. Everyone, from public universities to big businesses, is racing to cash in on what promises to be the future of information and communications.

A totally paperless, highly dynamic environment has been created in which ideas and images are exchanged free from the binds of the physical world. In this virtual space, the users are empowered to act with maximum freedom, as they do not have to wait for individual's liking or disliking for responding to their act. In that virtual space, what exists is the most massive amount of knowledge ever assembled on a common grid.

It is for this reason that an Internet connection is fast becoming the best way to reach the masses and provide input into a large percentage of the earth's composite knowledge. How will the business traditions of the past fit into the binary stream of the future? The world of mass marketing is evolving at an amazing rate. The market is gradually driven by the philosophy of 3As—that is, **Anything, Anywhere and Anytime**. And the vehicle, which will bring the business of the future to the doorsteps of everyone, lies in the web of the Internet.

Even the government is marketing its image on the Internet. This is extremely logical, as many citizens feel alienated by their government. The government site enables users to interact with the officials who run the country. The Internet provides a way for the government to become a more personal entity, and it also helps the government become more easily accessible. This marketing strategy makes it possible for the browser to gain information on new and debated issues of public policy. By making itself available on the Internet, the government boosts its image and almost gains public support because now everyone in the world has access to the more personal side of the government. As we move towards an Internet-based future, the government will coincide with the times. In the future, the presently overwhelming governmental system will become more accessible, understandable, and personable. This is perhaps the underlying philosophy of government to citizen service (G2C) concept manifested in e-governance to establish relationship with people. This is all a result of marketing on the Internet. The factors behind such high acceptability of Internet are as follows (Hamel and Breen 2007):

- Everyone has a voice.
- The tools of creativity are widely distributed.
- It is easy and cheap to experiment.
- Capability counts far more than credentials and titles.
- Commitment is voluntary.
- Power is generated from below.

- Authority is fluid and contingent on value-added.
- The only hierarchies are natural hierarchies.
- Communities are self-defining, individuals are richly empowered with information.
- Just about everything is decentralized.
- Ideas compete on an equal footing.
- It is easy for buyers and sellers to find each other.
- Resources are free to follow opportunities.
- Decisions are peer-based.

With all these facilities around, where is the need for the relationship manager to walk into the client's office for marketing interactions?

In the traditional concepts, relationship is developed through inter-personal or inter-group transactions. In these days, the philosophy of smaller, cheaper, faster, easier is driving the society and business. Many of the things have started becoming slick and small as well as simpler in operations.

Some organizations have already started augmenting one-man-office for marketing their product and this is supported by technology. In the insurance sector in India, such micro offices are already in operations in remote locations. In future, there need not be any office unless and otherwise it is absolutely essential. People would operate through laptops, and Personal Digital Assistants from home.

## EFFECT OF TECHNOLOGY

The shape of Relationship Marketing, in the future can be assessed now. Although it would be outlandish to comment 'man-less office', it speaks of self-automated office with a highly efficient high-calibre bare minimum workforce. Needs and demands of the customers would be catered by technology and organizations that would embrace cost-effective technology more and more in future. By leveraging the benefits of technology, the market would conveniently reach the clients, customers, and consumers instead their running to the market.

There are number of foreign banks and some PSU banks offering anywhere banking facilities to fulfil the objective of reaching people. Even in our social life, the Internet has even pervaded in the highly personalized family relation building process of match making. With such trend in marketing and social practice, where does relationship figure in the future marketing game plan? Would there be any genuine need for an individual to walk into the client's office in the early hours of the day saying 'Good Morning—here is a piece of good news for you'?

The answer is 'yes'—there is no substitute of human presence despite everything being available in technology. In future, it would be a costly proposition as its importance would be highly elevated. This would be done in a restricted manner. Web Portals would be very much in place to provide necessary human oriented routine relationship building support, for example, round-the-clock services in the call centres, and periodic review through web or portals about the feedback given the clients, customers. For consumer products or durables, there would be delivery people for handing over the required product—rather a large section of human force would be utilized to increase the reach at a lower cost.

# REAL AND VIRTUAL RELATIONSHIP

In the densely and highly populated Asian Subcontinent where physical presence of an individual still reigns at the top of individual's mind, the role of individual presence or personal interactions is certainly not going to fade away. This would continue to be on demand. But its look and feel would be somewhat different—a portion of it would be supported by technology, which embodies the spirit of 'virtual organization and virtual relationship'.

## Virtual Organization and Virtual Relationship

The phenomenon of virtual organization is quite recent and in constant evolution, implying that it is difficult to give any clear and definitive answer to what a virtual organization is. There seem to be five essential elements that are present in every virtual organization (Gummesson 1996):

- Network organization
- Goal-oriented activity
- No conventional limits
- Cooperations
- Sharing resources

If there is a difference between the virtual organization (VO) and the imaginary organization, then it could be the following:

Whereas the concept of VO is usually associated with IT, the concept of imaginary organization is broader and stresses both IT and human aspects. Hence, the concepts of imaginary and virtual organizations can be considered as very close.

Gummesson (1999) sees the concept of Relationship Marketing as recognition of a new type of organization which needs a new type of management. He describes "virtual or imaginary as a web of relationships, organized by continuous creation, transformation and maintenance of networks and amoeba-like, dynamic processes and structures," that epitomizes e-relationship.

Thus, the management of this web of relationships together with the challenges of changing markets and the necessity of flexible adjustments, builds a need to meet these requirements in a systematic and long-term oriented way.

## VIRTUAL RELATIONSHIP CIRCLE

The Virtual Relationship Circle (VRC) demonstrates the interrelationship between the main factors establishing virtual organizations in the dynamic environment and perspective where the client may not meet its service provider physically (Figure 13.1).

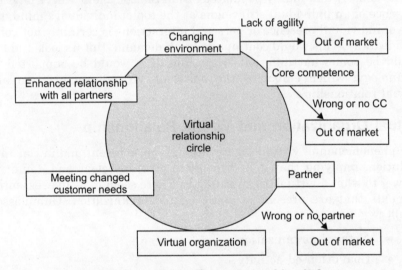

**Figure 13.1 The virtual relationship circle.**

As described above, companies nowadays are facing a changing environment characterized by accelerating speed of change. Not only that competition is getting more intense and fiercer due to generally decreasing transaction cost, but customers also are better informed and therefore more demanding which companies need to cope with.

To fulfil changing customer demands, companies have to focus on core competencies and to develop knowledge base for new enhanced products for their customers. By doing so, customer needs are met on long-term perspective. Companies not focusing on core competence due to more efficient specialized competitors would be forced out of market.

A natural consequence of specializing on core competencies is seeking for partners, which join the value creation process with their core competencies. Obviously, choosing wrong partners leads to minor valuable offerings (at least by producing at higher costs) and therefore will force the partnership in a weak market position, if not out of it. Think of leisure portals where customers are serviced in a virtual space.

The expectations out of such virtual relationships are clear—virtual customers should find it easy to use and it should have very high response time. This calls for IT enabling of business using the best tools offered by technology.

In this new generation of products and marketing, partners would always look forward to life-time clients—this view would not change but it would become tougher with time. Marketers would have to exert themselves to protect the reputation of something like 'life-time value' and market would be more and more flooded with 'use & throw', modular type items. Nobody can do anything about it—as a small differential change in any of the market driving event would force to change the configuration of products and the frequency would rise more with time—as a result, life of products become shorter and shorter.

## VIRTUAL VALUE CHAIN

In the last decade, the advancement of IT and the development of various concepts in manufacturing, like **Just In Time** (JIT) have led to the situation where businesses no longer focus on purely the physical aspect of the value chain as the virtual value chain is equal in importance.

Porter (1985), creator of the value chain, stated that there is no value added by the **Internet** itself; however, the Internet should be incorporated into the business' value chain. As a result the Internet affects primary activities and the activities that support them in numerous ways. Porter describes the value chain in the following: The value chain requires a comparison of all the skills and resources the firm uses to perform each activity.

Every business today competes in two worlds: a physical world of resources that managers can see and touch, and a virtual world made of information. The latter has given rise to the world of electronic commerce, a new locus of value creation. We call this new information world the marketspace to distinguish it from the physical world of the marketplace (Rayport and Sviokla 1996).

A few examples illustrate the distinction. When consumers use answering machines to store their phone messages, they are using objects made and sold in the physical world, but when they purchase electronic answering services from their local phone companies, they are utilizing the marketspace—a virtual realm where products and services exist as digital information and can be delivered through information-based channels. Banks provide services to customers at branch offices in the marketplace as well as electronic online services to customers in the marketspace; airlines sell passenger tickets in both the "place" and the "space"; and fast-food outlets take orders over the counter at restaurants and increasingly through touch screens connected to computers.

Executives must pay attention to the ways in which their companies create value in the physical and virtual worlds alike. But the processes for creating value are not the same in both. By understanding the differences and the interplay between the value-adding processes of the physical and information worlds, senior managers can see more clearly and comprehensively the strategic issues facing their organizations. Managing two interacting value-adding processes in the two mutually dependent realms poses new conceptual and tactical challenges.

The products and services the business supplies to the market need to conform to a channel that fits the customer's needs. Therefore, this channel controls the strategy of the business. The channel comprises different events, and each of these events should be in accordance to the overall strategy of the business.

In the virtual value chain (VVC), information has become a dynamic element in the formation of a business' competitive advantage. The information collected is utilized to generate innovative concepts and 'new knowledge'. This translates to a new value for the consumer. An examination of the VVC model informs the business to what function they have in the chain, and if they are not currently offering services that are information based (i.e. Internet services), how they can make the transition to the information based model.

In the virtual value chain, the 'virtual' indicates that the value adding steps are performed with information. The transfer of information between all events and among all members is a fundamental component in using this model. In the VVC, the creation of knowledge/added value involves a series of five events: **gathering**, **organization**, **selection**, **synthesization**, and **distribution** of information. The completion of these five events allows businesses to generate new markets and new relationships within existing markets. The process of a business refining raw material into something of value and the sequence of events involved is similar to that of business collecting information and adding value through its cycle of events.

## Geffen Records—Example of Virtual Value Chain

An examination of Geffen Records, a unit of MCA's music division, illustrates the use of information to create value. The traditional product of a major record label such as Geffen is a package of prerecorded music captured on an audiocassette or compact disc. The product is the end point of a set of value-adding processes that occur in the physical world. Those processes include discovering new musicians, screening them for potential marketability, recording their work in a studio, editing and, selecting their music, creating master tapes, producing CDs or cassettes, and finally, packaging, promoting, and distributing the products.

Increasingly, new competitors for Geffen's business are emerging in the marketspace. These entrants are viable because of the new economics of doing business in the world of information. For example, groups such as the Internet Underground Music Archive (IUMA) are posting digital audio tracks from unknown artists on the network, potentially subverting the role that record labels play. Today's technology allows musicians to record and edit material inexpensively themselves, and to distribute and promote it over networks such as the World Wide Web or commercial on-line services. They also can test consumers' reactions to their music, build an audience for their recorded performances, and distribute their products entirely in the marketplace.

The point here is simple: Bringing music to market can sometimes be done faster, better, and less expensively in the marketspace. Hence the challenge for Geffen. The company has a site on the World Wide Web devoted to the label's bands and uses it to distribute digital audio and video samples and to provide information about the bands' tours. The Web page has become Geffen's showroom in the marketspace and a potential new retail channel. It is also an information mirror of an activity that traditionally has occurred in the physical world—a stage in a virtual value chain that parallels a stage in a physical value chain.

The future holds a new digital marketplace in store for the people. An existence in which everyday errands are undertaken not in the family caravan but through the modem and mouse. With the promise of a brighter fiscal tomorrow, a corporate citizen stands ready to pounce on Internet users and inundate them with product information on demand. Shopping, paying bills, entertainment, and banking are all ready to enter every home through a more efficient channel, offering their services to the world for nominal cost in advertising. Interesting, many have noted, but how soon are we to see these changes appear on the net? The harbingers of change are already in place and they promise to redefine the lifestyles of every man, woman, and child on the planet. In fact, it is time to get ready for the greatest shift of consumer values for fifty years. New consumer values will demand new approach to marketing. Fundamental attitude/fashion changes are about to sweep through society. Those would be more powerful than Internet, biotech and globalization combined and would be accelerated dramatically by recent events, chaos and uncertainty. There would be a significant future impact on all marketing activity, business and personal decisions leading to experience certainty.

# IMPLEMENTATION OF VIRTUAL RELATIONSHIP

Various studies have shown that, on an average, only 11% of B2B leads generated made a purchase within 3 months of their inquiry, and that another 42% made a purchase in 4 to 12 months. This means that, at any given time, there are nearly four times as many qualified but longer-term prospects than there are immediate selling opportunities (Balegno, Sergio 2008).

Unfortunately, these qualified but less-immediate opportunities often fall through the cracks because seldom are efforts made to build a personal relationship with longer-term prospects. The reason? Few marketing and sales organizations have time today for the constant personal contact required... *unless it's done virtually.*

The goal of Virtual Relationship Marketing (VRM) is to get prospects to qualify themselves and tell you when they are in the buying mode. Done correctly, VRM will create the perception of personal contact in a way that is welcomed by the prospect and establishes trusted advisor status for the sales person. "Welcomed contact", as defined by a prospect, is being kept informed by someone who understands their problems and offers relevant information and solutions.

Virtual Relationship Marketing Processes and Automation will demonstrate how to use automated marketing processes to build these highly-personalized virtual relationships with prospects and customers, and generate the constant flow of qualified and timely selling opportunities that sales force and channel partners leverage to achieve profitable growth of business.

## Virtual Relationship Marketing Processes and Automation

Before proceeding with your first VRM campaign, there are two critical tasks that need to be completed—mapping clear and repeatable campaign processes, and implementing web-based solutions to automate these processes.

1. **Mapping your VRM campaign processes.** Begin by defining the sequential stages of core marketing-sales pipeline, which typically includes marketing communications, lead generation, prospect qualification, and opportunity identification and sales conversion.

   The next step is to map a clear and repeatable VRM campaign process that aligns with each stage of the pipeline. Sales channels vary by market segment, you will need to map a process for each segment.

2. **Implementing solutions to automate your processes.** The best solutions will be designed and configured specifically for automating VRM processes, and will seamlessly integrate the

following key functions in a secure and accessible marketing and sales web portal:

- **Contact management.** Store and manage critical prospect and customer information. Capture online and offline leads. Alert sales force and channel partners of high-probability selling opportunities and enforce follow-up rules.
- **Campaign management.** Segment contact lists for targeted email, direct mail and telemarketing. Compose and deliver mass-personalized, one-to-one emails (not categorized as spam), and track responses to VRM campaigns.
- **Content management.** Easily produce custom landing pages for email, direct mail and search engine marketing campaigns. Update website content.
- **Performance metrics.** View dashboard graphics and summary tables of marketing and sales performance metrics linked to detailed marketing reports.

## Virtual Relationship Marketing Campaign Workflow and Best Practices

By following the VRM campaign workflow and best practices below, one can achieve the highest level of performance in every campaign.

1. **Define the campaign objectives and strategic offer.** Begin by defining a clear objective for every campaign. Is the objective to trigger a qualifying response from unverified leads or to identify qualified prospects with an immediate need? Will the campaign be timed to generate trade show traffic or make prospects aware of a product launch. What segment will be targeted and what type of offer will be most relevant and of interest to that segment?

2. **Search and segment to create a campaign target list.** The contact database should contain field pick-lists for key market segments by region, application, industry, pipeline stage, etc. to make the creation of target lists fast and accurate. As with any direct marketing campaign, the list is one of the most critical factors to the success of a VRM campaign (Figure 13.2).

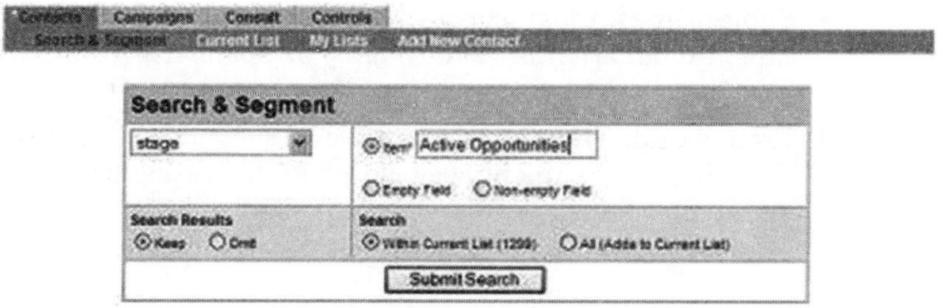

Figure 13.2  Creation of campaign target list.

3. **Compose and personalize the offer enticement email.** The most important principle of VRM is personalization. The email must appear, for all intents and purposes, to be a personal message from one individual to another. It should be written in the same tone you would use when writing an email to any business peer. Mass-personalization requires crafted message carefully and property merged contact data fields that add relevance to the recipient (Figure 13.3).

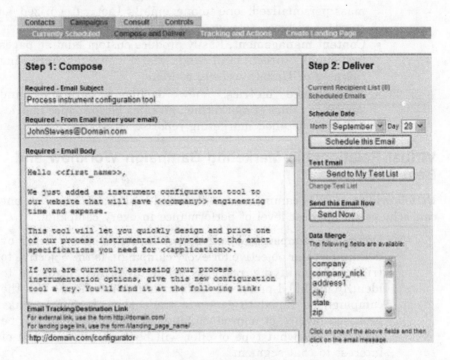

**Figure 13.3 Personalized e-mail.**

4. **Optimize email for deliverability and reader credibility.** The email message must also be crafted to bypass spam filters and the recipient's initial scrutiny in order to be opened, read and responded to. Some of the key best practices for optimizing deliverability and credibility include:

   • **Subject lines.** Clear, concise and relevant to the message. No caps, exclamation or dollar signs, or spam triggering words like free or save.

   • **From email.** The sender's email and the subject line are the first things a recipient sees, and will determine whether the email is opened or disregarded. Use only an individual sender's email, not a generic like sales@domain.com.

- **Email body.** Keep in mind that the purpose of the email is not to provide in-depth information about the offer, but simply to entice the reader to respond by clicking the tracking link if the offer is of interest, so keep the message brief. Plain text emails or HTML emails without formatting, graphics or colours are far more likely to be perceived as a one-to-one communication by both recipients and spam filters. If HTML is used, be sure to create a text version for recipients that have their email program default setting on text.

- **Tracking link.** Direct your recipient to a landing page that fulfils the offer.

- **Closing lines.** Be sure the name and contact information in the closing matches the email sender's.

5. **Create the offer fulfilment landing page.** If there is not an existing page on your website that fulfils the offer, you will need to create a landing page specifically for the campaign. If the solution you have implemented to automate the VRM campaign processes includes a content management system, this will be a quick and easy non-technical task.

6. **Schedule, test and deliver the email campaign.** B2B email campaigns scheduled and delivered early in the week generate higher rates of response than later in the week. Before delivering, it is always wise to trial your email and tracking link on an in-house email test list.

7. **Track campaign responses and identify sales opportunities.** Response tracking will show how well the campaign performed and give a real-time view of who responded. Depending on the objective of the campaign, tracking responses can identify the qualified and timely selling opportunities the sales force and channel partners will value and pursue.

8. **Distribute sales opportunities alerts and enforce follow-up.** The campaign process may provide for either the automated distribution of respondents to the assigned sales person or partner, or respondents may be manually reviewed prior to the distribution of sales alerts. In either case, automated follow-up rules and enforcement reminders are suggested. Studies have shown that the most effective and welcomed follow-up contact is by telephone or email made within hours of the original recipient's response.

9. **Consult and analyze key performance metrics.** An effective strategy for VRM analytics focuses on key performance metrics that will clearly mark a path to the most important outcome of

them all—sales growth. Concise dashboard graphics and summary tables of key marketing and sales performance metrics linked to detailed marketing reports are illustrated in Figure 13.4.

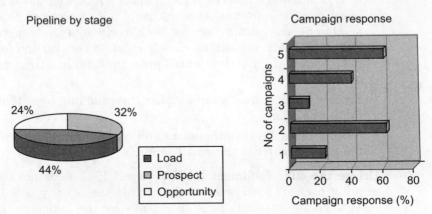

**Figure 13.4 Performance dashboards.**

Implementing a VRM strategy to build highly personalized relationships with prospects and customers will generate more of the qualified and timely selling opportunities to the organization's sales force.

## CONCLUSION

With the advent of state-of-the-art technology, the global market place is going through a drastic transformation from its traditional concepts of Relationship Marketing to Virtual Relationship Marketing. Using the benefits of IT and communications technology, users would relate themselves to the portal in the virtual market. Human intervention would be present while delivering the products and services. Transactions would take place in the virtual organization where the partner has to compete strongly and perpetually to assert their existence in the Virtual Relationship Cycle. The users would challenge the concept of life-time value every moment and the partner would have to survive through such tests leveraging the best offerings of technology. There are processes as well as best practice for the implementation of Virtual Relationship Marketing.

**Keywords***: Real and virtual relationship, Virtual organization, Virtual relationship circle.*

## Exercises

1. How do you visualize the function of Relationship Marketing in the virtual organization with specific relevance to the leisure sector?

2. How is the essence of virtual relationship perceived in the healthcare sector?

3. How does technology empower government to cultivate its relationship with the citizens?

4. Examine the best practice illustrated in the virtual relationship marketing campaign and give your analysis as to how you can relate this to the mobile phone service provider.

Fill in the blanks:

5. The market is gradually driven by the philosophy of 3As, that is, _____, _____ and _____ and the vehicle, which will bring the business of the future to the doorsteps of everyone, lies in the _____ of the Internet.

6. The _____ _____ _____ demonstrates the interrelationship between the main factors establishing Virtual Organizations in the dynamic environment and perspective where the client may not meet its service provider physically.

7. For implementing solutions to automate VRM processes, the best solutions will be designed and configured for automating VRM processes, and will seamlessly integrate the following key functions in a secure and accessible marketing and sales web portal:
   (a) _____
   (b) _____
   (c) _____
   (d) _____

8. Every business today competes in two worlds: a physical world of resources that managers can see and touch and a virtual world made of _____. The latter has given rise to the world of _____ commerce, a new locus of _____ creation. We call this new information world the _____ to distinguish it from the physical world of the _____.

9. In the _____ value chain, information has become a dynamic element in the formation of a business' competitive advantage. The information collected is utilized to generate innovative concepts and '_____ _____'.

# References

Balegno, Sergio, 2008, Virtual Relationship Marketing Best Practices. White Paper, www.ascend2.com

Brady, Nemmers M., 2005. 'The changing face of marketing', 'Wake up—its time' white paper College of Literature, Science and Arts, University of Michigan, Ann Arbor, USA.

Gummesson, Evert, 1996. Relationship Marketing and Imaginary Organizations: A synthesis, *European Journal of Marketing*, Vol. 30, No. 2, pp. 31–44.

Gummesson, Evert, 1999. *Total Relationship Marketing: Marketing Management, Relationship Strategy and CRM Approaches for the Network Economy*, Butterworth Heinemann, An Imprint of Elsevier, Oxford, p. 7.

Hamel, Gary and Breen, Bill, 2007. *The Future of Management*, Harvard Business School Press, Boston.

Porter, Michael E., 1985. *Competitive Advantage*, Free Press, New York, p. 37.

Rayport, F. Jeffrey and Sviokla, John J., 1996. Exploiting the Virtual Value Chain. *The Mckinsey Quarterly*, No. 1, pp. 20–36.

Snellman, Kaisa (Course Instructor), Ahonen, Mikko, Bechneim, Christian, Goux, Pierre, and Schöler, Andreas, 2000. Research Paper for Virtual Marketing (White paper), Source: arcor.de.

Websites

http://www-personal.umich.edu/~brady/intro.html
www.b2bmarketingtrends.com

# CHAPTER 14

# Customer Managed Relationship

## INTRODUCTION

What is CMR? Is it the acronym for Company Managed Relationship or Customer Managed Relationship? The answer is clearly the second one: Customer Managed Relationship. It might be more than just semantics. Disney Destinations Marketing has a new department: *Customer Managed Relationships. CMR is almost the version of CRM—just a slight nuance regarding the traditional philosophy that our guests invite us into their lives and ultimately manage our presence/relationship with them (Harrison 2007).* CMR is a value added change in the traditional concept of Relationship Marketing as well as Customer Relationship Management. CMR truly subscribes to the philosophy of 'living inside the customers' DNAs. The purpose of CMR is, by and large, to address the threat of falling product margins and increasing competition. Unfortunately, the emphasis for most is now cost cutting, driven by the overall economic downturn. But there are some clever and intelligent ones who think about how to get the balance right for the long term. They are none but the ones obsessed with the philosophy of CMR— Customer Managed Relationship. They are moving their mindset away from the belief that 'mother knows best' to the mentality that the customer knows what they want and you need to supply it on their terms. CMR is the new customer-driven marketing model where the customer drives the car and the company provides the roadmap to a rewarding lifetime relationship. And CRM is the old company-driven marketing model where the company drives the truck and the customer is supposed to ride in the back. The difference between the two is huge, and the new Internet-enabled, technology-wired customer market is well on its way to a new era of marketing where the customer really is king and the trip promises to be one of the most exciting adventures ever to be experienced by modern day commerce.

## CMR VERSUS CRM

Customer Managed Relationship relies upon the actions of the customer to drive performance while traditional marketing supported by current data base marketing and CRM technologies rely on actions of the company to drive performance.

If one looks at the term CRM—customer relationship management—it is all about companies managing relationships. Yet, if one thinks about it, the last thing customers want is to be managed. They do not want to be tracked down and directed and categorized. They simply want the organizations with which they do business to make their lives easier and less stressful. So instead of CRM, we should be practising CMR, or customer management of relationships. We have to put the customer in charge. Otherwise, CRM is about the company, not the customer.

CMR will, however, replace most of the costly, complicated, company-driven data base marketing technologies and software currently employed in the marketplace, and drive a more efficient application of most CRM technologies that were designed to serve the back-end.

In other words, many of us today believe that CRM technology got ahead of itself over the past decade and got the horse squarely before the cart and many companies are now paying the price for this costly mistake, i.e. CRM systems were developed for the most part to serve the needs of sales force management and customer service. But one tends to forget that no one needs sales force management and customer service until somebody sells something and the customer relationship is acquired and in place. The result—failure of many CRM technologies to deliver any meaningful level of customer satisfaction and measurable profit gain by those who paid large sums for an over-promised answer that was reversed in its application and ahead of its time in arriving at the marketplace.

In the current market scenario, customers do not want to be managed. Customers want to manage themselves—be in control of when and where and how they do business with you. There is no value in the one-sided relationship and that is what businesses have created and why the return on investment has not materialized. CRM initiatives have shown a recurrent failure to address three key aspects of the customer behaviour.

1. Customers view their interactions with you from their side of the fence. Their interactions must feel part of a logical process and deliver an end-to-end experience. Businesses rarely take this 'outside in' view.

2. The more you know about a customer, the more they expect you to 'get it right'. Businesses, in many instances, are weak at leveraging the customer data to improve their overall performance whether in product development, process improvement, sales targeting or the operational management. Excellent analytics have to be at the core of the business.

3. Technology is an enabler to offer self-service, and put the customer in control, for all customer types. The critical aspect is using it to make the services accessible to customers when they need them. Otherwise, it is simple, they will not use them.

To address these aspects of the customer behaviour you need to think in terms of a customer focused approach, hence CMR. Combining the three aspects one can create a great customer experience by taking the customer view of the interaction, generating revenue by leveraging information and people through great analytics and managing costs through technology enablers.

The critical aspect is building the best set of initiatives in all three areas to suit where you need to be—a sustainable economic model that has the right balance between revenue, costs and customer experience.

So, CMR is much more than just creating self-service applications on the web. It is more than good process design. It is more than successful campaign management.

*Source:* Naylor, David, 2007. www.budd.uk.com

## CMR APPROACH

If you take the customer view, you must do business with them on their terms. All too often though the customer is 'blamed' for not following the process or, for example, not using the frequently asked questions section on the website before calling. The problem is that many businesses try to fix the symptoms like delays in responding to emails or long call queue times rather than addressing the root causes.

Amazon has proven that you can build a successful business online. It still maintains 93% of contact with customer through the web and email rather than via the phone. Ryanair, the low cost airline, manages to achieve similar levels. Amazon calls it 'contact elimination'. Investigating why customers contact them via the telephone and eliminate the need, more often than not it is the clarity of the process or instructions on the web or similar issues that can be addressed relatively easily. Amazon has been obsessive about the analytics and the need to eliminate these problems. It has gathered the right information, done the analysis and fixed the root cause quickly.

The customer also needs to feel in control from two perspectives. In control of their data is one, and control of the process is the other. The long distance freight companies were the first to give the customer control of both. Vodafone has now done the same for corporate customers. These customers are now able to manage the activation of and updates to all their corporate mobile accounts themselves through a single view.

But businesses also need to realize that they cannot give with one hand and take away with the other. Offering a great experience in one area does not give the excuse for failing in another. Automating core processes like Vodafone has done the foundation, but when problems do arise, it is even more important to see things from the customer's perspective. Providing issue tracking numbers is one approach that has been adopted by many companies. But this often breaks down when exception handling processes are unclear, departments do not communicate and visibility of ownership and responsibility is poor. The customer still feels frustrated about the lack of control. A CMR approach links all the stakeholders together across the process and allows true collaboration to resolve the issues. This may even mean involving the customer in the discussions and decisions where appropriate. This not only saves time, but the transparency of the activity will result in mutual appreciation and great trust from the customer.

And trust is a key factor in creating customer lock-in—getting the customers to invest their personal data in you so that they remain long term, help you to get a clear picture of their needs through the analytics, and enable you to target them with more appropriate services and products. One example is the service offered by Carphone Warehouse that allows you to store all your phone numbers securely on their database. First you need to trust the business, of course. Then the chance of repeat purchase is increased because of the ease of transferring all your telephone book. A simple strategy but a powerful one.

But lock-in is not about capitalizing on customer apathy as the banks have done. Collecting sufficient data about customer activity and importantly, changes in their activity over time is critical. Using this data to do things that will 'wow' the customer is the aim.

The final factor to consider when taking the customer's view is the human factor. This combines many of the thoughts above such as putting the customer in control or considering the  customer's view of the end-to-end process. The human factor needs to address the way customers think and most importantly, the way customers buy.

If I want to go on holiday, I may know very clearly where I prefer, when I can go and how much I want to spend. That is how most web sites that help you select a holiday are set up. If I was to say I like sunny holidays with lots of adventure activities but do not like travelling more than 4 hours by plane, and so on, I would end up back at the travel agents shop or sticking a pin in a map! So, the first part of the process I need to go through is much less about how many tickets I need and more about the psychology of choosing a holiday.

Another human factor example is the old favourite of IVR systems. For example, if one wants to change the 'Hallow' tune of the mobile, one has to pass through quite a few menu options or operator intervention. However, advances in speech recognition technology would lead to the 'conversation flow' which is far more natural without complex menu handling process.

Considering the human factor and all the angles of the customer view is, therefore, simply a case of putting yourself in the customer's shoes. It is critical to view every interaction as part of an end-to-end customer experience. From a process perspective, the customers believe they behave logically and so the business needs to ensure the processes can withstand the 'outside in' test.

## TRENDS OF PERFECT MARKET

There are many reasons why CMR will soon catch and pass most of the competition that is currently out there on the racetrack. We are now in a customer-managed world where business value means customer value. We remain a long way from a 'perfect market'—the concept that the four trends described below would destroy the boundaries between customers and suppliers.

1. **Availability of information.** Most customers in developed markets will soon have Internet access that enables unparalleled depth of research.

2. **No barriers to entry and exit.** Barriers to market entry and exit remain, but they are being broken down by partnerships. Partnerships increasingly dominate business.

3. **Equilibrium price.** Equilibrium price applies to products and services that can be directly compared. In a truly transparent world, how you can survive if you are not cheap? Only when the offerings are differentiated, can you break out from being forced to drive down price.

4. **Perfect matching.** In the ultimately connected world, the gap between the supplier and the customer is non-existent: customers can find exactly what they want from exactly the

right supplier when they want it. We are rapidly approaching this situation.

The way to deliver customer value is through accepting that the customer is in control and adapting how you do your business to suit customer needs. This is the age of the customer managed relationship.

In customer managed relationships, what you offer, how you offer it, how you price it and how you partner to construct it are all adapted to how you attract, acquire and retain individual customers. This demands that you mass acquire and retain individual customers. This demands that you mass customize:

- your products (or services)
- your prices
- your processes
- your partnerships.

Customer managed relationships are not some ethereal vision in which you continue doing the same things while talking the talk of customers being in control. You have to reengineer how you create value.

## Mass Customize Your Products

Mass customization of products through reengineering the business around the smart use of technology has not worked as rapidly, or as completely, as its prophets forecast. The reason for this comparative failure is that in general the technology has not been up to the job. Simply, the problem is that it has been impossible to reconcile customer intimacy (individual product and service) with operational excellence (efficiency and low costs).

But the technology is getting better through an iterative process of competitive innovation across different industries. We are starting to see mass customization, if not at the level of the individual customer then for increasingly granular customer segments, across many sectors, such as insurance and car manufacturing. In insurance, customers increasingly expect to be able to include or exclude different policy features (cafeteria style benefits as insurers increasingly call them), and insurers are becoming able to deliver this flexibility without charging excessive premiums by using innovative policy management technologies. In car manufacturing, customers are given an increasing range of options and transparent pricing models at ever-lower prices. Simultaneously, lead times are falling as new technologies allow cars to be built to order.

Mass customization used to be about product. But we need to extend that agenda: It is no longer just about product, but process, price and partnership.

The Octopus card, which is widely used in Hong Kong, can be cited as one of the ideal examples of mass customization where technology has been leveraged to extend its use to penetrate into larger volume of population in different market segments.

The **Octopus card** (Figure 14.1) is a rechargeable contactless stored value smart card used to transfer electronic payments in online or offline systems in Hong Kong. Launched in September 1997 to collect fares for the city's mass transit system, the Octopus card system has since grown into a widely used payment system for virtually all public transport in Hong Kong. It is also used for payment at convenience stores, supermarkets, fast-food restaurants, on-street parking meters, car parks, and other point-of-sale applications such as service stations and vending machines.

The Octopus card has been internationally recognized, winning the Global IT Excellence Award for being the world's leading complex automatic fare collection and contactless smartcard payment system, and for its innovative use of technologies. According to Octopus Cards Limited, operator of the Octopus card system, there are more than 17 million cards in circulation, more than twice the population of Hong Kong. The cards are used by 95 per cent of the population of Hong Kong aged 16 to 65, generating over 10 million daily transactions worth a total of about US $ 3.7 billion a year.

**Figure 14.1  The Octopus card.**
*Source:* www.octopuscard.com, www.wikipedia.com

## Mass Customize Your Prices

Many firms are increasingly able to consider the mass customization of price. In today's relatively transparent market, customers understand supply and demand pricing better than ever before. A powerful combination is now on offer:

- Price sensitive customers understand better what is cheap and what is expensive, and accept and expect supply and demand to drive pricing.
- Technology allows real-time pricing at a more granular level than ever before.

In the new world, businesses can change prices more quickly and they can make more sophisticated information available to their customers.

## Mass Customize Your Processes

From a CRM perspective, mass customization of process enables customers to dictate their touch-points with a business process at no, or very little, incremental cost to the firm. Companies that have complex processes in which process status changes frequently (insurance claims, bespoke furniture orders) used to tell customers when the status changed at their convenience—if at all. Soon customers will dictate when and through what medium they want to be told of status changes.

## Mass Customize Your Partnerships

Competition is already increasingly about partnerships competing with partnerships, rather than individual firms competing with each other:

- In the fast-food industry, of course McDonald's competes with Burger King. But those firms line up powerful partnerships with Coca-Cola and Pepsi. It is the combination that competes, albeit through different brands.

Historically, such partnerships were pre-defined, structured relationships in which taut definitions of products or services to be supplied were entrenched within complex contracts pored over by lawyers. Yet, increasingly partnerships must be flexible to customer needs. The hotel that partners with the car rental firm will no longer have a rigid price tariff. The receptionist needs real-time access to real-time pricing and availability information to offer a discount on those hard-to-shift compact cars that are the only ones left in the rental car park. This requires reengineering across corporate boundaries—in which customer value is created by seamless connection.

The customer's experience in dealing with a firm is informed by knowledge of the partner's capabilities at that specific point in time. The essential component for the success of mass customization of partnerships is connectivity in real time. Connecting customer orders through the supply chain will drive huge savings in the interfaces between firms. The more extensive the reliance upon partnerships, the greater the savings that can be obtained.

Partnerships once created interfaces that were exposed to customers: for years, the customer has been the glue between partners solving the 'disconnect' between partners when the customer wants an individual response. As station guards shout on the London Underground: 'Mind the gap'. It applies as much to partnerships as the distance between train and platform. Customer Managed Relationships will force you to change that. Are, then, you ready to mass customize... everything (Molineux 2007).

## The Challenge of the 4Cs

We are now in a customer-managed era where business value means customer value. Businesses have to rethink how they serve and manage customers because of the 4Cs.

**Customers:** Customers have more options than ever before and are very discriminating. Customers can find exactly what they want from exactly the right supplier when they want it.

**Competition:** It is easier for competitors to begin offering similar services and products and get into markets they were unable to before.

**Communication:** Customers have higher access to information than ever before. Most customers have Internet access that allows access to information of competing products and services at a click. In a networked world, the communication gap between buyers and suppliers can be bridged rapidly.

**Commoditization:** The first 3Cs mean that there is a general industry trend towards commoditization of financial services. Products and services have become so similar that they can be directly compared. Only when products are differentiated, can businesses break out from competitive pressure to reduce prices.

Because of automated processing and multiple channels of delivery, financial service companies face the threat of commoditization.

Commoditization occurs when businesses face downward pressure on prices because their products are very similar to competing products. It is a magnet that businesses have to resist to remain profitable (Figure 14.2).

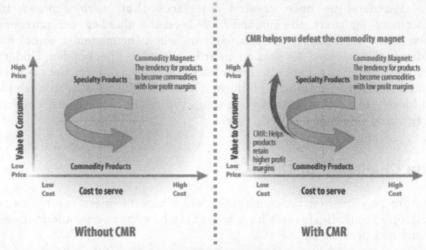

Figure 14.2 CMR and commodity magnet.

*Source:* www.infonox.com

## Essential Elements of Successful CMR Marketing

A successful CMR-based marketing system is dependent upon a behavioural design that recognizes and rewards the customer for the performance of the following five essential actions:

1. **Engagement.** Willingness to accept the company's marketing promise or value proposition as the motivating premise for building the relationship. This positions the company's marketing programme well ahead of customer need, giving the engaged customer a strong reason to choose the company when his need naturally arises. (This process eliminates current costly database marketing methodologies aimed at manufacturing customer need.) It is indeed hard to refute the logic that an engaged customer relationship will be more productive than an unengaged or open-ended relationship where the customer has agreed to nothing new or different before the marketing process starts.

2. **Consolidation.** This is the first area of greatest relationship marketing opportunity, motivating the customer to consolidate all of his business with just one company—yours!

3. **Future needs fulfilment.** If the customer is meaningfully engaged and recognized and rewarded for positive performance, he will naturally turn to your company for fulfilment of his future needs when they arise. His buying decisions will not require unnecessary sales pressure from the company to make this choice. Just remember, your existing customers are always your first and best source for new business.

4. **Referrals.** A well-designed CMR system will reward existing customers heavily for referring family and friends, motivating your existing customers to become your sales force.

5. **Retention.** The ultimate prize in all of marketing is to keep the customer for a lifetime. CMR marketing does this through the delivery of a higher level of customer satisfaction, which converts into lifetime retention.

Until now, the introduction of CMR-based marketing has been waiting for the arrival of supporting technology to ensure its effective delivery, waiting for the development of tracking software with the ability to efficiently track and configure the lifetime loyalty of every customer without being encumbered by dirty data and inadequate processing power. That wait is over. The new technology has arrived, and the future of CMR grows brighter with each new day.

The early proof of CMR is already visible in the travel, retailing and banking industries. Loyalty marketing programmes are fast evolving in all of these industries as the awareness of the power and potential of customer-driven marketing becomes more and more evident. New methodology that focuses on recognition and reward of customer performance and loyalty is the obvious model of the future.

And while the evolution of CMR is only in its infancy and many companies are just beginning to understand the conditions that genuinely motivate higher customer performance, recognition of the power of this new old consumer-driven force is undeniable and its current entry into the relationship management marketplace is unstoppable. It is now possible to track customer performance (loyalty) and justly reward its relative value for a lifetime.

Everything has a life cycle and many of us today believe that it is time to retire the old marketing equation of yesterday that relied on the performance of the old workhorse, the salesman, and replace it with the new 21st century marketing model that relies on the performance of the customer. Such a new and better model with the support of technology, can now reward customers for buying rather than salesmen for selling. It will be a right answer to building lifetime relationships with customers based on lifetime performance rather than short term company need and salesman's calls. This novel marketing paradigm engages the customer in the marketing promise of the company, and then lives up to that promise for a lifetime by delivering higher recognition and preferred pricing to every customer based upon that customer's lifetime record of performance, i.e. lifetime loyalty to the company. A marketing system that genuinely focuses on meeting the customer's expectations and eliminates redundant marketing effort aimed at satisfying the company and salesman's needs rather than focusing on the natural evolution of each customer's needs.

The concept of the customer-managed relationship is not a complicated one. It simply concentrates on measuring a customer's lifetime loyalty to the company, and then recognizes and rewards that lifetime loyalty based upon the performance of each customer; and the greater the customer's lifetime loyalty, the greater the recognition and reward for customer performance—an equation that eliminates much of the excessive direct and indirect marketing costs of the past, and the heavy reliance on the salesman to drive marketing success.

And in addition to all of this, the customer managed relationship has a place for every customer, not just the profitable customer of the moment.

In summary, those who see current and future value in every customer and are willing to cultivate that relationship through the implementation of low-cost customer-driven marketing that tracks lifetime loyalty and performance of every customer (not just those who appear to be profitable in a static picture of unreliable profitability) and recognizes that loyalty for its relative level of performance and value, will most certainly become the big winners in the future game of marketing in every industry.

# CONCLUSION

CMR is almost the version of CRM—just a slight nuance regarding the traditional philosophy that our guests invite us into their lives and ultimately manage our presence/relationship with them. Customers want to manage themselves—be in control of when and where and how they do business with you. Their interactions must be part of a logical process and deliver an end to end experience. Businesses rarely take this 'outside in' view, which is addressed in the CMR concepts. CMR endeavours to catch up with the trend of perfect market manifested in the following: availability of information, no barriers to entry and exit, equilibrium price and perfect matching. In customer managed relationships, what you offer, how you offer it, how you price it and how you partner to construct it are all adapted to how you attract, acquire and retain individual customers. This demands mass acquisition and retain individual customers. The essential elements of CMR are, namely, engagement, consolidation, future need fulfilment, referrals and retention. Marketers who see current and future value in every customer and are willing to cultivate that relationship through the implementation of low-cost customer-driven marketing that tracks lifetime loyalty and performance of every customer, will most certainly become the big winners in the future game of marketing in every industry.

## Exercises

1. What are the value added activities of Relationship Marketing that have been envisaged in CMR?

2. Where do you find CMR concept would be fast emerging? Justify your answer with suitable examples.

3. What is commodity magnet? How is it related to mass customization?

Fill in the blanks:

4. Barriers to market _____ and _____ remain, but they are being broken down by _____.

5. A well-designed _____ system will reward _____ customers heavily for _____ family and friends, motivating your existing customers to become your _____ _____. This process is known as _____.

## References

Harrison, Ralph, 2007. Harrison Company Website writeup. (Ralph Harrison is Managing Director of The Harrison Company, Aurora, CO, Developer of the Patented Loyalty Banking System.)

Molineux, Patrick, 2007. Patrick Molineux is Associate Director at Computer Sciences Corporation (CSC) and author of *Exploiting CRM: Connecting with Customers*, Published by Management Consultancies Association).

Naylor, David, 2007. The Shifting Balance of Power—Getting Results in a Customer Managed World, White paper, Source: www.callcenterhelper.com/customermanagedrelationship.htm.

Websites

www.harrisoncompany.net

www.budd.uk.com

# CHAPTER 15

||||||||||||||||||||||||

# Relationship Strategy and Enterprise Image

## INTRODUCTION

It is a fact that customers reign at the heart of Relationship Marketing. However, the concept does not end in itself though it appears to be the prime focus of marketing discipline. Time and knowledge have lent more values to the meaning of Relationship Marketing making its wings spread in domains beyond clients and consumers. It sounds more like marketing of relations with different interacting business entities than customer relationship marketing alone. All those entities, namely employee, investor, government, media, society, supplier and international community form the components of an organization's wholesome framework of relationship. It is like the limbs of a body; strength in each one of them leads to a pure and clean enterprise image. This chapter discusses those entities that impact the various relationship dimensions resulting in the confidence of the stakeholders in the organization.

## FRAMEWORK OF BUSINESS RELATIONSHIPS AND CORPORATE IMAGE

We have observed in the previous chapters the importance of different stakeholders in the business, such as clients, investors and employees. The fact is, if the enterprise ignores the other stakeholders of business, then it loses much of its 'quality of image' and here comes the context of perfect understanding and dressing of relationship parameters with other stakeholders who have a distinct role to play along with the key parameter: relationship with clients.

The other movers of business are not uncommon or new, as these are important business entities having significant roles in corporate image. Employees, investors, government, media, society, and international community are the ones with which the enterprise transactions are in perpetual endeavour to facilitate growth, stability, and comfort in business. This chapter focuses summarily on different dimensions of all those entities and how those enrich the enterprise image.

In the present context, the following relationship entities that contribute to enrichment of corporate image have been summarily discussed (Figure 15.1):

- Relationship with investors
- Relationship with clients
- Relationship with employees
- Relationship with vendors/suppliers/business partners
- Relationship with partners
- Relationship with government
- Relationship with media

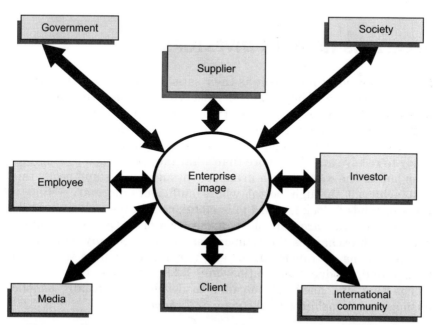

**Figure 15.1  Relationship lines with entities that influence enterprise image.**

- Relationship with society
- Relationship with international community

The concept underlying the effect of various internal and external relationships in enterprise image has been derived from 'Six Market Model' of Payne (1991). According to Payne, six markets are central to relationship marketing. They are: internal markets, supplier markets, recruitment markets, referral markets, influence markets, and customer markets. The traditional marketing plan has focused upon customers or consumers without recognizing the importance of supplier development, recruitment markets, referral sources or 'influencers'. However, each of these 'external' markets can have considerable impact upon performance in the customer/consumer market place (Payne, et al., 1995). This framework also contains Gummesson's concept of classical market relationship, special market relationship, mega relationship, and nano relationship (Chapter 1).

Various relationship dimensions that contribute to the enterprise image are discussed here. These constitute a network of entities and each one has some direct or indirect effect on the other. Key drivers for development of enterprise image in terms of market share and growth are: (a) clients, (b) investors, (c) employees and (d) suppliers. These four groups are the core groups for enterprise image. The other four groups are instrumental in adding values to the image in terms of 'Brand Physique': (a) government (b) media, (c) international community, and (d) society.

## RELATIONSHIP WITH INVESTORS

Investors are most important as their satisfaction ensures the existence of the enterprise. They are the most vital entities that are highly indispensible and absolutely result-oriented people. There is no place for any excuse to them. If they are not happy, they withdraw their investment and switch their investment somewhere else where they are ready to receive anything more than what they have been getting. Apart from one-to-one contact with investors through emails and posts, this is best achieved through portal where sufficient information that any investor tends to look forward to is mentioned. In the web site of Nikon, investors' queries are published in the form of FAQs. For example, in which stock exchanges the company share is listed, any plan for ADR receipts, name of transfer agent and register apart from the company background, product information, and R&D activities. Here are a few things that one needs to consider to develop a mutually beneficial business relationship with the company's investors.

1. Every company should have a contact person authorized to deal with the investors.

2. Know your financial structure well. This does not mean you have to be a financial wizard. However, the Investor Relation Executive will be knowledgeable enough to discuss the company's financial status, including cash flow, growth projections, servicing debt and so forth.

3. Withholding any information or to sugarcoat bad news upsets investors. Investors are not new in the field of business, so they do not expect a smooth ride all the time. When they have questions, do not keep them on hold and be timely with the delivery of either good or bad news.

4. When displaying your projections, be a bit conservative. One can talk about the numbers projected in the last or current quarter, but avoid misleading forecasts. When it comes to financial information, it is better to be forthright.

5. It takes only little effort to channelize your website for investors to visit. Via your company website, you can post investor news, financial statements and much more. Investors usually like it when they have easy access to information.

6. Investors generally make the decision to invest by evaluating business plans and markets, but this decision can also be based on business management. Try and be yourself, as it is your ability and skill that leads the company towards growth and this indirectly projects your worth.

7. Lastly, think of the investors as your potential partners and not as on-guard critics. Enjoy their support and experience.

*Source:* Business Relationships: Tips for Dealing with Your Investors, www.morebusiness.com Sept. 7, 2008.

Investor Relations (IR) is one of the "big four" standard components of a corporate website (along with 'Public Relations', 'Employment', and 'About Us'). In the modern world, investors assume that they can go to www.company.com to research a current or potential investment. While companies must provide IR information to attract and retain investors, they must also be realistic about the types of content and features that users need most. Simplicity and a coherent story about the company are better than drowning users in incomprehensible data. The contents of 'Investor Relations' are as follows:

- Company profile
- Financial results
- Annual reports
- Quarterly reports
- Roadshow presentation
- Corporate governance and ethics

- Articles of Association
- Stock information
- Shareholding pattern
- Financial calendar
- Transcripts of conference calls with financial analysts
- Investor relations contacts
- Press

Some organizations have downloadable 'Investor kit' as an item in the investor relation webpage, where key information files are clubbed together.

An example of website to illustrate investor relations is given in Figure 15.2.

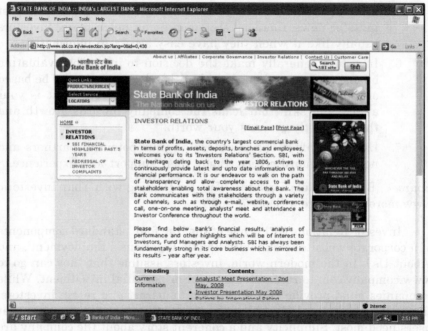

**Figure 15.2 Investor relationship.**

*Source:* www.sbi.co.in

# RELATIONSHIP WITH CLIENTS

Clients are the focus of relationship and various dimensions of client relationship have been discussed in the previous chapters.

# RELATIONSHIP WITH EMPLOYEES

Employees are key people within the enterprise. Satisfied clients are not achievable with dissatisfied employees. This is a specialized task, which is in the purview of Human Resource Development Department of the organization. It is the company's Employee Relationship Philosophy that addresses the employee satisfaction level within the organization. Software Engineering Institute's Capability Maturity Model has come out with the concept of development of quality people in their People CMM. This produces encouraging results with companies that are able to garner high level of loyalty from their employees. Such outlook varies from organization to organization—some organizations take equal concern in business and employee—as a result, those companies can successfully project 'best employer image' to attract talents from the market. These companies have employee feedback in their HR portal where their concern and grievances are noted and appropriately addressed. Companies publish House Journals that serve as a link between organization and employees, there are staff get-together to celebrate various events—all these are done with the basic purpose of encouraging the employee to act as a member in a family and such initiatives adopted by the HR department to boost up employee morale are very common.

# RELATIONSHIP WITH VENDORS/SUPPLIERS/ BUSINESS PARTNERS

Just like indispensable employees, business partners play a major role for mutual business benefits and this is possible through collaborative outlook. There are number of IT solutions available to facilitate this function. The concept of supply chain management is created to promote this activity.

The traditional systems that have been used for product development and procurement do not work anymore. Meanwhile, the potential downside cost and risk associated with managing supplier relationships has skyrocketed. These factors fuel the requirements for a fresh approach to managing relationships with suppliers.

This trend heading for more outsourcing and greater supplier value has also changed the economics of today's corporation. More and more companies have purchase spend exceeding 50 per cent of their top-line revenue. There are also growing concerns over the increased risk associated with aggressive outsourcing. In the old days, supply risk could be offset through split awards and effective management of second sources, but the trend toward suppliers designing, building and even directly shipping complete subsystems has nearly eliminated the second source option. Any time a supplier falls short on delivery or does not get a critical subsystem developed in time for a new product's launch, the top line suffers. This makes Supplier Relationship Management, or SRM, the best investment a company can make in design and procurement. It is the only system that can simultaneously reduce cost and risk.

Supplier Relationship Management (SRM) is a comprehensive approach to managing an enterprise's interactions with the organizations that supply the goods and services it uses. The goal of SRM is to streamline and make more effective the processes between an enterprise and its suppliers just as Customer Relationship Management (CRM) is intended to streamline and make more effective the processes between an enterprise and its customers.

SRM practices create a common frame of reference to enable effective communication between an enterprise and suppliers who may use quite different business practices and terminology. As a result, SRM increases the efficiency of processes associated with acquiring goods and services, managing inventory, and processing materials.

There is a fundamental power shift in the world of manufacturing. Suppliers are no longer simply supplying, they are critical players in the success of the business. For a growing list of features in OEM (Original Equipment Manufacturer) products, suppliers now own the intellectual capital that goes into creating the products. A few examples of this are computer monitors, automotive braking systems and passenger seating. If a supplier fails to develop and deliver competitive features, the OEM product is no longer competitive.

There are strategies and technologies to manage supplier relationship. Keiretsu is one such example (Chapter 4) that endeavours to promote this philosophy. As regards technology, there are number of offerings from organizations like Microsoft, SAP, Oracle, available in the market to cater to such requirements.

## RELATIONSHIP WITH GOVERNMENT

Government liaison is an essential part of business activity and especially interactions with the Central and the State governments at all levels need to be continuous and meaningful. Organizations work closely with relevant ministries and departments to comply with business regulations.

In the context of Indian business scenario, as a consequence of economic reforms since 1991, the process of obtaining governmental permissions has become relatively simple, allowing for a better liaison with the Centre or State governments. In this environment, it is necessary to establish effective working relationships with governments. This implies the ability of the organization to negotiate, amplify the business objectives, and secure necessary permissions and clearances for the clients to further their business interests. This also helps to monitor developments or amendments in issues such as ideological shifts, proposed changes in policy, regulatory framework, new laws and de-licensing, etc. all factors critical to corporate decision making.

Besides, the behaviour of a business enterprise as that of a law-abiding citizen elevates the relationship with government. Adherence to the rules and regulations of government, sending necessary information and returns on time to government keeps the corporate image clean and chaste. As a part of corporate governance, now it has become a common practice to teach and propagate among the employees the Code of Conduct of the organization. Tata Group companies have Ethics Counsellor, and Tata Code of Conduct Coordinator to ensure fair business practice within the corporation as well as with the customer and other stakeholders of the business.

## RELATIONSHIP WITH MEDIA

To update media with maximum transparency allows media to speak volumes about the enterprise and this acts positively for the corporate image. According to one definition, Public Relations is 'the management function that identifies, establishes and maintains mutually beneficial relationships between an organization and the various publics on whom its success or future depends' (Cutlip et al. 1985). The media relationships can be split into three types (Gummesson 2002):

- The relationship between an organization and the media
- The relationship between the media and their audiences
- The relationship between an organization and the media audience.

According to Bill Dugovich, President of Dugovich & Associates Inc. Public Relations in Kent, "CEOs, superintendents and business owners do not like to admit it, but the media can make or break them and their organizations. Nixon lost his presidency. Enron lost its reputation. Princess Diana spread goodwill. In every case, it was the media that carried their message to the masses. And the vehicle was news stories, not advertising space."

Prastising good media relations is really quite simple—one needs to be honest, one needs to be helpful and avoid being a nuisance to media. Doing these three things and it is possible to avoid all major media disasters. This will also not only protect the company's reputation; over time, it will enhance it immensely. Mistakes taught organizations and people the hard way that the press could not be fooled. It is hard to admit mistakes, especially personal mistakes. But take a moment and think about someone who admitted a mistake to you. Instead of getting diluted, this has enriched the impression of people who admits mistakes proving the transparency of their actions. The same applies for organizations.

Being helpful is also essential for good media relations. Being helpful means being available, even at home late at night or early in the morning. Reporters work on deadlines, not an individual's timeline. The presses stop for no one. Every moment delayed returning a call from a reporter is a moment the reporter is available to talk with someone else. That someone may not be a friend to share an individual's viewpoint. Worse, they may have inaccurate information or lack the background needed to convey the situation from that viewpoint.

Zealot media relation's people are always a nuisance. They waste reporters' time by pushing events or topics with marginal news value and then waste more time with multiple call-backs asking about coverage. These tactics undermine the fundamental reason behind all media relations' efforts—to enhance the reputation of the organization. In the end, the organization suffers as does the media relations' specialist's professional reputation.

To succeed at media relations, it helps to have a basic understanding of how the media works. And here lies the area where most efforts fail. The watchdog mentality is alive and well in the press. Reporters view themselves as keeping an eye on things for the public. Society needs that. It was Thomas Jefferson, one of the greatest champions of democracy, who said, "Were it left to me to decide whether we should have a government without newspapers or newspapers without a government, I should not hesitate a moment to prefer the latter."

Whether or not an organization decides to buy into the watchdog role makes no difference. People in the media believe it. It is what motivates them to go to work every day. They own the presses and the broadcast towers. Organizations get the picture.

Finally, it helps to like reporters and editors. That does not mean one has to agree with everything one reads in the newspaper or hear on the 11 o'clock news. But a person who does not like to talk to reporters or editors, who does not like to read newspapers and watch television news, should not be a corporate spokesperson. That may seem basic, but it happens more than people think.

It takes a dose of maturity and humility to practice solid media relations. It is not easy being honest all the time. It is not easy facing the fact that the organization's "big news" holds little value for someone else. But if the media relation's effort follows the rules, the treatment would be fair. In the world of media relations, that is what really counts.

The corporate communications department looks after this task. Calling press conferences, timely media briefing, keeps everyone linked with the business up-to-date with the happenings of the organization and it develops confidence of all concerned in the organization.

*Source:* http://www.bizjournals.com/seattle/stories/1999/11/08/focus8.html.

The following lines from a book on 'Celebrity Marketing' succinctly sum up the importance of the media relationship (Rein et al. 1987): 'Because the media make up the most powerful of channels, they are crucial to winning high visibility. Other channels are capable of moving celebrity images out of the warehouse and into the marketplace, but none approaches the cost-effectiveness and audience impact of the mass media (Karas 1991, Hadenius and Weibull 1993).

To promote relationship with media, some organizations set up webpage having information relevant to the media. The webpage of Standard Chartered Bank on media relations is one such example (Figure 15.3).

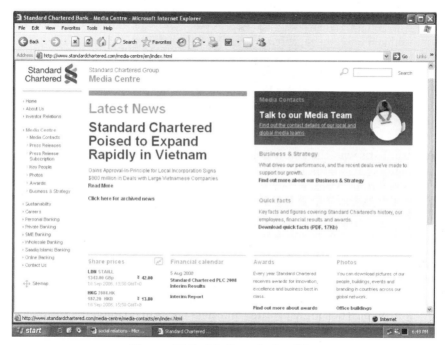

**Figure 15.3   Media relationship.**
*Source:*   www.standardchartered.com

# RELATIONSHIP WITH SOCIETY

Business and society are connected with each other intimately. Enterprise concerns for the society and social development show the human face of business.

## The Legend of Tata

Jamsetji Tata was more than an entrepreneur who helped India to take her place in the league of industrialized nations. He was a patriot and a humanist whose ideas and vision shaped an exceptional business conglomerate (Figure 15.4).

**Figure 15.4  Jamsetji Tata.**

Jamsetji Tata was the main person behind the idea to start an iron and steel factory. His sons fulfilled his dreams, when they started the Tata Iron and Steel Factory in 1907, three years after his death. The industrial town of Jamshedpur or Tatanagar is a spectacular example of industry's contribution to the society and citizen. He established the Indian Institute of Science Bangalore (IISc). His successors furthered his vision by establishing world-class institutes to serve the society in the avenues of medical sciences, technology, management, social science and many such fields. Tata Memorial Hospital in Mumbai is one such example where any common person can afford to undergo treatment.

Many of the high-profile business organizations in India are already pursuing this activity and this helps them earn respect from different quarters of the society. The relationship that shows concern and respect for an individual and society is the theme behind corporate social responsibility. Some of the examples are as follows:

1. **Amway Opportunity Foundation.** Amway Opportunity Foundation, or AOF for short, looks after the social responsibility of Amway India Enterprises. Amway had commenced work in the social sector well before commercial launch under the banner of the AOF, which was then an internal unit of Amway.

Amway's corporate vision is focused on the concept of helping people live better lives. According to Amway, "In all aspects of our products, businesses and social responsibility, we strive to make a meaningful difference in the communities in which we operate.

Consistent with this corporate vision, AOF sponsors organizations and projects that empower people to lead better lives. We are particularly interested in supporting groups:

- Committed to and work on social issues and causes
- Work in the field of rehabilitation and education of the disabled, as well as children
- Carry out research on issues which have a larger impact on society.

This translates into:

- Projects that demonstrate strong potential for making meaningful and lasting change in the community
- Projects that focus on health, education, and rehabilitation of the disabled, children as well as the underprivileged
- Projects in the vicinity of the Amway umbrella
- Proposals for personal causes, scholarships or loans, are not considered
- Projects which impact the beneficiary as directly as possible.

Thus, Amway's work in the social sector, through the AOF, has concentrated on areas for children, the underprivileged, the differently abled, and the blind.

2. **Infosys Foundation.** Infosys is an Information Technology organization which was started in the year 1992. It has grown to a magnificent height in a span of a decade. As a part of Corporate Social Responsibility, Infosys has their community service wing—Infosys Foundation to promote industry relations with the society. Sudha Murthy heads this foundation and in the seven years since the foundation was set up, it has built up orphanages, hospitals, relief centres, more than 10,000 small libraries in schools of rural Karnataka. She speaks of Jamsetji Nusserwanji Tata and JRD Tata as her inspiration (*Business Today,* June 8, 2003).

The Foundation has constructed:

- Orphanages at Banapur and Kalahandi in Orissa, Shedgeri in Karnataka and Kalahandi in Orissa
- A free girls hostel at Maharshi Karve Sthree Shikshana Samsthe, Hingne, Pune
- A girls hostel for the blind in Banapur, Orissa, Jagruthi Blind School in Pune, Sri Ramana Maharshi Academy for the Blind in Bangalore and Sri Sharada Andhara Vikasa Kendra in Shimoga, Karnataka
- Relief shelters in several parts of Orissa
- Sri Ramakrishna Students Home in Chennai, Tamil Nadu

- Shakthidhama Destitute Centre for Women in Mysore, Karnataka
- A hall for people with a physical disability in Belgaum, Karnataka

Other activities include:

- Steps to improve the living conditions of 'Devadasis' in Karnataka
- Improvised a rehabilitation centre in Chennai for mentally retarded women
- Improving the lives of children with leprosy and those living on the streets, platforms and in slums
- Organizing an annual 'mela' for the distribution of sewing machines to destitute women, to help them earn their livelihood, in different parts of the country including Bangalore and Sedam in Karnataka, and Chennai in Tamil Nadu
- Relief work in Osmanabad district of Maharashtra, the tribal areas of Kalahandi in Orissa, drought-hit areas of Andhra Pradesh, etc.

There are plenty of success stories of advertising agencies in development of advertising campaign for social cause. One such example is Ogilvy & Mather India's famous 'Mile Sur Tera Hamara' (Let there be unification of our melodies) campaign for promoting national integration. There are many such activities of O&M undertaken for social cause, as shown in Figure 15.5.

Figure 15.5 Relationship with society.
*Source:* www.ogilvyindia.com

# RELATIONSHIP WITH INTERNATIONAL COMMUNITY

When an enterprise operates on a global level, it has to establish its credibility and integrity. The relationship with international community in terms of business depends much on the visibility of that enterprise of terms of its business potential in the international market as well as business behaviour that conforms to the norm of the nations across the world. Globally, competitive organizations have an edge over positioning their enterprise in the global chart, for example, Fortune 500. In the emerging liberalized economy, the picture is getting more and more encouraging. Government permission to raise funds for investment through issue of ADR/GDR without prior government approval, easing the norm for Indian companies to make acquisitions abroad, allowing 100% investment abroad out of the ADR/GDR, etc. are some the examples to promote Indian business abroad. Organizations, namely, TISCO, Bajaj, Dr Reddy's Lab, L&T, ISPAT group, Infosys, TCS, Wipro have already garnered international recognition in terms of their corporate image. In this regard, it is a fact that ethical aspects of business are vital in international market. Business practices and customs in different national markets differ considerably. Business behaviour of a country is represented by the enterprise of that country. It is as good as the national behaviour, character or culture of that country. (A minor aberration in such behaviour can result in a devastating consequence which might even generate stress in government to government relation.) Strict adherence of GAAP (accounting standard in USA), or any other standard followed by a particular country, voluntary disclosure of correct facts and figures in the annual report, operational transparency, international certifications on the processes followed, observing the norms of World Trade Organization (WTO) for overseas trade practices, are some of the areas that have vital importance in sustaining steady relationship with overseas clients.

# CONCLUSION

The business mission of an enterprise points to client acquisition, and retaining through their satisfaction. Along with the company's endeavour to garner customer satisfaction to improve the company's credibility, there are other relationship entities that play critical role in influencing the decision of the client directly or indirectly. The enterprise needs to address those relationships through appropriate strategies. Those are, namely investors, government, society, media, employees, international community, vendors/suppliers or partners. These are like the limbs of a body to enable its balanced functioning of an enterprise. True that customer is being the focus of all activities, but nurturing the relationships with other stakeholders of the business facilitates an enterprise to further strengthen customer relationship. In such circumstances, corporate focus is essential to gear up activities that preserve and promote the connectors of those relationships, and thereby building up stronger rapport with those entities. In an ideal situation, the relationship profile of each of the stakeholders described before must be strong, robust and exemplary and only then the organization can achieve to have pure, clean and shining image to all concerned.

> **Keywords:** *Investor, Supplier Relationship Management (SRM), ADR, People CMM*

## Exercises

1. What do you understand by the term 'enterprise image'? Why relationship with different entities of business is important in building up the image?

2. How is corporate governance related to business relationship?

3. What is the role of employees in Relationship Marketing?

4. Give an example of an organization that has cultivated successful media relationship and discuss the salient features of the relationship.

5. Name two organizations which, in your views, present excellent enterprise image.

6. What do you understand by 'relationship with international community'?

7. What is media's role in relationship marketing? Discuss with suitable examples.

Fill in the blanks:

8. Key drivers for development of enterprise image are: (a) _____, (b) _____, (c) _____ and (d) _____. These four groups are the _____ groups for enterprise image. The other four groups, who are instrumental in adding value to the image on successful relationship, are: (a) _____, (b) _____, (c) _____ and (d) _____.

9. Corporate _____ department looks after this task of calling _____, timely _____, keeps everyone linked with the business up-to-date with the happenings of the organization and it develops confidence of all concerned in the organization.

10. Satisfied _____ are not achievable with dissatisfied _____.

# *References*

Cutlip, S.M., Center, A.H. and Broom, G.H., 1985. *Effective Public Relations.* Prentice Hall Inc., Englewood Cliffs, New Jersey, p. 4.

Gummesson, Evert., 2002. *Total Relationship Marketing, Marketing Management, Relationship and Strategy and CRM Approaches for the Network Economy,* Butterworth-Heinemann, Oxford, p. 173.

Hadenius, Stig and Weibull, Lennert, 1993. *Mass Media: A Book about the Press, Radio and Television,* 5th ed., Bonnier Alba, Stockholm, Sweden.

Karaszi, Peter, 1991. *Use the Press,* PK Information, Stockholm, Sweden.

Payne, A., 1991. Relationship Marketing: The Six Markets Framework (working paper). Cranfield, England: Cranfield University, School of Management.

Payne, A., Christopher, Martin, Clark, M. and Peek, Helen, 1995. *Relationship Marketing for Competitive Advantage: Winning and Keeping Customer,* Butterworth-Heinemann, Oxford, pp. 10–11.

Rein, Irving, Kotler, Philip and Stoller, Martin R., 1987. *High Visibility,* Heinemann, London, p. 255.

Websites

www.proximity.ro/en/relationship/dictionary.php?term= relationship_marketing

www.amwayindia.com/NewFolder/our_story.htm#90

www.bizjournals.com/seattle/stories/1999/11/08/focus8.html

www.infosys.com

www.morebusiness.com

www.sbi.co.in

www.standardchartered.com

www.ogilvyindia.com

# CHAPTER 16

# Thoughts on Relationship

## INTRODUCTION

The look and feel of a healthy relationship is developed through an evolutionary process where both client and partner play pivotal roles. Depending on the past learning and experience in various situations, the future of relationship is shaped.

It is not far from the truth that history and individual experience are ideal repositories of lessons for learning and comprehending customer relationship. In business, unpleasant history repeats only if one fails to learn the lessons out of it.

Today, every touchpoint of business, be it a person or an object, carries the essence of relationship. Back in the past at Chennai Airport, while I was heading for the check-in counter, a smiling Jet Airways executive approached me with a 'Spot Boarding Pass Machine' and issued me the boarding pass instantly saving my time from standing in the queue. I cannot recall his name neither do I recall his face. But his action promoted my relationship with the 'Jet' brand, because it was a complete 'WOW' experience for me.

Perhaps that is one of the reasons why the brand 'Jet' commands respect from its flyers. Indigo airlines in-flight service staff, while selling food packets to the passengers, carries the list of passengers and addressing them in person certainly adds some point towards relationship building. Spicejet staff helped me in recovering my mobile, which I left it behind at Kolkata Airport. Many such events, like this, are good enough to position brands in the pleasant side of the memory. I may not always be travelling in Spicejet, but certainly I shall not be speaking foul about them till I have any negative experience encounter.

The contents of this chapter narrate certain events, some myths, myopias, facts around key and major touchpoints of customer relationship. The views do not present any ultimate or absolute solution for success of relationship. It is like a bundled experience, guidelines that can help marketers to devise strategic approach towards relationship building, maintenance as well as troubleshooting.

Here I have one confession to make: for writing these pieces of articles on relationship marketing, I was inspired by the book *Outcries and Aside,* authored by renowned English essayist J.B. Priestley— certainly an outcome of a very special relationship I developed with that book almost 30 years ago.

## NERO AND LEVERAGING CUSTOMER LOYALTY

Remember the Bhopal Gas Disaster. On the night of December 3, 1984, an explosion at Union Carbide's pesticide plant caused 40 tonnes of lethal gas to seep into Bhopal. This explosion caused immediate death of thousands of people and led to life-long suffering for almost 120,000 survivors.

Warren Anderson, Union Carbide (UC) CEO, was wanted in India to face charges of culpable homicide over the deaths of 20,000 people since the disaster. There were many among them who were UC's stakeholders in terms of employees, consumers, etc. Anderson flew to India after the disaster and police investigating the disaster immediately arrested him. He subsequently jumped bail.

Perhaps, Anderson was aware of this bitter event, nevertheless realized it was time he should be around in India despite police action. With controversies still trailing behind his escepe, the CEO perhaps did not totally disown the societal responsibilities at that moment and showed up to express his solidarity with the people who suffered.

### Nero and the Client–Partner

History and individual experience are exemplary repositories of lessons for learning and comprehending customer relationship. There is a saying: history repeats itself only if one does not learn the lessons from it. Individual decision on how to weigh and act on a relation, emerges out of experience, and perception of historical event. Consider the situation, which constitutes Nero's dilemma.

To be situated is to be set in relation to other things. It is assumed Nero is in a safe place enjoying music; there are relations holding between him, the fiddle, the part of the earth on which he stands, the attendants around him and the sounds he makes on the fiddle. He might choose to limit his situations to factors as these, isolating him from the burning city to which, however, he also stands for various relations—good or evil.

But we are assuming that he has observed the city to be on fire and he knows there are people burning in it. Whether he likes it or not, he is within the wider situations. It is an ethical situation—i.e. a situation to which judgments of good and evil are relevant.

## Avoid or Stay Through the Crisis?

The question that confronts him is, then, whether or not music-making is good? that question is already answered; nor is it whether saving people's lives is good? that question may also be regarded as answered; nor is it the pseudo-question whether enjoying music is better than saving lives? it is the question whether in this definite situation it is better to stop fiddling to put out the fire. There would be no dilemma if to stop fiddling were not to give up something good. There would have been no dilemma if Nero had given up fiddling, which is sacrificing something good, at the cost of something better and thereby responding to a moral demand.

If the buildings in the city have no value, if the lives of the citizens have no value, then there cannot be a moral demand to save either from destruction. Moral values depend upon non-moral values. If Nero did not stand in definite relations to the city and its inhabitants, there could not be any demand upon him to take action with regard to them. But he does stand in relation to them and upon these the moral demand is based (Stebbing 1944).

In a client-partner relationship context, Nero can be taken for a symbol of gross indifference and Nero-like indifference in the industry is not an uncommon exhibit. The partner inadvertently offers a solution that accidentally spreads fire in the client's operating environment. The partner has multiple commitments to different stakeholders as well as to self and he has the option of setting it right in due course of time. In such a crisis, the partner knows his presence in the client place would not extinguish the fire, rather the client would jump on him but certainly he would not be killed but at the end, his presence would be appreciated.

## Like a Bridge over Troubled Waters

Should the partner avoid the client's rebuff or become bold enough to live with him through this turmoil? Suppose the partner decides to be present with the client. It may instil the very confidence that partner has not run away. In times of crisis, the partner's presence with the client is very much like a 'bridge over troubled waters' than to manoeuvre clever exit through some possible escape route to evade any unpleasant situation, passing the blame to someone in the organization.

To be with the client in crisis calls for courage and integrity in the partner's representative and organization culture. This approach elevates value and image of partner and enables to leverage assured customer loyalty.

*Source:* Reprinted with some modification from Business Standard Guest Blog in July 26, 2006. Acknowledgement to Mr. Govindaraj Ethiraj (now with UTV) whose editing touches had lent better flavour to the initial draft.

## WHAT HAPPENS TO THE TRAIN WHEN THE DRIVER JUMPS OFF

When Sun Chief Operating Officer Ed Zander left after 15 years there, Sun's stock fell 14%, shaving $ 2 bn from its market capitalization. When it was announced Zander was joining Motorola as CEO, Motorola's stock rose 4.2%, adding almost exactly $ 2 bn to Motorola's valuation (Jason Stamper 2006).

Users of Oracle Corporation's database software had downplayed the likely impact they would feel from the resignation of Gary Bloom, an executive vice-president who was in charge of Oracle's database development activities and numerous other key functions at the company. Oracle announced Bloom would leave as of Dec. 15, 2000 to become president and CEO of Veritas Software Corporation, a Mountain View, California-based maker of storage management software. Bloom was the second high-ranking executive to leave Oracle in a span of five months, with his resignation following the July departure of Ray Lane, Oracle's former president and chief operating officer.

According to Phil Russom, an analyst at Hurwitz Group Inc. in Framingham, Massachusetts, the users he talked to seemed to be obsessed over changes in Oracle's product pricing and packaging: The users have no interest in Oracle's management changes. Bloom's departure from Oracle is just another short-term glitch. Other analysts were not so sure about Oracle's ability to withstand the resignation of a second senior-level executive in less than six months. Many had considered Bloom to be a potential heir-apparent to Ellison, particularly after Lane left the company following a falling-out with Oracle's CEO (IT World, Canada).

## The Market Thinks Differently

But the stock market reflected the effect in this piece of news. Oracle slid $ 4.06 to $ 24.75. Veritas Software Corp., a maker of software that runs websites, said it named Gary Bloom, an executive vice president at Oracle, its chief executive. Veritas gained $ 2.88 to $ 107.25. Bloom, a 14-year Oracle veteran, was seen as a possible successor to Chairman Larry Ellison and was the latest executive to leave the company following the resignation of President Ray Lane in July. UBS Warburg's chief global strategist, Ed Kerschner, removed Oracle from the firm's 'Highlighted Stocks' list.

In India, look at Samsung's case. Samsung India had officially written to *Channel Times*, claiming the Vivek Prakash resignation story as "unsubstantiated". However, it failed to answer channel partner concerns on who the new chief would be and whether he would fulfill the commitments made by Prakash. Samsung said that while Prakash has put in his papers, the company has not yet accepted them. However, conversations with several sources within the company indicate that they would get accepted.

Vivek Prakash's abrupt resignation had, however, sent a section of Samsung partners into a tizzy. "Vivek Prakash is one of the persons who has written Samsung's success story during the last five years, and [lack of] coordination with the new man might disturb the channels," said one of the channel partners. A few others expressed doubts about the vendor's policies.

## Will Customer and Relationship Manager Click?

The probability that new customer and new relationship manager both can click evenly may be high. Both share the same starting trouble, together undergo the process of learning and once there is success, they become friends. With greater client-partner interactions towards positive direction, there is promotion of relationship constructs, namely adaptation, trust, confidence, cooperation, etc. culminating to the spirit of working as one team.

## Winning Work is about Relationships

Professional service firms win work when prospects trust them to solve their problems. "Trust" is the cornerstone of winning work and retaining clients. For most purchasers of professional services, trust begins with the key person (rainmaker) who really cares about the client's problem and can orchestrate a solution. Relationship-based selling is the single most powerful method of securing new clients and keeping existing ones.

People do not care how much you (or your firm) know until they know how much you (and your firm) care. It is a person-to-person business (Schrag 2003).

Relationship-based issues account for 70 per cent of the total impact for winning work, according to Lore International Institute research. The role of the rainmaker in establishing faith and maintaining communications and trust is critical in the process of winning work.

An effective relationship manager can even command the power equation and assume the role of business advisor-cum-mentor of the client, lending thought–leadership for strategy and planning. The relationship manager acts as the first guard of the organization to ensure seamless business interest integration with the client. The value proposition embedded in the role of the relationship manager in high-end service-oriented business is intangible, but it is enormous.

## Is there a Cycle for a Relationship?

In IT and service industry, the relationship managers are the key persons tackling issues from business negotiations to delivery for both sides—client and partner. It is their goodwill that enables acquisition of new business through cross-sell and up-sell. 'Rainmakers' are the manifestations of relationship managers who live with the clients.

Is there any pre-defined life cycle of such continued relationship? How long can the client and partner enjoy such comfort level of this partnership? The answer is: as long as there is least or no irritation lies in between. There could be issues of product, delivery, after sales service and so many others with the client and partner. The relationship manager can play a vital role to negotiate issues, resolve conflicts. To cap it all, after relationship stabilization, his mere physical presence helps clients to proactively address the problems.

But nothing is permanent except change. If the change of person is concurrent in both the camps, new faces on both sides once again reciprocate each other's comfort and discomfort to have a smooth sailing in relationship building process. Possibility of such concurrency can be remote. The client may suddenly change person to handle the business or else the client's person may quit either.

## Departures are Common Now

From the partner's end, the existing relationship manager can also quit the job. True, when he rediscovers his own worth through the client's mirror. These situations in the industry are not uncommon. The fall-out affects business performance of an organization. In the Indian BPO sector, the attrition rate is around 15–20 per cent in top tier companies whereas in medium sized industry, it is 20–30 per cent.

There are other ways of tackling this change. According to one Vice President of East Coast Specialty Consulting Engineering Firm in US: "The departing seller and replacing seller met face-to-face with each client. They tried to focus the meeting on the positive energy of the firm in providing seamless service. Usually a senior executive would also attend this relationship transfer meeting. There was enhanced communications during the first few months of the transition. Because of the problem of rainmakers leaving the firm, the organization is seeking more employees within the firm who can have a relationship with the client organization."

With expanding globalization and free flow of FDI, this is very common issue in the Indian industry. The pervasive nature of such 'Rainmakers' turnover is predominant in many sectors in the industry, namely IT, professional education and training, media, FMCG, etc. Companies with large of pool of professional can survive this change of guards. For others, the only option left is to perish or to be acquired when there is mass exodus of such change in the guard if such exodus is not handled with care.

## Problems Down the Line

The preceding discussions have focused on the outcome when any or some of the top executives of management pyramid quit. In the middle level where a senior executive, who builds up a day-to-day rapport with the customer, quit, the company's business also suffers a visible setback. In the contextual plane of relationship marketing, partners should endeavour to take necessary preparation from the vendor's end to live with such change.

If the first guard is fairly successful, he can use his experience and learning to tackle matters when there is a change in the customer's person. But when the first guard quits the job, have pity for the next person in command for pitching in as he has to live up to the expectation of the client. Longer and successful the relationship, it becomes more painful for the new driver of relationship to drive the vehicle with the same speed with lesser jerks. The reason is simple: it is difficult to assimilate in a short span of time the experience, the learning that the other has acquired over a period of time.

If the client is less critical about the person (its likelihood would be very less), the second guard will be lucky enough to pass the test. Normally, the client demands much more than 'the already enjoyed comfort level' with the previous guard. Incidentally, this is the reality in business.

## New Guard must Work Harder

The new guard is expected to stretch and exert multiple times of the previous guard's effort, just to reestablish some degree of the client's earlier confidence. This is an enormous task and entails great responsibility. The irony is, there is always an advantage of being the first that the second can never have even if the first has just one feather in his cap. Hence, the struggle for establishing the identity of the second guard begins right from introduction and it is a painstaking exercise.

Clients subscribing traditional and conservative business value system (highly prevalent in Indian social system), a change in person triggers tremendous psychological impact in their perceptual map for successor's acceptance. It is observed that the client always refers the earlier successful relationship manager as the role model and insists his style, methodology should be followed. Therefore, sufficient and adequate care needs to be taken to plan this activity. If it fails, the relationship gets a dent and becomes fragile.

There is one point to note. While tackling the change, the first and foremost concern is the selection of the right replacement of the first guard. The replacement of old guard is expected to have enough capability and potential to sustain the existing relationship and thereafter take it forward. However, apart from briefing the new guard, it is preferable that there is a simulation of business fire walk for the new person for sometime. Such situation takes the new guard somewhat close to the reality.

## Get it Insured as Well

To mitigate such risk of key person's exit, a new category of insurance cover, known as Key Person Insurance, has been introduced in some countries. Key person insurance is designed to minimize disruption to business if one of the key staff members is taken out of the picture. Regardless of the worth of a business in terms of equipment, property, inventory, goodwill, etc., the biggest asset is usually those people whose efforts and skill drive it.

They are the people who provide the ideas, initiatives and talent that generate the profits needed for the survival and growth of the business. The sudden loss of a key person can have an adverse effect on the sales and profits of the business and, until a suitable replacement is found, the business could be faced with recruitment costs, possible loss of clients, and negative impact on goodwill and credit rating.

## Succession Plan

There are leaders and there are leaders: the visionaries and the minor leaders who are needed at various levels of the organization. A simple test, however, can help determine if one is the leader in the truest sense: Can the leader develop leaders? Consider the much-discussed example of Jesus Christ. In another day and age, he built a team of 12 leaders who went around executing his thoughts with a commitment and passion and changed the global order—not only in religious terms but also in economic terms—as later day events would prove.

Building leaders is not about succession planning; it is about creating the human resource that will form the basis of succession planning. Did Jesus allow the cream among his disciples to simply rise and take over? One does not know. In today's networked world, where everything is far flung and virtual though, it would be difficult to expect leaders to rise and shine. Corporations have to play a part in building them and yet not all corporates do so conscientiously and meticulously (Roy Ghatak, 2008).

*Source:* Reprinted with some modifications from Business Standard Guest Blog in August 24, 2006.

## IS EVERYTHING OKAY?

If one senses something is going wrong in the morning, it is advised not to wait till evening to collect more problems and then escalate. The act of living patiently with a client's problem is akin to holding a bomb in the chest when the countdown has already begun. This is normally the case with demanding clients who tend to keep their partner on the tenterhooks. In case one is unable to act, it is better to let someone else act immediately to diffuse the bomb rather than getting it blown off. The consequence is obvious—one who holds the bomb is blown. There can be another analogy—if you discover smoke or smell of smoke, there must be fire somewhere near. Ask the client the simple question: Is everything okay? Read and understand from the body language the answer, that is the source of smoke. If there is any, contain the fire forthwith before it spreads to disaster.

For example, in the corporate education and training programme, it is advised to take feedback from the participants. This feedback provides the trend about the progress of the course but that is not everything. The involvement of the trainer with the participants should be deeper enough to anticipate matters beyond the feedback. Once such issues become visible, actions to correct the same can be undertaken promptly and this is where the relationship factor comes into play.

## TENSION IN THE STATION

The coach, that was supposed to be there in the train, was shunted just ten minutes before the departure. The passengers until then were running from one end to the other along the platform in anxiety. This created undue tension among the passengers. This could have been avoided by some display message or some announcement. Just another simple example—you are there with your clients to attend a meeting. Your colleague is supposed to join you and yet to reach the meeting venue. Possibly, he may be stuck in a traffic jam. You have a mobile phone and you can easily locate your colleague before the meeting and feel free to communicate it to the client beforehand.

## LOAN, PHONE AND INSURANCE

Two to three calls a day for any working man or woman or even housewife is not very uncommon these days. Some of them offer home loan, some offer mobile connection, and some offer insurance cover. Sometimes they call you up when you are in a meeting. If the meeting is pleasant, the caller is lucky or else he or she has a bad day. But they have to do their job and keep on calling their clients to have one-to-one relationship and market their services. Insistence or too much pressure, even when the client is ready to listen, does not yield favourable results. With the prospect's permission, mail the necessary information or send a representative.

## WHY DID NOT YOU SAY THESE TO ME BEFORE?

Lack of timely and transparent communications is a common grievance of the client community. Sometimes the clients are not told about the requirements at the outset. If it is done inadvertently, or out of ignorance, then it is a mistake and needs correction. If it is done with intention, then the consequences are disastrous. But in many cases, it is found that persons guiding the client are themselves not very well versed about what they want to convey. When a prospect meets the sales person in banks or other financial institutions (FIs) offering for home loan, he or she answers, it is simple and quick—just fill up the form and get a copy of your photo-id, salary certificate and bank statement, walk away with the money and buy the house. The borrowers feel happy to find it so simple. In the subsequent call, the salesperson asks for a number of legal documents, search certificate, and so on and so forth and all these pull the client down with a dismal feeling—"You could have told this before!"

## CLIENT-AGENCY RELATIONSHIP

To sustain in the wake of increasing and intense competition, the clients have become more demanding than before and this is one of the factors that are responsible for putting the client-agency relationship under duress. Some clients have a rating method for their agencies, whereas others continue their search for the right working relationship with the right agency. Switching over to another agency being the ultimate action, some clients also prefer to spread their budget on more than one agency. Some clients prefer appraisal system for the agency. A client sometimes switches over to new agencies when the creative team of the old agency moves out to a new agency just to maintain "brand continuity". When an advertiser leaves one ad agency and switches over to another, it is known as client-turnover. The various reasons for such client-turnover are as follows (Chunawalla and Sethia 2008):

- The account is not profitable.
- The advertiser is interested in a new medium with which the present agency is not familiar.
- The client and the agency perceive the ad strategy in a drastically different manner.
- Lack of coordination between the top executives of the client and the agency.
- International alignments may cause a change.
- Management changes.
- Change for the sake of change.
- Product conflicts with mergers, takeovers or new product introductions.
- Disenchantment with each other.
- Brand failures.
- Staff changes also lead to client-turnover.
- Perceived unreasonableness of the other party.
- Loss of confidence.
- Client's dislike of the ad programme conceived by the agency.
- Separation of the client and the agency is an easy thing to bring about.

Researchers have identified as many as 40 factors which influence the sale of product, advertising being one of them. But the agency is almost blamed if something goes wrong, particularly when the product incurs substantial amount of advertising expenditure, resulting in termination of relationship. There are three reasons for this:

1. It is very difficult to measure the advertisement's contribution to the success or failure of a product.
2. Legally, it is simple to terminate a relationship (e.g. a few weeks' notice).
3. New people in the client's office might like to have a change.

There are instances where dictatorial clients with control freak tendencies stay with agencies they can bully. The relationships are seldom happy because the agencies, in turn, are forced to apply bullying tactics towards the consumers. And, like everyone else, most consumers resent bullying and stop patronizing the brand. History also reveals that agencies hobbled by their clients' prejudices are less able to retain a creative edge and begin to slip down the agency league. Good clients believe in exceptional advertising talent. They are aware that such talent possesses an ability to empathize with their consumers by producing exciting stimuli. Good clients such as Sony, Volkswagen, Whitbred, Diego and Volvo have good advertising because it is part of their corporate culture. They actively plan for it because they desire it. And they desire it because experience has shown them that good advertising has been more beneficial to their bottom line than bad advertising (Len Weinreich 1999).

Cao and Gruca (2005) have pointed out that attempts at cross-selling or up-selling will encounter adverse conditions when the firm has not chosen the right clients. Shapiro et al. (1987) used the dimensions 'cost to serve' and 'price received' to create a model that contained clients whose cost to serve were low but price received were high; therefore these were considered profitable.

Here is another perception that a good non-customer is worth much more than a bad customer. A good non-customer spreads positive word of mouth while a bad customer spreads negative word of mouth and can even damage the brand equity of the product and the company (Singh 2008). There is some truth in it but the fact is, the purpose of Relationship Marketing is fully defeated the moment the customer turns sour. Because partners aim at relationship with good people, not with bad ones. If a customer is a hard critic of the product and services, it is definitely a healthy sign and should not be taken in negative spirit as it gives the organization the opportunity of improving the product and becoming competitive in the market. It is rather an alarming sign if the customer suddenly becomes silent and quiet without any noise or complaints. Evidently enough, it carries the obvious hints of smoke somewhere.

## TREATING THE CUSTOMER AS KING

According to Mr. Ratan N. Tata, Chairman of Tata Sons: In today's world, what customers are looking for, I believe, are products that suit their purpose best—in terms of price, features, quality and appearance. They expect to be treated as kings and to receive sales and service support for products like vehicles and air conditioners. They expect to receive timely and competent attention, along with a definite solution to their problems from our service people, dealers or channel partners. Our concern ought to be the interface with our customers. We have to ensure that it is excellent. This would involve training of our channel partners and improving the interface between them and us so that they can give the customer the service he or she wants.... Some of our policies are framed almost on the basis that everybody abuses, and that a customer has to prove his bona fides. That is what we need to change. Where we have direct dealings with our customers, it is important that, at the middle-management levels, they are shown courtesy, dealt with fairly, and made to feel that they are receiving the attention they deserve. The interface with the customer should be a seamless one (Noronha 2008).

Another excerpt of an interview of Shah Rukh Khan, conducted by *The Hindu* (Kulkarni 2008):

*Interviewer: How do you react when people call you King Khan?*

*SRK: I get really embarrassed. I never call myself the King. I'm a mere worker, an employee of the audience who works very hard. There are many people who have contributed to making me what I am and I think they deserve the title collectively.*

## THE MYTH OF 'IT IS DIFFERENT!'

'It is different' has become the catchphrase of the marketing of the current decade. For example, with repetitive and hackneyed run-of-the-mill concepts, multiple films are produced and many of them go off the rocker and then slid into box-office gloom. The fact is, people are now interested to know how different would be the benefits. One can take troubles to prepare the script to make the same thing differently but the question is: Are members of the audience able to perceive and appreciate the benefits of difference? Seven notes are common in any music but its arrangement in different order gives rise to unique melodies. But so what—as long as you can create different melodies! Are you sure that your audience would enjoy it at the first impact without having to preach them saying—'It's different and you must enjoy it'? Anything new can have a unique selling proposition provided that it has a positive impact in the space of customers' value. The trend of the day is: the market is coming close to the customers instead of customers' going to the market. It is time the marketers read the writings on the wall. This is possible only if they are related to them through constant interactions and involvement.

Way back in 1976, a film called 'Enter the Dragon' and its hero Bruce Lee made Martial Art a craze among the youths. It was a new kind of film introducing Marital Art not popularly known among people. The film was well directed and from the beginning to the end, it kept the audience glued to the seat. Thereafter, many films were released on

Marital Art. Excepting a very few, most of them could not get off the ground. Because simple replication did not attract the masses. But then, replication with a great deal of innovative touches can help people feel the difference. Run Run Shaw's 'Thirty Six Chambers of Shaolin' did precisely that. It was different and a box office hit, although based on the same theme.

Or think of 'Titanic' by James Cameron! The basic storyline of Titanic is similar to the one in black and white released long ago. But the storybuilding, direction, script, photography, technology, and music everything taken together has lent a great experience to the audience. In 2009, James Cameron once again presented the audience with a magnificient 3D experience: Avatar. It is a different experience for those who have seen the film.

# PRODUCT IN THE LAB AND PRODUCT IN MARKETPLACE

When a product grows in the lab, it is nurtured, reared to survive in the protected mode before it sees the light of the day. Its makers in the lab dislike seeing it under attack whatever be the circumstances—because there is an emotional attachment, almost similar to human affection that keeps the product safe and protected there. As per common human nature, people generally do not volunteer their evaluation by others. Likewise, there is a varying degree of internal resistance, when it comes to testing their product.

Nevertheless, in the interest of the clients, the lab is often transformed into a testing ground, lending it a ruthless look and feel towards the product. Because the product in the market has to survive in the unprotected mode. It is like facing the rough weather in a voyage. The product should be robust enough to withstand customer onslaught, hammering, grinding, shredding. Ultimately, it has to prove—it is the fittest and it can survive in the market like a Bollywood hero, who, apart from acting, is capable of singing, dancing, and fighting when required.

Therefore, all types of screen test should be done, simulating possible events, to ensure the client does not reject it. With such quality, the product would be capable of laying the foundations of relationship.

Therefore, the firm has to ensure that products are not introduced in the market without proper performance and quality tests. MRF claims its tyres are tested under the tough Himalayan terrain as well as in the worst rural tracks of India. Because if the product is faulty, no relationship construct works. Think of legendary Passenger Reservation Software of the Indian Railways that has brought comfort to millions and millions of common people who used to stand in the queue for hours in the heat and dust. Right from the beginning, every version of the application had to pass through all painstaking tests making it capable of running smoothly on the track in the live scenario.

## ARE YOU CONVINCED OF YOUR COMPANY'S PRODUCT?

The relationship manager must first be convinced himself of these two entities—the company and the product he represents. If he is in constant conflict with these two entities, then the obvious question arises, how would he make his clients owner of the product or services, which he himself disowns from the heart? Before the client, he is the face of the company and a speaker for the product. The relationship manager should not live in the client's DNA like a virus. He should live like an energizer to boost the client's morale promoting the success of partnership. If there is a problem in the product, he should be ready to own it through the expressions he shows to the client—it should resemble the pain of the parents whose child fails to pass an examination. The client is ready to give you the chance provided you own the product and every time your act, your involvement proves how close you are to your product.

## INNOVATION AND EXCELLENCE CREATE LEGENDS

Admittedly, excellence is a relative term. When we come across something better, we exclaim—wow! That's excellent! There is no pre-defined threshold level for innovation or excellence. But for legends, there is always a class that lives beyond the boundaries of time and place. The contributions of Newton, art of Da Vinci or works of Shakespeare elevated international science, art and literature to an exalted height and thus we call them legends. The genius behind their innovative and imaginative thinking is simply amazing and difficult to be cloned.

The plane and parameters of excellence change with time. Hence, it is important to note the time as well as the changing norms of excellence. People and organization-striving to keep pace with the changing norm can stand apart and make themselves clearly visible amidst the crowd. The same applies in the case of innovation. What can one do to reinvent oneself? There are companies who have reinvented themselves. IBM is one of the classic examples. It was close to oblivion 15 years ago and then it reinvented itself as monstrous IT services company (Birkinshaw 2008).

In the race of innovation and excellence, when organizations in their conscious effort cross excellence, they become legends. Legends emerge from excellence and once the legend is known, the market is driven towards the legends. In this context, it is well known that Xerox Corporation changed user's vocabulary of photocopying—in the shop windows one can see 'Xeroxing done here' in the nook and corner of the country. This is one simple example of the legend.

Brands and organizations, e.g. Coke, IBM, Microsoft, Infosys, Tatas, Wipro, Unilever, and selective several like them would remain to be remembered as legends. Because they thought something novel and they performed not just excellent but something beyond what others could think of.

# PEOPLE

Some years ago, Gallup conducted a survey of 6,000 consumers and found that the fifth "P" of the marketing mix, people, is by far the most important determinant of customer loyalty to brands than the other "Ps" of Place, Promotion, Product and Price. For example, in motor retailing, Gallup found that customers who feel their dealer representatives "stand out from all others" were ten to fifteen times more likely to choose that same make of vehicle for their next purchase. This same ratio held true for the airline industry, while in the banking sector the influence of people is even greater with customers saying they were ten to twenty times more likely to repurchase from organizations with outstanding employees. Even in telecommunications, employees are three to four times as important in driving loyalty as other factors (Smith 2008).

Right sets of people are the key drivers of business relationship. They may be presented in a variety of roles, such as relationship manager, and client servicing manager, but they own the responsibility of creating a positive impact about the organization right from day one of interaction with the client. He or she needs to be adequately dressed up with information, facts, and data so that the clients relish the comfort level of selecting the right partner. Because he or she is the face of the partner to the client. Some of the salient issues that come up while handling clients in the business transaction are discussed in this section with relevant examples.

We shall be talking about an advertisement in simplifying the role of 'People' in Relationship Marketing. In the accelerated world of print advertising, most new campaigns are lucky to survive six months. Then there is McGraw-Hill's famed "Man in the Chair" ad, which has been around for almost 40 years (Figure 16.1)—this is what can be termed legend of an advertisement.

The ad, exhorting business-to-business advertising, was recently updated for only the fourth time since first appearing in 1958. Two new versions were shot, one featuring a different man (and a different chair), and another with an Asian woman standing before a darkened backdrop (no chair). Despite its visual evolution over the decades, the ad's emphatic, blunt copy has remained constant:

*"I don't know who you are.*

*I don't know your company.*

*I don't know your company's product.*

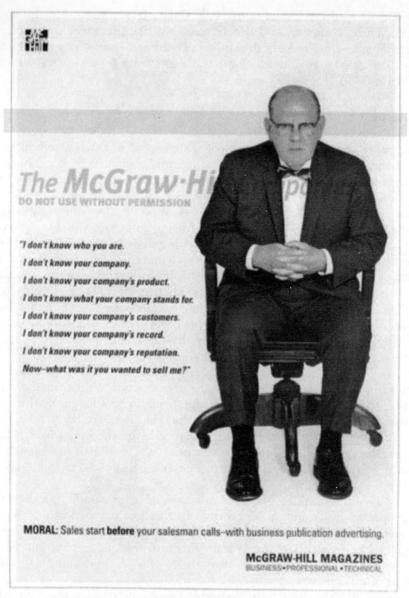

**Figure 16.1 The McGraw-Hill ad—Man in the Chair.**
*Source:* www.mcgraw-hill.com.

I don't know what your company stands for.
I don't know your company's customers.
I don't know your company's record.
I don't know your company's reputation.
Now—what was it you wanted to sell me?

> *Moral—Sales starts before your salesman calls—with business publication advertising"*

Nowhere in the ad does McGraw-Hill list its titles, and the campaign can be read as encouraging all business-to-business advertising. In fact, the universal nature of its message may explain why the ad has held up so long. "The creative hits home," says Tricia Reeson, Director of marketing services for *Business Week*. "I think everyone who's in sales has had to face down this type of tough customer at one point or another in their career. It goes straight to the heart of problems that salespeople face." The original black-and-white version ran in *Business Week*, a McGraw-Hill title, and Advertising, which named it one of the 10 best ads of 1958. Updated in 1968 and 1972, the ad has been translated into French, German, Italian, Russian and Chinese.

Yet the ad's basic message is still valid. "The concept of facing a tough customer hasn't changed," says Reeson. "It is as true today in the world of the Internet and digital communication as it was in 1958" (Garigliano 1997).

In the present-day context (with humble apologies to the creator of this ad the late Henry Sleser), one can think of rewriting the moral as *"Relationship starts before marketing calls."* The role of people in building business relationship with the client is evident from the message of this advertisement.

## PRODUCT AND PEOPLE

Both product and people are important in business transactions. In the service sector, more important is the person. If the person clicks, he can easily carry the product and company goodwill. In new business development, the relationship is established through product rationale, which is once again a person-oriented activity. In service industry, the products generally undergo microscopic evaluation, and the success of marketing depends on how the relationship manager takes the clients along with him. If the relationship manager fails to defend the product, even if it is rich with inherent strengths, the case is lost.

In the context of product and person, the following examples have been cited in the introduction. At Chennai Airport, while I was heading for the check-in counter, the Jet Airways executive approached me with a 'Spot Boarding Pass Machine' and issued me the pass. I do not know his name neither do I recall his face. But his action deepened my relationship with the brand because it was a complete 'WOW' experience for me.

Perhaps, that is one of the reasons why the brand 'Jet' commands respect from its flyers. Indigo airlines in-flight service staff, while selling food packets to the passengers, they carry the list of passengers and addressing them in person certainly adds some point towards relationship building. Spicejet staff helped me in recovering my mobile, which I left behind at Kolkata Airport. Many such events, like this, are good enough to position the brands in the pleasant side of the memory. I may not always be travelling in Spicejet, but certainly, I shall never be speaking foul about them because it is the concern and good work of the people of Spicejet that motivated me to respect the brand.

## STORY OF A GENT'S SALON

One customer walked into a gent's salon for a shave. The salon had a very good ambience and as far as the service, hygiene and cleanliness were concerned, those too were excellent—the barber dipped the scissors, knife into antiseptic liquid every time he was using it. But he was a chain smoker and the customer was a non-smoker. Every time he touched the knife to his cheek, his fingers had the pungent smell of tobacco that caused the customer nausea. The customer decided not to enter there next time.

The moral of the story is: Check the tools but, then, never ignore the fingers that make the tools work. The right product or solution may be delivered to a client on time, nevertheless it is also important to ensure that the channel (when it is people) through which it moves is acceptable by the client because he or she is responsible for explaining it to the client. This is summarily the fifth P of marketing mix, which is 'People'.

## "MR. HANIF" AND "MR. RANBIR"

While talking about characters and roles, the imaginary names, Mr. Hanif and Mr. Ranbir, may clear things a little. Their names are changed here, but they are the real characters and well-known faces of an organization as they lend their vehicles for hire. They have been doing this business since the mid-70s and they have grown from this business only. They are not well versed in English language or academically gifted as their clients; but these two persons almost live from morning to night in their client's office sitting on a stool (listening to songs and programmes from a primitive transistor radio) next to the security guard at the main gate. They are courteous and committed people. As and when the administration manager asks for vehicle, they are up and ready with action, arrange it immediately. They know the names, residence of almost each and every staff of that company, they know the customer locations of that company, they know company guest house locations in the city, they know the names of the corporate heads and whenever there is need for a vehicle—everyone knows that its either Ranbir or Hanif going to come with their vehicle. This is a comfort level that everyone in that organization has been enjoying in those two names. They are even there to see off the staff to drop him home on the superannuating day.

Things may change tomorrow, somebody else may come in their place. But having a business base for almost thirty years is simply amazing illustration of relationship where every now and then somebody else is waiting on the doorsteps to grab the offer. Is there any magic in those names? The answer is described in their profile. There is no magic in those names, nor is it a difficult task, but they have related themselves with the organization.

## SPEAKING IN CLIENT'S LANGUAGE

For convenience sake, a French tourist in India would prefer to be in the company of an Indian who is conversant in French. But that is not a great news in India. Rather, if the French is conversant in Hindi, Bengali or Tamil, then undoubtedly it is great news and a 'WOW' to us.

The relationship person should understand the business language of the client—this is where people think of having 'domain expert' in the client place who would be conversant about the problems of the client and can act as a consultant rather than a conventional troubleshooter.

The impact of first interaction with the client is very critical. For example, if the client is from a banking sector, he would expect the partner's persons to be fully conversant with the banking business, like what is it all about, who are the players, competition, policies and regulations. This would help reinforcing confidence in the client about the capability and competence of the relationship manager. The relationship manager must constantly upgrade himself with knowledge in technology and domain for making himself ready for acceptance by the clients.

## WHERE HAVE ALL THE AUDIENCE GONE?

While the committee members of an office recreation club were planning a cultural evening, five different performing groups, music, drama, skit, etc., comprising the employees, demanded some fixed time slots. The organizers apprehended that the audience would not have the time and patience to enjoy all the items. While they expressed their apprehension to the performing groups, they were not convinced—all those five groups claimed they were also professional entertainers and they had evidence in the past that nobody had left the auditorium when they were performing. The organizers finally submitted to what they demanded.

On the scheduled day, when the last programme was put on the stage, barely 2-3 persons were in audience and the rest had left. Incidentally, the auditorium was located in a place from where getting public transport posed a problem and although the programmes were interesting, nobody was in the mood to stay back. While planning the programme, the performers ignored the convenience of audience. As a result, the audience deserted the performers.

Give the client as much as and as long as he can take and digest. Being over-proactive or over-active has its own dangerous consequences. The relationship manager must have the control on the others in his organization to regulate any overenthusiastic activity. One should think ahead of time but move with time.

Overactive approach is never discouraged but sometimes it implies waste of time and energy without bringing in visible results. Proactive approach goes in line with business and goals. Action and dedication are keys to success, but there should be a sense of balance and proportion without which the entire exercise becomes meaningless, sometimes detrimental to both client and partner's objectives inviting undue complications in the relationship.

Sometimes, such overenthusiastic approach leads to perdition marketing. The **Osborne effect** is exhibited when a company's revelation of information about future products results in customers not purchasing (or delaying purchases of) the current offering. Its origin is a purported suicidal marketing mistake made by the Osborne Computer Corporation in the 1980s when its announcement of a successor to its Osborne 1 system led to a sharp reduction in sales, and the delay of the successor system created a revenue vacuum from which the company did not recover.

## WHY DO PEOPLE PRAY TO GOD?

The purpose of the statement 'Why people pray to God?' is not to challenge the individual's faith in god. People have faith in god for many reasons. One of the reasons is god is harmless. If there is anything good, the common saying is, it is all his blessings. When it is otherwise, people cry—Oh god! Why did you punish me?

What an amazing interaction of god with billions and billions of his devotees! What is his strength? Is there any visible proof of 'the act of god' (as written in the agreements) about his power, like the way a superhero in Bollywood acts on the crooked villain and his people?

Perhaps, god's only strength is: he is a patient listener and that is what makes him great. People pray for wealth, good health, and welfare or for many other physical or material comforts in life. When people pray, god silently listens to it.

Patient and honest listening enables the listener to create a special role for himself in the eyes of the client. In times of crisis, the relationship manager may not be equipped with all the solution, but the client finds exit route of his emotion, it may be anger or irritation, in the relationship manager once he is empathetic to his distress. The patient listening of his woes dilutes much of his pains and brings in lots of psychological comfort in the client; at least, the client finds a shoulder to cry upon—the way we do with god.

## CONCLUSION

Points discussed under different sections are consolidation of general perception, research findings, articles, and events about how Relationship Marketing works in various business transactions. Relationship Marketing has been developed into a discipline since the mid-90s and it is different from the concepts of traditional or conventional marketing. During interactions with clients, there are issues and conflicts and sometimes these may assume critical proportions where even top management may have to intervene and resolve. Those issues require careful tackling by the relationship manager, who has to keep his eyes and ears open while acting with the client. There is nothing like a copybook solution for relationship marketing, as situation may be varying depending on the client and the partner's work culture and business scenarios. Accordingly, the relationship manager is expected to think and act with proper judgment to situations and circumstances.

### *Exercises*

1. How is innovation related to customer relationship? Explain with suitable examples.

2. When departures are common today, what should be the strategy for service providing companies to overcome 'exit crists'?

3. What is the difference between 'product in the lab' and 'product in the market place'? What is their relevance with relationship?

4. Why is it important to speak in the client language? Discuss with examples.

5. 'Know your client before you meet'—What is the information required to gather about the client and what are its sources?

6. In service marketing, 'people' have significant role to play—what are your views on this statement?

7. As a Relationship Manager, how do you plan to develop the relationship when the client refers to better options than your product and services?

# References

Birkinshaw, Julian, 2008. Innovate or Die, *Indian Management*, Jan., Vol. 47, No. 1, p. 52.

Cao, Young and Gruca, Thomas S., 2005. Reducing Adverse Selecting through Customer Relationship Management, *Journal of Marketing*, Vol. 69, No. 4, pp. 219–229.

Chunawalla, S. and Sethia, K.C., 2008. *Advertising Business, Foundations of Advertising—Theory and Practice*, Himalaya Publishing House, New Delhi, pp. 124–127.

Garigliano, Jeff, Magazine for Magazine Management, Jan 1997, Media Central Inc, Gale Group (website: findarticles.com)

Jason Stamper's Blog: July 2006 Archives:

Kulkarni, Reshma, S., 2008. King Khan on a Roll, Centrestage, *The Hindu*, p. 8.

Noronha, Christabelle, 2008. Treating the Customer as King—An Interview with Ratan Tata, *Tata Review*, Jan., pp. 12–13.

Peppers, Don and Rogers, Martha, 1999. Which Came First: The Web or the Business Model, Marketing1to1, Peppers and Rogers Group, The Business forum online, website: www.businessforum.com/m1to1.

Roy Ghatak, Aditi, 2007. Building Leaders: Beyond Succession Planning, *The Contemporary Manger*, Vol. 12, Nov., No. 3.

Schrag, Dennis M. (Ed.). The Longview Group and The University of Iowa, Henry B Tippie College of Business CPSM, Retaining Clients when the Rainmaker Leaves, White Paper Presented to the Society for Marketing Professional Services Foundation (SMPS), Professional Service Markets Association National Conference, Phoenix, Arizona, August 2003.

Shapiro, B., Rangan, V.K., Moriaty R. and Ross, E., 1987. Manage Customers for Profits (not for sales), *Harvard Business Review*, Vol. 65, pp. 101–108.

Singh, Ramendra, 2008. Tapping the Hidden Potential, *Indian Management*, Jan., p. 135.

Smith, Shaun, 2008. Branded Experience Training, website: www.crmguru.com

Stebbing Susan, L., 1944. *Ideals and Illusions*, Watts and Co, London, pp. 93–99.

Weinreich, Len, 1999. 11 *Steps to Brand Heaven*, Kogan Page, London, p. 97.

Websites

www.itworldcanada.com/a/ComputerWorld/
www.leleux.be/leleux/JLCHome.nsf
www.findarticles.com
www.businessforum.com (Peppers and Rogers)
www.crmguru.com (Branded Experience)

# CHAPTER 17

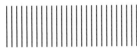

# Institutes Promoting Relationship Marketing

❖ Centre for Relationship Marketing, Buffalo School of Management, New York
❖ Centre for Relationship Marketing and Service Management (CERS)
❖ Institute for Relationship Marketing, Graz—Austria
❖ Journal of Relationship Marketing

## CENTRE FOR RELATIONSHIP MARKETING, BUFFALO SCHOOL OF MANAGEMENT, NEW YORK

The mission of Centre for Relationship Marketing is to conduct scholarly research to identify marketing strategies to enhance corporate profitability through superior relationships with customers. To achieve this, the Centre employs the power of supercomputing, the latest developments in computer technology, management information systems, and the Internet. The Centre develops and applies new methods and tools to help enterprises create and capture values in the marketplace.

### Goals

- Develop strong linkage between theory and practice. To achieve this, CRM works closely with industry for gathering support and test bed for implementation of our solutions.
- Integrate into educational curriculum, the results of research and the problems of the current management practices.
- Fund cutting-edge research by the faculty members and Ph.D. students.
- Identify critical research issues and provide a focus for such research.
- Conduct workshops, conferences, and lectures to exchange knowledge and information between world-class researchers, business leaders, educators, and students.

- Develop an honours programme to train undergraduate students in the use of information technology, statistical models, and point-of-sale data to help enterprises deliver greater value to customers and shareholders.
- Sponsor prominent researchers from peer institutions for short-term residency at Buffalo. During their stay, visitors would offer workshops and engage in joint research with faculty and Ph.D. students.
- Develop training programmes utilizing point-of-sale data and statistical modelling for industry.

## CENTRE FOR RELATIONSHIP MARKETING AND SERVICE MANAGEMENT (CERS)

Centre for Relationship Marketing and Service Management (CERS) was founded in 1994 as a unit associated with the Department of Marketing at the Swedish School of Economics and Business Administration. The Centre focuses on research and management education in relationship marketing and service management. The mission of CERS is to provide intellectual leadership in these areas, with the goal of improving business thought and practice.

CERS strives to create frontline academic knowledge in interactions with its international academic network and the surrounding business community. In the international academic community, CERS has become widely recognized as a leading research and knowledge centre in its field. Since the foundation of CERS, 28 doctoral theses have been defended and published. Currently, 13 senior researchers and 35 doctoral students are associated to CERS, of which one-third acting as full time researchers.

Through a dialogue with business, CERS serves as a bridge between the academic and business communities. Three concepts constitute and build this bridge of interaction with business:

- CERS partnership including *NEXT PRACTICE* ™
- CERS award
- CERS executive education.

### International Academic Partners of CERS

- Centre for Service Leadership, Arizona State University, USA
- The Centre for Hospitality Research, Cornell University, USA
- CTF Centrum for Tjänsteforskning (Service Research Centre), University of Karlstad, Sweden

- Centre for Service Management, Cranfield School of Management, UK
- Relationship Marketing, Emory University, USA
- Service Management Research Programme, Nankai University, PR China
- Relationship Marketing, University of Auckland, New Zealand
- Centre for Services Marketing, University of Maryland, USA

## CERS Research Areas

The mission of CERS is to provide intellectual leadership in relationship marketing and service management, with the goal of improving business thought and practice (Figure 17.1).

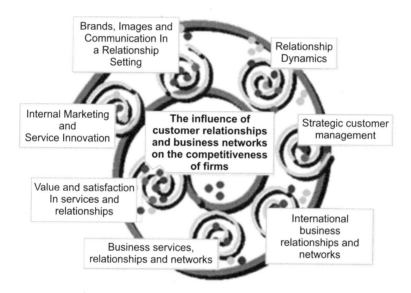

Figure 17.1 CERS research areas.

# INSTITUTE FOR RELATIONSHIP MARKETING, GRAZ—AUSTRIA

The Institute of Relationship Marketing (IRM) is the first one in the German speaking countries, which has Relationship Marketing at the heart of its operations. Being a university spin-off, this institute offers a vast range of advantages:

- Targeted use of synergies and reduced costs through a holistic approach.
- International scientific cooperation network—Marketing, Management and Psychology professors—ensuring the implementation of the state-of-the-art findings.

- Detailed analyses as a basis of decision making.
- Customers—their motivations, emotions, values, experiences and aims—at the heart of decisions.
- All services, e.g. analyses, concepts, and implementation—provided by one institute. Focus: Customer Relationship Management (CRM), Sales Management, Communication Management, Customer Research and Marketing.

For the establishment and development of customer oriented business models, the Institute offers a vast range of services:

1. Analyses and business-oriented research: Through a comprehensive analysis of companies' situations, the IRM supports in creating a fundamental basis for decision-making. Various methods are combined in order to get as much information as possible and to ensure relevant results.

2. Consulting, teaching and management training: Offer/provide with the customers a range of consulting services, e.g. from the development of long-term strategies and concepts to support in their implementation.

3. Content focus of the IRM: Customer Oriented Management, Customer Relationship Management (CRM), Sales Management, Communication Management, Customer Research and Marketing.

## JOURNAL OF RELATIONSHIP MARKETING

The *Journal of Relationship Marketing* is a quarterly journal that publishes peer-reviewed and invited conceptual and empirical papers and original works that make serious contributions to the understanding and advancement of relationship marketing theory, research, and practice. Under the editorship of Dr. David Bejou, this journal is a valuable literary resource for marketing researchers and managers in all sectors of today's ever-changing economy.

All articles in *Journal of Relationship Marketing* are written by international academicians and professionals with extensive experience and interest in the areas listed below. Each article is reviewed by the journal's distinguished Editorial Board members, which are listed in each issue. The journal strives to enhance customer service, customer relationship management processes, and strategies worldwide.

Examples of topics the journal addresses include:

- Evolution and life cycle of RM
- Theoretical and methodological issues in RM

- Determinants and consequences of RM
- Types of RM, networks and strategic alliances
- Internal and external customer relationship management strategies
- Psychological underpinning of RM
- Communication quality, style, and frequency in RM
- Quality, trust, commitment, satisfaction, loyalty, and dissolution in RM
- Applications of RM in different disciplines and industries
- International perspectives in RM
- Interdisciplinary nature of RM
- RM strategies in services economy
- RM strategies in higher education
- RM strategies in e-commerce
- RM, technology, and the web
- Profitability in RM
- Case studies and best practices in RM
- Future role of RM

The journal's website at http://www.uni-kl.de/icrm/jrm/

Websites

mgt.buffalo.edu/crm/abt_goals.shtml
www.hanken.fi/public/en/hankencers
http://www.uni-kl.de/icrm/jrm/
http://mgt.buffalo.edu/crm/index.shtml

# APPENDIX

# Marketing Glossaries

## AMERICAN DEPOSITARY RECEIPT (ADR)

A security issued by a company outside the US, which physically remains in the country of issue, usually in the custody of a bank, but is traded on US stock exchanges. ADRs are issued to offer investment routes that avoid the sometimes expensive and cumbersome laws that apply to non-citizens buying shares on local exchanges. The first ADR was issued in 1927.

## ADVERTISING

The term 'advertising' originates from the Latin word *adverto*, which means to turn round. Advertising thus denotes the means employed to draw attention to any object or purpose.

In the marketing context, advertising has been defined 'as any paid form of non-personal presentation and promotion of ideas, goods or services by an identified sponsor'. Through an advertisement, the advertiser intends to spread his ideas about his products/offerings among his customers and prospects.

Advertising is certainly one of the tools of promotion and thus facilitates marketing power. Advertisers try to extrapolate direct tangible benefits from the advertisements—for example, how sales figure has improved, what is the growth in the level of product awareness and how it has improved the market share. Media and outdoor advertising certainly has its benefits particularly in the context of FMCG and consumer durable. While thinking about high value industrial product, high value services marketing—does such media coverage play any role? Not much and not needed to the extent of FMCGs.

Limited corporate advertising campaigns certainly carry some intangible benefits. Just like the persons who are seen in the media definitely stand little apart from the commoners. Corporate advertising, corporate marketing programme, and public interaction open the information channel freely and make it easily available to the clients.

The crux of the success of advertising and promotional campaigns lies in the synergy of relationship between the agency and the client to devise appropriate marketing and advertising strategy in understanding and addressing the end clients' requirements.

## BRAND

A brand is defined as a 'name, term, symbol, design, or a combination of them, which is intended to identify the goods and services of one seller and to differentiate them from those of competitors'.

Brand building exercise today involves an exhaustive exercise of identifying the consumers' psyche with respect to their social, cultural and behavioural attributes and mapping the same with the message that the brand intends to communicate. Both the ends should match, else the exercise needs to be reworked. However, there are certain aspects of a brand that need to be understood at the time of augmenting such exercise. Some of them are described here.

## BRAND AMBITION

The role the brand aspires to play in people's mind.

## BRAND AUDIT

It is the process that describes the make-up of brand.

## BRAND EQUITY

It is a set of assets such as name, awareness, loyal customers, perceived quality and associations (e.g. being "pure" and "it floats") that are linked to the brand (its name and symbol) and add (or subtract) value to the product or services being offered (Aaker 1991).

## BRAND EXTENSION

It occurs when a firm that markets a product with a well-developed image uses the same brand name but in different product category. One consequence of brand extensions is that consumers develop an image for the new brand by transferring associations and affect from the brand's original set of associations to the brand extension.

## BRAND LOYAL

Broadly speaking, it can be categorized into two groups: Single Brand Loyal and Multi Brand Loyal.

- **Single brand loyal.** User of one product. This is the effect of long-term relationship with the brand and associated elements of it.
- **Multi brand loyal.** User of more than one brand and loyal to all these. This can be classified as:
  - ➤ Generic product based multibrand loyal, *for example, persons using paste for mouth washing are loyal to couple of paste brands.*

➤ Season based multibrand loyal, *for example, persons may use Liril in summer but Dove in winter because of seasonal effect.*

## BRAND PHYSIQUE

A brand by virtue of its attributes is capable of communicating with the client, end-user. In the case of consumer goods, products and services, through product usage, brand advertising, the brand assumes an intangible physical entity that the customers can identify with their own self-image. Whereas for industrial products or services, the physical image of the brand is formed through its feedback from users, partner's organization image and culture, and persons interacting on behalf of the partner. Summarily speaking, it comprises the following points:

- Personality—how does it behave while communicating? It is known as a set of associations that reflects the personification of the brand. In other words, if the brand were a person what type of person would it be? (Plummer 1985)
- Culture—What are its values and beliefs?
- Self-image—How the users of the brand perceive themselves?
- Reflection—How do brands want its users to be perceived?
- Relationship—How the brand and users are expected to interact with each other?

## BRAND POSITIONING

The concept of positioning was introduced by Al Ries and Jack Trout in 1969 and was elaborated in 1972. To understand the concept of positioning, we can consider the human mind as consisting of a perceptual map with various brands occupying different positions in it. This concept of perceptual space forms the theoretical basis for brand positioning. This leads to the perception of the consumer, which decides the positioning of any brand. It is important to note that what a marketer does is to find a position for its brand in the perceptual space of the consumer and place it at the most lucrative point.

Hence, positioning is not what you do to the product; it is what you do to the mind of the prospect. It is a new approach to communication and has changed the nature of advertising. It can be of a product, service, company or oneself.

The perception of a consumer is a function of consumer's values, beliefs, needs, experience and environment. According to Subroto Sengupta, "the core thought behind brand positioning—the idea that each brand (if at all noticed) occupies a particular point or space in the individual's mind, a point which is determined by that consumer's perception of the brand in question and in its relation to other brands. Thus, in the perceptual map, the spatial distance between the points on which brands are located reflects the subject's perception of similarity or dissimilarity between products or brands.

The origin of positioning comes from the following:

**Product era:** The product features and customer benefits were of importance. With technology being easily available, the product was no longer the unique selling proposition.

**Image era:** In this phase, the reputation and image of the company became more important than the product. But similar companies sprung up and this advantage was no longer a distinct one.

**Positioning era:** To succeed in today's over-communicated society, a company must create a position in the prospect's mind, a position takes into consideration not only the company's own strengths and weakness but those of competitors as well. In the positioning era as stated earlier, you must be the first to get into the prospect's mind.

*The ladders in the mind:* In a particular category, people have learned to rank the products and brands in the minds, e.g. in soft drinks, we generally have Coke followed by Pepsi followed by Thumsup. Thus if a new soft drink is to be introduced, the company must decide upon the way it will position itself, viz. the product ladder position.

*Positioning a company:* Positioning can also be applied to an organization in general. The companies who have a high position in the minds of the prospect, i.e. the students' mind absorb the cream of the crop from institutes. Similarly, companies visit only those campuses who have a high position in the mind of the company (the company becomes the prospect in this case).

7-Up exhibits the importance of positioning in the success of a brand. Originally considered as a mixer for hard drinks, it was later positioned as an Un-Cola soft drink. The result was that it became the third largest soft drink after Coke and Pepsi.

As Trout and Ries say, "You will not find an Un-Cola idea inside a 7-Up can. You find it inside the cola drinker's head."

Aaker (1991) considers positioning so central and critical that it should be considered at the level of the mission statement representing the essence of the business.

Positioning plots not only consumer perceptions but also preferences of a given consumer segment in a particular category or product market. Consumers express such preferences in terms of the benefits, whether they are getting the benefit, if it is important, to what extent are they missing something. These are called ideal points on a perceptual map.

Thus, this gives the idea as to how close we are to where we should be, that is, the position of the brand on the perceptual map vis-à-vis the ideal points. The next implication of the mapping is, that it earmarks the vacant spaces on the perceptual map which are nothing but opportunities, which can be exploited for positioning. Thus, identify the gaps, which new or repositioned products can fill by offering what current products do not provide. This gives the skeleton for making the strategy for future.

## BRAND REPORT CARD

A clear articulation of the campaign objectives against which a campaign's performance can be evaluated, for example, benefits, relevance, value perceptions, positioning, consistency, sustenance, support, etc.

## BRAND SCAN

It is the discovery of the health of a brand on six core equities—product, image, customer, visual, channel and goodwill.

## BRAND SWITCHING

Brand switching is a customer's normal behaviour and all marketing and promotion strategy is focused on how to control the customers from switching brands or precisely making them brand loyal. This can be analyzed from the perspective of various categories of users. The users, based on their experience of the brand, start developing loyalty that ultimately transforms into an intimate relationship.

### New Category Users

- **Negative new category users**—Those who do not need the generic product. For example, persons who live in places where electricity has not reached cannot be users of new electrical products.
- **Unaware new category users**—They are users of generic product but unaware of the new brand.
- **Positive new category users**—They are aware and they can be pursued to use the brand.

## BRAND SWITCHERS

**Regular favourable brand switchers.** The users find something better giving real value for money and they switch. Their change is not hasty. They take time to think over and then do it.

**Experimental brand switchers.** The users switch for trial purposes but in practice they normally do not switch unless there is a genuine problem in using that brand. They use it once to see how the product is like with the remote possibility of embracing the product.

**Experimental favourable brand switchers**. These categories of users, after a trial use, go for repeat purchase. In case the users achieve satisfaction in this stage, there is sure success of turning them into regular category. In industries, the brand switching may happen due to these two major factors (Roos 1999):

- **Pulling determinants**—The switching determinant that makes a customer patronize to switch over to other alternative.
- **Pushing determinants**—The switching determinant that the customer perceives as a reason for switching.

## CO-BRANDING

Co-branding is a form of cooperation between two or more brands with significant customer recognition, in which all the participants' brand names are retained.

## CONSUMER AND BUYER BEHAVIOUR, BUYING MOTIVE AND BUYER BEHAVIOUR

All the three concepts are interwoven with their objectives of exploring the forces, instincts, science, and logic persuading a consumer or customer to buy, purchase products or services for consumption.

Consumer Behaviour refers to the study of how a person buys products. Although the study of how person buys products is of interest to marketers, consumer behaviour involves quite a bit more. A more complete definition is:

Consumer Behaviour (Jacoby 1976) reflects the totality of consumers' decisions with respect to the acquisition, consumption, and disposition of goods, services, time and ideas by (human) decision-making units (over time). Consumer behaviour is a dynamic process meaning more that just buying can involve many people and decision (Hoyer & MacInnis 1999) like:

- Whether to acquire/use/dispose
- What to acquire/use/dispose
- When to acquire/use/dispose
- How to acquire/use/dispose
- Where to acquire/use/dispose
- How much acquire/use/dispose
- How long to acquire/use/dispose.

This is very important from the viewpoint of relationship building. However, there is no unified tested and universally established theory of buyer behaviour. Instead, concepts and theory have taken hints from economics, psychology, sociology, and anthropology. But before all, it is Abraham Maslow's hierarchy of need that states any human activity is directed towards meeting five-fold category of needs in the following hierarchy:

1. Self actualization—Self-development, fruition of one's own capabilities
2. Esteem needs—Recognition and status
3. Social needs—Sense of belonging
4. Safety needs—Security and protection
5. Psychological needs—Basic human needs for survival

## Buying Motive

Buying motives are basically of two kinds: (i) product motives and (ii) patronage motives (Ramaswamy & Namakumari 2002). It is often said that the dissatisfaction of human beings creates new products and new markets. And a product is a bundle of satisfactions. At least, it is expected to be so. Buying motives can be defined as all the impulses, desires and considerations of the buyer, which induce him to purchase a given product. Those impulses, desires and considerations that make people buy a given product, are called *product motives*. The influences that explain why they buy from particular firms/shops are called *patronage motives*.

## Product Motive

Product motives are of several types and they can be classified in several ways. One classification that is linked to the nature of satisfaction sought by the buyer puts them into the following two categories:

- Emotional product motives
- Rational product motives

**Emotional product motives** are those impulses that appeal to the buyer's pride or ego, his urge to imitate others, or his desire to be distinctive. The emotional motives may persuade a consumer to buy a certain product without evaluating the plus and minus points of such action. Careful reasoning or logical analysis need not be found behind such purchases.

**Rational product motives,** on the contrary, involve a logical analysis of the intended purchase—the purpose expected to be served by the product, the various alternatives available to the buyer, etc. Relevant and valid reasons that justify the purchase are characteristics of rational product motives.

## Patronage Motive

Patronage motives arise when there is buyer patronage of selected sellers/shops. Just like product motives, patronage motives also can be grouped into emotional and rational categories. Emotional patronage motives are those that persuade a buyer to buy from specific shops, without much logical reason behind that action. He may like the place for purely subjective reason and may consider the shop as his 'favourite' shopping place. However, if the buyer selects the shop because he knows that it offers a wide selection, or the latest models, or good after-sales service, then he is influenced by rational patronage motive. Nevertheless, every patronage is a combination of the rational and emotional motives.

### Models of Buyers, Behaviour

Following models are available to account for buying decision:

- **Economic model**—Buying decisions are governed exclusively by the purchasing power, maximum utility and benefits offered by the product.

- **Learning model**—It has taken a one from Pavlovian Stimulus-Response Theory where buying decisions are governed by basic drive, stimuli, and responses of the buyer.

- **Psychoanalytical model**—This model is based on Freudian psychology, which states that hidden motives, suppressed desires can govern buying decisions.

- **Sociological model**—According to this model, the buyer is influenced by society and the buying decisions are governed by intimate groups, social classes, social compulsions, buyers' aspirations to emulate, follow and fit in the immediate higher environment.

- **Nicosia model**—Francesco Nicosia, an exponent in consumer behaviour, put forward his model of buyer behaviour in 1966. The model tries to establish the links between a firm and its consumer—how the activities of the firm influence the consumer and result in his decision to buy. The messages from the firm first influence the predisposition of the consumer towards the product. Depending on the situation, he develops a certain attitude towards the product. It may lead to a search for the product or an evaluation of the product. If these steps have a positive impact on him, it may result in a decision to buy.

- **Engel–Kollat-Blackwell model**—In this model, introduced in the year 1968, the focus is on decision-making process, which is impacted by inputs, how information is processed, specific decision process variables and external influences.

- **Howard–Sheth model**—John Howard and Jagdish Sheth put forward the Howard-Sheth model in 1969, in their publication entitled *The Theory of Buyer Behaviour*. The logic of the model is as follows: there are inputs in the form of stimuli. There are outputs beginning with attention to given stimulus and ending with purchase. In between the inputs and the outputs, there are variables affecting perception and learning that are manifested in perceptual and learning constructs respectively. These variables are considered 'hypothetical' since they cannot be directly measured at the time of occurrence.

- **Blackwell–Miniard–Engel model or consumer decision model—** Since these early modelling efforts, the field of consumer behaviour has advanced into a more established discipline. Newer and more focused buyer behaviour models have evolved over time. One such model, the Consumer Decision Process (CDP) model of Blackwell, Miniard and Engel (2001), has become one of the established models of buyer behaviour. Its origins date back to 1968 (when it was known as the EKB model after its original developers Engel, Kollat and Blackwell). Since then the model has been periodically revised and refined as the knowledge of consumer behaviour has developed over time. The dawn of the Internet era has triggered renewed interest in understanding consumer behaviour, especially in the online world of electronic commerce.

In the CDP model, the starting point for any purchase decision is when a consumer recognizes some need or problem. Need recognition occurs when a consumer perceives a difference between an ideal versus the current state of affairs. A complex mosaic of stimuli and influences affect the way in which consumers perceive their current state of affairs and their problems and needs. Culture, social class, personal influences, family, reference group, motivation, knowledge, attitudes, personality and values are but a few of the influences that may trigger need recognition. Furthermore, as consumers' change and progress through life stages, so do their problems and needs evolve and change. These complex dynamics ultimately manifest in consumer trends that marketers need to constantly monitor and develop appropriate strategies.

## CROSS-SELLING AND UP-SELLING

Cross-selling and up-selling are some of the major derivatives of Relationship Marketing. Cross-selling and up-selling techniques are deployed to provide customers easy access to products they may want or need.

**Cross-selling** consists of displaying or linking to products related to the one(s) the user is already viewing or in possession. For example, in the garment store, after you buy a ready-made shirt, the counter salesperson shows you a variety of ties or else if you buy a trouser, you are offered to buy a shirt.

**Up-selling** consists of displaying or linking to a more expensive alternative to the one the customer has chosen. Up-selling can help users understand what is available at the next higher price level, and how much the additional function or quality would cost. For instance, if the customer intends to buy an expensive trouser, he may be offered a suit.

## CUSTOMER EQUITY

The customer equity model enables marketers to determine which of the three drivers—value, brand or retention equity—are most critical to driving customer equity in their industry and firm. Using this approach, marketers can quantify the financial benefit from improving one or more of the drivers.

## CUSTOMER LOYALTY

The term customer loyalty is used to describe the behaviour of repeat customers, as well as those that offer good ratings, reviews, or testimonials. Some customers do a particular company a great service by offering favorable word of mouth publicity regarding a product, telling friends and family, thus adding them to the number of loyal customers. However, customer loyalty includes much more. It is a process, a programme, or a group of programmes geared toward keeping a client happy so he or she will provide more business.

## CUSTOMER MANAGEMENT OF RELATIONSHIP

CMR is almost the version of CRM—just a slight nuance regarding the traditional philosophy that our guests invite us into their lives and ultimately manage our presence/relationship with them. CMR is a value added change in the traditional concept of Relationship Marketing as well as Customer Relationship Management. CMR truly subscribes to the philosophy of 'living inside the customers' DNAs'.

## CUSTOMER RELATIONSHIP MANAGEMENT (CRM)

Customer Relationship Management is a comprehensive strategy and process of acquiring, retaining and partnering with selective customers to create superior value for the company and customer.

## CUSTOMER VALUE CHAIN

Every activity performed by the firm creates some value, which reflects finally in the firm's product offer, and that these activities are linked into a chain. Porter calls it the firm's Value Chain.

## e-CRM

In simplest terms, e-CRM provides companies with a means to conduct interactive, personalized and relevant communications with customers across both electronic and traditional channels. It utilizes a complete view of the customer to make decisions about messaging, offers and channel delivery. It synchronizes communications across otherwise disjoint customer facing systems.

## GLOBAL DESPOSITARY RECEIPT (GDR)

Similar to the ADR described before, except the GDR is usually listed on exchanges outside the US, such as Luxembourg or London. Dividends are usually paid in US dollars. The first GDR was issued in 1990.

## LIFE TIME VALUE

Calculating Life Time Value (LTV) assists a company in a variety of applications for product development and marketing. LTV is a value added component to marketing return when marketing strategy is executed through relationship mode instead of conventional product marketing mode.

## MARKETING DEFINITION

The following definitions were approved by the American Marketing Association Board of Directors:

## MARKETING

Marketing is the activity, set of institutions, and processes for creating, communicating, delivering, and exchanging offerings that have value for customers, clients, partners, and society at large. (Approved in October 2007).

The following definition of **Marketing** by Kotler et al. 2009 states: "Marketing is a societal process by which individuals and groups obtain what they need and want through creating, offering and freely exchanging products and services of value with others.

## MARKETING MIX

It was Jerome McCarthy, the well-known American Professor of Marketing, who first described the marketing mix in terms of the four Ps. He classified the marketing mix variables under four heads, each beginning with the alphabet 'P'. Those are product, price, promotion and place.

## MARKETING RESEARCH

With the increasing complexity of business processes as a whole, there is a need to monitor routine problem, non-routine problems, short- and long-term problems related to any of the components of marketing. There is also a need to have a foresight of market in the future. Marketing research findings provide the business with necessary feedback based on which the marketers can design and plan their decision for marketing.

As per American Marketing Association, Marketing Research is the function that links the consumer, customer, and public to the marketer through information—information used to identify and define marketing opportunities and problems; generate, refine, and evaluate marketing actions; monitor marketing performance; and improve understanding of marketing as a process. Marketing research specifies the information required to address these issues, designs the method for collecting information, manages and implements the data collection process, analyzes the results, and communicates the findings and their implications. (Approved in October 2004). According to Philip Kotler (1999), Marketing Research is systematic problem analysis, model building and fact finding for the purposes of decision-making and control in the marketing of goods and services.

The research may be conducted on various aspects of marketing, for example, consumer, market/demand, product/brand, competition, distribution, price, advertising and promotion, sales method.

With reference to Relationship Marketing, consumer research plays a very dominant role. There can be many factors, which need to be addressed for research. Some of them are as follows:

- Motivation research
- Buying behaviour research
- Consumer psychographic research
- Customer satisfaction survey
- Study of consumer dissatisfaction
- Study of consumer acceptance pattern of innovation, etc.

## MARKETING STRATEGY

One common strategy, which is considered by the marketers, is segmentation. A market segment is a subgroup of people or organizations sharing one or more characteristics that cause them to have similar product needs.

Market segmentation is the process in marketing of dividing a market into distinct subsets (segments) that behave in the same way or have similar needs. Because each segment is fairly homogeneous in their needs and attitudes, they are likely to respond similarly to a given marketing strategy. That is, they are likely to have similar feelings and ideas about a marketing mix comprised a given product or service, sold at a given price, distributed in a certain way, and promoted in a certain way.

Broadly, markets can be divided according to a number of general criteria, such as by industry or public versus private sector. Small segments are often termed niche markets or specialty markets. However, all segments fall into either consumer or industrial markets. Although industrial market segmentation is quite different from consumer market segmentation, both have similar objectives.

Market segmentation can be seen from a top-down approach (Dey, 1980): *one* can start with the total population and divide it into segments.

Another alternative model is called the bottom-up approach. In this approach, start with a single customer and build on that profile. This typically requires the use of customer relationship management (CRM) software or a database of some kind. Profiles of existing customers are created and analyzed. Various demographic, behavioural, and psychographic patterns are built up using techniques such as cluster analysis.

## PERMISSION MARKETING

Permission marketing is about building an ongoing relationship of increasing depth with customers. It is all about turning strangers into friends, and friends into customers." Permission marketing has been hailed as a way for marketers to succeed in a world increasingly cluttered with marketing messages. (Godin 1999).

## PEOPLE, PROCESS AND PHYSICAL EVIDENCE—THE FIFTH, SIXTH AND SEVENTH Ps

All the Ps in marketing mix have strong relevance from the point of product planning, and launching to its stabilization in the market. However, for service industries, the fifth, sixth and seventh Ps are:

- People
- Process
- Physical evidence

### People

In the service industry, 'People' determine the success of the product. Training, attitude building, right compensation and company ownership of the people lead to the growth of the best persons. A set of excellent people can deliver a company like TCS, Infosys, Biocon, HDFC, etc. Similarly, a set of wrong persons can destroy even a Fortune 500 company, that is what happened to Enron.

### Process

The importance of the process enriches the competence of the firm to differentiate the offer and customize the product and services to leverage maximum client satisfaction. International bodies, Quality Assurance Institutes, International Standards Organizations, etc. award Quality Certifications after thorough evaluation of the processes undertaken by the organization.

### Physical Evidence

Physical evidence implies the ambience in which the customer is being served. This implies not only the quality of the food but also the plate on which the food is served, the décor of the room, the surrounding. All these add to the value of physical evidence. When a customer is invited for a product demonstration or training, the ambience of the place, the facilities arranged for the demo must suit the customer's taste or expectations. Or take the case of reference. The reference should be good enough to provide adequate supporting evidence to the partner's good work to the prospect.

## PLACE

It is one of the components of marketing mix. Channels of distribution and delivery are the key processes one can think of. It depicts channel design, types of intermediaries, and location of outlets, channels remuneration, and dealer–principal relations. Physical distribution covers the areas of transportation, warehousing, inventory order processing related activities.

The trend now is getting different. There is home delivery, showing market is reaching for the consumers. Direct marketing is one such example—it is the process by which a firm approaches its customers on one to one basis and markets its products directly to them. It relies on customized production, individualized distribution and individualized communications. In view of its individualistic approach, it is also known as 'Demassifed Marketing'.

Direct Marketing has an edge over mass marketing when it comes to building customer relations. As the marketplace gets more competitive, product clutter intensifies and consumers become more discerning, it is only through direct marketing that facilitates consumer attraction and retention. When mass marketers are separated from the customers by the wholesalers, distributors and retailers, direct marketers maintain direct touch with the customers.

### Multilevel Marketing

Multilevel marketing is a modified version of direct selling. Multilevel marketing allows sellers to build a business through their own sales efforts and by inviting others to become sellers. Remuneration is based on a seller's personal sales and on the combined sales of those people they have sponsored, trained and motivated. For example, Amway, Avon, Oriflame International are among the largest multilevel marketing outfits in the world—their personal care products are not sold through retail chain stores but through their representatives.

This is one example that pre-empted the philosophy of Relationship Marketing where selling activity is exercized primarily through social bonding.

Amway began in 1959 with two young entrepreneurs in the United States—Rich DeVos and Jay Van Andel. Their concept for an innovative business opportunity, centred on person-to-person marketing, established itself as a leader among one of today's fastest-growing industries. Today, more than 3 million independent business owners distribute Amway products in more than 80 countries and territories. Amway generates US$5 billion (FY1999) in sales at estimated retail through this global product distribution network.

Banking and insurance organizations have come out at large with their offer of various products and services. For example, companies marketing credit cards, such as Standard Chartered Bank, Citibank make direct call to the prospects and send representative to their home. The clients never have to visit their office excepting for payment of outstanding amount. These services are also extended through telephone, Internet or normal post mail.

## PRICE

It refers to pricing policies, margins, discounts and rebates, terms of delivery, payment and credit terms. Price has a distinct role to play, particularly with respect to FMCG consumer durables of daily use. The pricing of products has always been a matter of great concern for organizations dealing with FMCG and consumer durables. Because of price wars, small time operators with least production costs are slowly eating off the market shares of big players.

The following are the various approaches taken up by the firms for determining the pricing strategy:

- **Premium pricing**—High price for its uniqueness, used for luxuries, for example, expensive hotels.
- **Penetration pricing**—Low pricing for gaining market share.
- **Economy pricing**—Cheaper pricing for commodities of daily usage.
- **Price skimming**—Charging high price leveraging competitive advantage.
- **Psychological pricing**—This approach is used when the marketer wants the consumer to respond on an emotional rather than rational basis. For example; 'price point perspective' 99 Rupees, not one hundred.
- **Product line pricing**—Where there is a range of products or services, the pricing reflects the benefits of parts of the range. For example, car washes. Basic wash could be Rs. 100, wash and wax Rs. 200, and the whole package Rs. 150.
- **Optional product pricing**—Companies will attempt to increase the amount customers spend once they start to buy. Optional 'extras' increase the overall price of the product or service. For example, airlines may charge for optional extras such as guaranteeing a window seat or reserving a row of seats next to each other.

- **Captive product pricing**—Where products have complements, companies will charge a premium price where the consumer is captured. For example, a razor manufacturer will charge a low price and recoup its margin (and more) from the sale of the only design of blades which fit the razor.

- **Product bundle pricing**—Here sellers combine several products in the same package. This also serves to move old stock. Videos and CDs are often sold using the bundle approach.

- **Promotional pricing**—Pricing to promote a product is a very common application. There are many examples of promotional pricing including approaches such as BOGOF (Buy One Get One Free).

- **Geographical pricing**—Geographical pricing is evident where there are variations in price in different parts of the world. For example, rarity value, or where shipping costs increase price.

- **Value/perceived pricing**—This approach is used where external factors such as recession or increased competition force companies to provide 'value' products and services to retain sales. It is also a method of pricing in which the seller attempts to set price at the level that the intended buyers value the product. It is also called value-in-use pricing or value-oriented pricing. This approach is used for marketing services.

## PRODUCT

Product implies design, features, brand name, models, style, appearance, quality, warranty, service, packaging design, material appearance and labelling as well as post-sale servicing, quality of service and service charges. From marketing point of view, products are classified into the following categories:

- **Core product**—Cooking oil, flour, rice, etc.
- **Branded product**—Sunflower oil, Dell laptop, Lux soap.
- **Differentiated product**—To reach the specific segment, for example, Colgate gel to address the young generations.
- **Customized product**—The right examples are the 'made-to-order' pieces of furniture by interior decorators.
- **Augmented product**—Examples are existing products with additional features, like extra large, extra facilities, like a mobile phone with inbuilt Internet facilities.

## PROMOTION

Personal selling, advertising, sales promotion, publicity and public relation are the components of promotion. Once the product, price and channel of distribution are ready, promotion augments the psychological sale of the product by carrying the benefits, image of the product to the prospects.

## PUBLIC RELATIONS AND PUBLICITY

The British Institute of Public Relations defines PR Practice as a "deliberate, planned and sustained effort to establish and maintain mutual understanding between an organization and public". The Dutch Association defines PR as "the systematic promotion of mutual understanding between an organization and its public". The International Public Relations Association, in its declaration, maintained that PR is a management function of a continuing and planned character, through which public and private organizations seek to win and retain the understanding, sympathy and support of those with whom they are—or may be concerned by evaluating public opinion about themselves, in order to correlate, as far as possible, their own policies and procedures, to achieve by planned and widespread information, more productive cooperation and more efficient fulfilment of their common interests (Banik 2005).

If you want to reach large audiences as inexpensively as possible, public relations is the way to go. Public relations, or PR, are the popular terms for *publicity*. It is one of the tools under the gamut of Promotion that is one of the 4Ps of marketing. But actually PR includes much more, as it is explained below.

**Publicity** is the creation and distribution of information, primarily in the form of stories, published or broadcast by mass media such as newspapers, magazines, television and radio. Because the media does not charge for publishing these articles, but deem them valuable for their readers, publicity has the power to reach millions of people for very little money.

**Public relations** also include newsletters, information brochures, community relations, speeches, government relations and many other forms of communication in which time and space are not charged by the media.

Benefits of Public Relations and Publicity

- The most economical way by far to reach mass audiences.
- Stimulates awareness of and demand for your company products or services.
- Develops a stronger, more controlled image for your firm.
- Creates the perception that the company is active, "on the move."
- Has *seven times the credibility of advertising*, studies show.
- Provides an advantage over competitors who do not use 'PR' effectively.

*Source:* http://www.lciweb.com/PR.htm

## Public Relations Society of India

The Public Relations Society of India today is a premier national body of PR and Corporate Communication Professionals, attempting to steer Public Relations into the mainstream of management. A National Council, consisting of representatives elected by all the Regional Chapters manages the society. The Society has thirty-one Chapters across the Country with a total membership exceeding 8,000. The international Public Relations Association recognizes it.

## QUALITY SYSTEM

A quality system is the means by which an organization manages its quality aspects in a systematic, organized manner and provides a framework for planning, implementing, and assessing work performed by an organization and for carrying out required quality assurance and quality control activities.

## RELATIONSHIP EQUITY

It is the wealth-creating potential that resides in the firm's relationships with its stakeholders.

## RELATIONSHIP MARKETING

Relationship Marketing is the ongoing process of engaging in collaborative and cooperative activities, programmes with immediate and end-user customers to create and enhance mutual economic value at reduced cost. The emphasis is on the words "ongoing" and "collaborative".

## RELATIONSHIP SIGNALS

In a client partner business (B2B) scenario, Relationship Temperament, from business inception to product/service stabilization stage, is the driving force to set the rhythm, pace and mood of the business. Relationship signals are of fundamental importance as these represent body language, gestures, opinions, and expressions of the client in different communications channels conveying satisfaction or dissatisfaction right from the start. The understanding and anticipation of those signals help in deepening and broadening relationship, averting any possible conflict and strain leading to termination of the business. The signals have much to do with the temperament. Favourable signals are marked by cooperation and cordiality in client-partner operations. This is a healthy sign for mutual business growth. The cohesiveness in their mode of operations projects an integrated client-partner image.

## RETENTION MARKETING

The Retention Marketing and zero defection emphasize the relationship to existing customers. The latter term is paraphrasing the 'zero defects' quality strategy. This strategy says that company should continuously improve its quality and deliver defect-free goods and services.

## RFM MODEL

Recency, Frequency and Monetary Value is a concept which is used to rank the Lifetime Value and 'likelihood to respond' of customers relative to each other.

## SALES MANAGEMENT CHALLENGES

Managing sales is not difficult while a company is small, customer count and sales persons count are limited, and sales process is simple and transparent. However, when sales start to grow, companies understand that it is very hard to manage enlarged sales workflow as effectively as they did before. Managing increased sales volumes is more difficult because sales management process becomes more complicated and sales department has to deal with all aspects of the process. Not only the number of sales tasks grows but also grows the number of regions, customers and products. It is almost impossible for salespersons to handle with sales grows without a special system for planning, tracking, analyzing, reporting, and controlling all aspects of sales activity, projects and tasks. Sales project and task management software helps sales departments develop comprehensive, prioritized sales plans, track their completion and create real-time reports.

## SALES MANAGEMENT PROCESS

The four phase-model of management process comprises planning, tracking, reporting and control. This model is cyclical, so it is a constant/ continuous process. It consists of Sales Planning, Sales Reporting, and Sales Tracking.

## SALES PLANNING

When the business is growing, customers need more products, service and customization, this individual activity-oriented approach can become a barrier for sales to grow because unfocused and uncoordinated activity decreases effectiveness. Hence, sales department must be reorganized, and sales people should specialize and co-operate with each other as well as other departments. After setting sales goals, salespersons' activities should be planned by regions, clients, channels, managers, products, etc. Sales team leader or sales department head should choose volume and operational metrics to evaluate sales managers' effectiveness and to motivate them from achieved result. While planning it is important to consider market potential and structure, company's strengths and weaknesses, customer relations history, etc. that's why sales planning software must be able to store all sales-related information and allow a flexible searching, filtering, grouping and showing statistics (i.e. flexible customer, task and order forms, calculated fields, tables, schedules and charts).

## SALES REPORTING

The sales reporting includes the key performance indicator of the sales force. The Key Performance indicator indicates whether or not the sales process achieves the results as set forth in the sales planning and enables the sales managers to take corrective action in time in case the indicators deviate from the projected values. Sales reporting is a source for motivating sales managers, because awarding best managers without accurate and reliable sales reports is not objective. Also, sales reports are made not only for internal use or top management. If other divisions' compensation plan depends on final results, it is needed to present results of sales department's work to other departments. Finally, sales reports are required for investors, partners and government, so the sales management system should have advanced reporting capabilities to satisfy needs of different target audiences and help sales force to be more effective and make more sales. As a result, management finds it convenient to monitor and control the sales activities thus enabling the sales team align with the business goals.

## SALES TRACKING

Sales tracking is an integral part of sales management. Without tracking sales tasks, it is hard to find out if everything goes right and estimated intermediate results are achieved in time and in the limits of expected resources. If anything is out of expected range, you can analyze the details, talk to a sales manager responsible for this task and take corrective actions. Sales tracking tracks selling activities as opposed to revenue tracking which focuses on tracking the progress of forecast opportunities. Software used for sales tracking should allow sales team leaders to control sales tasks completion by using reminders and notifications, highlighting overdue tasks, analyzing task history, etc. If your sales task management system is really great and duly implemented, you are informed about all details of your company's sales process in real time and know who does what, when, and how.

## SALES PROMOTION

It is another important component of Marketing Communications Mix and a tool of Promotion—one of the 4Ps of marketing. It is essentially a direct and immediate inducement adding extra value to the product and hence prompts the dealer/consumer to buy the product. In a competitive market, sales promotion comes handy to a marketer, to solve several of the short-term hurdles.

According to American Marketing Association, 'In a specific sense, sales promotion includes those sales activities that supplement both personal selling and advertising, and coordinate them and make them effective, such as displays, shows, demonstration and other non-recurrent selling efforts in the ordinary routine'.

The following are the commonly used techniques for Sales Promotion:

- Demonstrations
- Trade Fair and Exhibition
- Coupons, Premiums, Free Offers, Price-offs, etc.
- Free Samples
- Joint Promotion
- Contests—Consumer Contests, Dealer Contest
- Merchandising and Displays
- Offers on the Web

## SELLING

Selling implies a legal and social process that signifies transfer of ownership of a product from the seller or seller's representative to the buyer or buyer's authorized representative in exchange of cash or kind over a period of time, mutually understood or agreed by both.

In selling the motif of profit may or may not exist but the process is driven by the sellers' intention to transfer the ownership in exchange of cash or its equivalent with the aid of various persuasion techniques.

## VIRTUAL RELATIONSHIP CIRCLE

Virtual Relationship Circle (VRC) demonstrates the interrelationship between the main factors establishing Virtual Organizations in the dynamic environment and perspective where the client may not meet its service provider physically.

# *References*

Aaker A., David, 1991. *Managing Brand Equity: Capitalizing on the Value of a Brand Name,* Free Press, New York.

Banik, G.C., 2005. *The Meaning of PR: A Literary Review,* Jaico Publishing House, New Delhi, pp. 1–2.

Blackwell, Roger, D., Miniard, Paul, W. and Engel, James F., 2001. Consumer Behaviour, South-Western College Publishers, Cincinnati, Ohio.

Day, G., 1980. "Strategic Market Analysis: Top-down and bottom-up approaches", working paper #80-105, Marketing Science Institute, Cambridge, Mass.

Godin, Seth, 1999. Permission Marketing: Turning Strangers into Friends and Friends into Customers, Simon & Schuster, New York.

Hoyer Wayne D. and MacInnis, Deborah J., 1999. Introduction to Consumer Behavior, Houghton Mifflin Company, Orlando, USA, pp. 3–11.

Jacoby, Jacob, 1976. Consumer Psychology: An Octennium, in Paul Mussen and Mark Rosenzweig (Eds.), *Annual Review of Psychology*, pp. 331-358.

Kotler, Philip, 1999. *Kotler on Marketing, How to Create, Win and Dominate Markets, 'Acquiring, Retaining and Growing Customers'*, The Free Press, New York.

Kotler, Philip, Keller, Kevin, Lane, Koshy, Abraham, and Jha, Mithileswar, 2009. *Marketing Management—A South Asian Perspective*, 13th ed., PHI Learning, New Delhi, p. 6.

Marketing Definition, Japanese Marketing Association, 1990. Source: http://www.jma-jp.org/eng/eteigi.htm

Plummer, Joseph T. 1985. How Personality Makes a Difference, *Journal of Advertising Research*, Dec-Jan 84-85, pp. 27–31.

Ramaswamy V.S. and Namakumkari, S., 2002. *Marketing Management —Planning, Implementation and Control, Global Perspective and Indian Context*, Buyer Behavior, Chap. 17, Macmillan, New Delhi, pp. 226–227.

Ries, Al., and Trout Jack, 2001. *Positioning: The Battle for Your Mind*, Chap. 1, McGraw Hill, New York.

Roos, Inger, 1999. Switching Processes in Customer Relationships, *Journal of Service Research*, Vol. 2, No. 1, August 1999, Sage Publications, Inc., Los Angeles, p. 14.

Sengupta, Subroto, 1993. *Brand Positioning*, Tata McGraw Hill, New Delhi.

Websites

www.crm-forum.com
www.lciweb.com/PR.htm
www.gatewayforindia.com
www.marketingteacher.com
www.consultancymarketing.co.uk

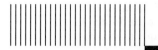

# Index